The Internet and the 2016 Presidential Campaign

The Internet and the 2016 Presidential Campaign

Edited by
Jody C Baumgartner and
Terri L. Towner

LEXINGTON BOOKS
Lanham • Boulder • New York • London

Published by Lexington Books
An imprint of The Rowman & Littlefield Publishing Group, Inc.
4501 Forbes Boulevard, Suite 200, Lanham, Maryland 20706
www.rowman.com

Unit A, Whitacre Mews, 26-34 Stannary Street, London SE11 4AB

British Library Cataloguing in Publication Information Available

Library of Congress Cataloging-in-Publication Data Available

ISBN 978-1-4985-4296-8 (cloth : alk. paper)
ISBN 978-1-4985-4298-2 (pbk. : alk. paper)
ISBN 978-1-4985-4297-5 (electronic)

∞™ The paper used in this publication meets the minimum requirements of
American National Standard for Information Sciences—Permanence of Paper
for Printed Library Materials, ANSI/NISO Z39.48-1992.

Printed in the United States of America

Terri would like to dedicate this book to her Mom and Dad,
Sharron and Russell: Thank you.

The book is also dedicated to Jody's daughters, Alicia and Anna.

Contents

Tables and Figures

TABLES

FIGURES

Preface

The Internet and the 2016 Presidential Campaign

Terri L. Towner

It has become clear that online tools are fully imbedded into every aspect of politics, including political campaigning, citizen mobilization and participation, constituency service and outreach, political information gathering, newsmaking, and political communications. In 2008 and 2012, Barack Obama was the first presidential candidate to effectively employ social media as a major campaign tool. During his eight years as president, Obama regularly tweeted on @POTUS, posted official reports and videos on Facebook, held Twitter town hall meetings, uploaded weekly fireside chats on YouTube, and sat for post–State of the Union *Fireside Hangouts*. By the 2016 presidential campaign, the digital media landscape had dramatically changed. There were a larger number of social media tools—Facebook, Twitter, Google+, Tumblr, Instagram, Snapchat, YouTube—all of which were used by the major 2016 presidential candidates. In addition, an increasing number of citizens of a variety of ages and races adopted and used the Internet and social networking sites.

The Internet and social media tools are now central forms of political communication. Debates, speeches, interviews, and events are all live-streamed, tweeted, Instagrammed, and Facebooked. In fact, President Trump's administration has made it clear that presidential correspondence is no longer limited to White House press conferences, Rose Garden speeches, and formal interviews. During his first 100 days in office, President Trump tweeted about relevant cabinet selections, border control, illegal immigration, voter fraud claims, *The Apprentice*'s television ratings, Neil Gorsuch's Supreme Court nomination, and more. Many of President Trump's tweets originated from his personal feed (@realDonaldTrump) and some were also retweeted to his verified @POTUS Twitter account. The latter is a clear break with precedent, as President Obama tweeted only on the verified @POTUS account during his presidency. From the early 2000s to 2016, online tools in politics and campaigning have leaped from a few "get-out-the-vote" emails to daily tweets from the president of the United States. But how did we get here?

ORIGINS

The Internet's role in politics can be traced back to the late 1990s, with the creation of FreeRepublic.com, a conservative online forum, in 1997, followed by MoveOn.org, an online liberal, advocacy group, in 1998. Then, in the 2000 presidential campaign, John McCain and Howard Dean claimed to raise $500,000 in donations via online websites in less than 24 hours.[1] Not to be outdone by McCain and Dean, George W. Bush employed email to persuade loyal voters to mobilize and get-out-the-vote. Building on his previous "cybercash" experience in 2000, Howard Dean utilized blogs, "MeetUp," "Dean TV," and "Get Local" to encourage his supporters to volunteer and self-organize in his 2004 presidential primary campaign.[2] Dean's online success and official blog led other candidates to do the same: George W. Bush and John Kerry used blogs in their 2004 presidential bids to send information to voters.[3] By the 2006 midterm elections, candidates further developed their online strategies, incorporating YouTube and MySpace alongside their campaign blogs and websites. As Gueorguieva[4] argued, these new digital tools brought benefits to campaigns, including more low-cost exposure and the ability to raise donations and recruit volunteers. In addition, these tools brought challenges, namely, less control over candidate image and message. For instance, Senator George Allen (R-VA) lost control of his message (and lost the election) when a YouTube video of him using a racial slur went viral. Despite these challenges, the Internet is a truly powerful campaign medium, excelling at maintaining relationships with voters: recruiting, mobilizing, and messaging.

But, no political candidate harnessed the power of online tools like Barack Obama in the 2008 and 2012 presidential campaigns.[5] In 2008, Barack Obama dominated the social media scene, employing Facebook, Twitter, and YouTube to mobilize his base, recruit volunteers, target new voters, collect donations, and communicate about his campaign. Obama's challenger, John McCain, rarely used social media tools, largely using get-out-the-vote emails and some Facebook and Twitter posts late in the fall campaign.[6] By 2012, Obama had a well-oiled, social media machine up and running, using other platforms such as Flickr, Google+, and Instagram as well. The Republican challenger, Mitt Romney, did not ignore these online platforms, notably using a wide variety of digital tools during the 2012 campaign. However, Obama's existing social media foundation, including his number of followers and fans alone, gave him a clear online advantage over Romney. For example, the Obama campaign was more active than Romney's, with Obama garnering more likes and re-tweets than Romney.[7]

By the 2016 presidential campaign, no candidate in the race for the White House could deny the importance of the Internet and social media tools. Campaign organizations had staff dedicated to their campaign's online presence, including social media, fundraising, outreach, organization, and mobilization efforts. Hillary Clinton and Donald Trump's campaigns were expected to spend an estimated $1 billion on digital advertising, not including digital spending from outside groups.[8] As the Pew Research Center[9] reported, the level of social media activity by the 2016 presidential candidates far outpaced the 2012 presidential candidates. Clinton and Trump posted, shared, and tweeted more, linking voters to their websites and news media articles, offering online video of speeches and events, and frequently mentioning (attacking) their opponent. Not surprisingly, the public did not ignore tweets and posts from the candidates.

CITIZEN USE OF ONLINE TOOLS

Since the Internet's widespread adoption, online tools ranging from websites, blogs, and social media have increased in adoption and use among citizens.[10] During the 2008 presidential election, a Pew Research Survey reported that television (77%) was the most common source for election news, followed by newspapers (28%) and the Internet (26%).[11] Among those Internet users, 60% went online to find news and information about the 2008 campaign, accessing blogs, candidate websites, social networking sites, and video sharing websites.[12] Eight years later, television sources (78%), particularly local and cable news, still remain the top outlets for learning about the 2016 presidential election.

However, citizens are now learning more about elections from online sources (65%), such as news websites, social networking sites, issue-based group websites, apps, or emails, and candidate/campaign websites, apps, or emails.[13] An eclectic news diet remains the norm, with Americans consuming mostly television and supplementing television watching with online sources. According to a Pew Research Survey, Facebook (37%) remains the dominant source for learning about the 2016 presidential election, followed by YouTube (11%), Twitter (9%), Google Plus (6%), Reddit (3%), and Instagram (3%).[14] These online sources gave citizens the opportunity to stay current with what their favorite candidate was doing and offer their support, whenever and wherever they found it convenient. Citizens could interact with candidates and the campaign by posting videos and images that were subsequently viewed by large numbers of people online and sometimes covered by traditional news organizations. But do citizens' political Internet and social media usage influence their attitudes and behaviors?

THE INTERNET AND SOCIAL MEDIA EFFECTS

Prior research indicates that the increased centrality of the Internet in citizens' lives has had an effect on how they learn about, view, and interact with campaigns and candidates. Taken together, however, much of the research examining social media' influence on citizen attitudes during previous midterm and presidential elections is often inconclusive. For example, employing the Internet for political information and debate has been found to be positively related to some forms of political participation.[15] However, some scholars offer evidence suggesting that the Internet only has a small impact on political participation.[16] Research on social media's impact on democratic norms is also rather mixed, with attention to social platforms having varying effects on government trust and political efficacy.[17] Interestingly, there are more conclusive findings on social media's influence on political knowledge. Studies indicate that the Internet and social media's role in creating a more informed citizenry is minimal, with many suggesting that social media sites are more a form of entertainment rather than an information-gathering tool.[18] As Internet technology has become a natural part of our political lives, perhaps online tools would have had a greater (or maybe less?) influence on citizens in 2016.

OVERVIEW OF THE BOOK

The previous discussion does not exhaust the ways in which the Internet is used by campaigns, organizations, and citizens to cover, engage in, and interact with presidential campaigns, and how these interactions may have a reciprocal effect. The online campaign has now evolved into an extensive, sophisticated, and integral part of presidential electioneering. Although many developments surrounding the Internet campaign are now considered to be standard fare, there were a number of new developments in 2016. Therefore, we have assembled original research in this volume in order to examine the Internet's role in the 2016 U.S. presidential campaign. We have gathered a number of authors who are experts in a variety of areas, including electoral campaigning, political communications, information technology and politics, and political marketing, to contribute their cutting-edge research. How were the Internet and social media platforms used to disseminate political news and information to a variety of audiences, including voters, professional journalists, citizen journalists, current officeholders, and political challengers, during the campaign period? To examine this and other questions, the book is divided into three sections.

Section I, "Campaign Organizations and Political Networks," focuses on the Internet and social media's role in political campaign organizations, issue advocacy groups, and other political networks. In particular, digital tools, such as email, websites, Facebook, and Twitter, have opened up new possibilities for political communication, helping parties, groups, and activists gain direct access to the citizenry. The first two chapters examine how the 2016 congressional campaigns utilized websites and social media to reach, communicate with, and inform voters.

In Chapter 1, James Druckman, Martin Kifer, and Michael Parkin offer a peek behind the digital curtain, asking campaign insiders how they viewed and used congressional websites during the 2016 elections. Despite the unusual campaign and surprising electoral outcome in 2016, the authors find that it was mostly "business as usual" for congressional campaigning via websites. Campaign websites remain at the heart of the congressional campaign, employed as a primary platform to communicate the campaign's overall strategy. The goals of campaign websites focused largely on increasing awareness of the candidate's issues position and background and less on coordinating volunteers and providing information about opponents.

In Chapter 2, Casey Frechette and Monica Ancu provide a detailed examination of Twitter adoption by Senate and House candidates in 2016. Twitter appears to be a standard tool for congressional campaigning, particularly among Democrat and Republican incumbents. The authors' analysis of Twitter posts centers on types of candidates (incumbents v. challengers, Democrats v. Republicans) and how they used this social media tool. Some results are surprising, such as the fact that third-party candidates were unlikely to use Twitter. Other findings were not new to 2016, particularly that Twitter remains a purely one-way campaign communication tool.

Anne-Bennett Smithson and Emily K. Vraga's examination of disagreement on Twitter at the gubernatorial level in Chapter 3 is especially relevant, given the current contentious political environment. Their focus on "disagreement" is on the presentation of opposing views and/or behaviors on social media, in particular, on Twitter. The authors coded tweets for the presence or absence of disagreement, along with the type of tweet (basic communication, personal characteristics, or policy), target (own party, opposing party, or political elites), and tone. They then set out to determine if disagreement differs by type of race (incumbent v. challenger) and party affiliation. Which party was more likely to present what types of disagreement in 2016 gubernatorial tweets, Republican or Democrats?

In Chapter 4, Steven Nawara and Mandi Bates Bailey move beyond congressional and gubernatorial adoption and use of digital tools to examine the social media strategies of the 2016 presidential candidates.

By monitoring the Twitter, Facebook, and Instagram accounts of Donald Trump, Hillary Clinton, and Gary Johnson, the authors seek to determine which platform emerged as "king" in 2016. Most important, they seek to discover which presidential candidate used each platform the most: the established politician, the businessman, or the libertarian. The authors then conduct a careful analysis of the content posted across the candidates' social media platforms as well as the tone they employed. Acknowledging the growing importance of visuals, they also explore the content and tone of images and videos candidates posted across platforms, hinting that perhaps visuals and text differ.

In Chapter 5, Heather K. Evans, Kayla J. Brown and Tiffany Wimberly delve into the role of gender in politics, an oft-studied topic of research since Democrat Geraldine Ferraro's 1984 vice presidential candidacy. In the 2016 presidential race, gender was particularly important given that Hillary Clinton was the first woman to receive a major party presidential nomination. In previous campaigns, female candidates have often utilized digital platforms to "go negative" and post or tweet about "women's issues." In the 2016 election, the authors compared Donald Trump and Hillary Clinton's tweet style, examining how they tweeted about policy issues and attacked their opponent. Do candidates use social media channels to play the gender card or keep it in the stack?

In Chapter 6, Girish J. "Jeff" Gulati and Christine Williams follow the money, examining how much outside groups, such as the NRA and Planned Parenthood, spent on traditional and digital media advertising during the 2012 and 2016 presidential elections. The authors clearly illustrate that the investment into digital media is increasing, but then look deeper, showing how much money is being invested into digital versus traditional media as well as who is investing the most into digital advertising. Numerous spending patterns emerge, indicating that outside groups spend more on Republican than on Democratic candidates.

Section II, "Political Messages: Production, Consumption, and Effects," focuses on the intersection of the Internet and mainstream media in political newsmaking. Internet sources, such as blogs, Facebook, Twitter, and YouTube, have been adopted as additional platforms and news sources for mainstream journalists as well as political candidates. During the most recent election cycles, the Internet and other technologies have transformed the campaign media machine, changing the ways in which journalists cover the campaign, how candidates battle for office, and how citizens consume political news. This section includes chapters that examine this multilayered communication, or "hybrid" media environment, in political campaigning, with a specific focus on the role of online sources for news production and reporting by journalists and usage by political candidates and citizens.

In Chapter 7, Diana Owen focuses on citizens' use of social media during political campaigns, particularly how digital platforms give citizens the opportunity to have a louder voice and more active role in the political arena. Of course, the amount of voice and activity may depend on how citizens actually use social media. Some social media users are simply looking for political information and watching campaign ads, other users are interacting by "liking" or sharing campaign content. Still others are joining campaign-related social media groups, organizing events, and donating online. Owen finds that most social media use in the 2016 election was for information gathering rather than for the more time-consuming forms of campaign engagement. As social media users read, watch, share, post, and join, it is likely that these actions may lead to offline information seeking, interactive expression, and campaign engagement.

In a "post-truth" Internet era, it has become critical to examine whether citizens can discern fact from fiction, or real versus "fake" information. What are you more likely to believe, a tweet or a newspaper headline? In Chapter 8, David Morris conducts an experiment to investigate how much credibility respondents assign to campaign messages from mainstream media headlines versus campaign messages from Twitter. He found no significant differences between those who were exposed to campaign messages from *USA Today* and those exposed to tweets during the heart of the election. It seems that citizens support, believe, and agree with political information from both mainstream and social media outlets. Perhaps this "faith" placed in social media messages may have contributed to Donald Trump's surprising victory?

In Chapter 9, Peter Francia tackles the latter question, suggesting that Trump may have won the White House in part due to his controversial tweets and criticisms of the press. In other words, candidate Trump was successfully able to "go public" by eschewing the costly mainstream media. Drawing on media reports as well as public opinion data, he shows how Trump garnered free, wide-reaching media coverage and courted an already untrusting citizenry by criticizing the press.

The last chapter in this section ends with a little political humor. In Chapter 10, Jody Baumgartner explores how late night political comedy on television has migrated to the Internet. As more citizens watch less traditional television and consume more digital video, research on the televised content found online becomes more important. Addressing this, Baumgartner reports how many clips from late-night comedy shows, such as "Jimmy Kimmel Live" and "Conan," that focused on the 2016 presidential campaign were posted on YouTube. Which shows went politically humorless? Does the amount of political humor influence the show's popularity? There is also a hunt for political bias, whether Hillary Clinton was the subject of more punch lines or Donald Trump was the more frequent brunt of jokes. Baumgartner illustrates that political comedy is alive and well, especially online.

Section III, "Political Issues on Twitter and Instagram," looks beyond the traditional press conference, rally, and stump speech, focusing specifically on how candidates and campaigns use Twitter and Instagram to cover campaign events, discuss political issues, provide background information, and, most important, shape media coverage. Agenda-building research demonstrates that candidates and officeholders can influence what issues and topics the mainstream media cover.[19] Yet, given the increase in social media use by both journalists and political candidates, scholars have sought to examine how candidates employ Facebook, Twitter, YouTube, and Instagram to influence traditional media coverage. What is lacking is a detailed examination of how agenda building occurs between social media and traditional media.

In Chapter 11, Bethany Conway-Silva, Christine R. Filer, Kate Kenski, and Eric Tsetsi demonstrate that Twitter influenced the mainstream media's agenda during the 2016 presidential nomination periods. In fact, there is a clear reciprocal relationship between candidate and campaign Twitter posts and mainstream media reports, with the newspapers' issue agendas holding a bit more power over Twitter's issue agenda. In addition, the issues "owned" by Republican and Democratic candidates and campaigns on Twitter often predicted issue emphasis in newspapers.

In Chapter 12, Terri Towner and Caroline Lego Muñoz also examine agenda building, focusing on Instagram, a newer social media tool. Instagram is a photo-sharing platform that allows users to share pictures and videos to followers. Every major presidential candidate used Instagram in the 2016 presidential campaign, making this fertile digital ground for examination. Similar to Conway-Silva and others, Towner and Muñoz focus specifically on the agenda-setting effects between the presidential primary candidates' Instagram posts and mainstream newspaper articles. Their content analysis of issue mentions in both mediums suggests a reciprocal relationship between the issue agenda in Instagram and newspapers.

Finally, in Chapter 13, Mark Ludwig also examines Instagram, conducting an extensive content analysis of the 20 candidates' Instagram posts in the primary and general elections. Ludwig describes how Democratic and Republican candidates used Instagram, primarily covering campaign events followed by policy issues. Yet, the issues Democrats and Republicans posted on Instagram differed greatly. Democratic and Republican candidates tended to focus on particular issues owned by their political party on Instagram.

It can be argued that the 2016 presidential election was the first, true social media election. In previous election campaigns, Internet tools were simply supplementary or secondary forms of political communication. This book illustrates that campaign websites, Twitter, Facebook, Instagram, and online video are now strategically employed, campaign communication tools. For instance, websites and other social media serve as credible informational gateways about the campaign, Twitter is a megaphone for campaign information, attacks on opponents, and policy positions, candidate Instagram posts influence the issue agenda, and YouTube offers campaign comedy. Clearly, the Internet and social media's influence in the 2016 presidential election was stronger than it has ever been and this election cycle will shape campaigns for years to come. What does the future hold for the Internet and campaigning? The importance of the Internet in campaigning will assuredly expand. A winning political strategy in 2020 must embrace and leverage social and audio (i.e., Pandora) digital platforms that offer candidates access to a wide variety of voters.

NOTES

We would like to thank Amber Whitley and Brittney Hunt, both of East Carolina University's Masters of Public Administration program, for doing the lion's share of the work in compiling the index for this book.

1. Bruce Bimber and Richard Davis. *Campaigning Online: The Internet in U.S. Elections.* NY: Oxford University Press, 2003; John M. Broder. "The 2000 Campaign: The Money Race; His Success in New Hampshire Brings McCain an Overnight Infusion of Cybercash," *The New York Times,* February 3, 2000, accessed March 1, 2017, http://www.nytimes.com/2000/02/03/us/2000-campaign-money-race-his-success-new-hampshire-brings-mccain-overnight.html.

2. Matthew Hindman. *The Myth of Digital Democracy.* Princeton University Press, 2008; Joe Trippi. *The Revolution Will Not Be Televised.* NY: HarperCollins, 2004.

3. Andrew P. Williams and John C. Tedesco. *The Internet Election: Perspectives on the Web in Campaign 2004.* Lanham, MD: Rowman & Littlefield, 2006.

4. Vassia Gueorguieva. "Voters, MySpace, and YouTube: The Impact of Alternative Communication Channels on the 2006 Election Cycle and Beyond." *Social Science Computer Review* 26.3(2008): 288–300.

5. Terri L. Towner and David A. Dulio. "New Media and Political Marketing in the United States: 2012 and Beyond." *The Journal of Political Marketing* 11(2012): 95–119.

6. Monica Ancu. "From Soundbite to Textbite: Election 2008 Comments on Twitter," in *Techno-Politics in Presidential Campaigning: New Voices, New Technologies, and New Voters,* ed. Lynda L. Kaid and John Allen Hendricks (New York: Routledge, 2011), 11.

7. Pew Research Center. "How the Presidential Candidates Use the Web and Social Media." August 15, 2012, accessed on March 1, 2017, http://www.journalism.org/2012/08/15/how-presidential-candidates-use-web-and-social-media/.

8. Meg James. "Political Ad Spending Estimated at $6 billion in 2016," *Los Angeles Times*, November 8, 2015, accessed on March 1, 2017, http://www.latimes.com/entertainment/envelope/cotown/la-et-ct-political-ad-spending-6-billion-dollars-in-2016-20151117-story.html.

9. Pew Research Center. "Election 2016: Campaigns as a Direct Source of News." July 18, 2016, accessed on March 1, 2017, http://www.journalism.org/2016/07/18/candidates-differ-in-their-use-of-social-media-to-connect-with-the-public/.

10. Pew Research Center. "Social Media Usage: 2005–2015." October 8, 2015, accessed on March 1, 2017, http://www.pewinternet.org/2015/10/08/social-networking-usage-2005-2015/.

11. Aaron Smith. "The Internet's Role in Campaign 2008." Pew Research Center. April 2009, accessed on March 1, 2017, http://www.pewinternet.org/files/old-media/Files/Reports/2009/The_Internets_Role_in_Campaign_2008.pdf.

12. Ibid.

13. Jeffrey Gottfried, Michael Barthel, Elisa Shearer, and Amy Mitchell. "The 2016 Presidential Campaign: A News Event That's Hard to Miss." Pew Research Center, 2016, accessed March 1, 2017, http://www.journalism.org/2016/02/04/the-2016-presidential-campaign-a-news-event-thats-hard-to-miss/.

14. Jeffrey Gottfried, Michael Barthel, Elisa Shearer, and Amy Mitchell. "The 2016 Presidential Campaign: A News Event That's Hard to Miss." Pew Research Center, 2016, accessed March 1, 2017, http://www.journalism.org/2016/02/04/the-2016-presidential-campaign-a-news-event-thats-hard-to-miss/.

15. Shelley Boulianne. "Does Internet Use Affect Engagement? A Meta-Analysis of Research." *Political Communication* 26(2009): 193–211; Erik P. Bucy and Kimberly S. Gregson. "Media Participation: A Legitimizing Mechanism of Mass Democracy." *New Media and Society* 3(2001): 357–380; Dhavan V. Shah, Jack M. McLeod, and So-Hyang Yoon. "Communication, Context, and Community: An Exploration of Print, Broadcast, and Internet Influence." *Communication Research* 28(2001): 464–506; Dhavan V. Shah, Jaeho Cho, William P. Eveland, and Nojin Kwak. "Information and Expression in a Digital Age: Modeling Internet Effects on Civic Participation." *Communication Research* 32(2005): 1–35; Terri L. Towner. "All Political Participation Is Socially Networked?: New Media and the 2012 Election." *Social Science Computer Review* 31(2013): 527–541.

16. Bimber and Davis, *Campaigning Online*; Jacob Groshek and Daniela Dimitrova. "A Cross-section of Voter Learning, Campaign Interest and Intention to Vote in the 2008 American Election: Did Web 2.0 Matter?" *Studies in Communications* 9(2011): 355–375; Dietram A. Scheufele and Matthew Nisbet. "Being a Citizen Online: New Opportunities and Dead Ends." *The Harvard International Journal of Press/Politics* 7(2002): 55–75.

17. Gary Hanson, Paul M. Haridakis, Audrey W. Cunningham, Rekha Sharma, and J. D. Ponder. "The 2008 Presidential Campaign: Political Cynicism in the Age of Facebook, MySpace, and YouTube." *Mass Communication and Society* 13(2010): 584–607; Matthew Kushin and Masahiro Yamamoto. "Did Social Media Really Matter? College Students' Use of Online Media and Political Decision Making in the 2008 Election." *Mass Communication and Society* 13(2010): 608–630; Terri L. Towner and David A. Dulio. "The Web 2.0 Election: Does the Online Medium

Matter?" *Journal of Political Marketing* 10(2011a): 165–188; Terri L. Towner and David A. Dulio. "An Experiment of Campaign Effects during the YouTube Election." *New Media and Society* 13(2011b), 626–644.

18. Jody C Baumgartner and Jonathan Morris. "MyFacebookTube Politics: Social Networking and Political Engagement of Young Adults." *Social Science Computer Review* 28(2009): 24–44; Daniela Dimitrova, Adam Shehata, Jesper Stromback, and Lars Nord. "The Effects of Digital Media on Political Knowledge and Participation in Election Campaigns: Evidence from Panel Data." *Communication Research* 41(2014): 95–118; Groshek and Dimitrova. "A Cross-section of Voter Learning, Campaign Interest and Intention to Vote in the 2008 American Election"; Kelly Kaufhold, Sebastian Valenzuela, and Homero Gil de Zuñiga. "Citizen Journalism and Democracy: How User-Generated News Use Relates to Political Knowledge and Participation." *Journalism and Mass Communication Quarterly* 87(2010): 515–529; Josh Pasek, Eian More, and Daniel Romer. "Realizing the Social Internet? Online Social Networking Meets Offline Civic Engagement." *Journal of Information Technology and Politics* 6(2009): 197–215; Terri L. Towner. "Information Hubs or Drains?: The Role of Online Sources in Campaign Learning," in *Handbook of Research on Citizens Engagement and Public Participation in the Era of New Media*, ed., Marco Adria and Yuping Mao (IGI Global, 2017), 157; Towner and Dulio, "The Web 2.0 Election."

19. See Jesper Stromback and Spiro Kiousis. "A New Look at Agenda-Setting Effects—Comparing the Predictive Power of Overall Political News Consumption and Specific New Media Consumption across Different Media Channels and Media Types." *Journal of Communication* 60(2010): 271–292.

balance the incentives for change against practical political motivations such as the desire to win support from undecided voters and the ability to communicate broad messages. This leaves us with the question: Did the unique aspects of the 2016 presidential election upend congressional campaign strategies such that they viewed and used their websites differently than in the past while also engaging with the presidential candidates?

We start in the next section by describing our survey and data. We then present our results in two main sections. The first focuses on how respondents viewed and used the web in 2016, compared to previous years. This includes an analysis of target audiences, likely visitors, and the website's relative effectiveness compared to other forms of communication. This section also includes results on website goals and whether the site was used to go negative against the opponent. The second results section focuses on the tendency of congressional campaign websites to mention the presidential candidates. We conclude with a brief discussion of our findings.

2016 CAMPAIGN SURVEY DATA

Between 2008 and 2014, we conducted four surveys of those involved with the creation and maintenance of online congressional campaigns. Each survey captured basic information about the candidate, the race, and how respondents viewed and used the Internet.[11] We replicated this survey in 2016 with additional questions about online references to the presidential candidates.[12]

As in past years, we used Project Vote Smart to create a list of all major party general election congressional candidates. We then searched each candidate's website for contact information, such as the names, emails, and phone numbers of possible respondents (e.g., Campaign Manager, Communications Director). In mid-September, we sent an email request either to the specific contact or to the campaign more generally asking for someone "involved in the construction and/or maintenance of the [campaign] website" to complete a brief, confidential survey via an online link or email. We repeated our request up to three more times either by email or phone (when available), including a final request in the days immediately following the election.

We sent our requests to the 830 campaigns for which we had a workable email address (n = 772) or online inquiry form (n = 58). We received 118 responses, leading to an overall response rate of 14.2%, which is not far off the typical range for these types of web surveys.[13] In our analysis, the Ns are slightly smaller due to item non-response.

To confirm that we had contacted appropriate individuals, we posed an initial screening question asking respondents to indicate the extent to which they were informed about how the content of the site was determined, on a seven-point scale, with higher scores indicating more knowledge. The average response was 6.57 (standard deviation = 1.00, n = 115) with 76.52% of respondents rating themselves at the top of our scale (i.e., "very informed").

Respondents were then asked about the campaign for which they worked. This included questions about race competitiveness and the candidate's office level (House or Senate), party, gender, and incumbency status. Our sample reflects the actual population of 2016 congressional campaigns fairly well in terms of race competitiveness (toss-up: 15.52% sample / 6.81% population), office level (Senate: 11.02% sample / 7.67% population), party (Democratic: 55.56% sample / 50.16% population), candidate gender (male: 80.17% sample / 79.03% population), and incumbency status (challengers: 52.99% sample / 41.60% population).[14] While there are some discrepancies between our sample and the population, the modes are the same in all categories except candidate status, where we have a slightly higher number of responses from challenger campaigns. Nevertheless, we have plenty of responses from incumbent campaigns (n = 44), sufficient variation between incumbent and non-incumbent campaigns, and no clear basis to believe that respondents from incumbent campaigns systematically differ from those who did not respond.

Our survey asked respondents to indicate their perception of how often an average member of several groups (e.g., undecided voters, supporters, journalists) visited the site, on a seven-point scale, with higher scores indicating more frequent visits. Respondents used a similar scale to rate the priority of these same groups in terms of each being a target audience of the website, with higher scores indicating higher priority. We also asked respondents to assess, again with a seven-point scale, how they thought campaign websites compared to other communications (e.g., direct mailings, television ads, candidate speeches) in terms of "capturing the campaign's overall strategy," how websites compared to email and social media in terms of communicating directly with voters, and to rate the importance of various goals for their site (e.g., persuading undecided voters, increasing awareness of issue positions, fundraising). Respondents also noted whether their sites included any negative mentions of their opponent, and whether the site referenced either Hillary Clinton or Donald Trump.

It is important to reiterate that all responses were given on the promise of complete anonymity, so we have no way to know exactly which campaigns responded. This means that we are unable to match individual survey results to other measures such as actual website contact, fundraising data, or district partisanship. We believe a survey of those involved in campaign website design and maintenance has particular advantages over relying on content analysis data of the websites.[15] Specifically, it allows us to isolate the expressed motivation of campaign insiders. Moreover, repeating the survey conducted in earlier years (2008–2014) allows us to assess how their motivations might have changed in 2016.

VIEWS AND USES OF CONGRESSIONAL CAMPAIGN WEBSITES IN 2016

In this section, we analyze how campaign personnel view *and* use their campaign websites. We address each topic—views and uses—in turn. For each, we compare the stable trends we uncovered from 2008 through 2014 to data from 2016 to answer the question of whether this particular election affected (e.g., interrupted) what had become typical. This is an interesting question given the unique nature of the 2016 presidential campaign. For example, intensifying polarization and incivility at the national level might have led congressional campaigns to shift their website target audience from voters in general to supporters, and to see supporters as even more likely to visit their sites than in past years.[16] The general campaign also could have stimulated greater negativity such that even incumbents—who historically avoid negative campaigning[17]—go negative. Additionally, the emphasis on social media at the presidential level may have led congressional campaigns to rethink their website goals and to see their websites as relatively less effective at communicating with voters. The bottom line is that 2016 appears to be a strong test case for stability. If campaigns maintained their traditional strategies in 2016, it would be powerful evidence that the place of websites in congressional campaigns is quite stable.

Views of Websites

There are reasons to expect continuity in how congressional campaign insiders view their websites. This possibility stems from three key premises. First, campaigns have limited control over the audiences that visit their websites. Regardless of technological advancements and targeted appeals, the decision to visit a campaign website still requires deliberate choice and action by individuals. The implication is that those most engaged in the campaign—engaged voters, journalists and bloggers who write about the campaign, and supportive voters and activists who selectively expose themselves to media[18]—are expected to visit much more often than the typical voter. Second, this lack of control does not constrain who campaigns target. Campaigns ought to realize that any items placed on their websites can potentially become central to the campaign narrative—it takes only a journalist or an opponent to make it so.[19] For this reason, campaigns need to be cognizant of the latent audience of all voters, regardless of the frequency with which average voters access the site. Thus, the main targets are likely to be voters in general and undecided voters. Third, websites are a relatively unique media insofar as they provide an unmediated and virtually unlimited presentation of information.[20] This contrasts with other media (e.g., television news) that do not allow campaigns to communicate directly or communications with time and space limits (e.g., speeches, mailers, most other digital media such as email and Twitter). This means websites, relative to other media, can potentially serve as digital hubs that encapsulate their entire campaign platform. These three points, in theory, are exactly what we found in our 2008 to 2014 surveys, both in aggregate and year-to-year results.[21] But do these trends hold in the uniquely polarized, fragmented, and uncivil environment of the 2016 election?

We begin to explore this in Figure 1.1, where we present the averages and standard deviations from our questions about the perceptions of the frequency of website visits (black bars) and the primary target audiences (gray bars). The black bars show that campaigns perceived highly engaged voters, supportive voters, supportive activists, journalists, and then bloggers as the most frequent visitors in 2016. There is then a statistically significant drop in perceived frequency of visits by voters in general and undecided voters, with opponent's voters and non-voters considered the least likely to visit (comparing bloggers to voters in general gives t_{98} = 1.767, p = .080 in a two-tailed test). The gray bars in Figure 1.1 further show that campaigns targeted voters in general and undecided voters over all others (comparing undecided voters to highly engaged voters gives t_{100} = 2.364, p = .020 in a two-tailed test). Thus, even with the polarized nature of the 2016 campaign where people may have been particularly likely to be selective in media exposure,[22] congressional campaign strategy on the web did not change when it came to targets. The reality of "potential" access to all meant the targets remained voters writ large.

Stability in views of the website audience is accentuated by the fact that the results in Figure 1.1 are virtually identical to the results from our 2008–2014 surveys.[23] In fact, the relative rankings and absolute values given to each group are remarkably similar. For example, respondents gave highly engaged voters an average target rating of 5.37 and an average frequency rating of 4.79 between 2008 and 2014, compared to 5.38 and 4.62 respectively in 2016 (comparing highly engaged voters' target rating between 2008–2014 and 2016 gives t_{559} = 0.045, p = .964 in a two-tailed test and comparing highly engaged voters' frequency rating between 2008–14 and 2016 gives $t_{522} = 0.995$, $p = 0.320$ in a two-tailed test). Thus, congressional campaigns clearly did not change how they viewed their likely visitors and targets in 2016. Rather than adapting to the context, congressional campaigns stuck to their original perceptions of who visits and to whom they should tailor their website.

The realities of voter behavior and technological limits and opportunities, and not the uniqueness of the 2016 campaign, drove views of websites. Moreover, the consistency of the approach is an important reminder to avoid confounding the perceived frequency of visitors with the intended targets of the website. Certain groups may be seen as more important even if they visit less often.[24] This disconnect also demonstrates the danger, particularly in a highly polarized environment like 2016, of targeting supporters with websites that might alienate some other crucial group of voters. Focusing the website on a broad audience may do little to fire up the base, but it ensures that potentially persuadable voters will not be turned off, even if they do not visit all that often.

We also mentioned that technological realities might lead campaigns to continue to view their websites as digital hubs reflecting their entire campaign platform. This could be the case both because of the unmediated and infinite information capacity of websites and also because the main target audience of voters in general would be best persuaded by full information, rather than potentially contrary targeted information.

We asked respondents to rate how well campaign websites, candidate speeches, informal conversations, mailings, media coverage, and television ads "capture the campaign's overall strategy." Figure 1.2 presents averages and standard deviations, and shows that respondents in 2016 estimated websites to be more representative of their overall strategy than all other forms of communication. Campaign websites are rated slightly higher than candidate speeches and informal conversations while clearly outpacing the ability of mailings, media coverage, and television ads to capture the campaign's platform.[25] Moreover, these results match those from previous years. For example, campaign websites received an average rating of 5.85 between 2008 and 2014, compared to 5.81 in 2016, while candidate speeches and informal conversations were basically unmoved from 5.59 to 5.60 and from 5.48 to 5.49 respectively.[26] In fact, the only change over time that approaches statistical significance is with television ads, which dropped from 4.75 to 4.28 (comparing television ads between 2008–2014 and 2016 gives $t_{354} = 1.661$, $p = .098$ in a two-tailed test), which may reflect an increasingly fragmented television market and thus a move towards more targeted advertising.[27] Campaign insiders clearly still value websites for their ability to present an unlimited and unmediated portrait of their entire campaign strategy.

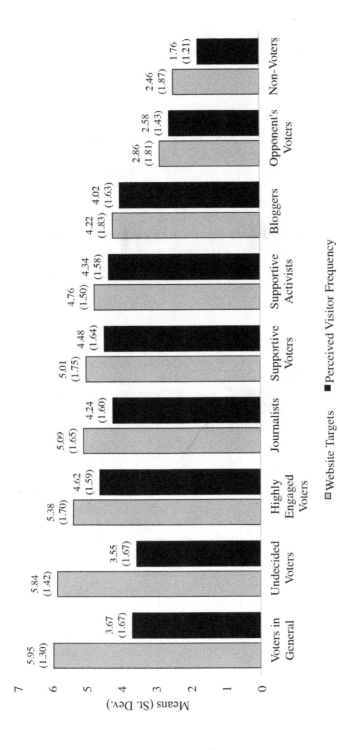

Figure 1.1. Website Targets and Perceived Visitor Frequency (2016)

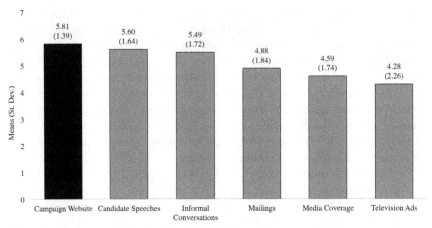

Figure 1.2. Communicating the Campaign's Overall Strategy (2016)

Our last inquiry into how campaigns view their websites concerns the relative effectiveness of different new media. We measured perceived effectiveness by asking respondents to rate how much their campaign used campaign websites, email, and various social media to communicate with voters in 2016—the idea being that media use reflects perceived effectiveness. The results in Figure 1.3 show that respondents used websites moderately, although significantly less than Facebook and email (comparing email to campaign websites gives t_{93} = 5.090, p = .000 in a two-tailed test). While congressional campaigns also used Twitter moderately in 2016, they reported much less use of YouTube, Instagram, LinkedIn, and other social media, indicating a nuanced view of social media as a direct communications tool (comparing Twitter to campaign websites gives t_{92} = 0.362, p = .718 in a two-tailed test, campaign websites to YouTube gives t_{91} = 5.806, p = .000 in a two-tailed test). Perhaps campaigns resist relying on social media that constrains their communication in terms of length (Twitter) or written content (Instagram), even if the communication is active and targeted. It could also be that campaigns feel there are simply too many social media platforms to maintain with limited staff resources or they worry that social media will promote open, two-way communication (unlike websites) that they would rather avoid.[28]

We have less data on trends when it comes to this issue as our past work only explored it in 2014. Nevertheless, the results above replicate those we received in 2014 when we asked about websites, email, Facebook, and Twitter. In fact, the only significant differences between 2014 and 2016 were with email, which marginally increased from 5.39 to 5.79, and Twitter, which dropped from 5.39 to 4.76 in terms of use.[29] The fact that websites maintained a relatively lower ranking than Facebook and email is sensible insofar as websites, despite providing an opportunity for holistic messaging, are limited in terms of reach. As mentioned above, individuals must make a concerted effort to visit a campaign website, which means that only a select portion of the population is likely to visit. Websites represent a passive form of communication compared to email and social media that can be used to actively distribute information to subscribers and followers. Thus, campaigns are relatively unsure that website information is reaching the intended voters, but they can be fairly certain that email and social media posts are being received. This makes emphasizing Facebook and email sensible.

This ostensible stability means that even though 2016 was purported to be the ultimate social media campaign,[30] little changed in terms of how much congressional campaign websites were used to communicate with voters. The consistency between media also reflects the fact that, despite all of the social media hype in 2016, we find campaigns holding consistent views on the fundamental differences between social media, email, and campaign websites in terms of their inherent ability to communicate with voters—i.e., their fundamental qualities have stayed the same. It may take a more dramatic shift for congressional campaigns to rethink how they communicate with voters online.

All of these results present a virtually unchanged view of congressional campaigning on the web in 2016. Those who design and maintain campaign websites clearly resisted the opportunity to reassess their approach in the context of a historic election, which speaks to the power of fundamental strategic incentives over technological trends and changes in the political environment. Congressional campaigns continue to see their websites as digital hubs, ideally suited for presenting broad messages

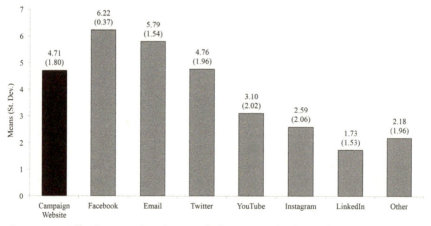

Figure 1.3.   Effectiveness of Various Media in Communicating with Voters (2016)

to voters in general while favoring email and Facebook for communicating directly with supporters and engaged voters. Moreover, in results available from the authors, we find limited variability in these findings across campaign types—the views of websites reported here are virtually constant regardless of race competitiveness, candidate party, office level, incumbency, or gender. The realities of voter behavior and technology apply across campaigns, which speaks to the fact that these views are based on powerful premises that are largely constant across both time and electoral context. Even the 2016 campaign could not dislodge views of websites, at least at the congressional level. This also speaks to perhaps the potentially limited direct impact that presidential campaigns have on congressional campaigning.[31] The lesson is *continuity*.

Website Uses

While campaigns may have a fairly uniform and stable *view* of their websites, this does not necessarily mean that they all *use* their websites in the same way. Indeed, the logic underlying website usage may differ from the aforementioned key points about how they view their websites. This is because different types of candidates—even if they all view voters in general as the central target—may have distinct incentives on what type of message to put forth. The central point of variation in message preference concerns incumbency status.

It is well known that incumbents enjoy an edge over challengers, all else constant. Their status alone can generate up to a 10% advantage in vote share,[32] which has meant that House and Senate incumbents have historically won more than 85% of the time.[33] This gives incumbents scant incentive to actively campaign, and instead they would be best served by focusing on what makes incumbents preferable, namely their backgrounds, which involves having ties to the district and experience.[34] In contrast, challengers need to get voters' attention, which they can do by going negative,[35] and they must also mobilize people to vote and persuade them to focus on issues and other items that can counter the incumbency advantage. These are the exact trends we found from 2008 to 2014,[36] which could hold in 2016 given the fundamental nature of these incentives.

In 2016, we assessed these dynamics with a question that asked respondents to rate the importance of various website goals (i.e., how they used their websites) on seven-point scales. Figure 1.4 shows that, overall, the primary goal of most campaigns is to increase awareness of issue positions, followed by increasing awareness of the candidate's background and persuading undecided voters. The graph then shows a gradual decline from fundraising to providing information on the opponent's

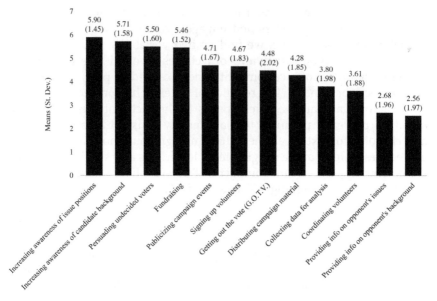

Figure 1.4.   Campaign Website Goals (2016)

background. This order is almost entirely consistent with the goals expressed by campaign insiders in previous years.[37]

Of more importance is the fact that these goals differ based on incumbency status, as they have in past years. We analyze the role of incumbency in Table 1.1, where we regressed each goal on a variety of campaign features. The results show that incumbent campaigns continue to use their websites to promote the candidate's background much more than non-incumbent campaigns, while non-incumbent campaigns put more emphasis on all other goals. These other goals include the aforementioned efforts to counteract the incumbent's advantage by promoting issues and active campaigning (e.g., fundraising, persuading, and distributing material). While past results were a little more robust, the fact remains that, in 2016, website goals continue to differ between incumbent and non-incumbent campaigns. We also, in Table 1.2, studied if non-incumbent campaigns go negative more often. We find that 2016 was no different than past years in that non-incumbent campaigns continue to use their websites to attack their opponents much more often than incumbent campaigns.

Taken together, these results paint a clear picture of how congressional campaign insiders viewed and used their websites in 2016. They targeted voters in general while recognizing that engaged voters and supporters were more likely to visit, and they saw their websites as digital hubs, better suited for capturing their entire strategy than communicating directly

Table 1.1. Campaign Website Content Goals (2016)

	Promote Issues	Promote Background	Fundraise	Persuade	Distribute Material	Sign Up Volunteers	Publicize Campaign Events	G.O.T.V.	Coord. Volunteer	Opp. Background	Opp. Issue
Democrat	-.213	-.337	-.199	-.099	.135	-.083	-.394*	-.063	.058	-.083	-.115
	(.247)	(.244)	(.231)	(.235)	(.224)	(.225)	(.226)	(.227)	(.228)	(.242)	(.238)
Senate	-.493	-.785*	.760*	-.878**	-.830*	-.418	-.158	.003	-.226	-.387	-.491
	(.402)	(.414)	(.429)	(.395)	(.397)	(.394)	(.388)	(.429)	(.393)	(.438)	(.439)
Competitiveness	-.104	-.021	.103	-.230	-.301*	-.077	-.122	.055	.130	.175	.029
	(.172)	(.167)	(.168)	(.166)	(.162)	(.161)	(.160)	(.163)	(.163)	(.171)	(.170)
Incumbent	-.646**	.668***	-.238	-.374	-.523**	-.414*	-.573**	-.209	-.285	-.275	-.250
	(.257)	(.260)	(.244)	(.246)	(.243)	(.240)	(.241)	(.241)	(.242)	(.262)	(.257)
Female	-.067	-.075	-.282	-.102	.038	.019	.010	-.027	.392	.125	-.027
	(.289)	(.285)	(.269)	(.273)	(.262)	(.261)	(.261)	(.266)	(.269)	(.286)	(.283)
Log Likelihood	-132.217	-137.078	-148.780	-148.672	-168.941	-178.022	-170.644	-177.809	-175.235	-143.159	-150.013
N	96	96	96	95	95	96	96	95	94	95	95

Note: Entries are ordered probit coefficients with standard errors in parentheses. *** p < .01; ** p < .05; * p < .10 for two-tailed tests. Test statistics available from authors on request.

Table 1.2.   Going Negative (2016)

	Negative Mention of Opponent
Democrat	.085
	(.305)
Senate	.629
	(.483)
Competitiveness	.278
	(.187)
Incumbent	−.973***
	(.329)
Female	.278
	(.376)
Log Likelihood	−53.512
N	95

Note: Entries are probit coefficients with standard errors in parentheses. *** p < .01; ** p < .05; * p < .10 for two-tailed tests.

with supporters. Non-incumbent campaigns also used their websites much more aggressively than their incumbent counterparts. What is perhaps most remarkable, however, is how consistent these results are with those from previous years. On nearly every measure, congressional campaign insiders reported virtually identical responses, despite the fact that 2016 provided an opportunity to reassess their approach to online campaigning—the emphasis on social media and the unique nature of the 2016 presidential campaign *did not change incentives in congressional campaigns*. The fundamentals of congressional campaigning seem invulnerable to technological trends and contextual changes, at least in the face of the historic 2016 presidential campaign. That said, one area where the presidential election may have crept in concerns when campaigns engage with the presidential race by mentioning either Hillary Clinton or Donald Trump. We now turn to this question.

MENTIONING 2016 PRESIDENTIAL CANDIDATES ON CONGRESSIONAL CAMPAIGN WEBSITES

The most notable political story by far in 2016 was the presidential race, and at first glance it might make sense for congressional campaigns to raise their profiles by engaging and mentioning that race. The 2016 presidential campaign was novel in a number of respects, including the backgrounds, characteristics, and behavior of the candidates themselves. In Hillary Clinton, Democrats had the first woman to be nominated for president by a major American political party, a politician with years of experience who had wrapped up the vast majority of in-party endorse-ments,[38] and a politician with a history of some negative baggage. In Donald Trump, Republicans had nominated a billionaire outsider who had never held political or military office and promised to transform American government,[39] a reality television personality who had shaped his brand through controversy, and a provocateur who made numerous outlandish statements on the campaign trail and in his prior professional life, including statements about women.

Together, these candidate qualities brought extraordinary attention to the open seat presidential contest. Indeed, there were relatively large seg-ments of the voting public who did not like the candidates, albeit for very different reasons. Both major presidential candidates had historically low favorability ratings with the country as a whole and the electorate,[40] and coverage of the presidential campaign itself was overwhelmingly nega-tive.[41] So, congressional campaigns had difficult choices to make about whether they would associate themselves with or mention (potentially negatively) the campaigns of Donald Trump or Hillary Clinton. There may have been some risk in doing so.

Trump's outsider status, controversial campaign style and statements, and low ratings with the electorate overall could conceivably give his own partisans reasons to distance themselves from him and Democrats motivation to attack him online to energize base voters.[42] On the other hand, and despite low overall favorability ratings, Hillary Clinton's his-toric candidacy and popularity with the Democratic base might lead more Democrats to associate themselves with her campaign.

One key dynamic in the race was the combination of Clinton's historic candidacy as the first female nominee of a major American political party and Trump's history with and statements about women. The intensity of attention to these aspects of the campaign could have made this an elec-tion in which congressional candidates and their campaigns were more acutely aware of gender (and discussion of gender) and its perceived ef-fects on voters.

The older conventional wisdom when it comes to gender and congres-sional campaigns is that there is stereotyping by voters, gendered patterns in how the different sexes communicate through campaign advertise-ments, and differences in press coverage of men's and women's candida-cies.[43] However, more recent research casts some doubt on whether there are still significant differences between male and female candidates in how their campaigns communicate and how the news media covers their candidacies.[44] Hayes and Lawless argue that gender gaps in issue agendas and word usage in campaign communications have more to do with dif-ferences across political parties than the gender of the candidates.

There is, however, a shortage of research on how congressional candidates of different genders relate to presidential candidates. It is possible that Trump's behavior was not an "issue" in the sense that types of policy programs constitute issues and his actions and comments about women prompted Democrats and female candidates to mention him more on their websites.

To test these ideas, we added a new item to our 2016 survey of congressional campaign insiders that asked whether their websites mentioned any of the presidential candidates. Campaigns in general reported very few mentions of either Clinton or Trump—they cautiously stayed away from the potentially polarizing candidates. Table 1.3 shows only 17.09% of campaigns reported mentioning Trump and a slightly higher percentage—18.80%—mentioned Clinton. In other words, the vast majority of campaigns did not mention the presidential candidates at all. Beyond that, there appear to be some interesting partisan differences. Democratic campaigns mentioned Clinton (25%) significantly more than Republicans (10%), while Republicans were only marginally more likely to mention Trump (22%) than Democrats (14.06%) (comparing Clinton mentions by Democrats and Republicans gives $t_{114} = -1.851$, $p = .067$; comparing Trump mentions by Democrats and Republicans gives $t_{114} = 1.001$, $p = .319$). These differences suggest that when presidential candidates were mentioned, there was a slight partisan slant which is perhaps not surprising given the polarized environment. Overall, though, the campaign did not cause the majority of congressional candidates to engage with the presidential race.

Table 1.3. Descriptive Statistics on Presidential Candidate Mentions (2016)

		Clinton		Trump	
		%	n	%	n
	All Candidates (117)	18.80	22	17.09	20
Party	Democrats (64)	25.00	16	14.06	9
	Republicans (50)	10.00	5	22.00	11
Gender	Female (23)	30.44	7	30.44	7
	Male (93)	16.13	15	13.98	13
Office	House (104)	20.19	21	16.35	17
	Senate (13)	7.69	1	23.08	3
Status	Incumbent (44)	25.00	11	15.91	7
	Non-Incumbent (72)	15.28	11	18.06	13
Competitiveness	Solid (62)	20.97	13	16.13	10
	Leaning (36)	16.67	6	22.22	8
	Toss-Up (18)	16.67	3	11.11	2

There also appear to be some differences between male and female congressional candidates. Female candidate campaigns mentioned both Clinton and Trump on 30.44% of their websites, while male candidate campaigns were marginally less likely to mention Clinton (16.13%) and significantly less likely to mention Trump (13.98%) (comparing Clinton mentions between female and male candidates gives $t_{114} = -1.570$, p = .119; comparing Trump mentions between female and male candidates gives $t_{114} = -1.883$, p = .062). Again, while the vast majority of congressional campaigns avoided any mention of either presidential candidate, it seems as though some female candidate campaigns were drawn in more than their male counterparts.

Table 1.4 shows logit coefficients and standard errors for separate regressions for reported Clinton and Trump mentions. The results substantiate the findings above. First, Democratic campaigns are significantly more likely than Republican campaigns to mention Clinton on their websites; however, there is no party difference when it comes to mentioning Trump, all else constant. Second, we find that female candidate campaigns are marginally (p = .114) more likely than male candidate campaigns to mention Clinton and significantly more likely to mention Trump.

We believe these findings suggest that, overall, congressional campaigns reacted cautiously to the presidential campaign context. Most avoided any mention of either presidential candidate on their campaign websites. However, of those that did enter the fray, there was a tendency among Democratic and female candidate campaigns to become more involved than their counterparts. Republicans and male candidates ostensibly had fewer incentives or felt it would be riskier to mention either Trump or Clinton. While this suggests that the political environment may

Table 1.4.   Presidential Candidate Mentions (2016)

	Clinton	Trump
Democrat	1.116**	–.521
	(.568)	(.533)
Senate	–.732	.292
	(1.11)	(.773)
Competitiveness	–.084	–.106
	(.355)	(.358)
Incumbent	.760	–.460
	(.546)	(.564)
Female	.901#	1.078*
	(.571)	(.561)
Log Likelihood	–51.4356	–50.4996
N	115	115

Note: Entries are logit coefficients with standard errors in parentheses. *** p < .01; ** p < .05; * p < .10; # p < .115 in two-tailed tests.

have prompted a small group of congressional campaigns to mention the presidential contenders, the point remains that even major environmental forces, like the intense partisanship and gendered dynamics of the 2016 election, have a limited ability to cause most congressional campaigns to deviate from the message they present online.

CONCLUSION

The nature and outcome of the 2016 presidential campaign surprised most scholars, pundits, and citizens. Many point to its polarizing nature, but regardless, if nothing else, it was unique for its inclusion of a clear political outsider (i.e., Trump is the first president to have neither prior political nor military experience) and a major party woman candidate. There were also numerous reports about the perceived importance of social media and its potential to change the nature of campaigning.[45] We sought to assess whether these realities altered how congressional candidates campaigned on the web. We did so by following up on our prior work that entailed surveys of campaign website personnel from 2008 through 2014.

Perhaps surprisingly, we find amazing continuity in how campaigns view and use their websites. National politics does not dislodge historic congressional campaign practices, at least when it comes to web campaigning. Congressional campaign websites continue to serve as digital hubs, capturing the campaign's overall platform and being used strategically depending on a candidate's status. Whether these trends will sustain going forward, as new technologies develop, is a question for future research. We also find that the intense partisanship and gendered dynamics of the 2016 presidential race had limited impact on congressional candidate mentions of Trump and Clinton. Despite, or perhaps because of, powerful narratives at the national level, the vast majority of congressional campaign websites stayed away from the presidential race. We see all of this as quite remarkable given the incentives that congressional campaigners had to change, even if only slightly, their approach to online campaigning. The 2016 campaign was a strong test case for change, and yet the results are clear: congressional campaign use of the Internet remains consistent and cautious.

NOTES

1. We thank the National Science Foundation (1627413, 1627431) for generous research support. We also thank Edward Douglass, Sam Gubitz, Lena Kesden, Kendall Mahavier, Brady Marks, Devon McMahon, Bit Meehan, Jacob Rothschild, Richard Shafranek, Gabe Steller, and Zelda Wengrod for research assistance.

2. James N. Druckman, Martin J. Kifer, Michael Parkin, and Ivonne Montes. "An Inside View of Congressional Campaigning on the Web." *Journal of Political Marketing,* forthcoming.

3. Pew Research Center. "Partisanship and Political Animosity in 2016." Last modified June 22, 2016. http://www.people-press.org/2016/06/22/partisanship-and-political-animosity-in-2016/.

4. Maeve Duggan and Aaron Smith. "The Political Environment on Social Media." *Pew Research Center,* Last modified October 25, 2016. http://www.pewinternet.org/2016/10/25/the-political-environment-on-social-media/.

5. Katie Leslie and Jordan Rudner. "Clinton, Trump and Gender Dynamics Pose 'Unprecedented Political Spectacle' at Presidential Debate." *Dallas Morning News,* September 23, 2016. http://www.dallasnews.com/news/politics/2016/09/23/clinton-trump-gender-dynamics-pose-unprecedented-political-spectacle-presidential-debate.

6. Vassia Gueorguieva. "Voters, MySpace, and YouTube: The Impact of Alternative Communication Channels on the 2006 Election Cycle and Beyond," *Social Science Computer Review* 26.3 (2008): 288–300; Jennifer Golbeck, Justin Grimes, and Anthony Rogers. "Twitter Use by the U.S. Congress," *Journal for the American Society of Information Science and Technology* 61.8 (2010): 1612–1621.

7. Jennifer Stromer-Galley. *Presidential Campaigning in the Internet Age.* (New York: Oxford University Press, 2014); Bruce Bimber. "Digital Media in the Obama Campaigns of 2008 and 2012: Adaption to the Personalized Political Communication Environment," *Journal of Information Technology and Politics* 11.2 (2014): 130–150.

8. Aja Romano. "The Year Social Media Changed Everything," *Vox,* December 31, 2016. http://www.vox.com/2016/12/31/13869676/social-media-influence-alt-right; also see Amanda Hess. "Memes, Myself and I: The Internet Lets Us All Run the Campaign." *New York Times,* November 6, 2016. https://www.nytimes.com/2016/11/06/arts/memes-myself-and-i-the-internet-lets-us-all-run-the-campaign.html?_r=0.

9. David McCabe. "Welcome to the Social Media Election." *The Hill,* August 17, 2015. http://thehill.com/policy/technology/251185-welcome-to-the-social-media-election.

10. Pew Research Center. "As Election Nears, Voters Divided Over Democracy and 'Respect.'" Last modified October 27, 2016. http://www.people-press.org/2016/10/27/as-election-nears-voters-divided-over-democracy-and-respect/.

11. For more information on these surveys, see Druckman et al. "An Inside View of Congressional Campaigning on the Web."

12. A full copy of the survey is available from the authors.

13. Mick P. Couper. *Designing Effective Web Surveys.* (New York: Cambridge University Press, 2008), 340.

14. Population competitiveness comes from the Cook Political Report. For House results, see Cook Political Report, October 27, 2016, http://cookpolitical.com/house/charts/race-ratings/10124. For Senate results, see Cook Political Report, November 2, 2016, http://cookpolitical.com/senate/charts/race-rat-

ings/10145. All other population figures are based on data from Project Vote Smart; see http://votesmart.org.

15. For example, Kirsten A. Foot and Steven M. Schneider. *Web Campaigning.* (Cambridge: MIT Press, 2006); James N. Druckman, Martin J. Kifer, and Michael Parkin. "Congressional Campaign Communications in an Internet Age." *Journal of Elections, Public Opinion, and Parties* 24 (2014): 20–44.

16. Andrew Soergel. "Divided We Stand: Political Polarization Drives Presidential Race to the Bottom." *US News and World Report*, July 19, 2016. http://www.usnews.com/news/articles/2016-07-19/political-polarization-drives-presidential-race-to-the-bottom; Pew Research Center. "As Election Nears, Voters Divided Over Democracy and 'Respect.'"

17. Kim Fridkin Kahn and Patrick J. Kenney. *No Holds Barred: Negativity in U.S. Senate Campaigns.* (Upper Saddle River, NJ: Pearson, Prentice-Hall, 2004).

18. Charles S. Taber and Milton Lodge. "Motivated Skepticism in the Evaluation of Political Beliefs." *American Journal of Political Science* 50.3 (2006): 755–769.

19. Emilienne Ireland and Phil Tajitsu Nash. *Winning Campaigns Online: Strategies for Candidates and Causes,* 2nd ed. (Bethesda, MD: Science Writers Press, 2001), 14–15; Diana Owen. "Media: The Complex Interplay of Old and New Forms." In *New Directions in Campaigns and Elections,* edited by Stephen K. Medvic, 145–162. (New York: Routledge, 2011); Mike Gruszczynski. "New and Traditional Media Reportage on Electoral Campaign Controversies." In *Controlling the Message: New Media in American Political Campaigns,* ed. Victoria A. Farrar-Myers and Justin S. Vaughn, 113–135. (New York: New York University Press, 2015).

20. James N. Druckman, Martin J. Kifer, and Michael Parkin. "Campaign Communications in U.S. Congressional Elections." *American Political Science Review* 103.3 (2009): 343–366.

21. Druckman et al. "An Inside View of Congressional Campaigning on the Web."

22. Markus Prior. "Media and Political Polarization." *Annual Review of Political Science* 16 (2013): 101–127.

23. For details, see Druckman et al. "An Inside View of Congressional Campaigning on the Web."

24. See, however, Judith S. Trent, Robert V. Friedenberg, and Robert E. Denton, Jr. *Political Campaign Communication: Principles and Practices,* 7th ed. (New York: Rowman & Littlefield, 2011), 368–369.

25. Although websites have the highest absolute mean, the differences between websites, candidate speeches, and informal conversations fail to reach conventional levels of statistical significance (comparing campaign websites to candidate speeches gives $t_{93} = 1.093$, $p = .277$ in a two-tailed test and campaign websites to informal conversations gives $t_{94} = 1.555$, $p = .123$ in a two-tailed test). There is, however, a significant difference between campaign websites and mailings, media coverage, and television ads (comparing informal conversations to mailings gives $t_{91} = 2.080$, $p = .040$ in a two-tailed test). The lack of statistical significance on the first two comparisons with campaign websites is almost certainly the result of sample size, as the absolute differences are nearly identical to the statistically significant differences we found for campaigns between 2008 and 2014 (see, Druckman et al. "An Inside View of Congressional Campaigning on the Web").

26. Two-tailed t-tests between 2008–14 and 2016 yield no statistically significant results on websites (t_{511} = 0.234, p = .815), candidate speeches (t_{507} = 0.062, p = .951), or informal conversations (t_{509} = 0.065, p = .949).

27. Erika Fowler, Michael M. Franz, and Travis N. Ridout. *Political Advertising in the United States*. (Boulder, CO: Westview Press, 2016), 104–109.

28. Jennifer Stromer-Galley. "On-line Interaction and Why Candidates Avoid It." *Journal of Communication* 50.4 (2000): 111–132.

29. Two-tailed t-tests between 2014 and 2016 yield the following: on website use (t_{178} = 0.440, p = .660), Facebook (t_{176} = 0.390, p = .697), email (t_{177} = 1.879, p = .062), and Twitter (t_{176} = 2.508, p = .013).

30. McCabe, "Welcome to the Social Media Election"; Romano, "The Year Social Media Changed Everything."

31. Gary C. Jacobson. *The Politics of Congressional Elections*, 8th ed. (Boston: Pearson, 2013).

32. Stephen Ansolabehere and James M. Snyder. "Using Term Limits to Estimate Incumbency Advantages When Officeholders Retire Strategically." *Legislative Studies Quarterly* 29 (2004): 487–515: 487; Alan I. Abramowitz, Brad Alexander, and Matthew Gunning. "Incumbency, Redistricting, and the Decline of Competition in U.S. House Elections." *Journal of Politics* 68 (2006): 75–88; Jacobson, *The Politics of Congressional Elections*; Jens Hainmueller, Andrew B. Hall, and James M. Snyder, Jr. "Assessing the External Validity of Election RD Estimates: An Investigation of the Incumbency Advantage." *Journal of Politics* 77.3 (2015): 707–720.

33. Roger H. Davidson, Walter J. Oleszek, Francis E. Lee, and Eric Schickler. *Congress and Its Members*, 15th ed. (Los Angeles: CQ Press, 2016), 94

34. Morris P. Fiorina. *Congress: Keystone of the Washington Establishment*, 2nd ed. (New Haven: Yale University Press, 1989); Paul Gronke. *The Electorate, the Campaign, and the Office: A Unified Approach to Senate and House Elections*. (Ann Arbor: University of Michigan Press, 2000), 142; Jacobson, *The Politics of Congressional Elections*; also see Druckman, Kifer, and Parkin. "Campaign Communications in U.S. Congressional Elections," 343–366; James N. Druckman, Martin J. Kifer, and Michael Parkin. "Timeless Strategy Meets New Medium: Going Negative on Congressional Campaign Websites, 2002–2006." *Political Communication* 27 (2010): 88–103.

35. George E. Marcus, W. Russell Neuman, and Michael MacKuen. *Affective Intelligence and Political Judgment*. (Chicago: University of Chicago Press, 2000); James N. Druckman and Rose McDermott. "Emotion and the Framing of Risky Choice." *Political Behavior* 30 (2008): 297–321.

36. Druckman, et al. "An Inside View of Congressional Campaigning on the Web."

37. Two-tailed t-tests between 2008–14 and 2016 yield few statistically significant results. The only differences that reached statistical significance are on increasing awareness of issue positions (t_{529} = 1.792, p = .074), signing up volunteers (t_{528} = 1.720, p = .086), and providing information on opponent's issues (t_{525} = 2.546, p = .011). See Druckman, et al. "An Inside View of Congressional Campaigning on the Web."

38. Clinton won the nomination by securing insider and elite support and defeating an outside candidate—Senator Bernie Sanders—who had always run

for U.S. House and Senate as an independent (see Linda Qui. "Is Bernie Sanders a Democrat?" *Politifact.com*, Last modified February 23, 2016. http://www.politifact.com/truth-o-meter/article/2016/feb/23/bernie-sanders-democrat/). Fivethirtyeight.com featured an "endorsement primary" tracking influential elected officials who had endorsed presidential candidates (see Aaron Bycoffe. "The Endorsement Primary," *Fivethirtyeight.com*, Last modified June 7, 2016. https://projects.fivethirtyeight.com/2016-endorsement-primary/).

39. Trump, who had not always been a registered Republican, ran as the consummate outsider candidate with statements and tactics that defied primary and general election campaign norms. Trump's victory in the primaries despite the vocal opposition from establishment party figures was seemingly at odds with expectations that the "party decides" presidential nominations (see Marty Cohen, David Karol, Hans Noel, and John Zaller. *The Party Decides: Presidential Nominations Before and After Reform*. [Chicago: The University of Chicago Press, 2009]; Steve Kolowich. "The Life of 'The Party Decides.'" *The Chronicle of Higher Education*, May 16, 2016. http://www.chronicle.com/article/The-Life-of-The-Party/236483).

40. Lydia Saad. "Trump Leads Clinton in Historically Bad Image Ratings." *Gallup*, July 1, 2016. http://www.gallup.com/poll/193376/trump-leads-clinton-historically-bad-image-ratings.aspx; Pew Research Center. "Partisanship and Political Animosity in 2016."

41. Thomas Patterson. "News Coverage of the 2016 General Election: How the Press Failed the Voters," *Shorenstein Center*, Last Modified December 7, 2016. https://shorensteincenter.org/news-coverage-2016-general-election/.

42. Stephen Ansolabehere and Shanto Iyengar. *Going Negative: How Political Advertisements Shrink and Polarize the Electorate. (*New York: Free Press, 1995).

43. Kim Fridkin Kahn. "Gender Differences in Campaign Messages: The Political Advertisements of Men and Women Candidates for U.S. Senate." *Political Research Quarterly* 46.3 (1993): 481–502; Kim Fridkin Kahn and Edie N. Goldenberg. "Women Candidates in the News: An Examination of Gender Differences in U.S. Senate Campaign Coverage." *Public Opinion Quarterly* 55.2 (1991): 180–199; Dianne G. Bystrom, Mary C. Banwart, Lynda Lee Kaid, and Terry A. Robertson. *Gender and Candidate Communication: VideoStyle, WebStyle, NewsStyle*. (New York: Routledge, 2004).

44. Danny Hayes and Jennifer L. Lawless. *Women on the Run: Gender, Media, and Political Campaigns in a Polarized Era. (*New York: Cambridge University Press, 2016); Jennifer L. Lawless. "Female Candidates and Legislators." *Annual Review of Political Science* 18 (2015): 349–366.

45. Romano, "The Year Social Media Changed Everything."

2

Campaigning in 140 Characters

A Content Analysis of Twitter Use by 2016 U.S. Congressional Candidates

Casey Frechette and Monica Ancu

In November of 2016, Americans elected 34 U.S. Senators and 435 U.S. House Representatives. Prior to the election, Democrats held 44 Senate seats, Republicans held 54, and independents held 2. In the months prior to Election Day, most opinion polls favored Democrats, even suggesting they might regain their Senate majority. Of the 34 seats being contested, Democrats were defending only 10 and Republicans were defending 24, with 10 of these Republican seats viewed as competitive. Republicans controlled 246 seats and Democrats 186 in the House of Representatives, but polls forecasted very few surprises there. Control of the House was expected to stay Republican, with only 23 of the seats considered competitive. In this context, how did congressional candidates use Twitter, a social media communication tool that has become a new mainstay in campaign communication?

Studying how political candidates communicated through Twitter during the 2016 campaign is especially relevant given Donald Trump's numerous headline-grabbing tweets. Among the top 10 global trends on Twitter in 2016, "#Election2016" ranked second (after the Olympics' "#Rio2016"), while "#Trump" ranked eighth.[1] This chapter documents how U.S. congressional candidates used Twitter in 2016 and compares the results to what we know about Twitter use from prior election cycles. Twitter has evolved from a novelty in the 2008 and 2012 election cycles to become a major global social media platform with widespread adoption among the U.S. population. Therefore, research is needed to track how politicians use this medium for campaign communication. Among the questions explored are: How many candidates used Twitter? How often did they do so? What did they tweet about? At what rate did they interact with other users? And, to what degree did they use all the features (text, visuals, links, and conversation) of the platform? The research can help us understand how political innovation and social communication technology diffuse from presidential campaigning to lower-level campaigns.

Launched in 2006, Twitter has become a critical communication tool for political candidates, parties, groups, the media, voters, and in general anyone with a political agenda. Though not the biggest social networking site, Twitter has surged in popularity among political candidates due to its immediacy and speed. With Twitter, candidates can communicate information in real time, bypass mainstream media filters, and reach voters directly. Unlike other social sites such as Facebook or YouTube, Twitter can be used to publish short bursts of information instantly and frequently. On other sites it is frowned upon to publish numerous updates, but on Twitter frequent and repeated posts are considered acceptable—even desirable. This capacity for real-time communication, combined with unfettered access (anyone, even those without accounts, can read most updates) makes Twitter a valuable campaign communication asset.

A SHORT HISTORY OF TWITTER
AS A CAMPAIGN COMMUNICATION TOOL

The most popular social networking websites today launched between 2004 and 2006, just in time for the 2008 U.S. general election. Facebook launched in February 2004, YouTube in February 2005, and Twitter in July 2006. The very first attempts to campaign with social media took place during the 2006 midterm elections, when political candidates experimented with Facebook, MySpace (launched in August 2003, popular at the time, but obsolete today), and YouTube.[2] Facebook created public pages for each candidate in the U.S. congressional elections, then invited the candidates to take over their pages. Only about 32 percent of Senate candidates and 13 percent of House candidates took advantage of Facebook's invitation to manage their public page.[3] On MySpace, only 21 percent of Senate candidates and only 2.7 percent of House candidates had profiles.[4] And just 13 of 130 Senate candidates (10%) set up a YouTube account, while none of the 1,102 House candidates used YouTube.[5]

Though the 2006 adoption rate of social media might seem low, it was actually a good start. The Internet had already become mainstream among American voters, but only 85 percent of Senate candidates and 79 percent of House candidates had a campaign website in 2006.[6]

In 2006, Twitter was too new to receive much attention. But, in 2008, Barack Obama gained acclaim as a political innovator with his use of both Facebook and Twitter. By Election Day, Obama had tweeted 262 times and accrued half a million followers, compared to John McCain's 25 tweets and 45,000 followers. Research shows that Obama's campaign, through Twitter and other social media platforms, went beyond educating the public about the candidate to creating an energized network of supporters who donated, volunteered, and participated in his campaign.[7]

However, in 2012, Twitter was used in full force for political campaigning. During the 2012 election cycle, politicians realized that social media is a powerful tool to communicate an agenda that reaches not only voters but the media as well.[8] By this point Twitter was well established as one of the major social media platforms in the world, ranked by Alexa.com in the top 10 most trafficked websites. Quickly posting messages, linking to other users (by including @usernames), linking to external content, and classifying messages (with hashtags) makes Twitter a uniquely democratic, all-inclusive communication channel.[9]

The adoption of social networking sites by political candidates grew in parallel with the broader population's adoption. In 2006, only 11 percent of the U.S. adult population were social media users.[10] By the 2008 election social media use had jumped to 25 percent of the adult population. In 2010 it reached 46 percent, and in 2012 a little over half (55%) of all adults in the U.S. were using social sites.[11] In 2016, Pew Internet Research reported that about 86 percent of all Americans were Internet users, while 79 percent of all Americans used Facebook, 32 percent used Instagram, and 24 percent used Twitter.[12]

Political campaigns quickly recognized Twitter's value. In 2008, Obama pioneered the use of Twitter, among other social media platforms. His rival, John McCain, appeared technologically out of touch after stating in an interview with the *New York Times* that he did not know how to use email or navigate the Internet.[13] By 2012 both Obama and Mitt Romney clearly understood the importance of social media. Their "communications staffers' goals [shifted] away from winning individual 24-hour news cycles . . . toward domination of shorter windows of time on social media, especially Twitter."[14]

WHAT DETERMINES TECHNOLOGY
ADOPTION IN POLITICAL CAMPAIGNS?

The likelihood of political candidates embracing a new communication tool is influenced by a number of factors. Below, we briefly introduce and discuss those that research has found to be important.

First, candidates in higher-level races (such as the Senate) are more likely to adopt new technologies, compared to lower-level campaigns (such as the House). This is because senatorial candidates typically have more resources, bigger budgets, larger staffs, and more volunteers. They also have to target a more diverse electorate across an entire state than do House candidates.[15]

Second, competitiveness of the race and candidate status seem to be important. A competitive race, regardless of level, is more likely to prompt candidates to adopt diversified communication tools. Research on Facebook adoption in 2006, the very first election after the site was launched, showed that challengers, better-financed candidates, and candidates running in competitive races were most likely to update their Facebook profiles.[16] Other studies showed that challengers might be more willing to adopt new technologies in an attempt to gain an advantage over incumbents.[17]

Third, party affiliation seems to matter as well. Democrats were more likely than Republicans, independents, and third party candidates to use Facebook in 2006, the first time congressional candidates used the platform. This difference could be explained by a political ideology more sensitive to "netroots" mobilization strategies. In races for the Senate, 61 percent of Democratic candidates used Facebook, compared to only 39 percent of Republican candidates.[18] However, political theory suggests that the minority party is more motivated to adopt new technology in order to gain majority status, in addition to compensating for the fact that traditional media coverage tends to focus on existing leaders and thus underemphasize lesser-known candidates.[19]

Fourth, constituency demographics play a role in adoption rates. Research shows that candidates running in precincts with more educated and affluent voters are more likely to adopt new technologies.[20] Partisanship may also be a factor, with candidates running in polarized or swing voting precincts more likely to adopt new and innovative technology.[21]

Fifth, candidates' demographics have an effect, with younger candidates more likely to adopt new technology such as Twitter. This may be the result of belonging to a cohort that grew up with social media.[22] In addition, a 2012 study showed that gender influenced Twitter adoption by U.S. House candidates, with major-party, incumbent women more likely to use Twitter compared to male candidates.[23]

Several other factors can also impact the likelihood of a political candidate using a new technology. For example, candidates who are early adopters of other communication technologies are more likely to embrace emerging technologies.[24] In addition, the demonstrated success of the use of newer technologies in one election makes adoption by others more likely in subsequent elections. This list is not comprehensive. It should also be noted that not all these factors affect all races at all times. For instance, during the 2006 midterms, the only factor that predicted whether a Senate candidate used Facebook was race competitiveness. None of the other factors (budgets, constituency, party affiliation, etc.) made a signifi-cant difference.[25]

WHEN CONGRESSIONAL CANDIDATES
TWEET, WHAT DO THEY TWEET ABOUT?

Political candidates' Twitter feeds have been undergoing scrutiny consis-tently from 2010, when Twitter was a campaign novelty, to every election since. A study on the 2010 U.S. congressional election found that nine incumbent Senators and 159 incumbent Representatives used Twitter accounts for their reelection campaigns.[26] About 60 percent of the time these incumbents posted mainly informational tweets with links to news stories about themselves, to their blog posts, or to campaign communica-tion such as ads and press releases.

In about 27 percent of the tweets, candidates communicated their pres-ence at a campaign event or a specific location (e.g., the name of a restau-rant where the candidate stopped to dine). About 5 percent of the tweets talked about official business candidates performed as incumbents. Direct communication between candidates and citizens was a less popular activ-ity, with only 7 percent of the tweets directed to another Twitter account, like their followers.[27] Interestingly enough, this study found that the 2010 U.S. congressional candidates almost never retweeted (only five tweets out of almost 5,000 were re-tweets). Similarly, another popular phenom-enon at the time on Twitter, the use of hashtags, was absent from 2010 electioneering tweets. Only 7 percent of all tweets examined included a hashtag, prompting researchers at the time to speculate that congressio-nal candidates were either lacking understanding of Twitter etiquette or that they simply disregarded the practice.[28]

A study of 67,000 tweets posted by 1,119 candidates for the House dur-ing the 2012 election campaign identified 10 thematic categories, includ-ing attack, issue, campaign, and mobilization.[29] Candidates were classi-fied by party, gender, incumbency, and race competitiveness. Differences were found across groups in both the frequency and style of tweets. On average, 18 percent more women than men tweeted, and Democrats and Republicans were over three times more likely to tweet as third party candidates. Incumbents tweeted 32 percent more than challengers, and candidates in competitive races tweeted 13 percent more than those in noncompetitive races.

With regard to party, the same study found that Republicans and Dem-ocrats had similar styles, but third party candidates were more aggres-sive, had significantly fewer followers, and tweeted significantly more.

Women had more followers, tweeted more, and used a more aggressive style than men. Challengers attacked more, discussed campaign issues more, mobilized more, and interacted with followers more. Incumbents focused more on issues and personal statements. Attack tweets were more common in competitive races, along with tweets about campaign events.

Another content analysis focused on tweets posted by 2012 Republican presidential candidates showed that when mentioning policy issues, candidates tended to focus on issues owned by their parties. In 2012, Republican candidates posted predominantly about energy and very little about the economy, while Obama and the DNC tweeted predominantly about taxes.[30] During the main phase of the 2012 congressional election, Senate candidates mentioned policy issues only about 21 percent of the time and candidate image and traits only 12 percent of the time, while campaign updates made up the majority of election tweets.[31] In terms of retweets, candidates tended to retweet from familiar, favorable, and vetted sources, such as family, friends, fellow politicians, media organizations, their own political parties, and established entities such as nonprofit and advocacy groups.[32]

Building on existing research, we designed our study around the following questions: (1) What was the Twitter adoption rate among 2016 U.S. congressional candidates? (2) What factors were related to Twitter adoption among 2016 congressional candidates? (3) What were some dominant conversational themes in the tweets posted by congressional candidates? and (4) How sophisticated and platform savvy were 2016 congressional candidates in their use of Twitter?

METHOD/STUDY DESIGN

We first created a list of all registered candidates (Republican, Democrat, independent, and third party) in every congressional election in November 2016. The list came from Ballotpedia.org, a nonprofit, nonpartisan site that tracks each general, state, and local election in the U.S. Ballotpedia maintains accurate, comprehensive records, including even candidates who withdraw before Election Day. After elections, Ballotpedia publishes election results, including the number and percentage of votes received by each candidate. Using a custom computer program, we scraped Ballotpedia pages to generate the list of candidates, then spot-checked against other records (such as election commission records) to ensure accuracy. Our script captured candidates' names, states, party affiliation, and the races in which they were running. Whenever possible we also captured information about campaign Twitter accounts directly from Ballotpedia, although these links were not always listed. After removing duplicate records and those candidates who withdrew before Election Day, the final list included 1,033 candidates with the following characteristics:

- 84 candidates for the Senate, and 949 for the House;
- 39 percent Democrats, 39 percent Republicans, 22 percent third party (including independents, for the sake of a more compact analysis);
- 34 percent incumbents, 66 percent challengers;
- 80 percent men, 20 percent female.

With this list we programmed a second script to find Twitter accounts for the roughly 50 percent of candidates without social media information listed on Ballotpedia. The script ran web searches combining "Twitter" and the candidates' full names and returned the top 20 most relevant results from twitter.com, which we manually reviewed to determine official Twitter campaign accounts. This required a review of Twitter account names, biographies, and recent tweets.

We found Twitter accounts for 71 percent of congressional candidates. Using Twitter's application programming interface (API) we downloaded tweets published from these accounts between Labor Day (September 5) and Election Day (November 8). This resulted in 77,365 tweets. Using Twitter's API enabled us to extract key information from each tweet, including publication date, number of retweets, number of likes, and number of hashtags. Because hand-coding such a high volume of tweets would be very time-consuming, we next created a randomly constructed one-week sample, narrowing the number to 7,685 tweets posted by 540 candidates. The constructed week includes Monday, Oct. 3, Tuesday, Sep. 20, Wednesday, Nov. 2, Thursday, Sep. 8, Friday, Oct. 28, Saturday, Oct. 22, and Sunday, Sep. 25. These dates can be considered typical in that no presidential debates, breaking news, scandals, or other unusual events occurred. This approach allowed us to understand the frequency and content of regular, everyday tweeting, apart from events that could cause irregular publishing patterns.

The two authors hand-coded the sampled tweets to classify their content. Descriptive information for each tweet (such as number of likes, retweets or replies, and presence of links, visuals, and video) was coded using a custom computer program. Content was classified with coding categories established by prior studies of political tweets that included informational tweets. These were then categorized into those focused on issue/policy discussion, candidate image, and political statements that do not qualify as either issue or image (e.g., "To me, it's not about party. It's about moving our country forward by working together," a tweet by Democratic House candidate Brad Ashford, or "Change is coming!"). A second category included campaign tweets, of those about campaign

appearances, campaign communication (ads or press releases), endorsements, horserace updates, news reports, and media content about the
campaign. A third dealt with tweets about official business (incumbents
tweeting about their current activities and achievements), while a fourth
was more personal in nature (opinions, photos, inspirational quotes, etc.).
Other categories included mobilization (volunteering, get-out-the-vote)
tweets, donation requests, opponent attacks, and supporter communication (replies to followers, thank-you messages).[33] Given the controversies
surrounding the 2016 presidential candidates, we also coded separately
for mentions of Trump and Clinton. Finally, a small group of the sampled
tweets were labeled as no content (those with no text update, broken
links, or broken visuals).

The researchers manually coded the content category, but the rest of the
categories were coded automatically by the computer scripts. The scripts
captured candidates' gender, party affiliation, status, and office sought,
as well as Twitter account information such as followers, likes, number of
hashtags, and number of visuals and links. The researchers spot-checked
through the sample to make sure the information was accurate and found
no errors. The only hand-coded category was the content of the tweets.
To establish inter-rater reliability, the two authors each coded the same
set of 500 tweets (6% of the sample) and obtained 96 percent agreement.

Differences came from the fact that some tweets could have been classified into more than one category, and moving forward researchers
decided to code for the dominant category. For instance, a tweet like "I'll
be going on the House Floor in a few minutes to discuss our student loan
debt crisis. Tune into C-SPAN to watch live!" (California Congressman
John Garamendi, @RepGaramendi, September 6, 2016) includes both
policy issue information (student debt) and a campaign event. The coders determined that the dominant intention of the tweet was to inform
followers about an immediate campaign event rather than to express a
policy position, and the tweet was therefore coded as campaign-related.

FINDINGS

What Was the Twitter Adoption Rate by 2016 U.S. Congressional Candidates?

Out of 1,033 candidates running for House and Senate, 71 percent had
an official Twitter account, defined as a Twitter profile page managed
by the candidate or the candidate's campaign. However, this is far from
saying that most candidates adopted Twitter, because some opened an
account but did not use it at all, others used it only occasionally during
the campaign, and some tweeted with less sophistication than others. For

instance, about 12 percent of candidates who had opened a Twitter account posted no tweets at all, about 11 percent did not personalize it with a biography, and 15 percent tweeted less than 100 times.

Overall, more Democrats had Twitter accounts than Republicans, and both major party candidates had accounts at almost four times the frequency of third party and independents (χ^2=338, df=2, p<.01; see Table 2.1). Senate candidates had a lower adoption rate (66%) than did House candidates (72%), but this difference was not statistically significant. Almost all incumbents (99%) used Twitter, compared to just over half of challengers (57%), and women's adoption rates were higher than men's (85% compared to 68%).

Table 2.1. Percentage of Candidates Using Twitter in the 2016 Congressional Race

	All Candidates	Senate Candidates	House Candidates
Democrats	90%*	87%	90%*
Republicans	80%*	93%	79%*
Independents	24%*	32%*	22%*
Senate	66%	n/a	n/a
House	72%	n/a	n/a
Incumbents	99%*	100%*	99%*
Challengers	57%*	56%*	57%*
Men	68%*	63%	69%*
Women	85%*	91%	85%*

*Chi-square significant at p < .05.

What Factors Were Associated with a Candidate's Likelihood of Using Twitter?

In terms of party affiliation, Democrats demonstrated a significantly higher adoption rate than Republicans, especially in the House races (χ^2=310.544, df=2, p<.01). However, more Senate Republicans than Democrats used Twitter, though the difference is not significant. The highest gap in terms of partisanship is between the major party candidates (Democrats and Republicans) and independent and third party candidates in both the House and Senate.

With regard to candidate status, Twitter penetration among both Senate and House incumbents is at full capacity (99–100%). On the other hand, only about half of all challengers (56% in the Senate, 57% in the House) used Twitter during the 2016 election (χ^2=197.775, df=2, p<.01). However, it is worth noting that, in the Senate, almost all the challengers without Twitter accounts ran as third party candidates, and only three Democratic and two Republican challengers did not use Twitter. In the Senate, all the candidates running in the nine competitive states had active Twitter accounts, with the exception of a Nevada Republican and one third party candidate in Pennsylvania.

In the House, the connection between a candidate's challenger status and party affiliation is a little more nuanced. As stated above, only 57 percent of House challengers used Twitter. Of this group, more than half (57%) were independent and third party candidates, followed by Republicans (29%) and a few Democrats (14%). The incumbents (99%) all had active Twitter accounts despite their party affiliation, similarly to the Senate incumbents.

Gender seemed to make a difference in Twitter adoption as well. Overall, female candidates significantly outnumbered male candidates in Twitter adoption (χ^2=21.846, df=1, p<.01). In the Senate, out of 11 women candidates, 10 had Twitter accounts, and the only one who did not was a third party challenger. In the House, 96 percent of female Democrats adopted Twitter, a significantly higher rate than Republicans (82%) and independent and third party candidates (38%) (χ^2=51.278, df=2, p<.01).

Beyond the mere existence of a Twitter account, a second way to measure Twitter adoption is to see how many and how frequently candidates tweeted in a fixed time period. Our constructed week sample included 7,686 tweets from 540 candidates. On average, a little over half of all congressional candidates tweeted over the duration of this one-week period. The frequency of tweets ranged from only one tweet to a record 201 tweets posted by Democratic Senate candidate Maggie Hassan, who ran as a challenger to Republican incumbent Kelly Ayotte in New Hampshire. This was probably one of the closest and most competitive Senate races in 2016. Out of the 540 candidates who tweeted during the sampled week, only six posted more than 100 tweets, and 49 candidates (9%) tweeted only once, while the average number of tweets per candidate (excluding the 6 outliers) was 13. These numbers show that on the whole, while congressional candidates adopted Twitter at high rates, they did not use it with any frequency.

What Did Candidates Tweet About?

Overall, the 540 candidates sampled most often tweeted about campaign events and locations (31% of all tweets). These were followed by informational tweets (20% of tweets), personal tweets (12%), opponent attacks (11%), tweets about the two presidential candidates (7.2%) and replies to supporters (7%), calls to action (6%), official incumbent business (5%), tweets without valid content (1%), and fundraising requests (0.5%).

Informational tweets were classified as either policy issue, image, or vague political statement. We found that tweets expressing a policy stance made up 13 percent of all tweets. Tweets discussing candidate qualifications and other image-related information were only 4 percent, while tweets containing other types of political statements that were related to neither issues nor image registered 4 percent of the sample.

Upon further analysis, tweets classified as campaign-related were mostly about specific campaign events and locations that the candidate attended or was scheduled to attend (20%). A smaller number were endorsement announcements (5%), links to campaign public relations posted on other sites (3%), links to media articles about the campaign (3%), and horserace-related tweets announcing the latest polls that favored the candidate's chances of winning (2%).

What Did Senate Candidates Tweet About?

In the 761 tweets posted by Senate candidates in our sample, the highest frequencies were campaign tweets (28%), opponent attacks (27%), and informational tweets (23%). The remaining tweets were classified as personalizing (8%), official business (5%), tweets about the two presidential candidates (4%), calls to action (3%) and supporter communication (3%), and a trivial number of donations requests (0.5%).

Party affiliation created significant statistical differences in these overall priorities. Republicans posted three times more campaign tweets than Democrats, eight times more official business tweets (to be expected, given that more Republicans were incumbents than Democrats), and six times more personalizing information (χ^2=210.791, df=18, p<0.01). Although the number of tweets was too low to yield significant statistical differences, they also posted three times more calls for volunteers, all donation requests, seven times more supporter replies, and twice the number of tweets about the two presidential candidates compared to Democrats. On informational tweets, both parties posted at about the same frequency. The only category where Democrats significantly outnumbered Republicans was opponent attacks, with 55 percent of all of the Twitter attacks made by Democrats, 32 percent by Republicans, and 13 percent by third party candidates.

Third party candidates did not differ much from either Republicans or Democrats in their tweeting patterns. They also mostly tweeted about campaign events (25%, similar to Republicans and Democrats), followed by opponent attacks (16%), personalizing (16%), and informational tweets (15%). They did, however, post a higher number of tweets about the presidential candidates (12%) and the highest tweets of supporter communication compared to the major parties (11%). Figure 2.1 shows how often members of each party running for seats in the Senate tweeted about the nine identified topics.

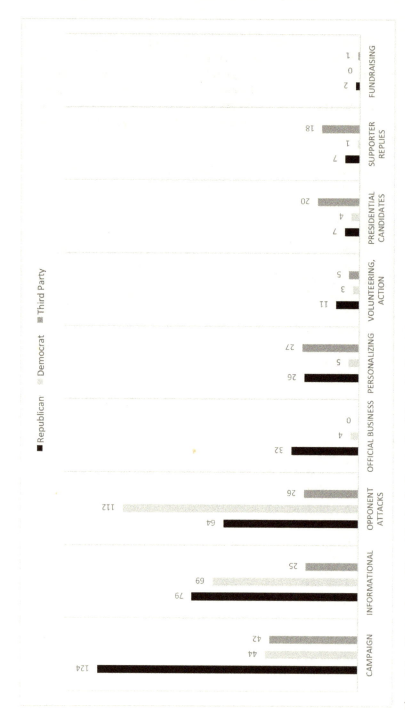

Figure 2.1.   Comparison of Tweet Topics for Senate Candidates, by Party ID
Numbers indicate counts; bar columns in descending order for Republicans.

A more in-depth analysis of informational tweets shows that neither party excelled at policy discussion. Tweets about policy amounted to only 15 percent of the tweets for each side. Democrats, however, talked twice as often as Republicans about their image and qualifications, while third party candidates posted the majority of vague political statements such as "Let's restore values to our Senate."

Our data analysis also identified some significant differences between incumbents and challengers, with incumbents posting twice as many campaign tweets as challengers. In turn, challengers posted three times more supporter replies than incumbent, and tweeted three times more about the two presidential candidates, mostly attacking both Trump and Clinton. Challengers also posted twice as many attack tweets against the incumbents (χ^2=87.062, df=18, p<0.01). Figure 2.2 shows how often incumbents and challengers running for seats in the Senate tweeted about the nine identified topics.

What Did House Candidates Tweet About?

Our sample included 6,924 tweets from House candidates, with 57 percent of these tweets posted by Democrats, 38 percent by Republicans, and 4 percent by third parties. Democratic House candidates tweeted 1.5 times more than the competition. Overall, House candidates discussed campaign events most frequently (31% of all tweets), followed by informational tweets (20%), personalizing (13%), opponent attacks (10%), presidential candidates (8%), supporter communication (7%), calls to action (6%), official incumbent business (5%), and fundraising requests (less than 1%).

Compared to Republicans, Democrats tweeted three times more calls to action, two times more opponent attacks, and significantly more campaign announcements, official business, and personalizing information. In all of the other categories both major parties, as well as third party candidates, were equal in volume (χ^2= 219.584, df=18, p<0.01). Figure 2.3 shows how often members of each party running for seats in the House tweeted about the nine identified topics.

Incumbents also posted more informational tweets than challengers, specifically tweets discussing policy issues and personalizing information. Challengers, on the other hand, had twice as many calls to action and supporter replies, two and a half times the number of opponent attacks, and all of the fundraising requests. They also posted three times more horserace tweets and endorsement announcements compared to the incumbents (χ^2=713.010, df=22, p<0.01). Figure 2.4 shows how often incumbents and challengers running for seats in the House tweeted about the nine identified topics.

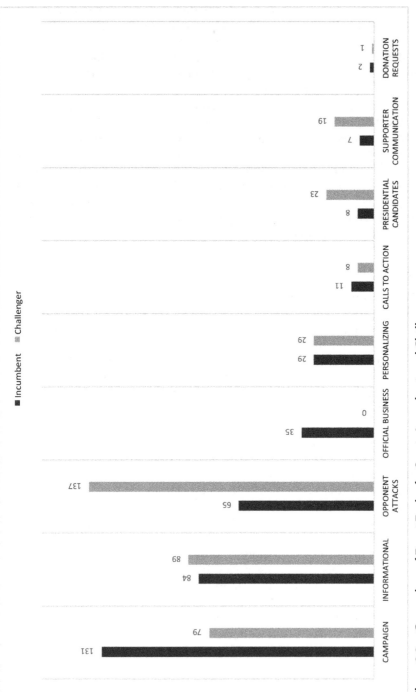

Figure 2.2. Comparison of Tweet Topics for Senate Incumbents and Challengers

*Numbers indicate counts; bar columns in descending order for incumbents. No "official business" category for challengers because these are tweets posted by incumbents about their current activity in office.

■ Incumbent ▨ Challenger

Topic	Incumbent	Challenger
CAMPAIGN	131	79
INFORMATIONAL	84	89
OPPONENT ATTACKS	65	137
OFFICIAL BUSINESS	35	0
PERSONALIZING	29	29
CALLS TO ACTION	11	8
PRESIDENTIAL CANDIDATES	8	23
SUPPORTER COMMUNICATION	7	19
DONATION REQUESTS	2	1

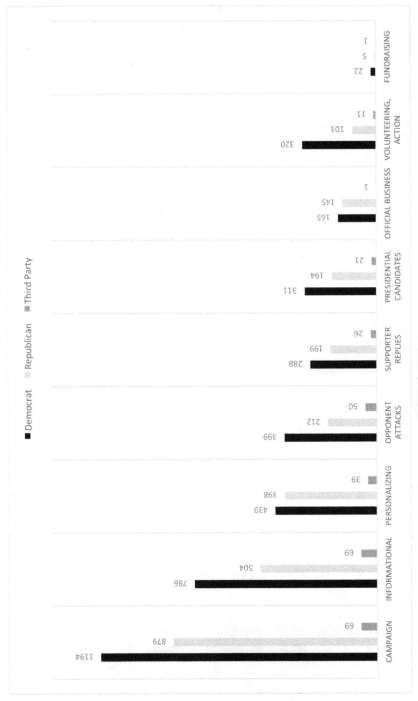

Figure 2.3. Comparison of Tweet Topics for House Candidates by Party ID
*Numbers represent counts. Bar columns in descending order for Republicans.

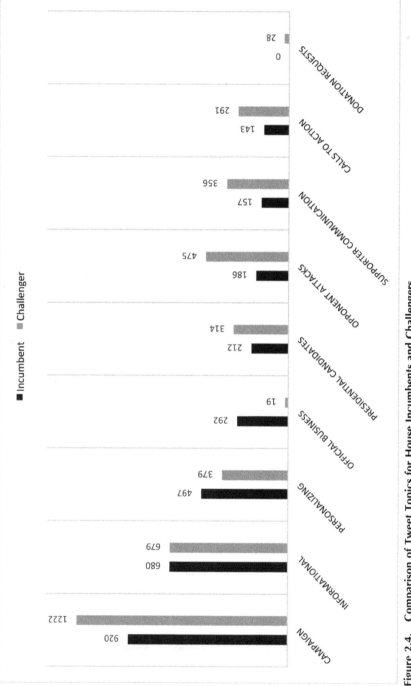

Figure 2.4. Comparison of Tweet Topics for House Incumbents and Challengers

*Numbers represent counts. Bar columns in descending order for incumbents. Some "official business" counts for challengers because some were occupying other political offices while running.

How technologically savvy were congressional candidates in their use of Twitter? We measured this along three dimensions: (1) interactivity, or the extent to which candidates engaged with other Twitter users via retweets, mentions, replies, and likes; (2) popularity, or the number of followers candidates accrued and the extent to which candidates' tweets generated engagement in the form of likes and retweets; and (3) sophistication, or the use of hashtags, links, and media within tweets.

Overall, candidates retweeted an average of 3.98 times, replied to others' tweets an average of once, mentioned other accounts an average of 5.81 times, and liked an average of 320 tweets from their accounts. By Election Day, candidates had accrued an average of 22.5 likes per tweet and 13.25 retweets per tweet on the posts we analyzed. Candidates used an average of .48 hashtags per tweet, .5 links per tweet and .15 pieces of media per tweet. Their accounts had an average of 10,123 followers.

Democrats were more likely to mention others in their tweets, averaging .44 mentions per tweet, compared to .35 mentions per tweet for Republicans and .34 mentions per tweet for third party candidates ($F_{(2, 528)}$ = 3.31, p < .05). Third party candidates, meanwhile, were more likely to reply to others' posts, doing so an average of 20 percent of the time, compared to 6 percent of the time for Democrats and 5 percent of the time for Republicans ($F_{(2, 528)}$ = 16.77, p < .01). No statistically significant differences were observed with regard to popularity across party affiliation.

Republicans used more hashtags in their tweets, averaging .55 hashtags per tweet, compared with .46 hashtags per tweet for Democrats and .47 hashtags per tweet for third party candidates ($F_{(2, 528)}$ = 5.44, p < .05). However, Democrats were more likely to include hashtags in their tweets, doing so 44 percent of the time, compared to 38 percent for Republicans and 28 percent for third party candidates ($F_{(2, 528)}$ = 4.77, p < .05). Republicans averaged the most links per tweet, .55, compared to .46 for Democrats and .47 for third party candidates ($F_{(2, 528)}$ = 5.44, p < .05). Republicans were also the most likely to send tweets with links, doing so 60 percent of the time, compared to 52 percent of the time for Democrats and 48 percent for third party candidates ($F_{(2, 528)}$ = 5.66, p < .05). Republicans included media in their tweets 20 percent of the time, compared to 18 percent of the time for Democrats and 9 percent of the time for third party candidates ($F_{(2, 528)}$ = 3.11, p < .05).

Senate candidates mentioned other accounts an average of .45 times per tweet, compared to .34 times per tweet for House candidates (t=3.30, df=2, p<.01). House candidates replied to others an average of 1.67 times per account, compared to the Senate candidate average of .41 times per account (t=5.00, df=2, p<.001). Likewise, 10 percent of House candidate tweets were replies, compared to 3 percent of Senate candidate tweets (t=-5.89, df=2, p<.001).

Senate candidates were more popular, with an average of 32,666 followers compared to House candidates' average of 8,526 followers (t=3.13, df=2, p < .001). Differences in likes or retweets received were not significant between Senate and House candidates. Senate candidates included links in 58 percent of their tweets, compared to 52 percent of House candidates' tweets (t=.36, df=2, p<.05). Hashtag and media usage were not different by office.

Nor were Senate incumbents and challengers different in how they retweeted others' posts, but they did interact in different ways. Incumbents mentioned other accounts an average of .45 times a tweet, compared to an average of .34 times a tweet for challengers (t=3.29, df=2, p<0.01). Replies comprised 10 percent of challengers' tweets and 3 percent of incumbents' tweets (t=-5.89, df=2, p<.001). Challengers also liked far more tweets, 420.34 on average compared to 270.24 on average for incumbents (t=-2.46, df=2, p<.05).

Senate incumbents had an average of 17,609 followers, compared to 2,313 followers for challengers (t=3.99, df=2, p<0.001). Incumbents also garnered far more likes and retweets per tweet, but these differences were not statistically significant due to several high-profile outliers such as Rand Paul, who drew far more attention to their accounts than did the typical Senate incumbent.

Senate incumbents and challengers displayed a similar level of Twitter savvy, using both hashtags and media with the same frequency. Incumbents included an average of .53 links per post, compared to an average of .47 links per post for challengers (t=2.07, df=2, p<0.05). Incumbents also used links more often. They appeared in 58 percent of their posts, compared to 52 percent of posts for challengers (t=2.36, df=2, p<0.05).

DISCUSSION

Ideally, social media sites like Twitter would be used to promote participatory democracy, increase political transparency, serve as a two-way communication channel between politicians and voters, and generally better the political environment. Analyzing the spread and content of political candidates' Twitter provided insight into how far we are from fulfilling this dream of candidates and voters engaged in meaningful, productive, democratic conversation through the social media technologies currently available. Below we summarize our findings and discuss their implications.

All major party candidates show high Twitter adoption rates. A majority of candidates now use Twitter for campaigning (66% of Senate candidates, 71% of House candidates), showing that Twitter is becoming a standard, perhaps even required, campaign tool. In 2016 Election was only the third election cycle since the launch of Twitter, and arguably only the second since Twitter became a mainstream social media site. Twitter adoption rates in 2016 were similar to adoption rates for other online technologies. For instance, the first campaign websites were created in the 1996 general election cycle by the two presidential candidates, Bill Clinton and Bob Dole. Three election cycles later (2004) the website adoption rate among congressional candidates was estimated at around 60 percent.[34]

The adoption gap between major and third party candidates was noticeable. Congressional third party candidates stood out in their lack of Twitter adoption. Only 32 percent of those running for the Senate and only 22 percent of House candidates had Twitter accounts. This lower adoption rate compared to major party candidates is similar to third party adoption rates of new technology in past elections. As documented before, third party candidates have fewer resources and/or fewer incentives to adopt new technologies, due mainly to smaller budgets. They are amongst the later adopters of technology. In 2016, however, there was an exception. In the nine most competitive Senate races third party candidates were as likely to have Twitter as their Democratic and Republican competitors. In fact, all the third party candidates running in these nine races had Twitter accounts.

With few exceptions, all incumbents used Twitter in a frequent and systematic manner, compared to only about half of challengers, both in the Senate and the House. As in past elections, race competitiveness was a strong predictive factor in a candidate's adoption of technology. In 2016, all candidates in highly competitive races had active Twitter accounts, even third party candidates. Only one Republican and only one Democrat did not, and they were both challengers highly unlikely to win.

In terms of content, other patterns emerged. For example, Twitter does not seem to be a supporter mobilization (getting people to volunteer, make phone calls, vote, write letters to the editor, and engage in other political actions) tool. Congressional candidates in 2016 did not use Twitter with this goal in mind. Volunteering and get-out-the-vote (GOTV) requests made up only about 3 percent of all Senate tweets and 6 percent of all House tweets. Challengers tweeted the majority of volunteering and GOTV requests, perhaps being more motivated by small campaign budgets and a higher need for volunteers (recall that challengers are more likely to gain from higher voter turnout than incumbents).

Nor was Twitter used much as a fundraising tool. With all the talk about modern-day candidates shattering fundraising records through small donations, one would expect to find donation requests in the Twitter feeds of political candidates. Our analysis shows just the opposite: that for whatever reason candidates did not post such messages, regardless of party. Tweets asking followers to donate accounted for less than 1 percent of the 7,685 tweets in our sample, and were posted exclusively by challengers.

Further, Twitter was not used as a policy discussion tool. As established by prior research on political candidates' social media profiles, candidates do not discuss policy issues. Among Senate candidates, tweets about policies registered 14 percent of the sample, 12 percent among the House. It seems that House incumbents had a greater propensity toward policy discussion through Twitter, being the group with the highest number of issue statements.

Twitter is mostly a one-way communication channel. Very little conversation took place on the Twitter accounts of 2016 congressional candidates, with only 7 percent of all tweets in reply to another account, and about 27 percent retweets of content created by others. Half (51%) of all tweets were campaign announcements and informational tweets (with a minimum amount of discussion). The other half was made up of a variety of topics such as opponent attacks, personalizing information, discussion of the two presidential candidates, and calls to action. In the Senate, 80 percent of all tweets were split between campaign announcements, informational tweets, and opponent attacks. The remaining 20 percent included some personalizing (8%) and very little of anything else: no supporter communication, no fundraising, no calls to action. Incumbents did not talk about their Senate activities very much, either.

Candidate status seems to be the strongest predictor of message strategies. Republicans and Democrats scored similarly on most measures in our analysis. Significant differences resulted almost exclusively from a candidate's status as incumbent or challenger. For instance, in the Senate race, challengers tweeted more and outnumbered GOP candidates on attack tweets, which is a typical challenger strategy. They also talked more often about their own image and qualifications, another typical challenger strategy. Similar patterns (challengers tweeting more, outbidding incumbents on opponent attacks) held up among House candidates. We also observed that challengers tended to post more supporter replies, endorsements, and horserace-related tweets. On the other hand, incumbents seemed more willing to discuss policy.

Candidate gender also continues to be associated with technology use, with women leading men in adoption. This trend of female candidates using new technologies at a higher rate than male candidates was noted in 2012 studies of Twitter adoption by U.S. congressional candidates as well.[35]

Republican candidates adopted a less interactive approach but made the most use of the tools of the platform. Republicans mentioned other accounts in their tweets less often than Democrats, and they replied to others less than either Democrats or third party candidates. However, they displayed more sophistication in their use of the Twitter platform. Republican candidates used the most hashtags, the most links, and the most media.

Senate and House candidates interacted in different ways. Whereas Senate candidates focused on mentioning other accounts, House candidates spent more time replying directly to others. Senate candidates were also somewhat more likely to include links in their communications, although no other differences in Twitter savvy were noted with regard to congressional races.

Challengers focused on interaction, and incumbents focused on sharing content. Despite garnering far fewer followers, challengers spent more time than their incumbent counterparts reaching out to people by replying to others and liking their posts. Meanwhile, incumbents were more likely to use the platform's tools, in particular, links to news stories and other external content.

CONCLUSION

The 2016 election was the third general election cycle since Twitter was launched. Twitter's penetration is estimated at only 21 percent of the entire U.S. adult population (compared to 68% for Facebook), but the site received heavy attention during the campaign.[36] The company announced that users in the U.S. published 1 billion tweets about the election from the start of the nomination season (August 2015) to Election Day, November 8.[37]

Our study found Twitter adoption rates of about 80 to 90 percent for Democrats and Republicans, and almost 100 percent for incumbents, which shows that Twitter adoption is reaching a plateau among the major parties. For third party candidates, the situation is mixed, with high adoption rates only for the candidates in competitive races.

However, having an account does not mean a candidate is active on Twitter. How frequently candidates post, what they post about, and how savvy they are at using the platform also speak to the degree of technology adoption. While data point to high adoption rates, the frequency, content, and technical savviness paint a more nuanced picture. For instance, 82 percent of the tweets in our sample were text-only, 55 percent did not have a hashtag, and 50 percent did not have a link. These numbers show candidates did not take full advantage of the platform's potential to communicate. The Twitter feed algorithm prioritizes the most popular tweets by displaying them at the top of a user's timeline. So if a tweet receives lots of replies, retweets, and likes, that tweet will be shown to many more users for a longer period of time. Knowing this, one would think that political candidates would take advantage of every feature of the platform (such as including attention-grabbing visuals) to increase their reach.

It is also possible that political candidates are using Twitter to reach and influence the media, rather than regular voters. Frequent content throughout the campaign is public relations information such as campaign announcements (locations the candidate had campaigned or will campaign), links to endorsements, and links to other campaign-produced communication (press releases, ads, social media accounts, letters to editors, etc.).

While, in theory, Twitter encourages access to political discourse and participation, our analysis showed that congressional candidates' tweets lacked substance. Candidates centered around campaign events and announcements, and largely ignored opportunities to engage and converse with others on Twitter.

Candidates mainly posted one-way announcements and infrequently replied to followers, with the exception of challengers. However, for all the talk about polarization, negativity, and controversy created on Twitter by the Republican presidential candidate, our data show that opponent attacks were only 11 percent of the overall messages, and this was slightly higher among challengers. It seems that polarization and negativity did not seep from the presidential to the congressional level, where candidates posted mostly the expected things (campaign information, some personal information, and minimal numbers of issue and image statements).

Several limitations of this research are worth noting. First, we coded a sample of about 10 percent of all available tweets in our target time range. Working from a constructed one-week sample made it feasible to hand code for message category but also restricted the number of messages we were able to consider. Second, we did not consider race competitiveness as a predictor of Twitter use. Likewise, we did not examine candidates' ages or races, nor voter demographics in their districts, as potential predictive factors. Future research that accounts for these variables could shed additional light on how and why congressional candidates adopt technology.

In summary, our investigation into a week of campaign tweets shows that, during the 2016 election, Twitter was not utilized to its full social and interactive potential. The political campaigning and discourse coming from the 2016 congressional candidates was conventional in nature and not tailored to the social platform. Though overall adoption rates have gone up, candidates continued to use Twitter just as they did in prior elections, with little interaction with supporters, minimal transparency, and few discussions of policy issues.[38] In other words, on Twitter in 2016, the medium was not the message.

NOTES

1. Leslie Berland, "#ThisHappened in 2016," Twitter Blog, December 6, 2016, accessed February 2, 2017, https://blog.twitter.com/2016/thishappened-in-2016.

2. Monica Ancu and Raluca Cozma, "MySpace Politics: Uses and Gratifications of Befriending Candidates," *Journal of Broadcasting & Electronic Media* 53.4 (2009): 567–583. doi http://dx.doi.org/10.1080/08838150903333064.

3. Christine B. Williams and Girish J. "Jeff" Gulati, "Social Networks in Political Campaigns: Facebook and the 2006 Midterm Elections," (paper presented at the 2007 annual meeting of the American Political Science Association, Chicago, Illinois, August 30–September 2, 2007), accessed December 20, 2016, http://tranb300.ulb.ac.be/2012-2013/groupe141/archive/files/c65d6cf6f5d-34b49f79d9e68a315bb41.pdf.

4. Williams and Gulati, "Social Networks," 6.

5. Williams and Gulati, "Social Networks," 7.

6. Williams and Gulati, "Social Networks," 3.

7. Porismita Borah, "Political Facebook Use: Campaign Strategies Used in 2008 and 2012 Presidential Elections," *Journal of Information Technology & Politics* 13:4 (2016): 326–338. doi: 10.1080/19331681.2016.1163519; Monica Ancu, "From Soundbite to TextBite: Election 2008 Comments on Twitter," in *Techno Politics in Presidential Campaigning. New Voice, New Technologies, and New Voters*, ed. John A. Hendricks and Lynda Lee Kaid (New York: Routledge, 2011), 11–21; Terri L. Towner and David A. Dulio, "New Media and Political Marketing in the United States: 2012 and Beyond," *Journal of Political Marketing* 11:1–2 (2012): 95–119. doi: http://dx.doi.org/10.1080/15377857.2012.642748; Cheris Carpenter, "The Obamachine: Techno-politics 2.0.," *Journal of Information Technology and Politics*, 7:1–2 (2010): 216–225.

8. Bethany A. Conway, Kate Kenski, and Di Wang, "The Rise of Twitter in the Political Campaign: Searching For Intermedia Agenda-Setting Effects in the Presidential Primary," *Journal Of Computer-Mediated Communication*, 20.4 (2015): 363–380; Emily Metzgar and Albert Maruggi, "Social Media and the 2008 U.S. Presidential Election," *Journal of New Communications Research* 4.1 (2009): 141–165; W. Russell Neuman, Lauren Guggenheim, S. Mo Jang, and Soo Young Bae, "The Dynamics of Public Attention: Agenda-Setting Theory Meets Big Data," *Journal of Communication* 64 (2014): 193–214. Accessed February 18, 2017. doi: 10.1111/jcom.12088.

9. Julian Ausserhofer and Axel Maireder, "National Politics on Twitter," *Information, Communication & Society* 16:3 (2013): 291–314. Accessed February 20, 2017. doi:10.1080/1369118X.2012.756050.

10. Andrew Perrin, "Social Media Usage: 2006–2015," Pew Research Center, October 8, 2015, accessed December 20, 2016, http://www.pewinternet.org/2015/10/08/social-networking-usage-2005-2015/.

11. Ibid.

12. Shannon Greenwood, Andrew Perrin, and Maeve Duggan, "Social Media Update 2016," Pew Research Center, November 11, 2016, accessed January 2, 2017, http://www.pewinternet.org/2016/11/11/social-media-update-2016/.

13. "The Times Interviews John McCain," last modified July 13, 2008, accessed January 10, 2017, http://www.nytimes.com/2008/07/13/us/politics/13text-mccain.html.

14. David Uberti, "How Political Campaigns Use Twitter to Shape Media Coverage," *Columbia Journalism Review*, December 9, 2014, accessed December 20, 2016, http://www.cjr.org/behind_the_news/how_political_campaigns_use_tw.php.

15. Bruce Bimber and Richard Davis, *Campaigning Online: The Internet in U.S. Elections* (New York: Oxford University Press: 2003), 27; James N. Druckman, Martin J. Kifer, and Michael Parkin, "The Technological Development of Congressional Candidate Websites: How and Why Candidates Use Web Innovation," *Social Science Computer Review* 25:4 (2007): 425–442, accessed January 5, 2017, doi: https://doi.org/10.1177/0894439307305623.

16. Williams and Gulati, "Social Networks," 12.

17. Druckman, Kifer, and Parkin, "The Technological Development"; Paul S. Herrnson, Atiya Kai Stokes-Brown, and Matthew Hindman, "Campaign Politics and the Digital Divide: Constituency Characteristics, Strategic Considerations, and Candidate Internet Use in State Legislative Elections," *Political Research Quarterly* 60:1 (2007): 31–42, accessed January 5, 2017, doi: https://doi.org/10.1177/1065912906298527.

18. Williams and Gulati, "Social Networks," 8.

19. Tim Cook, *Governing with the News: The News Media as a Political Institution* (Chicago: University of Chicago Press, 2005), 151.

20. Bimber and Davis, *Campaigning Online*, 104–107; Kirsten A. Foot and Steven M. Schneider, *Web Campaigning* (Cambridge, MA: MIT Press, 2006), 171.

21. Andrew Kohut and Lee Rainie, "Internet Election News Audience Seeks Convenience, Familiar Names," Pew Research Center, December 3, 2000, accessed February 20, 2017, http://www.pewinternet.org/2000/12/03/internet-election-news-audience-seeks-convenience-familiar-names/.

22. Christopher A. Cooper, "Internet Use in the State Legislature," *Social Science Computer Review* 22:3 (2004): 347–354; E. Scott Adler, Chariti E. Gent, and Cary B. Overmeyer, "The Home Style Homepage: Legislator Use of the World Wide Web for Constituency Contact," *Legislative Studies Quarterly* 23:4 (1998): 585–595.

23. Heather K. Evans, Victoria Cordova, and Savannah Sipole, "Twitter Style: An Analysis of How House Candidates Used Twitter in Their 2012 Campaigns," *Political Science & Politics* 47:2 (2014): 454–462, doi:10.1017/S1049096514000389.

24. Adler, Gent, and Overmeyer, "The Home Style Homepage."

25. Williams and Gulati, "Social Networks."

26. Jennifer Golbeck, Justin M. Grimes, and Anthony Rogers, "Twitter Use by the U.S. Congress," *Journal of the American Society for Information Science and Technology* 61: 8 (2010): 1612–1621, doi:10.1002/asi.21344.

27. Goldbeck, Grimes, and Rogers, "Twitter Use."

28. Ibid.

29. Evans, Cordova, and Sipole, "Twitter Style."

30. Conway, Kenski, and Wang, "The Rise of Twitter."

31. Lindsey Meeks, "Aligning and Trespassing: Candidates' Party-Based Issue and Trait Ownership on Twitter," *Journalism & Mass Communication Quarterly* 93:4 (2016): 1050–1072, doi: 10.1177/1077699015609284.

32. Meeks, "Aligning and Trespassing."

33. Evans, Cordova, and Sipole, "Twitter Style."

34. Druckman, Kifer, and Parkin, "The Technological Development."

35. Evans, Cordova, and Sipole, "Twitter Style."

36. "Social Media Fact Sheet," Pew Research Center, accessed February 20, 2017, http://www.pewinternet.org/fact-sheet/social-media/.

37. Bridget Coyne, "How #Election2016 was Tweeted so far," Twitter, November 7, 2016, accessed February 20, 2017, https://blog.twitter.com/2016/how-election2016-was-tweeted-so-far.

38. Evans, Cordova, and Sipole, "Twitter Style"; Amelia Adams, and Tina Mc-Corkindale, "Dialogue and Transparency: A Content Analysis of How The 2012 Presidential Candidates Used Twitter," *Public Relations Review* 39:4 (2013) 357–359.

3

I Beg to Differ

Understanding Political Disagreement Presented By Candidates in Gubernatorial Primaries

Anne-Bennett Smithson and Emily K. Vraga

As candidates increasingly turn to social networking sites (SNS) to engage with potential voters, present ideas, and challenge opponents, not enough research has examined how candidates frame political disagreement online. When disagreement takes the form of communication from campaigns instead of occurring via interpersonal discussion, it can be a tool by which candidates expose their audience to divergent viewpoints and confront such views in a carefully crafted manner.

In a political network, candidates compete for limited attention.[1] This process is exacerbated during a primary, where similarities between candidate ideology render areas of disagreement "prized possessions" to help candidates distinguish themselves from their competitors.[2] The framing of political disagreement on social media during primary campaigns reflects a fundamentally different and understudied process as compared to inter-party disagreement during general elections.[3] Moreover, as such primary challenges become more frequent, especially among mainstream Republicans and Tea Party candidates,[4] it becomes increasingly important to explore this dynamic.

However, the *presentation* of disagreement online—as compared to its experience in interpersonal relationships[5] or its characteristic in a social network[6]—has not been adequately defined. Drawing from the political advertising literature,[7] we distinguish between the type of disagreement (e.g., a focus on personal characteristics versus policy), its target (e.g., other party members, the opposing party, or the Washington elite), and its tone (e.g., civil versus uncivil).

Moreover, the presentation of disagreement likely depends on a number of candidate and race characteristics, most notably (1) whether a candidate is an incumbent, challenger, or in an open race, and (2) a candidate's party affiliation. We expect that incumbents will adopt a "Rose Garden strategy" to focus on their successes in office and rarely mention disagreement with the opposition, while challengers will be more likely to criticize the incumbent and her record.[8] Strategies by candidates in an open race are less clear. Similarly, we know Republicans and Democrats differ in their worldview and tolerance for disagreement,[9] but have not tested whether that leads candidates to frame disagreement differently as part of their social media efforts.

In this chapter, we explore each of these forms of disagreement, and test whether certain forms of disagreement depend on characteristics of the campaign. To test these questions, we conducted a content analysis of the Twitter posts made by gubernatorial primary candidates in all of the states holding gubernatorial primary races in 2016 to understand how they present disagreement. We focus on gubernatorial elections, given the important consequences such elections have for state and national politics. At the state level, governors control the executive branch and have power over budgetary (e.g., taxes, spending), judiciary (e.g., appoint judges, issue pardons), and legislative decisions (e.g., setting policy directions, vetoing bills). At the national level, several Republican governors entered the run for the White House in 2016 (e.g., Jeb Bush, Chris Christie, John Kasich), and many of our recent presidents served as governors before becoming president (e.g., Ronald Reagan, Bill Clinton, George W. Bush). In short, it is important to study gubernatorial elections because their results can impact our country at both the state and national levels.

This project adds to the literature on campaign communication during primary campaigns, with special emphasis on the prevalence and characteristics of political disagreement in online spaces. This study provides an important step in understanding the manner in which candidates leverage social media to control the flow of information and strategically highlight points of divergence between the candidate and opponent(s), which can not only determine subsequent electoral success but also influence audiences' views of the political process and their own willingness to participate.[10] Understanding how candidates attempt to shape voters' perceptions is particularly relevant in 2016, a year in which voters paid more attention to the presidential election than at any point during any campaign since 1988.[11]

THE PRESENTATION OF DISAGREEMENT

The current scholarship focusing on political disagreement reveals considerable discrepancy regarding how the construct should be defined. Because many scholars study political disagreement as a product of interpersonal relationships, it is often conceptualized as it occurs in dyadic communication[12] and network communication.[13] At its heart, scholars define political disagreement as occurring when individuals confront political opinions that are different from one's own, which they see as a vital component of deliberative democracy.[14]

Despite its value, exposure to disagreement is not automatic. In fact, selective exposure theories predict that many individuals will attempt to actively avoid engagement with diverse political views.[15] Social media often create more opportunities for exposure to disagreement, as what people see online results from a combination of decisions made by an individual, by their friends, and by organizations and political actors, creating structural forces that encourage people to see more disagreement online.[16]

Most existing work has focused on individual or social decisions that contribute to exposure to disagreement online.[17] However, the content offered by politicians creates a structure for exposing people to disagreement, with candidates deliberately framing their relationship to particular issues and to other political actors. Social media allow politicians to present disagreement in the manner they choose and strategically address their points in a way that optimizes their overall message or position.

ELITE FRAMING OF DISAGREEMENT

In choosing when and how to present disagreement, politicians are essentially engaging in a form of framing. As Entman explains, "To frame is to select some aspects of a perceived reality and make them more salient in a communicating text."[18] In campaign communications, the key question is *how* candidates emphasize certain aspects of reality and draw attention away from other aspects in their messaging. Moreover, framing also allows the communicator to select which facts they want to emphasize.[19] When thinking about politicians, then, campaign communications allow candidates to strategically frame election issues in such a way that draws attention to items or ideas they want to emphasize while drawing attention away from issues that may be less helpful to the candidate's overall message.

When it comes to candidate communication, we conceptualize political disagreement as candidates' confrontation of opposing viewpoints/behaviors during an election and presentation of such discrepancies to an audience. While most research to date explores the *experience* of disagreement, our research explores the *presentation* of disagreement. Specifically, social networking sites (SNS) provide the candidate control of the message and allow her to present divergent viewpoints in the way she chooses. This raises the question: *How* do politicians expose the public to perspectives that are different than the candidate's own? After all, a candidate often must exhibit some type of disagreement between herself and her opponent to differentiate herself as the more desirable choice.[20]

Studying disagreement as presented by politicians allows us to examine political messages from a key source and understand how politicians are shaping audience perceptions of reality. Moreover, this approach allows us to complicate our definition of what "disagreement" looks like on social media during competitive primary campaigns. We argue that disagreement can take several forms, depending on its type, target, and tone.

Type. Political disagreement is a necessary part of the political process, especially for political figures. This is particularly true during a primary campaign, where a candidate cannot rely on party loyalties or political ideology to shape voter behavior.[21] Instead, candidates are likely to highlight personal characteristics or issue positions.[22] In fact, Benoit suggests that candidates in a primary may leverage more attacks based on character, as their policy positions may not be notably different from those of their intra-party competitors.[23] These studies open intriguing possibilities for different forms that disagreement can take. Therefore, our first research question (*RQ1*) examines whether disagreement is more common when discussing policy versus personal characteristics during the 2016 primary campaign.

Target. Disagreement is often studied as occurring across party lines.[24] But during a primary campaign in particular, disagreement with candidates of the opposing party is unlikely to be the only type of disagreement, and perhaps not the most common. Such disagreement with an opposing party may be used as a tool to encourage turnout among their voters or for candidates attempting to imbue their campaign with a sense of inevitability.[25] Alternatively, disagreement may be focused instead on highlighting differences *within* candidates' own party—particularly opposing candidates in the primary campaign.[26] Finally, an alternative form of disagreement that may become more common as approval ratings for the government overall decline occurs when candidates attempt to signal their status as mavericks or outsiders, separate from the Washington elite.[27] This form of disagreement is not necessarily *partisan* in nature, but instead is meant to emphasize a candidate's independence from political structures. Our second research question (*RQ2*) examines the target of disagreement—whether it focuses on disagreement with the opposing party, with members of the same party, or with the Washington elite.

Tone. In addition to examining the type and target of disagreement, we also explore the *tone* of that disagreement. By its very nature, the concept of disagreement lends itself to being conflated with negativity.[28] For example, Gronbeck explains that negativity happens when a candidate highlights "unattractive or undesirable images of one's political opponents,"[29] while Geer defines negative advertisements as simply any type of criticism leveled against one's opponents during a campaign.[30]

To differentiate content from tone, we turn to the concept of incivility. Incivility occurs when disagreement with an opponent includes inflammatory comments that indicate a "lack of respect"[31] toward an opponent without adding substance to a political message or discussion—for example, through "name-calling, contempt, and derision of the competition."[32] By adopting this definition to study campaign communication, we extend the current literature on the nature of disagreement—including its tone— to better understand how gubernatorial candidates are communicating with prospective voters. Our third research question (RQ3) explores the frequency of uncivil tweets overall.

CAMPAIGN CHARACTERISTICS
THAT INFLUENCE DISAGREEMENT

We contend that how candidates present disagreement depends upon a range of factors such as political party (e.g., Democrat or Republican) and incumbency status (e.g., incumbent, challenger, or open race) that can help us predict when and how certain candidates might adopt particular styles of disagreement when communicating their messages to prospective voters.

Republicans and Democrats

Perhaps unsurprisingly, research has shown that conservatives (e.g., Republicans) and liberals (e.g., Democrats) have fundamentally different worldviews, which can impact their political reasoning.[33] For example, senators[34] and Supreme Court justices[35] with liberal or moderate voting records are more likely to view policymaking as an exercise in weighing competing interests, while conservatives are more likely to see the policies they support as having wholly positive consequences and the policies they oppose as being completely negative. Tetlock also found that the viewpoints people hold often constrain the complexity of their reasoning when trying to decide upon policy issues.[36] Because the nature of one's ideology may impact the nature of one's reasoning, it follows that candidates with opposing ideologies frame disagreement differently in their messages.

Interestingly, research has also shown that even voters who identify as Republican may approach elections differently than voters who identify as Democrats. For instance, research on first-time voters has shown that Republicans tend to vote based on a belief that it is their duty as a citizen, while first-time Democratic voters choose to vote based on the issues in the election.[37] Further, Sweester found that Democratic voters generally embrace an external locus of control (e.g., events are controlled by others) while Republican voters hold an internal locus of control (e.g., events are controlled by oneself).[38] These party differences extend to social media practices, as research suggests Republicans are more likely to create congruent echo chambers for political expression on their social media than Democrats,[39] and Republicans who follow official party accounts on Twitter (e.g., from party leaders) also demonstrate more homophily in their networks.[40] As such, Democratic versus Republican candidates may have incentives to present disagreement differently, leading to our fourth research question (RQ4): Do gubernatorial candidates communicate disagreement differently based on their own party affiliation?

Incumbents and Challengers

With regard to campaign communication, literature has consistently shown that challengers and incumbents leverage different communication strategies when presenting their messages. For instance, Trent, Friedenberg, and Denton theorize that incumbents use communication strategies that cast them in a positive light, showing them as competent, successful, and worthy of the office they already hold.[41] In other words, the incumbent attempts to show that he or she embodies the office as such by demonstrating that s/he is solid, credible, and confident, which Popkin terms the "Rose Garden strategy."[42] Further, incumbents often attempt to cast themselves as reluctant leaders who are "above the fray" of politics or as statesmen who represent their electorate without desire for personal gain.[43] On the other hand, challengers tend to assume an offensive position and criticize both the incumbent and her record, highlighting differences between their goals and the actions of the sitting incumbent.[44] As such, we expect that incumbents will be less likely to present disagreement during the course of their campaign communications than challengers, although there is little empirical research explicitly testing this proposition.

Further, while there is limited research testing how open race candidates compare to incumbents and challengers in terms of their communication strategies, we theorize that open race candidates will be more similar to challengers than incumbents because, like challengers, open race candidates would benefit by demonstrating how they can effect positive changes within the state. This research sets up our fifth and final research question (RQ5), exploring how incumbents, challengers, and open race candidates differently present disagreement.

DATA AND METHOD

We explore the above differences in the context of campaign communication on Twitter, which has become an increasingly important method for political candidates to communicate with the public. In 2016, 98% of House members used Twitter,[45] and 25% of social media users followed candidates or political figures via SNS.[46]

To ensure a broad sample, we studied campaigns from each of the 12 states that held a gubernatorial election in 2016: Delaware, Indiana, Missouri, Montana, New Hampshire, North Carolina, North Dakota, Oregon, Utah, Vermont, Washington, and West Virginia. We realize that the states in our sample are not particularly large or wholly representative of the United States population, but these were the only states holding gubernatorial elections in 2016. The data collection period took place beginning three months before each state's primary date and concluded the date each primary was held. We randomly selected 10 Twitter posts per week from each competitive[47] candidate[48] to ensure comparability across candidates, given the range of tweets posted varied widely by candidate (*Min*=42, *Max*=1200). We coded each tweet for the presence or absence of disagreement, as well as the type, target, and tone of disagreement.

Upon completion of the primaries, we included tweets from 41 different candidates in the final dataset for the primary election period. As one can see in Table 3.1, competitive candidates posted a total of 13,643 times in the three months leading up to each state's primary. Since we sampled 10 tweets per week for three months preceding each primary, the dataset from the primary election contained 4,576 tweets, which represents roughly 33% of the total tweets posted. During some weeks, some candidates posted fewer than 10 tweets, which is the reason that this number is not divisible by 10. In those instances, we used all of the candidate's tweets posted that week in the final dataset. Of the 41 total candidates who received at least 15% of the vote in their state primary election, 18 (44%) ran as Democrats and 23 (56%) ran as Republicans. With regard to incumbency status, there were 6 incumbents (14.5%), 8 challengers (19.5%), and 27 open race candidates (66%) in the sample. This information is displayed in Table 3.1.

To analyze our data, we used a general coding scheme adapted from the work of Brader[49] who studied emotional appeals in television advertisements and of Gainous and Wagner[50] who explored how congressional candidates leveraged Twitter during the 2010 elections.

Tweet Type. For each tweet, we first coded whether it was best defined as (1) basic communicating, (2) highlighting personal characteristics, or (3) policy information based on categories provided by Gainous and Wagner,[51] as explained below. Each of these categories is mutually

Table 3.1. Total Candidate Tweets

Candidate	Vote %	Status	Party	Data Collection Period	Total Tweets
DE–John Carney	100%	Open Race	Democrat	June 13–Sept. 13	42
DE–Colin Bonini	70%	Open Race	Republican	June 13–Sept. 13	47
DE–Lacey Lafferty	30%	Open Race	Republican	June 13–Sept. 13	121
IN–Mike Pence	100%	Incumbent	Republican	Feb. 3–May 3	288
IN–John Gregg	100%	Challenger	Democrat	Feb. 3–May 3	888
MO–Eric Greitens	35%	Open Race	Republican	May 2–Aug. 2	284
MO–John Brunner	25%	Open Race	Republican	May 2–Aug. 2	1200
MO–Peter Kinder	21%	Open Race	Republican	May 2–Aug. 2	737
MO–C. Hanaway	20%	Open Race	Republican	May 2–Aug. 2	403
MO–Chris Koster	79%	Open Race	Democrat	May 2–Aug. 2	257
MT–Steve Bullock	91%	Incumbent	Democrat	Mar. 7–June 7	119
MT–Greg Gianforte	76%	Challenger	Republican	Mar. 7–June 7	232
NC–Pat McCrory	82%	Incumbent	Republican	Dec. 15–Mar. 15	387
NC–Roy Cooper	69%	Challenger	Democrat	Dec. 15–Mar. 15	90
NC–Ken Spaulding	31%	Challenger	Democrat	Dec. 15–Mar. 15	136
ND–Marvin Nelson	100%	Open Race	Democrat	Mar. 14–June 14	64
ND–Doug Burgun	59%	Open Race	Republican	Mar. 14–June 14	273
ND–Wayne Stenehjem	38%	Open Race	Republican	Mar. 14–June 14	156

Candidate	Percent	Race	Party	Dates	Count
NH–Colin Van Ostern	52%	Open Race	Democrat	June 13–Sept. 13	454
NH–Steve Marchand	25%	Open Race	Democrat	June 13–Sept. 13	302
NH–Mark Connolly	20%	Open Race	Democrat	June 13–Sept. 13	203
NH - Chris Sununu	31%	Open Race	Republican	June 13–Sept. 13	233
NH–Frank Edelblut	30%	Open Race	Republican	June 13–Sept. 13	144
NH–Ted Gatsas	20%	Open Race	Republican	June 13–Sept. 13	443
NH–Jeanie Forrester	18%	Open Race	Republican	June 13–Sept. 13	129
OR–Kate Brown	84%	Incumbent	Democrat	Feb. 17–May 17	456
OR–Bud Pierce	47%	Challenger	Republican	Feb. 17–May 17	178
OR–Allen Alley	29%	Challenger	Republican	Feb. 17–May 17	311
UT–Gary Herbert	72%	Incumbent	Republican	Mar. 28–June 28	297
UT–Jonathan Johnson	28%	Challenger	Republican	Mar. 28–June 28	432
UT–Mike Weinholtz	80%	Challenger	Democrat	Mar. 28–June 28	458
VT–Sue Minter	48%	Open Race	Democrat	May 9–Aug. 9	318
VT–Matt Dunne	37%	Open Race	Democrat	May 9–Aug. 9	393
VT–Phil Scott	61%	Open Race	Republican	May 9–Aug. 9	891
VT–Bruce Lisman	37%	Open Race	Republican	May 9–Aug. 9	989
WA–Jay Inslee	48%	Incumbent	Democrat	May 2–Aug. 2	113
WA–Bill Bryant	38%	Challenger	Republican	May 2–Aug. 2	109
WV–Bill Cole	100%	Open Race	Republican	Feb. 10–May 10	128
WV–Jim Justice	51%	Open Race	Democrat	Feb. 10–May 10	154
WV–Booth Goodwin	25%	Open Race	Democrat	Feb. 10–May 10	304
WV–Jeff Kessler	24%	Open Race	Democrat	Feb. 10–May 10	480

TOTAL: 13,643

exclusive. *Basic communicating* included general messages, often about upcoming events, where the candidate will be, or how to get involved in the campaign (e.g., donating money or volunteering). Messages that highlight *personal characteristics* were coded as either focusing on positive aspects of the candidate (e.g., honest, hardworking) or negative aspects of her opponent (e.g., Washington insider, liar). Finally, *policy messages* include information about the candidate's position or actions pertaining to an issue area or her opponent's position, statements, or prior actions regarding particular issue(s), and may also refer to other sources (like the candidate's website) for more information on policy details.

Disagreement. Turning to our focal variable of disagreement, we coded each tweet for messages in which a candidate highlights places of divergence with others, such as opposing candidates or opposing parties. This sometimes takes the form of *general disagreements* in which the candidate simply points out difference or provides reasons for a particular position.

During the process of reviewing tweets, we noticed that candidates directed their disagreement toward three specific types of entities: their own party, the opposing party, and Washington elite.[52] During the primaries, candidates often expressed disagreement with individuals within the same political party (e.g., candidates opposing them in the primary race and the supporters of those candidates), which were coded as *disagreement—same party*. Further, candidates also highlighted disagreement with candidates and groups on the other side of the political aisle. They did so by expressing disagreement with candidates within their state (e.g., the person running for governor in the opposing political party, criticizing a state legislature for passing legislation espousing the views of the opposite party) as well as at the national level (e.g., pointing to disagreement with presidential candidates in the opposing party), which we coded as *disagreement—opposing party*. Finally, there were tweets that highlight points of divergence between the candidate and the *Washington elite*. This seemed to be a salient point in this election, as multiple candidates framed themselves as being "political outsiders," as sharply contrasted with "career politicians," "political class," "Washington elite," or "special interests."

Tone. Candidates also present disagreement using a provocative tone that goes beyond pointing out differences and openly challenges a competitor using scornful and disapproving language. This is called *uncivil disagreement* and is a separate code that often overlapped with other types of disagreement (e.g., same party, opposing party, Washington elite).

To ensure reliability, two coders tested 300 tweets randomly selected from the four primaries that completed before the end of May (e.g., North Carolina, Indiana, West Virginia, and Oregon). Assessing reliability near the beginning of the data collection process allowed us to solidify the codebook early, identify any problems moving forward, and code tweets in real time as the rest of the election unfolded. After each individual coded a set of 300 tweets, we uploaded the data into a reliability calculator found at http://dfreelon.org/utils/recalfront/.[53] For many variables, our initial reliability test did not meet the standard for a reliable coding instrument; both coders met to discuss inconsistencies and clarify the codebook. Next, we selected a separate 300 tweets to recode. During the second round, the two coders were able to achieve reliability ranging from .8 to 1.00 for each of the coded constructs. After establishing reliability, we proceeded to hand-code all 4,576 tweets collected during the primary. After collecting and coding the data, we used SPSS to run statistical analyses, the results of which are explained in the following section.

RESULTS

To begin, we look at the full population of tweets from all of the competitive gubernatorial primary candidates in 2016. Overall, Republican candidates posted more total tweets (8,412, 61.7% of the total population) than Democrats (5,231, 38.3% of the total population) and open race candidates twice as many tweets (9,149, 67.8% of the total population) as incumbents (1,660, 12.2% of the total population) and challengers (2,979, 20% of the total population) combined. At first glance, this is not particularly surprising, as the population included more Republicans than Democrats and significantly more open race candidates than challengers or incumbents. However, as shown in Table 3.2, Republicans posted an average of approximately 336 posts during the primary election period, while the average Democrat posted approximately 275 tweets. Incumbents posted an average of 207 tweets during the primary election period, while chal-

Table 3.2.   Total and Average Tweets by Candidate Type for Population of Tweets

	Total Candidates	Total Tweets	Average Number of Tweets
Republican	23	8412	376
Democrat	18	5231	290
Challenger	9	2834	314
Incumbent	6	1660	207
Open Race	26	9149	351
Open Race-R	15	6178	411
Open Race-D	11	2971	297
Incumbent-R	3	972	324
Incumbent-D	3	688	229
Challenger-R	5	1262	252
Challenger-D	4	1572	393

lengers and open race candidates made an average of 314 and 351 posts, respectively. Overall, Republicans posted more often, on average, than Democrats in every category except challengers, in which Democratic challengers posted an average of 393 tweets, as compared to Republicans' average of 252 tweets.

Next, we turn to the sampled tweets that were coded for more detailed information. Among our sample, we found that 61% (2,798) of tweets focused on basic communicating with the public (e.g., general messages about where candidate will be or how to get involved). This finding aligns with Gainous and Wagner,[54] who argue that candidates predominately use Twitter to post surface-level information about the campaign in general and spend comparatively little time focusing upon policy points or character traits.

However, tweets focused on policy and character are by no means absent. In fact, 27% (1,225) of the tweets sampled addressed policy issues (e.g., messages about candidate's policy actions/positions), and 12% (553) focused upon personal characteristics (e.g., messages highlighting positive aspects of candidate or negative aspects of opponent). Tweets focusing on the candidate's own personal characteristics were much more common (8.6%, 394) than those focused on the personal characteristics of the opponent (3.5%, 159).

Disagreement

Next, we turn to our focal variable—the types of disagreement that occurred in these tweets. We found that 12.3% of tweets (563) presented at least one form of disagreement (e.g., disagreement with the candidate's same party, opposing party, and Washington elite). First, during the primaries, candidates often expressed disagreement with individuals within the same political party (e.g., candidates opposing them in the primary race and the supporters of such candidates). For example, in the following tweet posted on June 3, 2016, Republican challenger Jonathan Johnson expresses disagreement with Republican Governor Herbert's decisions regarding Common Core: "Reason #4 to #HireJJ: Gary Herbert chose #CommonCore for Utah students. Now it's your turn to choose a new governor." Such a tweet expresses disagreement with the candidate's intra-party opponent as well as with a policy decision made by Herbert.

Further, candidates also highlighted disagreement with candidates and groups on the other side of the political aisle (e.g., opposing party disagreement). They did so by expressing disagreement with candidates within their state (e.g., the person running for governor in the opposing political party, criticizing a state legislature for passing legislation espousing the views of the opposite party) as well as at the national level (e.g., pointing to disagreement with presidential candidates in the opposing party). For example, in the following tweet posted on June 28, 2016, Republican Peter Kinder expresses disagreement with the policies of the Democratic Missouri administration, "Liberal job-killing policies have harmed #mogov's economy. Missouri's economy needs #RightToWork and lower taxes."

Finally, there were many tweets that highlighted points of divergence between a candidate's platform and the Washington elite. This seemed to be a salient point in this election, as multiple candidates framed themselves as being "political outsiders," as sharply contrasted with "career politicians," "political class," and "special interests." For instance, Jim Justice attempted to distance himself from the elite in the following tweet, posted on March 15, 2016: "The political elites in Charleston wasted this session dividing our state, pointing fingers, and passing raw milk legislation.—Jim #wvgov."

While the majority of tweets in our sample only focused upon one of the areas of disagreement (same party, opposing party, Washington elite), it is important to note that 45% of disagreeable tweets (252) contained more than one type of disagreement, suggesting disagreement in a single tweet often extended to multiple domains.

RQ1: Does Disagreement Differ Depending on Tweet Type?

Our first research question explored whether disagreement would be more common with certain types of tweets—and especially whether policy or personal characteristics would more often coincide with the presence of disagreement. First, we examine the frequency with which these types of disagreement occur (Figure 3.1). Within tweets that presented disagreement, policy disagreement is the most common form of disagreement observed, occurring in 53% (299) of disagreeable tweets, while personal disagreement occurred in 38% (215) of disagreeable tweets.

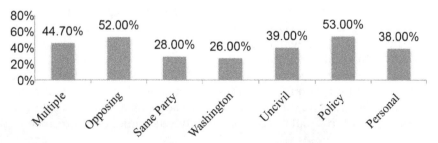

Figure 3.1. Types, Target, and Tone of Tweets Containing Disagreement

A chi-square test demonstrated that there is a significant relationship between type of tweet and the overall presentation of disagreement (χ^2 = 1497.308, df = 3, p < .001), regardless of its target or tone. The results suggest that candidates are especially likely to present disagreement when talking about an opponent's personal characteristics, with 96% of tweets (215) that discuss the opponent's personal characteristics also categorized as presenting disagreement. Disagreement was also more likely to occur when a tweet focused on policy information, as occurred in 18.6% of all policy tweets (299), although to a lesser extent than an opponent's personal characteristics. Meanwhile, disagreement was relatively rare when the tweet discussed the candidate's own personal characteristics (1.1%) or focused on basic communication (.08%). Thus, it appears that while gubernatorial primary candidates frequently present disagreement pertaining to policy information (e.g., "My opponent will raise your taxes"), they are more often tweeting about their own policies rather than their opponents'—but mentions of an opponent's character nearly always include disagreement.

RQ2: Does Disagreement Differ Depending on Target?

Turning to the target of disagreement, we find that disagreement with the opposing party was the most common target, occurring in 52% (293) of disagreeable tweets, followed by disagreement within the candidate's own party, which occurred in 28% (160) of disagreeable tweets. Finally, fitting narratives of the 2016 election as one in which candidates attempted to signal their disapproval of the unpopular Washington establishment, 26% (148) of tweets that contained disagreement (3% of all sampled tweets) by gubernatorial candidates highlighted disagreement with the Washington elite. Because these targets were not mutually exclusive, no chi-square test could be computed.

RQ3: Does Disagreement Differ in Tone?

Turning to the tone of the tweets that present disagreement, we find that incivility is relatively common. Thirty-nine percent of tweets (221) that presented disagreement (meaning 5% of the overall sample) were uncivil in tone, suggesting that disagreement was often presented in an uncivil manner. This information is displayed below in Figure 3.1. This is confirmed by chi-square statistics, which show that when candidates present disagreement, they are likely to do so using an uncivil tone (χ^2 = 1655.202, df = 1, p < .001) as compared to tweets without disagreement.

RQ4: Does Presentation of Disagreement Differ Based on Party Affiliation?

To answer the second research question regarding whether the presentation of disagreement depended on the party affiliation of the candidate, we conducted a series of chi-square tests of association. First, we tested whether there was a relationship between candidate party affiliation and presentation of disagreement of any type on Twitter. Results showed that there was no significant relationship ($\chi^2 = 1.644$, $df = 1$, p = .202) between overall presentation of disagreement and party affiliation—disagreement occurred in 12% of Democratic and 13% of Republican candidates' tweets.

However, these analyses ignore the possibility that the *type, tone,* or *target* of the disagreement differed by candidate party. For these analyses, we only examine these characteristics among those tweets that include disagreement.

In terms of disagreement *type*, we find that while Republicans and Democrats were equally likely to present policy disagreement, Republicans are slightly more likely than Democrats to present disagreement pertaining to personal characteristics. We present these results in Table 3.3, where percentages indicate the number of tweets that contain disagreement that have a particular characteristic.

Moreover, we found numerous differences between Republican and Democratic candidates in terms of the *target* of their disagreement. There is a significant relationship between party affiliation and expressing disagreement with someone in a *candidate's own party*, and the standardized residuals suggest that Republicans candidates were significantly more likely to express disagreement with their own party on Twitter while Democrats were significantly less likely to do so. In contrast, Democrats were more likely than Republicans to express disagreement with the *opposing party*. However, there was not a significant relationship between party affiliation and presenting disagreement with Washington elite, suggesting Democrats and Republicans were equally likely to be critical of the Washington elite.

Table 3.3.   Characteristics of Disagreement by Party Affiliation

	Uncivil	Same Party	Opposing Party	Washington Elite	Policy Disagreement	Personal Disagreement
Chi-Square	4.84*	25.39***	28.49***	3.37+	1.71	4.65*
Republican	35.6%	36.17%	42.9%	23.5%	50.8%	41.7%
Democrat	44.8%	16.6%	65.9%	30.5%	56.5%	32.7%

*$p < .05$, ** $p < .01$, ***$p < .001$

Finally, we found that there was a significant relationship between party affiliation and use of incivility, such that Democratic candidates were more likely than Republican candidates to present disagreement using an uncivil tone.

RQ5: Does Presentation of Disagreement Differ Based on Race Type?

To explore whether presentation of disagreement differs based on incumbency status, we again conducted a series of chi-square tests. Again, using a dichotomous variable that simply indicated whether disagreement was present without accounting for target, we found that there is a significant relationship between presentation of disagreement and incumbency status (χ^2 = 93.073, df = 2, p < .001). Results show that, overall, challengers were more likely to present disagreement (20% of tweets) than incumbents (5.3% of tweets) or open race candidates (11.3% of tweets).

Next, we applied a filter to explore how different types of disagreement were manifested in tweets that already contained some form of disagreement. We again begin by testing the type of disagreement. In this case, we find that although incumbents present disagreement least frequently, when expressing disagreement it is most likely to be about policy, followed by open race candidates and challengers. In contrast, within disagreeable tweets, challengers were most likely to tweet about disagreement with an opponent's personal characteristics, followed by open race candidates and incumbents. Therefore, the type of disagreement differs greatly depending on race characteristics. Results among disagreeable tweets are shown in Table 3.4.

Similarly, differences emerge in the target of disagreement depending on race type. We find that challengers were the most likely to post tweets expressing disagreement with members of their same party, followed by open race candidates, while incumbents were unlikely to express disagreement with members of their own party. However, within disagreeable tweets, incumbents were more likely to express disagreement with their opposing party than challengers or open race candidates during the primary. Finally—and interestingly in the political climate of 2016—open race candidates were most likely to highlight disagreement with Washington elite compared to incumbents or challengers, but we find no significant differences in the tone of tweets containing disagreement depending on race type.

Overall, our results present a complicated picture of disagreement between different types of races. Although all candidates were equally likely to take an uncivil tone in their tweets, challengers were the most likely to present disagreement overall, and were also more likely to attack other members of their own party or focus on personal characteristics.

Table 3.4. Characteristics of Disagreement by Race Type

	Uncivil	Same Party	Opposing Party	Washington Elite	Policy Disagreement	Personal Disagreement
Chi-Square	3.386	14.491***	17.571***	19.436***	17.291***	14.290***
Incumbent	31.5%	2.6%	84.2%	13%	84.2%	10.5%
Challenger	44%	33%	52%	17.5%	47.5%	43%
Open Race	37.2%	28.6%	48.3%	33.2%	52.9%	38.5%

*p < .05, ** p < .01, ***p < .001

In contrast, incumbents rarely presented disagreement—but when they did, it was nearly always policy-focused disagreement with the opposing party. Finally, open race candidates were the most likely to focus their attack on Washington elite, signaling their outsider status in the race.

DISCUSSION

This study examines how gubernatorial candidates presented disagreement on Twitter during the 2016 primary campaigns, as well as the campaign characteristics that shaped these communication strategies. Our results reveal a complex picture of how candidates present disagreement online, dependent both on the party affiliation of the candidate and whether the candidate is an incumbent, a challenger, or competing in an open race.

First, although the majority of tweets were focused on basic communicating, including fundraising or information about the candidate's public appearances,[55] many tweets were substantive in their approach: A quarter of gubernatorial candidates' tweets focused on policy, with another 10% focused on personal characteristics. And most importantly for this paper, 12% of tweets presented disagreement in some form. This disagreement often came in the form of policy disagreement, which might be considered one of the most beneficial forms of disagreement. After all, disagreement is inevitable, as candidates seek to distinguish themselves from their opponents and offer unique perspectives on the political environment—thus offering the voters discrete choices about candidates that best represent their values, interests, and beliefs.[56]

Perhaps less optimistically, we found references to the opponent's character were nearly inevitably associated with disagreement. We might expect the number of personal attacks to be higher during a primary campaign, when candidates have fewer policy differences to highlight as they compete with other candidates from their own party.[57] Future research should explore the frequency of personal versus issue-based attacks during the general election.

Additionally, our results complicate the narrative that social media is often a disagreeable and uncivil space for political communication.[58] Only 5% of all of tweets from competitive candidates during the gubernatorial primaries were uncivil—but 39% of tweets that contain disagreement were uncivil. That the candidates themselves serve as the source of incivility—which we define as lacking substantive information while demeaning the opposition[59]—is especially troubling, as it can create norms about appropriate discourse and shape the tone of subsequent commentary.[60]

Our results also point to specific campaign characteristics that created different strategies with regard to disagreement. As expected, we found that incumbents shy away from disagreement as compared to challengers or those competing in an open race. What is noteworthy is the size of these effects: incumbents present disagreement in 5% of their tweets, compared to 11% for open race candidates and 20% for challengers. When incumbents do engage in disagreement, they nearly always focus on policy disagreement with the opposing party, rather than their own. This strategy neatly fits what Popkin termed the "Rose Garden strategy," with incumbents attempting to appear above the competition in the primary.[61] Similarly, it may be that incumbents are attempting to activate strategic voting among their constituents by reminding them of the ultimate opposition—the other party.[62]

In contrast, challengers and open race candidates were relatively similar in their approach to disagreement on Twitter. Both were relatively likely to post about disagreement with the personal characteristics of their opposition, roughly as often as they posted about policy disagreements. Similarly, they focused on disagreement with members of their own party more than incumbents did (although still less than they discussed their disagreement with members of the other party). And this makes sense—both challengers and open race candidates cannot afford to rest on their accomplishments in office, and instead must highlight their differences with opposing candidates to get elected. This is especially true for open race candidates, who must not only set themselves apart from candidates within their own party, but must also overcome a candidate from the opposing party to reach the governor's office.

Open race candidates were also most likely to emphasize their disagreement with the Washington elite. Among open race candidates, nearly a third of tweets containing disagreement criticized the Washington elite or insiders—double the percentage of incumbents or challengers. Moreover, both Democratic and Republican candidates engaged in this criticism. We expect that these candidate attempts to define themselves as "outsiders" are driven by the unpopular political system in 2016,[63] but future research should examine whether candidate attempts to distance themselves from the system persist, and their effects on both perceptions of the candidates and of the political process.

However, it is not just the characteristics of the race itself that matter for campaign strategies regarding disagreement. Republican and Democratic candidates were similar in how often they presented disagreement overall and in the likelihood of focusing on policy or disagreement with Washington elites when they disagree. However, during the 2016 primary campaigns, Republicans were more likely to focus their disagreement on other members of their own party, whereas Democrats tended to highlight disagreement with the opposing party. These different strategies may result from the idiosyncratic nature of the 2016 election, especially given the fragmented primary that occurred for the presidential nomination among Republicans. Alternatively, it may reflect expected differences in how members of their party respond to disagreement and the nature of their online networks.[64] However, this focus on the opposing party in Democratic tweets may explain why these tweets tended to be more uncivil than Republican tweets. In drawing distinctions between themselves and other party members, Republicans may have to exercise caution to avoid alienating voters they would need in the general election, as compared to discussing an increasingly disliked opposing political party.[65] Future research should test whether these differences in strategic communication by party hold consistent across multiple campaigns, or whether they are unique to the 2016 primaries.

Of course, this approach has a number of limitations that must be acknowledged. First, our analyses focus only on those candidates who were competitive in their state's primaries, which we defined as achieving 15% of the vote. While this made our hand coding of the tweets more manageable, we would expect that non-competitive candidates might have different social media strategies than competitive candidates, which shape perceptions of the climate. Second, while we coded candidates from all the gubernatorial races in 2016, these states were often smaller in population and thus may not be representative of the experience of most American citizens. Future research should explore how Twitter strategies may differ between states. Third, although we can speak to the political climate that these candidates fostered through their campaigns on social media, we cannot discuss either the *motivations* of the candidates behind such efforts nor their effects on the public. We hope this study will provide a springboard to future efforts to understand the effects such campaign communication has.

Our results present a complicated picture of the nature of disagreement that originates with the political candidates themselves. We demonstrate that political disagreement is a meaningful part of nearly all candidates' strategic efforts on Twitter, but *how* candidates leverage different types of disagreement to frame their messages depends on characteristics of their race and of their political affiliation. Those considering the nature and effects of political campaigns online need to account for these differences. The candidates that individuals choose to follow during the primary campaign may dramatically shape their perceptions of the political process.

NOTES

1. Randall Collins, *The Sociology of Philosophies: A Global Theory of Intellectual Change* (Harvard University Press: 2000), 1–12.

2. Ibid., 12.; Lee Sigelman and Emmett H. Buell, "Avoidance or Engagement? Issue Convergence in US Presidential Campaigns, 1960–2000," *American Journal of Political Science* 48, no. 4 (2004): 650–661.

3. Casey A. Klofstad, Anand Edward Sokhey, and Scott D. McClurg, "Disagreeing About Disagreement: How Conflict in Social Networks Affects Political Behavior," *American Journal of Political Science* 57, no. 1 (2013): 120–134; Bryan M. Parsons, "Social Networks and the Affective Impact of Political Disagreement," *Political Behavior* 32, no. 2 (2010): 181–204; Diana C. Mutz, *Hearing the Other Side: Deliberative Versus Participatory Democracy* (Cambridge University Press: 2006); Robert Huckfeldt and Jeanette Morehouse Mendez, "Moths, Flames, and Political Engagement: Managing Disagreement Within Communication Networks," *The Journal of Politics* 70, no. 1 (2008): 83–96.

4. Elaine Kamarack, "Increasing Turnout in Congressional Primaries," Brookings Institution (July 26, 2014). Accessed January 9, 2017. https://www.brookings.edu/research/increasing-turnout-in-congressional-primaries/.

5. Casey A. Klofstad, Anand Edward Sokhey, and Scott D. McClurg, "Disagreeing About Disagreement: How Conflict in Social Networks Affects Political Behavior," *American Journal of Political Science* 57, no. 1 (2013): 120–134; Diana C. Mutz, *Hearing the Other Side: Deliberative Versus Participatory Democracy* (Cambridge University Press: 2006).

6. Elanor Colleoni, Alessandro Rozza, and Adam Arvidsson, "Echo Chamber or Public Sphere? Predicting Political Orientation and Measuring Political Homophily in Twitter Using Big Data," *Journal of Communication* 64, no. 2 (2014): 317–332; Emily K. Vraga, "Party Differences in Political Content on Social Media," *Online Information Review* 40, no. 5 (2016): 595–609.

7. William L. Benoit, "Election Outcome and Topic of Political Campaign Attacks," *Southern Journal of Communication* 69, no. 4 (2004): 348–355; Ted Brader, "Striking a Responsive Chord: How Political Ads Motivate and Persuade Voters by Appealing to Emotions," *American Journal of Political Science* 49, no. 2 (2005) 388–405; Ted Brader, *Campaigning for Hearts and Minds: How Emotional Appeals in Political Ads Work* (University of Chicago Press, 2006); Travis N. Ridout and Kathleen Searles, "It's My Campaign I'll Cry if I Want To: How and When Campaigns Use Emotional Appeals," *Political Psychology* 32, no. 3 (2011): 439–458.

8. Samuel L. Popkin, *The Reasoning Voter: Communication and Persuasion in Presidential Campaigns* (University of Chicago Press: 1994); Judith S. Trent, Robert V. Friedenberg, and Robert E. Denton, Jr., *Political Campaign Communication: Principles and Practices* (Rowman & Littlefield: 2011).

9. Elanor Colleoni, Alessandro Rozza, and Adam Arvidsson, "Echo Chamber or Public Sphere? Predicting Political Orientation and Measuring Political Homophily in Twitter Using Big Data," *Journal of Communication* 64, no. 2 (2014): 317–332; John T. Jost, Jack Glaser, Arie W. Kruglanski, and Frank J. Sulloway, "Political Conservatism as Motivated Social Cognition," *Psychological Bulletin* (2003): 339–375; Emily K. Vraga, Kjerstin Thorson, Neta Kligler-Vilenchik, and

Emily Gee, "How Individual Sensitivities to Disagreement Shape Youth Political Expression on Facebook," *Computers in Human Behavior* 45 (2015): 281–289.

10. Jody C Baumgartner, Jenn Burleson Mackay, Jonathan S. Morris, Eric E. Otenyo, Larry Powell, Melissa M. Smith, Nancy Snow, Frederic I. Solop, and Brandon C. Waite, *Communicator-in-chief: How Barack Obama used new media technology to win the White House*, Edited by John Allen Hendricks and Robert E. Denton Jr. (Lexington Books, 2010); Jason Gainous and Kevin M. Wagner, *Tweeting to Power: The Social Media Revolution in American Politics* (Oxford University Press: 2014); Judith S. Trent, Robert V. Friedenberg, and Robert E. Denton, Jr., *Political Campaign Communication: Principles and Practices* (Rowman & Littlefield: 2011); Diana C. Mutz, *Hearing the Other Side: Deliberative Versus Participatory Democracy* (Cambridge University Press: 2006); Terri L. Towner, "All Political Participation is Socially Networked? New Media and the 2012 Election," *Social Science Computer Review* 31, no. 5 (2013): 527–541.

11. Pew Research Center, "Campaign Exposes Fissures Over Issues, Values, and How Life Has Changed in the U.S." (2016). Accessed January 9, 2017. http://www.people-press.org/2016/03/31/1-views-of-the-primaries-press-coverage-of-candidates-attitudes-about-government-and-the-country/.

12. Robert Huckfeldt and Jeanette Morehouse Mendez, "Moths, Flames, and Political Engagement: Managing Disagreement Within Communication Networks," *The Journal of Politics* 70, no. 1 (2008): 83–96; Jason Bello and Meredith Rolfe, "Is Influence Mightier than Selection? Forging Agreement in Political Discussion Networks During a Campaign," *Social Networks* 36 (2014): 134–146.

13. Casey A. Klofstad, Anand Edward Sokhey, and Scott D. McClurg, "Disagreeing About Disagreement: How Conflict in Social Networks Affects Political Behavior," *American Journal of Political Science* 57, no. 1 (2013): 120–134; Bryan M. Parsons, "Social Networks and the Affective Impact of Political Disagreement," *Political Behavior* 32, no. 2 (2010): 181–204; Diana C. Mutz, *Hearing the Other Side: Deliberative Versus Participatory Democracy* (Cambridge University Press: 2006).

14. Casey A. Klofstad, Anand Edward Sokhey, and Scott D. McClurg, "Disagreeing About Disagreement: How Conflict in Social Networks Affects Political Behavior," *American Journal of Political Science* 57, no. 1 (2013): 120–134; Diana C. Mutz, *Hearing the Other Side: Deliberative Versus Participatory Democracy* (Cambridge University Press: 2006); Jennifer R. Brundidge, Kelly Garrett, Hernando Rojas, and Homero Gil de Zúñiga, "Political Participation and Ideological News Online: 'Differential Gains' and 'Differential Losses' in a Presidential Election Cycle," *Mass Communication and Society* 17, no. 4 (2014): 464–486.

15. Leon Festinger, *A Theory of Cognitive Dissonance* (Evanston, IL: Row, Peterson, 1957); Kelly R. Garrett, "Politically Motivated Reinforcement Seeking: Reframing the Selective Exposure Debate," *Journal of Communication* 59, no. 4 (2009): 676–699; Natalie J. Stroud, *Niche News: The Politics of News Choice* (Oxford: Oxford University Press, 2011).

16. Leticia Bode, "Political News in the News Feed: Learning Politics from Social Media," *Mass Communication and Society* 19 (2016): 24–48; Yonghwan Kim, "The Contribution of Social Network Sites to Exposure to Political Difference: The Relationships Among SNSs, Online Political Messaging, and Exposure to Cross-Cutting Perspectives," *Computers in Human Behavior* 27, no. 2 (2011): 971–977;

Dietram A. Scheufele, Matthew C. Nisbet, Dominique Brossard, and Erik C. Nisbet, "Social Structure and Citizenship: Examining the Impacts of Social Setting, Network Heterogeneity, and Informational Variables on Political Participation," *Political Communication,* 21, no. 3 (2004): 315–338; Kjerstin Thorson and Chris Wells, "Curated Flows: A Framework for Mapping Media Exposure in the Digital Age," *Communication Theory* (2015); Emily K. Vraga, Kjerstin Thorson, Neta Kligler-Vilenchik, and Emily Gee, "How Individual Sensitivities to Disagreement Shape Youth Political Expression on Facebook," *Computers in Human Behavior* 45 (2015): 281–289.

17. Leticia Bode, "Political News in the News Feed: Learning Politics from Social Media," *Mass Communication and Society* 19 (2016): 24–48; Yonghwan Kim, "The Contribution of Social Network Sites to Exposure to Political Difference: The Relationships Among SNSs, Online Political Messaging, and Exposure to Cross-Cutting Perspectives," *Computers in Human Behavior* 27, no. 2 (2011): 971–977; Emily K. Vraga, Kjerstin Thorson, Neta Kligler-Vilenchik, and Emily Gee, "How Individual Sensitivities to Disagreement Shape Youth Political Expression on Facebook," *Computers in Human Behavior* 45 (2015): 281–289.

18. Robert M. Entman, "Framing: Toward Clarification of a Fractured Paradigm," *Journal of Communication* 43, no. 4 (1993): 52.

19. Emily K. Vraga, D. Jasun Carr, Jeffrey P. Nytes, and Dhavan V. Shah, "Precision vs. Realism on the Framing Continuum: Understanding the Underpinnings of Message Effects," *Political Communication* 27, no. 1 (2010): 1–19.

20. Randall Collins, *The Sociology of Philosophies: A Global Theory of Intellectual Change* (Harvard University Press: 2000).

21. Joseph Bafami and Robert Y. Shapiro, "A New Partisan Voter," *The Journal of Politics* 71 (2009): 1–24; Angus Campbell, Philip E. Converse, Warren E. Miller, and Donald E. Stokes, *The American Voter* (New York: Wiley, 1960); Richard R. Lau and Daniel P. Redlawsk, *How Voters Decide: Information Processing in Election Campaigns* (Cambridge: Cambridge University Press, 1960).

22. Ted Brader, "Striking a Responsive Chord: How Political Ads Motivate and Persuade Voters by Appealing to Emotions," *American Journal of Political Science* 49, no. 2 (2005): 388–405; Angus Campbell, Philip E. Converse, Warren E. Miller, and Donald E. Stokes, *The American Voter* (New York: Wiley, 1960); Richard R. Lau and Daniel P. Redlawsk, *How Voters Decide: Information Processing in Election Campaigns* (Cambridge: Cambridge University Press, 1960).

23. William L. Benoit, "Election Outcome and Topic of Political Campaign Attacks," *Southern Journal of Communication* 69, no. 4 (2004): 348–355; William L. Benoit, "Beyond Genre Theory: The Genesis of Rhetorical Action," *Communications Monographs* 67, no. 2 (2000): 178–192.

24. Robert Huckfeldt, Paul E. Johnson, and John Sprague, *Political Disagreement: The Survival of Diverse Opinions Within Communication Networks* (Cambridge University Press: 2004); Diana C. Mutz, *Hearing the Other Side: Deliberative Versus Participatory Democracy* (Cambridge University Press: 2006); Robert Huckfeldt and Jeanette Morehouse Mendez, "Moths, Flames, and Political Engagement: Managing Disagreement Within Communication Networks," *The Journal of Politics* 70, no. 1 (2008): 83–96; Bryan M. Parsons, "Social Networks and the Affective Impact of Political Disagreement," *Political Behavior* 32, no. 2 (2010): 181–204.

25. Samuel L. Popkin, *The Reasoning Voter: Communication and Persuasion in Presidential Campaigns* (University of Chicago Press: 1994).

26. David W. Brady, Hahrie Han, and Jeremy C. Pope, "Primary Elections and Candidate Ideology: Out of Step With the Primary Electorate?" *Legislative Studies Quarterly* 32, no. 1 (2007): 79–105; Richard R. Lau and Daniel P. Redlawsk, *How Voters Decide: Information Processing in Election Campaigns* (Cambridge: Cambridge University Press, 1960).

27. Daniel Lipinski, William T. Bianco, and Ryan Work, "What Happens When House Members Run with Congress? The Electoral Consequences of Institutional Loyalty," *Legislative Studies Quarterly* 28, no. 3 (2003): 413–429; Emily K. Vraga, "Which Candidates Can Be Mavericks? The Effects of Issue Disagreement and Gender on Candidate Evaluations," *Politics and Policy* 45, no. 1: 4–30.

28. John G. Geer, *In defense of negativity: Attack ads in presidential campaigns* (University of Chicago Press: 2008); Glenn W. Richardson Jr., *Pulp Politics: How Political Advertising Tells the Stories of American Politics* (Rowman & Littlefield Publishers: 2008).

29. Bruce E. Gronbeck, "Negative Political Ads and American Self Images." In *Presidential Campaigns and American Self Images*, edited by Arthur H. Miller and Bruce E. Gronbeck, 62 (Oxford: Westview Press, 1994).

30. John G. Geer, *In Defense of Negativity: Attack Ads in Presidential Campaigns* (University of Chicago Press: 2008).

31. Deborah Jordan Brooks and John G. Geer, "Beyond Negativity: The Effects of Incivility on the Electorate," *American Journal of Political Science* 51, no. 1 (2007): 5.

32. Ibid., 1; see also Diana C. Mutz and Byron Reeves, "The New Videomalaise: Effects of Televised Incivility on Political Trust," *American Political Science Review* 99, no. 01 (2005): 1–15; Darrell M. West, *Air Wars: Television Advertising and Social Media in Election Campaigns, 1952–2012* (Sage: 2013).

33. John T. Jost and David M. Amodio, "Political Ideology as Motivated Social Cognition: Behavioral and Neuroscientific Evidence," *Motivation and Emotion* 36, no. 1 (2012): 55–64; John T. Jost, Jack Glaser, Arie W. Kruglanski, and Frank J. Sulloway, "Political Conservatism as Motivated Social Cognition," *Psychological Bulletin* (2003): 339–375; Jonathan Haidt and Jesse Graham, "When Morality Opposes Justice: Conservatives Have Moral Intuitions that Liberals May Not Recognize," *Social Justice Research* 20, no. 1 (2007): 98–116; Kaye D. Sweester, "Partisan Personality: The Psychological Differences Between Democrats and Republicans, and Independents Somewhere in Between," *American Behavioral Scientist* 58, no. 9 (2014): 1183–1194; Emily K. Vraga, Kjerstin Thorson, Neta Kligler-Vilenchik, and Emily Gee, "How Individual Sensitivities to Disagreement Shape Youth Political Expression on Facebook," *Computers in Human Behavior* 45 (2015): 281–289.

34. Philip E. Tetlock, "Cognitive Style and Political Belief Systems in the British House of Commons," *Journal of Personality and Social Psychology* 46, no. 2 (1984): 365–375.

35. Philip E. Tetlock, Jane Bernzweig, and Jack L. Gallant, "Supreme Court Decision Making: Cognitive Style as a Predictor of Ideological Consistency of Voting," *Journal of Personality and Social Psychology* 48, no. 5 (1985): 1227–1239.

36. Philip E. Tetlock, "A Value Pluralism Model of Ideological Reasoning," *Journal of Personality and Social Psychology* 50, no. 4 (1986): 819–827.

37. Natalie T. Wood and Kenneth C. Herbst, "Political Star Power and Political Parties: Does Celebrity Endorsement Win First-time Votes?" *Journal of Political Marketing* 6, no. 2–3 (2007): 141–158.

38. Kaye D. Sweester, "Partisan Personality: The Psychological Differences Between Democrats and Republicans, and Independents Somewhere in Between," *American Behavioral Scientist* 58, no. 9 (2014): 1183–1194.

39. Emily K. Vraga, "Party Differences in Political Content on Social Media," *Online Information Review* 40, no. 5 (2016): 595–609.

40. Elanor Colleoni, Alessandro Rozza, and Adam Arvidsson, "Echo Chamber or Public Sphere? Predicting Political Orientation and Measuring Political Homophily in Twitter Using Big Data," *Journal of Communication* 64, no. 2 (2014): 317–332.

41. Judith S. Trent, Robert V. Friedenberg, and Robert E. Denton, Jr., *Political Campaign Communication: Principles and Practices* (Rowman & Littlefield: 2011).

42. Samuel L. Popkin, *The Reasoning Voter: Communication and Persuasion in Presidential Campaigns* (University of Chicago Press: 1994).

43. Judith S. Trent, Robert V. Friedenberg, and Robert E. Denton, Jr., *Political Campaign Communication: Principles and Practices* (Rowman & Littlefield: 2011), 205.

44. Judith S. Trent, Robert V. Friedenberg, and Robert E. Denton, Jr., *Political Campaign Communication: Principles and Practices* (Rowman & Littlefield: 2011).

45. Twitter 2016. US House: A public list by Twitter government. Accessed November 1, 2016. https://twitter.com/gov/lists/us-house.

46. A pretest in 2015 suggested that Twitter was more commonly used by gubernatorial candidates, with governors posting about four times as many tweets as Facebook posts and generally having more followers on Twitter than Facebook (Authors).

Pew Research Center,"The Political Environment on Social Media" (2016). Accessed January 9, 2017. http://www.pewinternet.org/2016/10/25/the-political-environment-on-social-media/.

47. This guideline is based on the criteria set forth by the Commission on Presidential Debates (CPD) to determine whether a candidate will be invited to participate in a Presidential Debate. Essentially, the CPD guidelines state that a candidate must have at least 15% support nationwide to be included in a national debate. For this study, if a candidate obtained at least 15% of the vote in the primary election, we used a sample of his or her tweets in the final dataset.

48. Commission on Presidential Debates. 2016. "The Commission on Presidential Debates: An Overview." Accessed December 30, 2016. http://debates.org/index.php?page=overview.

49. Ted Brader, "Striking a Responsive Chord: How Political Ads Motivate and Persuade Voters by Appealing to Emotions," *American Journal of Political Science* 49, no. 2 (2005): 388–405; Ted Brader, *Campaigning for Hearts and Minds: How Emotional Appeals in Political Ads Work* (University of Chicago Press, 2006).

50. Jason Gainous and Kevin M. Wagner, *Tweeting to Power: The Social Media Revolution in American Politics* (Oxford University Press: 2014).

51. Ibid.

52. These three categories are not mutually exclusive. For instance, in a few cases candidates used more than one type of disagreement in their message, so it is worth noting that some data points may include more than one designation.

53. Deen Freelon, "ReCal: Intercoder Reliability Calculation as a Web Service," *International Journal of Internet Science* 5, no. 1 (2010): 20–33; Deen Freelon, "ReCal OIR: Ordinal, Interval, and Ratio Intercoder Reliability as a Web Service," *International Journal of Internet Science* 8, no. 1 (2013): 10–16.

54. Jason Gainous and Kevin M. Wagner, *Tweeting to Power: The Social Media Revolution in American Politics* (Oxford University Press: 2014).

55. Ibid.

56. Alan Abramowitz and Kyle L. Saunders, "Ideological Realignment in the US Electorate," *Journal of Politics* 60 (1998): 634–652; Anthony Downs, "An Economic Theory of Political Action in a Democracy," *The Journal of Political Economy* 65, no. 2 (1957): 135–150.

57. William L. Benoit, "Election Outcome and Topic of Political Campaign Attacks," *Southern Journal of Communication* 69, no. 4 (2004): 348–355; William L. Benoit, "Beyond Genre Theory: The Genesis of Rhetorical Action," *Communications Monographs* 67, no. 2 (2000): 178–192.

58. Ashley A. Anderson, Dominique Brossard, Dietram A. Scheufele, Michael A. Xenos, and Peter Ladwig, "The 'Nasty Effect': Online Incivility and Risk Perceptions of Emerging Technologies," *Journal of Computer-Mediated Communication* 19, no. 3 (2014): 373–387; Emily K. Vraga, Kjerstin Thorson, Neta Kligler-Vilenchik, and Emily Gee, "How Individual Sensitivities to Disagreement Shape Youth Political Expression on Facebook," *Computers in Human Behavior* 45 (2015): 281–289.

59. Deborah Jordan Brooks and John G. Geer, "Beyond Negativity: The Effects of Incivility on the Electorate," *American Journal of Political Science* 51, no. 1 (2007): 5.

60. Stephanie Edgerly, Emily K. Vraga, Kajsa E. Dalrymple, Timothy Macafee, and Timothy KF Fung, "Directing the Dialogue: The Relationship Between YouTube Videos and the Comments They Spur," *Journal of Information Technology & Politics* 10, no. 3 (2013): 276–292; Emily K. Vraga, Kjerstin Thorson, Neta Kligler-Vilenchik, and Emily Gee, "How Individual Sensitivities to Disagreement Shape Youth Political Expression on Facebook," *Computers in Human Behavior* 45 (2015): 281–289.

61. Samuel L. Popkin, *The Reasoning Voter: Communication and Persuasion in Presidential Campaigns* (University of Chicago Press: 1994); see also Judith S. Trent, Robert V. Friedenberg, and Robert E. Denton, Jr., *Political Campaign Communication: Principles and Practices* (Rowman & Littlefield: 2011).

62. Richard R. Lau and Daniel P. Redlawsk, *How Voters Decide: Information Processing in Election Campaigns* (Cambridge: Cambridge University Press, 1960).

63. Daniel Lipinski, William T. Bianco, and Ryan Work, "What Happens When House Members Run with Congress? The Electoral Consequences of Institutional Loyalty," *Legislative Studies Quarterly* 28, no. 3 (2003): 413–429; Gallup, "Congress and the Public," (2016) Accessed January 11, 2017: http://www.gallup.com/poll/1600/congress-public.aspx; Emily K. Vraga, "Which Candidates

Can Be Mavericks? The Effects of Issue Disagreement and Gender on Candidate Evaluations," *Politics and Policy* 45, no. 1: 4–30.

64. Elanor Colleoni, Alessandro Rozza, and Adam Arvidsson, "Echo Chamber or Public Sphere? Predicting Political Orientation and Measuring Political Homophily in Twitter Using Big Data," *Journal of Communication* 64, no. 2 (2014): 317–332; Emily K. Vraga, "Party Differences in Political Content on Social Media," *Online Information Review* 40, no. 5 (2016): 595–609.

65. Pew Research Center, "Partisanship and Political Animosity in 2016," (2016). Accessed January 11, 2017. http://www.people-press.org/2016/06/22/partisanship-and-political-animosity-in-2016/.

4

The Twitter Election

Analyzing Candidate Use of Social Media in the 2016 Presidential Campaign

Steven P. Nawara and Mandi Bates Bailey

On January 13, 2017, President-elect Donald Trump took to the social media platform Twitter to attack his recent opponent, former Secretary of State Hillary Clinton. Trump microblogged, "What are Hillary Clinton's people complaining about with respect to the F.B.I. Based on the information they had she would have never been allowed to run—guilty as hell . . . [sic]" Aside from the obvious concerns about a president who will be appointing judicial candidates assigning guilt to a political opponent, this tweet generally illustrates the overall negative tone perceived throughout the 2016 presidential election campaign and more specifically illustrates the way in which social media are revolutionizing American elections.

This election cycle saw both major-party nominees with "underwater" favorability numbers and each candidate was dogged by scandals that called into question their character and suitability for office. With no shortage of potentially damning information on either side, Twitter became a forum for 140-character (or less) personal attacks from candidates who could be characterized as having itchy Twitter fingers.

This chapter investigates presidential candidates' use of social media broadly as well as its use as a vehicle of negativity in the contentious 2016 election by looking across platforms. Specifically, we content analyze the official candidate social media account activity in the months preceding Election Day 2016 from the three most-prominent social media platforms, Twitter, Facebook, and Instagram. In addition to major party candidates Trump (the Republican nominee) and Clinton (the Democratic nominee), we also investigate the social media use of Libertarian candidate Gary Johnson.

Our goal is to present a comprehensive look at the social media campaign strategies of the 2016 presidential candidates. This type of in-depth investigation of candidate social media use is not only timely, it is becoming increasingly necessary in order to fully understand both how candidates campaign and how the public consumes political information. Not only is social media use growing across segments of the American population, candidates are increasingly using these media. In addition mainstream news organizations are both covering candidate social media use in the content of their news accounts and using social media to enhance delivery of the news. For instance, the *New York Times* ran an article on Election Day titled "For Election Day Influence, Twitter Ruled Social Media," while CNN and FOX News incorporated live social media posts into their coverage of presidential debates.[1]

In order to comprehensively review the 2016 presidential candidates' social media use, we begin by assessing Americans' use of social media and reviewing extant studies of candidates' social media use, which has largely focused on Congress, before turning to a broader look at negativity and discussing our expectations. We introduce our content analysis in detail and present our findings. We conclude that Twitter was the dominant social medium in the 2016 presidential race by a relatively large margin. We also find that while social media were often used to address campaign activities and opponents' character, these platforms were rarely used to delve into substantive policy discussion. Lastly, we find that in spite of Trump's reputation for negativity, the aggregate percentages of Clinton's and Trump's posts that were negative are nearly identical (Trump, however, was more negative on Twitter). In fact, despite the perception of the 2016 campaign as overwhelmingly negative, positive posts greatly outnumbered negative posts on social media.

AMERICAN SOCIAL MEDIA USE

Social media use is prevalent across a variety of American demographic groups.[2] In total, 68 percent of American adults have Facebook accounts while 28 percent and 21 percent of American adults, respectively, use Instagram and Twitter.[3] It is notable, however, that among American social media users, women outnumber men on Facebook and Instagram while men outnumber women on Twitter.[4] Social media use may be widespread, but do Americans get political information from it?

For those individuals active on social networking sites, political information is difficult to avoid. An October 2016 report on social media use by Pew found that younger users were more likely to use these platforms to seek out political information, and roughly one-third of social media users report that they participate in political discussions on these sites.[5] This same study found that both Republicans and Democrats are equally likely to participate in political dialogue via social media platforms.

While political information via social media sites is prevalent, users are not necessarily turning to these sites for varied perspectives on given issues. One study suggests that those users seeking out political information via social media are often looking for information that reinforces their existing opinions while actively avoiding information that is inconsistent with their political views.[6] Nevertheless, research suggests that social media use has a political impact. It is related to both political participation and political attitudes such as increasing support for freedom of expression and declining support (particularly among younger social media users) for the right to privacy.[7]

SOCIAL MEDIA IN PRESIDENTIAL ELECTIONS

Columnist Nathan Heller asserts that every election has a key medium. While Franklin Roosevelt dominated radio and Kennedy successfully utilized television, Twitter was the key medium for the 2016 presidential election.[8] Others have dubbed the 2008 election "The Facebook Election."[9] However, evidence suggests that the impact of social media was likely minimal in previous presidential elections. For instance, one study analyzed Facebook users' activity during the 2008 presidential nomination and general election seasons and found that while the medium generated attention from political parties, candidates, and mainstream media, it was not successful in mobilizing political participation.[10] Another report found that while presidential candidates increasingly used Twitter in the 2012 presidential election, that use did not translate into greater online public attention.[11]

In spite of certain limitations of social media in previous presidential elections, some generalizations can be drawn about its use by candidates and individuals. First, more than 1,000 Facebook group pages focusing on presidential candidates Barack Obama and John McCain during the 2008 campaign were created, with Obama receiving a greater amount of attention as well as more positive attention.[12] Second, an analysis of Twitter feeds by major and minor party candidates during the 2012 presidential primaries reveals that minor party candidates were more likely to tweet than were major party candidates.[13] Finally, use of Twitter by presidential candidates grew tremendously between the 2008 and 2012 presidential elections.[14]

LESSONS FROM CONGRESS

Going into the 2016 campaign, it was clear that candidates would increasingly use social networking sites and that the campaign would be the first national race in which social media would be viewed by practically all observers as a vital and a necessary tool to reach out to voters and disseminate information. While we have drawn some generalizations from literature directly addressing presidential candidates/campaigns, this research is still somewhat limited. Therefore, we look to research investigating Congressional use of social media to get a better sense of how political actors use social networking sites. We begin by addressing general use of social media by Congressmembers before addressing social media use in Congressional campaigns.

Presently, nearly every member of the 115th Congress has a social media presence. These networking sites allow members of Congress to repeatedly reach out to audiences that may have only visited a campaign website or blog once.[15] Thus, members of Congress have found social media to be an attractive, low-cost means of reaching their constituents and supporters while circumventing traditional media that could be critical or potentially obscure the messages they are trying to relay.[16] While Congress in general has embraced social media, research points to potentially differing patterns of use by party, however, suggesting that Republicans may be using Twitter more often than Democrats.[17]

The low-cost aspect of social media contributes to its attractiveness as a campaign tool. Incumbents and challengers may use social media to reach likely supporters and to influence more traditional media coverage. Moreover, one's voting activity may be influenced by the voting activity of those active on his/her social network(s), enlarging the size of candidates' pools of supporters.[18]

Undoubtedly, politicians have taken notice of social media's campaign potential and these platforms are now playing a growing role in Congressional elections. Research corroborates this view as it relates to Facebook.[19] One study found that candidates for the U.S. Senate used Facebook as a campaigning tool in 2010, with both challengers and incumbents posting more negative content if the race was electorally competitive.[20]

Generally, research suggests that men and women are very similar in their strategic approaches to campaigning.[21] In terms of Congressional campaigning via social media, however, evidence is mixed. This is particularly the case regarding candidate gender and the frequency and tone of messages (research is more unified as it relates to gender and policy messaging). One report suggests that women post more frequently and were more likely to go negative than men in the 2012 election cycle.[22] Another suggests that men in Congress tweet more often than women.[23] Another finds that gender differences are limited to women posting more pro forma official business and more frequently about social policies such as gay marriage, abortion, and women's issues.[24] Still another points to differences across gender, with female candidates posting more frequently about policy.[25]

NEGATIVITY AND THE "TWITTER ELECTION"

Pew reports that many Americans were largely dissatisfied with both of the major party presidential candidates in 2016 and also saw the campaign as excessively negative.[26] This same study reported that only 27 percent of voters thought the campaign was focused on important policy debate. The 2016 presidential campaign was seen as exceedingly negative and not focused on policy. A great deal of this negatively played out on social media, particularly Twitter.

Writing for *The New Yorker*, Heller referred to the 2016 presidential contest as "The Twitter Election."[27] This may not be an overstatement. Twitter's internal data collection indicates that users posted more than one billion tweets over the course of the nomination and general election seasons. Both candidates took advantage of a forum that allowed them to quickly and cost-effectively send campaign messages. For example, Trump addressed the email scandal plaguing Clinton as often as possible while Clinton jumped on Trump's frequent false statements and suitability for office. Trump's most retweeted post came on June 9, 2016, when he stated, "How long did it take your staff of 823 people to think that up—and where are your 33,000 emails that you deleted?"[28] This tweet was in response to the most retweeted post of the entire election by either candidate in which Clinton told Trump to "Delete your account" after Trump mocked President Obama for his endorsement of Clinton.

Of course the 2016 campaign did not take place entirely on Twitter, and Twitter did not represent the only social medium used by candidates. However, its frequent use by the candidates and 140-character format present fertile opportunity to explore social media's impact on American government and elections. As one observer claimed, "It isn't just that the service has become Trump's favorite bully pulpit, or a leading sloganeering platform for Clinton supporters. It's that the form of a tweet—short, fast, and easily passed on—is suited to a campaign season in which gaffes occur several times a day and health updates are released with a glow of drama benefitting 'General Hospital.'"[29]

What makes Twitter attractive for candidates is what also makes it attractive for those researching the impact of social media on elections. The short form of communication is relatively easy to manually code and analyze compared to the longer and often narrative approach on Facebook. Nevertheless, scholars are now systematically studying both Twitter and Facebook with regularity. Other social media platforms, such as Instagram, are not being analyzed with this same regularity even though Instagram is actually more popular among Americans than Twitter, with nearly a third of online Americans being Instagram users.[30] Furthermore, Instagram is continuing to experience rapid growth; there are now over 600 million worldwide users of the platform, with over 100 million joining between May 2016 and December 2016.[31] Though scholars have been slow to recognize Instagram's importance, politicians have not. Of the major-party candidates running for their party's presidential nomination, only Republican candidate Carly Fiorina did not have a public Instagram account.[32]

Studies have found that most social media posts by candidates are positive in tone.[33] However, there is also existing scholarship to support the expectation that candidates will "go negative" on social media. As one study notes, Twitter in particular "provides a context in which candidates feel more comfortable discussing the negative qualities of their competitors."[34] Moreover, the ability of campaigns to re-tweet links and content from others allows candidates to disseminate negative information about their opponents while personally distancing themselves from the attack.[35] Going negative on social media has been found to have positive electoral effects, especially if the candidate is also under attack by rivals.[36] Research into social media activity in recent elections reveals some patterns of candidate behavior: attacks on social media were primarily about opponents' policy preferences in gubernatorial campaigns;[37] attacks on Twitter increased as the Republican primaries approached;[38] and attacks were more common when there were fewer primary candidates.[39] However, findings are not monolithic. One study found that tweets generally become more positive in tone as elections approach,[40] while others[41] found that long-shot candidates are unlikely to run negative campaigns. Still others find that candidates in the 2016 Republican nomination season "punched upward" at those ahead of them in the polls in targeting their Twitter attacks.[42]

A general summary of the foregoing suggests the following:

1. Americans across demographic categories are increasingly using social media, but more women than men are on Facebook and Instagram while more men than women are on Twitter;[43]
2. Political information via social media is often a by-product, but younger generations use social media to seek out political information;[44]
3. Minor party presidential candidates are likely to use Twitter with greater frequency than are major party candidates;[45]
4. Congressional use of social media has proliferated;[46]

5. Social media are low-cost and are regularly used as campaigning tools;[47]
6. Republicans appear to use social media with greater frequency than their Democratic counterparts, though evidence for this is limited to Congress;[48]
7. Evidence is mixed regarding the impact of candidate gender on social media use;[49]
8. Twitter is the dominant form of campaign messages via social media;[50]
9. The 2016 presidential election generated a great deal of interest and was perceived to have been very negative.[51]

This summary provides a foundation for our expectations regarding how presidential candidates would use social media in 2016.

EXPECTATIONS

We expect all three candidates in our analysis to take advantage of all three social media platforms considered (Facebook, Instagram, and Twitter). However, we specifically expect to see Twitter emerge as the most frequently used social media platform.

We are somewhat conflicted in our expectations regarding which candidate is likely to post/tweet more often. If we extend studies of congressional campaigns to this election, we could say that Trump is more likely to post/tweet with greater frequency given that he is a Republican. Alternatively, the research suggesting that women in Congress tweet more often than men suggests that Clinton might post/tweet more than Trump. Finally, as Johnson has the least resources of the three presidential candidates and evidence suggests minor party candidates will tweet with greater frequency,[52] we might expect that he is more likely to post/tweet with greater frequency given the cost-effective nature of the medium.

Ultimately, given that Trump is not a typical Republican, the recent research pointing to women in Congress tweeting more often than men,[53] and the fact that there are more women than men on the two most-used social media platforms, we expect that Hillary Clinton will post/tweet more often than Trump or Johnson.

We also expect that all three candidates will use social media to go negative. The overall tenor of the election speaks to this. In spite of Trump's bombastic persona and a reputation for tweeting, we expect Clinton to tweet negatively more often than Trump given research suggesting that women in Congress are more likely to go negative on social media than men. Admittedly, this is a weak expectation as extant research does not directly address presidential candidate behavior on social media and Trump illustrated a willingness (if not a fondness) to attack opponents on social media. Nevertheless, as we are concerned with the quantity of negative posts/tweets per candidate as opposed to the degree of negativity within posts, we are confident in our expectation that Clinton will post/tweet more than her opponents will.

Finally, we expect to see Clinton post more about substantive policy issues than Trump. This expectation is based on research that points to women in Congress tweeting more often than men about issues, as well as the fact that Clinton, unlike Trump, has a professional history in government service.[54] We also expect Johnson to post about substantive policy issues with greater frequency than Trump given both his experience in public service and his need to illustrate to potential supporters his issue competency as a third-party candidate. The expectation relating to Johnson is also weak as there is little extant research addressing the use of social media by third party candidates.

We address these expectations as well as a more comprehensive look at the general social media strategy employed by all three presidential candidates below.

DATA AND METHODS

This study employs a content analysis of every post by candidates' official social media accounts during the final three months of the 2016 presidential campaign (August 15 through Election Day on November 8). The study monitored the Twitter, Facebook, and Instagram accounts of Clinton, Trump, and Gary Johnson.[55] Three undergraduate students analyzed each post on a weekly rotation across candidates and platforms.

Each post was treated as a separate observation and the candidate, platform, and date were recorded as separate variables. Coders were asked to classify the content of the post in one of 58 categories, which have been condensed into 35 categories for this chapter.[56] Table 4.1 lists these categories. Coders were also asked to note the general tone of the posts (negative, neutral, or positive), as well as the tone towards the Republican and Democratic Parties (negative, neutral, positive, or not applicable).[57] Finally, the coders noted if the post contained an image or video, the tone and content of any image/videos, and the length of any videos.

Table 4.1. Content Categories

Content Categories
Economy
Deficit, Spending, and Taxes
Education
Health Care
Immigration
Terrorism and ISIS
Foreign Relations
Military and Veterans
Crime and Police
LGBTQ Issues
Race
Women's Issues (including abortion, child care, and family leave)
Gun Issues
Climate Change and Environment
Polls
President Obama, Congress, or Other Politicians
Supreme Court and Judiciary
Running Mates
Campaign Activities (including rallies and endorsements)
Fundraising
Voter Mobilization (including voter registration and get out the vote reminders)
Clinton Email Scandals, DNC Hacking, and FBI Investigation
Candidate Foundations, Brands, and Financial Activities (including Trump University and candidate tax returns)
Media Appearances and Self-promotion
Debates
Character of Opponent
Giving Thanks
Honoring Deaths, Disasters, and History
Patriotic Appeals (including calls for unity and "Make American Great Again")
Corruption and Anti-Establishment (including criticisms of the two-party system, a "rigged" system, and "Drain the Swamp")
Critiquing Media Coverage
Personal Characteristics (including personal traits, health, leisure activities)
Candidate Families
Trump Sexual Assault Tape and Sexual Assault Allegations
Other

FINDINGS AND RESULTS

How Common Were Social Media Postings?

In total, there were 5,810 posts by the three candidates during this time frame: 3,355 tweets (57.8% of the total posts), 1,715 Facebook posts

(29.5%), and 740 posts to Instagram. In other words, a typical day during the campaign featured 39 tweets, 20 Facebook posts, and 9 Instagram pictures published by the three candidates. Clearly, the campaigns used social media extensively during the 2016 election.

If one just looks at the public's social media usage, it is surprising that Twitter was, by far, the most common platform for candidate postings. As of November 2016, 79 percent of online Americans were on Facebook, which is more than double the percentage that used Twitter (24%) or Instagram (31%).[58] That same study also showed that not only are more Americans on Facebook than Instagram or Twitter, but they are more likely to visit the site daily or several times a day: 55 percent report visiting Facebook more than once a day and another 22 percent do so daily. In comparison, only 35 percent of Instagram users visit several times a day (51% do so daily) and just 23 percent of Twitter users visit several times a day (42% visit daily).

The prevalence of tweeting in comparison to Facebook and Instagram suggests that campaigns are not efficiently targeting their social media posts to the platform with their largest potential audiences. So why are tweets so common? First, journalists use Twitter extensively. Practically all national journalists are active on Twitter, and candidate tweets might be an attempt to influence their coverage. Secondly, it is possible that citizens are more likely to seek out political information on Twitter than other social media platforms. Forty-eight percent of respondents mostly follow people they do not personally know on Twitter and another 37 percent follow mostly a mix of those they know and do not know personally. On Facebook, however, 66 percent of people mostly follow others they personally know.[59] It might be that whereas people use Facebook and Instagram primarily to keep up with personal relationships, they are using Twitter to keep up with current events, including political campaigns. Finally, Twitter may be a more effective way to respond quickly to current events. The 140-character limit of tweets necessitates brevity and prevents deep elaboration or analysis. However, these "micro-blogs" do allow for rapid statements in response to political critiques and developing news stories.

Figure 4.1 breaks down the posts by candidate and platform to assess whether there were any telling differences. First, for all three candidates, Twitter was the most commonly used platform, followed by Facebook and Instagram. Second, in terms of postings, Clinton dominated social media with 2,664 posts, compared to 1,922 posts for Trump and 1,224 posts for Johnson. Clinton posted more than her rivals on both Twitter and Facebook, though she also made the fewest Instagram posts. Third, despite Trump's reputation for tweeting, he tweeted 43 percent less than Clinton did. Also, just half (49.7%) of Trump's posts were tweets, com-

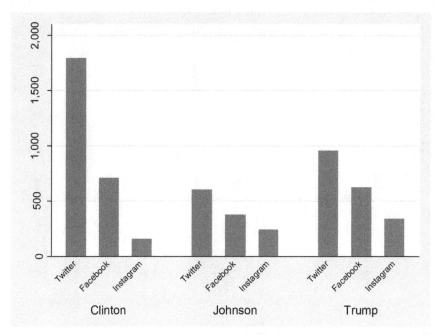

Figure 4.1. Social Media Posts by Candidate and Platform

pared to two-thirds (67.4%) of Clinton's posts. Trump's Twitter behavior might have been more candid, outlandish, and memorable, but Clinton's approach to Twitter appeared to be one of quantity. Finally, Gary Johnson's social media usage was unexpected. Given extant research suggesting that minor party candidates would tweet more than major party candidates, as well as the lack of media coverage and financial constraints that come with being a third-party candidate, we expected Johnson to be very active on social media, which could be a practically cost-free way to get attention and directly reach supporters. Instead, Johnson posted the least of all three candidates.

The Content of Social Media Posts

Figure 4.2 shows the primary topic of each post, classified into 35 content areas, including an "other" category. The first thing that jumps out is the sheer dominance of campaign activities as a topic of social media postings. Rallies, endorsements, and other routine campaign activities represented 23 percent of the candidates' posts on Facebook, Twitter, and Instagram, a full 12 percentage points higher than the second-place category, the character of one's opponent (11%). Voter mobilization (8%) and

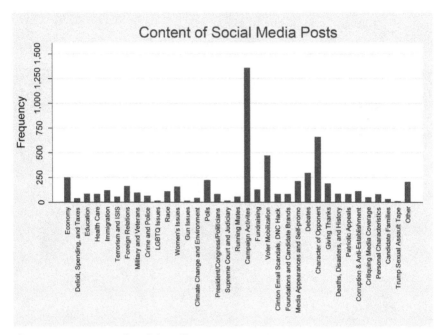

Figure 4.2. Content of Social Media Posts

the debates (5%) were the only other categories to consist of at least 5 percent of the total posts. Together, this means that 37 percent of posts were related to campaign rallies, endorsements, the debates, voter registration appeals, and get out the vote efforts. Clearly, modern political candidates view the documentation of routine campaign events as a major purpose for their social media presence.

This serves a purpose greater than simply recounting campaign stops and documenting public support, however. Instead, these posts are likely meant to rally supporters among their social media following. The average citizen is unlikely to attend a single campaign event, let alone several rallies. However, candidates can use social media to bring the rallies and campaign events directly to the screens of their followers, giving them a sense of participation and group belonging. These posts allow followers to feel like a part of the campaign, and their quantity serves as a constant reminder of the upcoming election. These reminders attempt to motivate followers to become stronger supporters or take some concrete action towards helping the campaign, such as registering to vote, volunteering, donating, or voting.

Perhaps the most surprising thing that comes out of Figure 4.2 is what is *not* the topic of many social media posts. Discussions of major political issues were simply not a priority for presidential candidates on social media. For example, despite a vacancy on the Supreme Court that was deadlocked in a 4–4 split between liberal and conservative justices, there were just 17 postings about the judiciary or the Supreme Court (0.29%). Combined, the categories "Supreme Court and the judiciary," "gun issues," "LGBTQ issues," "deficit, spending, and taxes," "climate change and the environment," and "terrorism and ISIS" accounted for a mere 3.2 percent of total posts. The only issue-based categories that accounted for more than 2 percent of total posts were the economy (4.3%), foreign relations (2.8%), women's issues (including abortion, childcare, and family leave; 2.7%), and immigration (2.1%). Candidates clearly do not see social media as the place to engage in policy-related discussions and instead prefer to focus on more prosaic topics such as campaign events (23%), polls (3.8%), media appearances and self-promotion (3.7%), thanking people (3.3%), and acknowledging historical events, deaths, and tragedies (1.5%).

Finally, despite the several scandals that will likely define the 2016 race in the historical record, the candidates did not make scandals a centerpiece of their social media strategies. While many posts generally related to corruption and took an anti-establishment stance (1.9%), just 1.4 percent of posts were about the Clinton email scandal, the DNC hacking, and the FBI investigation; 1.4 percent mentioned the two major-party candidates' controversial charitable foundations and other name-branded products and entities (such as Trump University); and just 0.2 percent of posts referenced the leak of Trump's *Access Hollywood* tape. Despite the undeniable importance of these scandals in explaining the 2016 race, these scandals largely played out in the mainstream media and among the candidates' supporters, not on the their official social media accounts.

Patterns in Content across Candidates

Table 4.2 shows every content category where Clinton or Trump posted at least 35 times more than his or her major-party rival did. While readers must keep in mind that Clinton made 742 more posts than Trump during this study, this table can nonetheless provide a snapshot of the issues that were disproportionately pushed by the major-party candidates on social media.

Clinton expended a great deal of effort attacking the character of Trump. While Trump made plenty of posts attacking Clinton's honesty and other character traits, he did not do so as often as Clinton and was out-posted by almost 300 posts in that content category. Clinton frequently posted about issues more than Trump, with women's issues, education, the economy, military and veterans, race, climate change and the environment, and foreign relations all appearing in Table 4.2, indicating

Table 4.2.   Content of Posts

	Clinton	Trump	Clinton-Trump
Character of Opponent	447	150	297
Voter Mobilization	321	86	235
Women's Issues	139	18	121
Education	84	1	83
Economy	138	73	65
Military and Veterans	67	17	50
Campaign Activities	497	449	48
Debates	105	60	45
Race	74	32	42
Climate Change and Environment	39	2	37
Other	95	59	36
Foreign Relations	85	50	35
Email Scandals, DNC Hacking, and FBI Investigation	16	63	−47
Critiquing Media Coverage	0	47	−47
Corruption and Anti-Establishment	5	75	−70
Polls	5	148	−143
Giving Thanks	5	168	−163

Note: Table only includes content categories with a difference of at least 35 posts across the major-party candidates.

at least a 35-post advantage to Clinton. The disparities were particularly stark regarding education (84–1) and climate change (39–2). Finally, 235 more of Clinton's posts fell in the category of voter mobilization, suggesting that the Clinton campaign put more faith in social media's ability to translate online support to real-world activities like voting.

Despite being dramatically out-posted by Clinton overall, Trump still out-posted Clinton in a handful of content areas. Clinton never issued a post that was primarily a critique of media coverage, but Trump did so 47 times. Trump made 75 posts about generalized corruption, the "rigged" system, and other anti-establishment sentiments (including his catchphrase "drain the swamp") while Clinton only made 5 posts that fell in that category. Similarly, Trump posted 143 more times about poll results than Clinton. Finally, one result that political observers might not have expected is that Trump was exceedingly more thankful on social media than his rival. A total of 168 posts were "thank you" notes to supporters, cities, and other groups.

Tone of Social Media Posts

Figure 4.3 shows the general tone (negative, neutral, or positive) for each platform and illustrates distinct differences in how the candidates

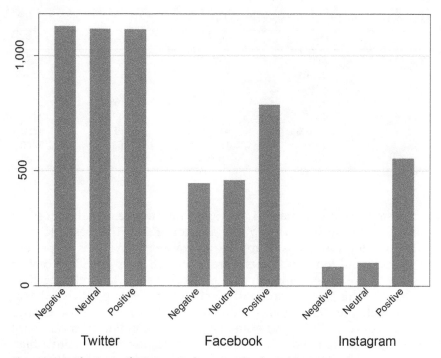

Figure 4.3. The Tone of Posts on Twitter, Facebook, and Instagram

approached the various social media platforms. Given the 2016 campaign's reputation for being nasty and negative, it is somewhat surprising to see that positive postings clearly outnumbered negative ones on social media. Across all platforms, 42 percent of posts were positive, another 29 percent were neutral, and 29 percent were negative.

Tweets were almost evenly divided between negative, neutral, and positive posts. This means, though, that Twitter was by far the most negative platform because positive posts outnumbered negative posts 47 to 26 percent on Facebook and 75 to 11 percent on Instagram. This difference in the tone of posts across the three platforms is statistically significant (F=199.81, df=2, p=0.000). Looking at t-tests of the means shows a 95 percent confidence that Twitter was more negative than Facebook and Facebook was more negative than Instagram.[60]

Table 4.3 looks at the tone of social media posts for each candidate. When it comes to negativity, both Clinton and Trump were nearly identical in the percentage of their posts that were negative, 33.4 to 32.5 percent, respectively, though Clinton's larger number of total posts means that she posted more negative content on social media than Trump. Clinton, however, was also the most positive candidate as well; 54 percent of

Table 4.3.   Candidate Tone on Social Media

	Clinton	Johnson	Trump	Total
Negative	890	149	615	1654
	33.4%	12.2%	32.5%	28.6%
Neutral	336	530	807	1673
	12.6%	43.3%	42.6%	28.9%
Positive	1437	545	471	2453
	54.0%	44.5%	24.9%	42.4%
Total	2663	1224	1863	5780
	100%	100%	100%	100%

her posts were positive and, in terms of raw frequencies, her positive postings out-numbered Trump's by a factor of 3–1. The reason for this is that Clinton rarely posted tonally neutral items. Whereas 43 percent of Trump's and Johnson's posts were neutral in tone, just 13 percent of Clinton's were. It is also worth noting that Johnson was rarely negative; 88 percent of his posts were almost evenly split between positive and neutral content. There is a significant difference in tone across the candidates (F=105.6, df=2, p=0.000). An examination of the candidates' mean tones shows that Clinton and Johnson were significantly more positive than Trump; though Clinton was more positive than Johnson, that difference just barely failed to reach significance at p<0.05.

Figure 4.4 expands on these results by breaking up candidates' posts by platform and examining their tone. Looking first at Clinton, we can see that a majority (51%) of her Twitter posts were positive, but she was quite frequently negative as well (36%). This negativity was much rarer on Facebook and Instagram, where she was more positive than negative by over a 2-to-1 margin. Gary Johnson rarely posted negatively on any platform and was overwhelmingly positive on Facebook and Instagram. He did diverge from his rivals on Twitter, where the clear majority (74%) of his posts were neutral in tone, this because his tweets often were strictly informational (e.g., dryly announcing campaign events and articulating policy positions). Finally, unlike Clinton and Johnson, Trump's tweets were far more likely to be negative than positive (42 to 12%). Trump's reputation for negativity on Twitter appears to be accurate. Trump was relatively more positive on Facebook, though negative posts still outnumbered positive posts 27 to 22 percent. It was only on Instagram that Trump was positive, with two-thirds of his postings positive compared to 16 percent negative.

own." This is a policy statement tweet because she never states what she wants to do about the issue of mental illness.

To see if either Clinton or Trump were discussing women's issues we used a key word search of specific terms and phrases associated with these issues. There is a large literature on women's issues and many authors define them somewhat differently; there is, however, considerable overlap.[53] We take our definition from Evans and Clark who include:

- Issues that affect women as a group more than men (health, welfare, education, and the environment);
- Feminist concerns (equality/equal rights, Gay, Lesbian, Bisexual, Transgender, Questioning, and Allied [GLBTQA] rights, poverty);
- Gendered crimes (rape and domestic violence);
- Women's health decisions (Plan B, abortion, pro-choice, and pro-life).

We also hand coded the tweets for negativity. If the candidate said negative things about their opponent, those were coded as attack tweets. We also coded for whether the candidate said negative things about one of the political parties (attack Democrat; attack Republican), the government (attack government), and the media (attack media). For example, on November 1, Trump tweeted "Look at the way Crooked Hillary is handling the e-mail case and the total mess she is in. She is unfit to be president. Bad judgement!" This is an attack tweet since he said negative things about his opponent. Similarly on October 11, Trump tweeted "Our very weak and ineffective leader, Paul Ryan, had a bad conference call where his members went wild at his disloyalty." This tweet is an attack Republican tweet since he said negative things about Paul Ryan, the Republican Speaker of the House.[54]

FINDINGS

Clinton sent a total of 2,179 tweets from July 1 through November 7, while Trump sent 1,184. When we examine those tweets for content we find that Clinton greatly out-tweeted Trump about the issues. Looking closer, Clinton sent significantly more tweets where she took a stand on a policy issue (issue position), but Trump sent more policy statement tweets. When we combine the two types of tweets into a single column, we find that 18 percent of Clinton's tweets were about policy, compared to only 5.4 percent of Trump's. Figure 5.1 displays the results.

After performing a key word search for women's issues that were discussed on both Twitter accounts, we find that only 5.6 percent of

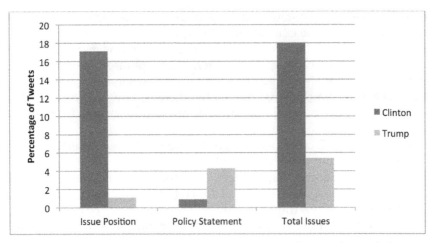

Figure 5.1.   Percentage of Issue Tweets Sent by Clinton and Trump from July 1, 2016, to November 7, 2016

Trump's tweets incorporated those words, compared to 17.4 percent of Clinton's tweets. Clinton spent a considerable amount of time tweeting about women and family, which together accounted for 11.1 percent of her tweets, while most of Trump's tweets related to women's issues were about the repeal of Obamacare (2.4% of his total tweets). Women's issues that were tweeted most by each candidate can be seen in Table 5.1.

One of the biggest contrasts between these two candidates was in their use of the words women, woman, girl, and female. As Table 5.1 details, these words were the most used on Clinton's list of tweeted women's issues. Overall, Trump had much fewer tweets about anything related to women's issues, and these words occurred in only 11 tweets. When we break out those tweets from the entire dataset we see that he mostly used these words within tweets where he said negative things about either Clinton or the press.[55] Clinton, on the other hand, used the words women, woman, girl, and female when she discussed issues like equal pay and the women's rights movement, as well as when she paid attention to women who were making history. She also used these words in tweets where she insisted the Trump ticket was bad for women, but most of these tweets were about her fight for women's rights.

In terms of "going negative" on Twitter, we find that Clinton posted more negative messages about Trump than he posted about her. Figure 5.2 gives the percentage of tweets that the two candidates posted that were negative about each other, Republicans, Democrats, the government, or the media.

Table 5.1. Most-Discussed "Women's Issues" by Each Candidate

Hillary Clinton	Donald Trump
Women (136 tweets–6.2%)	Health (29 tweets–2.4%)
Family (107 tweets–4.9%)	Family (17 tweets–1.4%)
Child (76 tweets–3.5%)	Women (11 tweets–0.9%)
Education (69 tweets–3.2%)	Poverty (5 tweets–0.4%)

Approximately 37.5 percent of the tweets coming from @HillaryClinton were negative about Trump, while 19.1 percent of the tweets on his page were negative about Clinton. Table 5.2 also illustrates that Trump was more likely to be negative about other people in government than was Clinton. He sent proportionately more tweets that were negative about Republicans than she did, and he sent many tweets attacking Democrats, government, and the media while she sent none. When we add up the various forms of negativity, we find that Trump sent 1 percent more attack-style tweets than she did (proportionately).

DISCUSSION

Results from this descriptive analysis demonstrate that Trump and Clinton took different approaches to discussion of policy issues and negativity

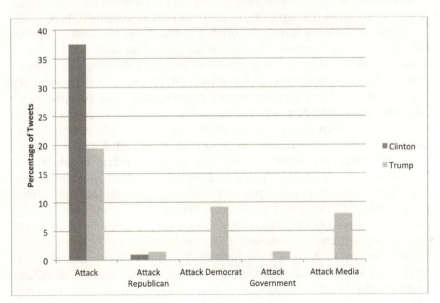

Figure 5.2. Negativity on Twitter

on Twitter. Clinton was far more likely to discuss policies and voice her position on policy issues than was Trump. While she was more active on Twitter than Trump, she sent more than three times as many policy position tweets than her opponent. She also sent more tweets about women's issues. When Trump did refer to women's issues, it was typically a reference to replacing Obamacare. Clinton tweeted three times more often about women's issues.

When we turn to negativity we find that Clinton targeted a greater percentage of her tweets at Trump than he about her. Trump sent more tweets attacking Democrats, the government, and the media than did Clinton, and surprisingly, he also attacked fellow Republicans more often than Clinton. On average though, the two candidates were approximately equal in terms of tweets with a negative tone.

Data from this analysis suggest that Clinton, similar to women running for congressional seats in 2010 and 2012, was more likely to "go negative" about her opponent on Twitter. More, not only did Clinton tweet more about policies, she frequently took a stand on them. This type of communication was largely absent from Trump's Twitter feed.

Clinton was also more likely to attack Trump on Twitter than he was to attack her. This should surprise anyone who followed the 2016 presidential campaign. Trump received far more media attention than Clinton, especially when he sent negative tweets about her. For instance, a piece from the *New York Times* by Barbaro, Haberman, and Rappeport was titled "As America Sleeps, Donald Trump Seethes on Twitter."[56] His late night tweets were often the topic of discussion by news commentators, while Clinton's tweets were largely ignored. Clinton, however, took to Twitter in ways similar to women who ran for congressional seats in 2012.[57]

We would like to caution researchers in terms of extending our research findings to all women who run for office. Clinton's run for the presidency is a special case. More cases of women running as a major party nominee for president would be needed before we can say that women use Twitter differently than men do at this level. We also need to examine these same topics in elections between two male candidates to see whether these differences are really due to gender or partisanship. Would a male Democrat running against Trump in 2016 have spent as much time talking about women's issues? Since some research suggests that the number of women in the race can affect what women talk about on Twitter,[58] would Clinton have been less likely to talk about women's issues if she had run against another woman? If Clinton had not been running against Trump, for instance, would she have sent so many tweets attacking her opponent? Would another Democrat running for president in 2016 have sent so many negative tweets about Trump? What role does partisanship play in issue discussion and negativity?

On November 8, 2016, Clinton lost the presidential election to Trump. Whether Twitter affected the election is yet to be determined. What is clear from these results though is that the two candidates adopted different styles of tweeting, especially in their use of negativity and issue discussion. Clinton spent more time playing the "woman's card" on Twitter, when we define playing it as the mention of specific women's issues in tweets. As others point out, however, all candidates play the "woman's card" during their elections, by either choosing to highlight these issues or ignoring them, and by adopting particular ways of interacting with one's opponents and dealing with gender norms.[59] Clinton adopted a more masculine campaign style on Twitter by sending a higher proportion of aggressive tweets towards her opponent, but she discussed women's issues more than Trump. The effects of both of these styles of tweeting are left for future inquiry. Future work should also examine whether Clinton was playing the "woman's card" in traditional television interviews and campaign advertisements.

NOTES

1. Richard L. Fox. *Gender Dynamics in Congressional Elections*. Thousand Oaks, CA: Sage, 1997; Herrnson, Paul S. and Jennifer C. Lucas. "The Fairer Sex? Gender and Negative Campaigning in U.S. Elections." *American Politics Research*, 34 (2006): 69–94; Kim Fridkin Kahn. *The Political Consequences of Being a Woman*. New York: Columbia University Press, 1996; Kim Fridkin Kahn and Ann Gordon. "How Women Campaign for the U.S. Senate: Substance and Strategy." In P. Norris (Ed.), *Women, media, and politics*. (New York, NY: Oxford University Press, 1997), 59–76.

2. Danny Hayes and Jennifer L. Lawless. "A Non-Gendered Lens? The Absence of Stereotyping in Contemporary Congressional Elections." *Perspectives on Politics* 13 (2015): 95–118; Kathleen Dolan. "Gender Stereotypes, Candidate Evaluations, and Voting for Women Candidates: What Really Matters?" *Political Research Quarterly* 67 (2014): 96–107.

3. Kim Fridkin Kahn. "Gender Differences in Campaign Messages: The Political Advertisements of Men and Women Candidates for U.S. Senate." *Political Research Quarterly*, 46 (1993): 481–502; Kim Fridkin Kahn and Edie N. Goldenberg. "Women Candidates in the News: An Examination of Gender Differences in U.S. Senate Campaign Coverage." *Public Opinion Quarterly* 55 (1991): 180–199.

4. Heather K. Evans and Jennifer Hayes Clark. "'You Tweet like a Girl!': How Female Candidates Campaign on Twitter." *American Politics Research*, 44 (2016): 325–352.

5. Heather K. Evans, Victoria Cordova, and Savannah Sipole. "Twitter Style: An Analysis of How House Candidates Used Twitter in Their 2012 Campaigns." *PS: Political Science and Politics*, 47 (2014): 454–462; Heather K. Evans and Jennifer Hayes Clark, "You Tweet like a Girl!"

6. Evans, Cordova, and Sipole, "Twitter Style"; Heather K. Evans, Jocelyn Ovalle, and Stephen Green. "Rockin' Robins: Do Congresswomen Rule the Roost in the Twittersphere?" *Journal of the Association of Information Science and Technology*, 67 (2016): 268–275; Evans and Clark, "You Tweet like a Girl!"

7. Evans, Cordova, and Sipole, "Twitter Style"; Evans and Clark 2016; Heather K. Evans. "Do Women Only Talk About 'Female Issues'? Gender and Issue Discussion on Twitter." *Online Information Review*, 40 (2016): 660–672.

8. Hillary Clinton's victory speech in Philadelphia after winning Delaware, Maryland, and Pennsylvania during the primary on April 26, 2016.

9. Thomas E. Patterson. "News Coverage of the 2016 General Election: How the Press Failed the Voters." *Harvard Shorenstein Center on Media, Politics, and Public Policy.* December 7, 2016. Available at: https://shorensteincenter.org/news-coverage-2016-general-election/.

10. Shawn W. Rosenberg, Lisa Bohan, Patrick McCafferty, and Kevin Harris. "The Image and the Vote: The Effect of Candidate Presentation on Voter Preference." *American Journal of Political Science* 30 (1986): 108–128; James N. Druckman. "The Power of Television Images: The First Kennedy-Nixon Debate Revisited." *Journal of Politics* 65 (2003): 559–571; Amy King and Andrew Leigh. "Beautiful Politicians." *Kyklos* 62 (2009): 579–593; Gabriel S. Lenz and Chappell Lawson. "Looking the Part: Television Leads Less Informed Citizens to Vote Based on Candidates' Appearance." *American Journal of Political Science* 55 (2011): 574–589; Sarah Macha. "Media Coverage of Female Presidential and Vice Presidential Candidates and Voter Perceptions of Competency." MA Thesis, Sam Houston State University, 2012.

11. Sarah Macha. "Media Coverage of Female Presidential and Vice Presidential Candidates and Voter Perceptions of Competency." MA Thesis, Sam Houston State University, 2012, p. 7.

12. Jennifer L. Lawless. "Female Candidates and Legislators." *American Review of Political Science* 18 (2015): 349–366.

13. Kim Fridkin Kahn. "The Distorted Mirror: Press Coverage of Women Candidates for Statewide Office." *Journal of Politics* 56 (1994): 154–173; Kahn and Goldenberg, "Women Candidates in the News."

14. Sean Aday and John Devitt. "Style Over Substance: Newspaper Coverage of Elizabeth Dole's Presidential Bid." *The Harvard International Journal of Press/Politics* 6 (2001): 52–73; Caroline Heldman, Susan J. Carroll, and Stephanie Olson. "'She Brought Only a Skirt': Print Media Coverage of Elizabeth Dole's Bid for the Republican Nomination." *Political Communication* 22 (2005): 315–335.

15. Fox, *Gender Dynamics*; Aday and Devitt, "Style Over Substance."

16. Hayes and Lawless, "A Non-Gendered Lens?"

17. Dolan, "Gender Stereotypes."

18. Deborah Jordan Brooks. *He Runs, She Runs: Why Gender Stereotypes Do Not Harm Women Candidates.* (Princeton, NJ: Princeton University Press, 2013).

19. Evans and Clark, "You Tweet like a Girl!"

20. Kathleen Hall Jamieson. *Beyond the Double Bind: Women and Leadership.* New York: Oxford University Press, 1995.

21. Dolan, "Gender Stereotypes."

22. Diana B. Carlin and Kelly L. Winfrey. "Have You Come a Long Way, Baby? Hillary Clinton, Sarah Palin, and Sexism in 2008 Campaign Coverage." *Communication Studies* 60 (2009): 326–343; Jamieson, *Beyond the Double Bind.*

23. Heldman, Carroll, and Olson, "She Brought Only a Skirt"; Carlin and Winfrey, "Have You Come a Long Way, Baby?"; Patricia Gilmartin. "Still the Angel in the Household: Political Cartoons of Elizabeth Dole's Presidential Campaign." *Women and Politics* 22 (2001): 51–63; Erika Falk. *Women for President: Media Bias in Nine Campaigns.* (Urbana, IL: University of Illinois Press, 2008).

24. Heldman, Carroll, and Olson, "She Brought Only a Skirt."

25. Lori Cox Han and Caroline Heldman. *Rethinking Madam President: Are We Ready for a Woman in the White House?* (Boulder, Colorado: Lynne Rienner Publishers, 2007), pp. 21–22; Joseph E. Uscinski and Lilly J. Goren. "What's in a Name? Coverage of Senator Hillary Clinton During the 2008 Democratic Primary." *Political Research Quarterly* 64 (2010): 884–896.

26. Uscinski and Goren, "What's in a Name?"; Janis L. Edwards and C. Austin McDonald. "Reading Hillary and Sarah: Contradictions of Feminism and Representation in 2008 Campaign Political Cartoons." *American Behavioral Scientist* 54 (2010): 313–329.

27. Uscinski and Goren, "What's in a Name?"; Carlin and Winfrey, "Have You Come a Long Way, Baby?"; Ann C. McGinley. "Hillary Clinton, Sarah Palin, and Michelle Obama: Performing Gender, Race, and Class on the Campaign Trail." *Denver University Law Review* 86 (2009): 709–725; Edwards and McDonald, "Reading Hillary and Sarah."

28. Macha, "Media Coverage."

29. Falk, *Women for President.*

30. Carlin and Winfrey, "Have You Come a Long Way, Baby?"

31. Rainbow Murray. *Cracking the Highest Glass Ceiling: A Global Comparison on Women's Campaigns for Executive Office.* (Santa Barbara, CA: ABC-CLIO, 2010).

32. Maureen Dowd. "Vice in go-go boots?" *The New York Times*, August 31, 2008. Available at: http://www.nytimes.com/2008/08/31/opinion/31dowd.html?_r=1and; Carlin and Winfrey, "Have You Come a Long Way, Baby?"

33. Rob Lever. "Twitter Shakes Up U.S. Election Campaign." *News 24.* August 26, 2012. Available at: http://www.news24.com/SciTech/News/Twitter-shakes-up-US-election-campaign-20120826.

34. Jason Gainous and Kevin M. Wagner. *Tweeting to Power: The Social Media Revolution in American Politics.* (New York, NY: Oxford University Press, 2014).

35. Evans, Cordova, and Sipole, "Twitter Style."

36. Evans, Cordova, and Sipole, "Twitter Style"; Evans and Clark, "You Tweet like a Girl!"

37. Evans and Clark, "You Tweet like a Girl!"; Evans, "Do Women only Talk About 'Female Issues'?"

38. Evans, "Do Women only Talk About 'Female Issues'?"

39. Kim Fridkin Kahn and Patrick J. Kenney. *The Spectacle of U.S. Senate Campaigns.* (Princeton, NJ: Princeton University Press, 2000).

40. Kim L. Fridkin and Patrick J. Kenney. "The Role of Gender Stereotypes in U.S. Senate Campaigns." *Politics and Gender* 5 (2009): 301–324.

41. Richard Lau and Gerald M. Pomper. *Negative Campaigning: An Analysis of U.S. Senate Elections.* (Oxford: Rowman and Littlefield, 2004); Richard Lau and Gerald M. Pomper. "Effects of Negative Campaigning on Turnout in U.S. Senate Elections, 1988–1996." *Journal of Politics* 63 (2001): 804–819.

42. Gainous and Wagner, *Tweeting to Power*; Evans and Clark, "You Tweet like a Girl!"

43. Jayeon Lee and Young-shin Lim. "Gendered Campaign Tweets: The Cases of Hillary Clinton and Donald Trump." *Public Relations Review* 42 (2016): 849–855.

44. McGinley, "Hillary Clinton."

45. Lee and Lim, "Gendered Campaign Tweets," pg. 3.

46. Jordain Carney. "Clinton Takes McConnell to Task for 'Gender Card' Comment." *The Hill.* July 7, 2015. Available at: http://thehill.com/blogs/ballot-box/presidential-races/248573-clinton-takes-mcconnell-to-task-for-gender-card-comment.

47. Clarity Campaign Labs, January 20, 2015. Available here: http://www.americanwomen.org/research/national-survey-paycheck-fairness-act.

48. Kate Black. "What We're Not Hearing from Republicans: Issues that Matter to Women and Families." *2016 Presidential Gender Watch.* October 28, 2015. Available here: http://presidentialgenderwatch.org/issuesthatmatter/#more-4748.

49. Kelly Dittmar. "Trump's Gender Miscalculations." Presidential Gender Watch. April 28, 2016. Available at: http://presidentialgenderwatch.org/trumps gendermiscalculations/#more-8007.

50. Jane C. Timm. "Trump on Hot Mike: 'When You're a Star . . . You Can Do Anything' to Women." *NBC News.* October 7, 2016.

51. Matt Kapko. "Twitter's Impact on 2016 Presidential Election is Unmistakable." *CIO.* November 3, 2016. Available at: http://www.cio.com/article/3137513/social-networking/twitters-impact-on-2016-presidential-election-is-unmistakable.html.

52. Tweet sent June 8, 2016, at 11:27 AM.

53. Kathleen A. Bratton. "The Effect of Legislative Diversity on Agenda Setting: Evidence from Six State Legislatures." *American Politics Research,* 30 (2002): 115–142; Deborah L. Dodson. *Reshaping the Agenda: Women in State Legislatures.* (New Brunswick, NJ: Center for the American Woman and Politics, 1991); Beth Reingold. *Representing Women: Sex, Gender, and Legislative Behavior in Arizona and California.* (Chapel Hill: University of North Carolina Press, 2000); Michelle Swers. *The Difference Women Make: The Policy Impact of Women in Congress.* (Chicago, IL: University of Chicago Press, 2002); Sue Thomas. "The Impact of Women on State Legislative Policies." *Journal of Politics,* 53 (1991): 958–976; Sue Thomas. *How Women Legislate.* (New York, NY: Oxford University Press, 1994); Christina Wolbrecht. *The Politics of Women's Rights: Parties, Positions, and Change.* (Princeton, NJ: Princeton University Press, 2000); Evans and Clark, "You Tweet like a Girl!"

54. Two of the authors split the data in half with one collecting and coding all of Clinton's tweets, and the other collecting and coding all of Trump's tweets. The lead author then went back through each tweet to check the coding for the first two months of data collection. The level of the authors' agreement across all data was 98.56%.

55. 63% of his tweets using the word woman, women, female, and girls were attack tweets aimed at either Clinton or the press. The other four tweets were references to something happening in the news or thanking people for helping with his campaign.

56. Michael Barbaro, Maggie Haberman, and Alan Rappeport. "As America Sleeps, Donald Trump Seethes on Twitter." *New York Times*, September 30, 2016. Available at: https://www.nytimes.com/2016/10/01/us/politics/donald-trump-alicia-machado.html.

57. Evans, Cordova, and Sipole, "Twitter Style."

58. Evans and Clark, "You Tweet like a Girl!"

59. Kelly Dittmar. "Everyone's Playing the Gender Card: The Question is How?" *Presidential Gender Watch*. August 2, 2015. Available here: http://presidentialgenderwatch.org/everyones-playing-the-gender-card-the-question-is-how/.

6

Digital Ad Expenditures by Outside Groups in the 2016 Presidential Election

Christine B. Williams and Girish J. "Jeff" Gulati

In the past decade, outside, non-candidate organizations including political action committees (PACs), 501(c) non-profit groups, 527 political committees, and Super PACs have invested heavily in federal elections through independent expenditures. Indeed, many times in the most expensive races, outside-spending was considerably more than that by the candidates themselves.[1] For example, in 2012 and 2014, outside groups sponsored nearly 30 percent of all congressional primary and general election ads. In the 2016 presidential race, they sponsored more than half of all the television ads in the Republican nomination contests.[2]

During this same period, individuals have changed the way they consume media by watching less live television and accessing more content over the Internet. Business organizations have responded to these trends by directing more of their advertising budgets to producing digital content that can be delivered online and targeted to specific audiences. Political candidates and organizations are slowly catching up but, to date, there is little academic research on the extent campaigns are allocating resources to digital media. This chapter concerns itself with how these outside groups allocated their campaign expenditures in the 2012 and 2016 presidential elections. Specifically, it investigates the division between traditional and digital advertising, the latter of which has increased steadily in recent election cycles. Of further interest in the 2016 presidential election are the considerable differences in the emphasis placed on digital advertising by the outside groups supporting the Democratic and Republican candidates.

We begin our analysis by tracking how outside group spending became such an important underwriter for federal campaigns. We then consider how online media are changing the targeting platforms and fundraising methods of campaigns. We follow this with an illustrative review of academic studies investigating these groups' fundraising activities and their effects. Next, we present our case study and data for the 2012 and 2016 presidential elections and conclude the chapter with a discussion of the larger implications of our findings.

OUTSIDE GROUP SPENDING TRENDS

A variety of factors have led to the substantial increase in the number of outside groups participating in federal elections and how much they have spent to influence those elections. Although the 1907 Tillman Act had prohibited direct contributions to candidates by corporations and the 1947 Taft-Hartley Act did the same for labor unions, federal legislation and Supreme Court rulings have eroded these prohibitions and changed the players and landscape of campaign fundraising. The 1978 and 1979 amendments to the Federal Elections Campaign Act (1971) allowed the use of "soft money" contributions to political parties for voter registration and get-out-the-vote drives, issue advertising, and generic party-building activities. The landmark 2002 Bipartisan Campaign Reform Act (BCRA) banned or restricted such soft money contributions and placed limits on issue ads. However, rediscovery of a 1975 tax code provision permitting ideological, union, and business organizations to fund candidates as independent voices (527s) resulted in a continued increase in outside groups' involvement in presidential and congressional races.

The ability of outside groups to try to influence elections expanded further in response to the Supreme Court's ruling in *Wisconsin Right to Life vs. FEC* (2007), which invalidated parts of BCRA and allowed 501(c)(4) non-profit, social welfare organizations to conduct issue advocacy advertising with few restrictions and no obligation to disclose their donors. In early 2010, the Supreme Court went further in their *Citizens United vs. FEC* (2010) decision. It ruled that the federal government could not ban express advocacy and other political spending by corporations or unions for independent expenditures when there was no coordination between the group and the candidate or political party. While limits on independent expenditures had been prohibited since *Buckley vs. Valeo* (1976), the district court ruling in *SpeechNow.org vs. FEC* lifted limits on contributions to independent expenditures-only committees (i.e., Super PACs) that were unaffiliated with a candidate. In 2014, *McCutcheon vs. FEC* lifted aggregate limits on how much an individual could donate to candidates, political party committees, and PACs. The cumulative effect of these rulings was that outside groups were poised to be an even more active force in the 2016 elections.

This trend becomes evident after 2002, when advertising by outside groups increases dramatically, in both total amount[3] and as a share of all ads.[4] It jumps from \$27,686,417 in 2002 to \$193,129,472 two years later in

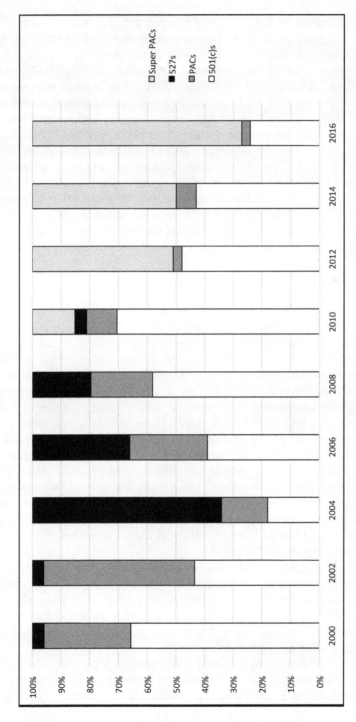

Figure 6.1. Proportion of Outside Spending by Type of Group for Republicans and Democrats, 2000–2016
Source: https://www.statista.com/statistics/611844/outside-spending-for-and-against-parties-2016-us-presidential-election/

2004, to $1.4 billion in 2016, a nearly 650 percent increase over the span of 12 years (6 election cycles).[5] Between 2000 and 2010 outside groups represented between 5 and 15 percent of total ad spending with a marked increase to near or more than 30 percent thereafter. Although 527 groups dominated in 2004, more recently Super PACs dominate as sponsors of outside ads (see Figure 6.1). In the 2016 presidential election, we see notable differences in spending for and against the Republican and Democratic parties. Whereas outside groups favoring Republican candidates spent $301,215,025, those favoring Democratic candidates spent only $66,255,483. On the other hand, outside group spending against Republicans totaled $272,744,967 but against Democrats it was $107,881,493.[6] This gave total Republican-oriented spending a roughly $70 million edge over the total for Democrats. Of course, there were many more Republican than Democratic candidates vying for the nomination in 2016, and there was outsized antipathy toward Donald Trump from those who otherwise would spend in support of Republicans.

Digital Media Spending Trends

There are several reasons why digital media have made significant inroads into the single-channel dominance of television for audio-visual content delivery. The number of hours that Americans consume live and linear television continues to decline in favor of time-shifting devices such as DVRs and video-on-demand devices. Many Americans have switched to subscription-based streaming services, and a growing number have dropped their cable television service. These declines are most pronounced among the young, but are evident among Americans between the ages of 30 and 49 as well.[7] More important in the context of political campaign fundraising, the tremendous influx of money has meant that the television ad buys available to candidates and groups are reaching their limit in swing states.[8] Furthermore, outside groups are not accorded the lowest unit rate that applies to candidate ads, making it more efficient for them to migrate away from television to digital advertising.[9]

Advertising trend data show that private sector businesses have led the way in adopting new technologies to improve efficiency and achieve their strategic objectives. Total digital ad spending in 2017 will surpass $77 billion, or 38.4 percent of total ad spending. Although television advertising spending by retailers will continue to grow by about 2 percent a year, more advertising dollars will flow to digital as a way of optimizing spending in challenging economic times.[10]

By way of contrast, digital media expenditures represent only 9.5 percent of their overall advertising budget.[11] However, for 2016 Borrell Associates projected $1.1 billion, and actual outlays reached $1.4 billion, a 14 percent market share that represents a nearly 800 percent increase in digital ad spending over the $159.21 million in the 2012 presidential election year[12] (see Figure 6.2). In the presidential election, Trump favored free media and social media. His campaign outpaced Clinton's in online advertising—$8.4 million to $132,500 in July, for example[13]—and spent about $5 million in get-out-the-vote digital advertising targeted in the final few days on states critical in his victory: Michigan, Wisconsin, Pennsylvania, and Florida.[14] While Clinton's campaign placed a far greater emphasis than Trump on traditional television advertising, outside groups supporting her did invest heavily in online ads. For example, the largest such group, Priorities USA Action, reported it spent roughly $116 million on television advertising, $2.5 million on radio, and $28 million or nearly 20 percent of their total on digital ads.[15] In 2012 it only spent a total of $65,166,859 on the presidential election.[16] Overall, the Obama campaign spent nearly double ($52 million) that of Romney's campaign ($26 million) for online ads in 2012.[17]

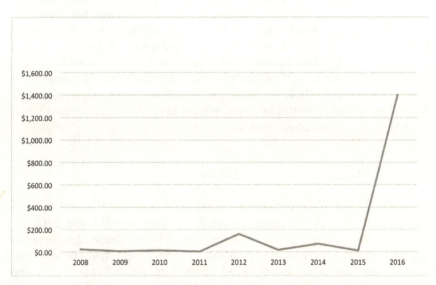

Figure 6.2. Total U.S. Digital Political Ad Spending in Millions, 2008–2016
Data sources: https://www.wired.com/2015/08/digital-politcal-ads-2016/; http://adage.com/article/media/2016-political-broadcast-tv-spend-20-cable-52/307346/

Advertising Effects

Research suggests that campaign advertising has had important effects on elections. Studies have demonstrated that it has changed both candidate strategies and outcomes. For example, spending by outside

groups enabled some weak, second-tier candidates to prolong the nomination contest by remaining in the race longer than their performance
warranted, or changed candidates' momentum.[18] Evidence also shows
that candidates and outside groups respond to each other's spending by
following one another into a state, reciprocating though not necessarily
coordinating their behavior.[19] Other studies[20] show that television advertising totaled for all sources has an impact on vote share, particularly
in non-battleground states and when candidates are less well known.[21]
Moreover, ads by outside groups are as effective, and possibly more so,
than candidate-sponsored ads.[22] We also know that the negativity of ads
is increasing,[23] and that Super PAC independent expenditures urging the
defeat of candidates often exceeds what is spent promoting and supporting candidates.[24]

Taking a long-term view, outside group spending trends have important consequences for democratic institutions and elections. First, they
are diminishing the candidates' control over their message.[25] At the same
time, their ascendance comes at the expense of political parties[26] who appear to be outsourcing their traditional role in campaign fundraising.[27]
As outside groups' ties to the parties weaken and they come more under
the control of wealthy donors, these groups' interests take on a more
ideological bent.[28] And because negative advertising by outside groups
receives less blowback,[29] negativity and advocacy against rather than
for candidates is likely to increase. Since independent groups raise their
money early and in multiple states, we are likely to see continued front-
loading of the nomination contest.[30]

DATA

We obtained the data to analyze digital media expenditures by outside
groups from the Independent Expenditures files for 2012 and 2016 collected by the Federal Election Commission (FEC).[31] These files included
54,134 individual entries of expenditure report filings made by any outside groups supporting or opposing a presidential candidate in 2012 and
81,200 such entries in 2016. Together there were nearly 50,000 unique
category entries that we sorted and organized to aggregate digital media expenditures and all other media expenditures for every committee
that filed papers with the FEC and made independent expenditures. We
classified an entry as a digital media expenditure if it included the terms
digital, Internet, e-mail, Facebook, YouTube, Twitter, blast, online, web
ads, or social in the "purpose" field. If the field included multiple purposes but also listed these terms, we still assigned the entry to the digital
media category. If, however, these entries were for expenditures such as
Internet service or email services only, we considered them to be similar

to electric, telephone, cable television, and other utilities services and did not classify them as digital media expenditures.

We used an automated computer sort function based on key words to assign entries to the digital media category. In addition, we carefully reviewed the entries that the automated process did not capture. A sample of specific expenditures either assigned automatically or manually as digital media include:

- Online ads
- Blogs and social media posts
- Digital communications
- Online advertising
- Facebook ads
- Twitter ads
- Internet ads
- YouTube ads
- Email blasts
- E-marketing
- Voter contact emails
- Google ads across 50 states
- Digital advertising production
- GOTV online advertising
- Digital ad buy
- Online media buy
- Online voter contact
- Anti-Trump memes

We combined reports for organizations that established more than one committee to make its independent expenditures into single cases. For example, American Crossroads, which supports Republican candidates, is organized as a 527 political committee, an independent expenditures-only Super PAC (i.e., a 527 political committee) that must disclose its contributors. American Crossroads' leadership established Crossroads Geopolitical Strategies and Crossroads Generations as 501(c)(4) committees that also make independent expenditures, but without having to disclose their donors because political activity is not their primary purpose. For this study, we assigned all of these groups' expenditures to American Crossroads.

ANALYSIS

Our coding and aggregating of the data identified 111 different organizations that made independent expenditures of $729,896,339 in 2012. In

2016, we identified 157 different organizations that made independent expenditures of $890,484,562. This increase represents about 22 percent more spending in independent expenditures on the presidential election from 2012 to 2016.

Our analysis of the data begins with a comparison of how much money outside groups spent on media on behalf of major party presidential candidates in 2012 and 2016 and then calculates the amounts and percentages spent on traditional and digital media. The data from the independent expenditures files shows a substantial increase in the amount that outside groups spent on digital media in the two presidential cycles. Whereas outside groups spent nearly $89 million on digital media during the 2012 election cycle, outside groups spent over $219 million in 2016. This represents an increase of almost 250 percent from 2012 to 2016.

With the costs of campaigns increasing every year and the ability to raise money expanding, it should not be surprising that there was a substantial increase in overall independent expenditures and digital media expenditures over the four years. Of course, both parties had contested nominations with more competitive candidates to support than was the case four years previous. Even considering all of these factors, the total amount that outside groups spent on the 2016 presidential election increased by only 21 percent. Whereas the combined total spent by outside groups in the 2012 presidential campaigns on all independent expenditures and electioneering communications was $730 million, they spent $885 million in 2016. Thus, the proportion of total expenditures that went to digital media also increased substantially between 2012 and 2016 from 12.2 percent to 24.8 percent. The ratio of digital media expenditures to total media expenditures also more than doubled in four years, from 0.16 in 2012 to 0.40 in 2016.

Since reaching voters through digital advertising is not yet an accepted campaign practice, we expected to find significant variation in digital media allocation in both election years. Many interest groups and their communication consultants are firmly established participants in the "air wars," but some of these groups may be in a better position to adapt to the new media environment because of their experience and resources. Groups emerging in the digital age may be unconstrained by conventional practices, but they also may not have the sophistication to be on the cutting edge in terms of utilizing new technology. Early studies of candidates' adoption of websites and social media not only show that variation is common when the first opportunities to use new communication technologies arise, but also that this variation is a result of differences in resources and political party.[32]

To explore this expected variation, identify early adopters, and discern patterns that might explain the variation, we selected the top 25 outside groups in terms of total independent expenditures. In addition to total expenditures, we display the amount spent on digital media, the percentage of the total spent on digital media, and the ratio of digital media expenditures to traditional media expenditures. We display these data and rankings in Tables 6.1 and 6.2.

Among these large Super PACs, conservative groups outnumbered liberal groups by a wide margin in both the 2012 and 2016 election campaigns. Whereas 17 of the top 25 Super PACs in 2012 supported Republican candidates, only eight of the top 25 supported Democratic candidates. This same unequal distribution occurred in the 2016 presidential election. Looking at just the 10 largest Super PACs, in both years most were conservative groups. In 2012, only two liberal groups—Priorities USA Action and the Service Employees International Union—were among the top 10 Super PACs in spending on independent expenditures in the presidential race. In 2016, Priorities USA was the only liberal Super PAC among the 10 largest in the presidential race, although their independent expenditures were greater than that of any other outside group.

In Tables 6.3 and 6.4, we display the data for the two election years sorted in order of the proportion of digital media expenditures to total media expenditures. The outside group that spent the largest proportion (62%) of their expenditures on digital media was the American Federation of State, County and Municipal Employees (AFSCME), a 501(c)(5) Super PAC that supported President Obama. Three other liberal groups were among the top 10. Planned Parenthood's Super PACs together spent over $3 million on digital media, which represented 26 percent of their total expenditures. Priorities USA spent $7.5 million, or 12 percent, of their independent expenditures to support President Obama. The Service Employees International Union only spent $1.5 million on digital media, but that represented 9 percent of their total expenditures, the tenth-highest proportion among outside groups in 2012.

The next four groups after AFSCME with a high proportion of independent expenditures allocated to digital media were all conservative Super PACs. Endorse Liberty, a single-candidate Super PAC working on behalf of Rep. Ron Paul (TX), spent $4.1 million on digital media and had the second-largest proportion at 55 percent. Both of these groups, moreover, spent more on digital media than on traditional media. The third largest was Winning Our Future at 45 percent ($22.6 million), which was created to support Newt Gingrich's primary campaign. Fourth was American Future Fund (39 percent; $7.6 million), a 501(c)(4) organization that supported Mitt Romney in the general election. The National Rifle Association (33 percent; $4.2 million) ranked fifth and also supported Governor Romney. Finishing eighth was Karl Rove's American Crossroads, which spent only 10 percent of their total expenditures on digital media, albeit

Table 6.1. Digital Media Expenditures for 25 Most Active Outside-Groups, 2012 Presidential Election

Rank	Group	View	Type	Digital Media Expenditures	Percentage Digital	Ratio Digital/ Traditional	Total Independent Expenditures
1	American Crossroads	C	501(c)(4)	$15,194,542	10.39	0.12	$146,181,859
2	Restore Our Future	C	Super PAC (Romney)	$2,513,035	1.75	0.02	$143,792,574
3	Priorities USA Action	L	Super PAC	$7,552,392	11.65	0.13	$64,822,242
4	Americans For Prosperity	C	501(c)(4)	$5,183,670	9.03	0.10	$57,405,763
5	Winning Our Future	C	Super PAC (Gingrich)	$22,583,926	44.61	0.88	$50,627,373
6	Republican National Committee	C	Political Party	$0	—	N/A	$50,294,711
7	American Future Fund	C	501(c)(4)	$7,553,793	38.65	0.73	$19,545,002
8	Service Employees Int. Union	L	501(c)(5)	$1,508,250	9.26	0.49	$16,296,033
9	Americans For Job Security	C	501(c)(6)	$790,000	5.19	0.05	$15,223,067
10	Nation Rifle Association	C	501(c)(4)	$4,150,153	33.08	0.85	$12,546,577
11	Planned Parenthood Votes/Action Fund	L	501(c)(4)	$3,034,707	25.64	0.41	$11,835,848
12	Ending Spending Action Fund	C	501(c)(4)	$1,143,948	9.85	0.16	$11,608,200
13	Freedom Committee	L	Super PAC (Obama)	$0	—	N/A	$10,500,000
14	Americans For Resp. Leadership	C	501(c)(4)	$0	—	N/A	$10,044,989
15	Red White And Blue Fund	C	Super PAC (Santorum)	$47,932	0.52	0.01	$9,154,751
16	Endorse Liberty	C	Super PAC (Paul)	$4,134,769	54.86	1.43	$7,537,217
17	Republican Jewish Coalition	C	501(c)(4)	$65,000	1.03	0.01	$6,329,766
18	The 60 Plus Association	C	501(c)(4)	$13,204	0.22	0.00	$ 6,128,784
19	Make Us Great Again	C	Super PAC (Trump)	$0	—	N/A	$4,126,124
20	American Fed. of State, County & Muncip. Em.	L	501(c)(5)	$2,500,000	62.07	2.50	$ 4,027,831
21	Our Destiny PAC	C	Super PAC (Huntsman)	$5,473	0.15	0.00	$3,629,700
22	Florida Freedom PAC	L	501(c)(4)	$0	—	N/A	$3,475,313
23	Workers' Voice	L	501(c)(5)	$2,880	0.10	N/A	$3,026,122
24	Conservative Majority Fund	C	501(c)(4)	$880	—	N/A	$2,947,095
25	Fair Share Alliance	L	501(c)(4)	$7,291	0.29	0.01	$2,555,899

Table 6.2. Digital Media Expenditures for 25 Most Active Outside-Groups, 2016 Presidential Election

Rank	Group	View	Type	Digital Media Expenditures	Percentage Digital	Ratio Digital/ Traditional	Total Independent Expenditures
1	Priorities USA Action	L	Super PAC	$30,018,845	22.06	0.29	$136,096,232
2	Right to Rise USA	C	Super PAC (Bush)	$1,232,500	1.42	0.02	$87,089,454
3	Conservative Solutions PAC	C	Super PAC (Rubio)	$6,445,186	10.99	0.13	$58,668,654
4	Get Our Jobs Back	C	Super PAC (Trump)	$50,019,666	100.00	N/A	$50,019,666
5	National Rifle Association	C	501(c)(4)	$1,483,522	3.87	0.05	$38,288,778
6	Future45	C	Super PAC (Trump)	0	—	N/A	$26,945,036
7	Rebuilding America Now	C	Super PAC (Trump)	0	—	N/A	$26,591,734
8	Great America PAC	C	Hybrid (Trump)	$3,582,505	15.05	0.15	$23,797,041
9	45 Committee Inc.	C	Super PAC (Trump)	0	—	0.00	$21,339,015
10	NextGen Action	L	501(c)(4)	$6,981,390	34.54	0.61	$20,212,709
11	America Leads	C	Super PAC (Christie)	$8,026,850	40.87	0.72	$19,639,035
12	Our Principles PAC	L	Super PAC (Clinton)	$1,321,172	6.94	0.10	$19,039,614
13	New Day for America	C	Super PAC (Kasich)	$491,693	3.10	0.03	$16,507,440
14	United We Can	L	501(c)(5)	$275,847	2.03	N/A	$13,617,502
15	Club For Growth	C	501(c)(4)	$1,811,412	13.97	0.16	$12,970,866
16	Women Vote!	L	501(c)(4)	$7,711,792	61.15	1.60	$12,612,086
17	Keep The Promise PAC	C	Super PAC (Cruz)	$2,141,621	17.84	0.23	$12,002,394
18	Stand For Truth	C	Super PAC (Cruz)	$1,434,093	13.97	0.16	$10,268,087
19	Lift Leading Illinois for Tomorrow	C	Super PAC (Anti-Trump)	$9,022,303	90.93	10.03	$9,922,028
20	American Future Fund	C	501(c)(4)	$173,000	1.74	0.02	$9,916,281
21	League Of Conservation Voters	L	501(c)(4)	$741,928	8.35	0.74	$8,888,357
22	Democratic Cong. Campaign Comm.	L	Political Party	0	—	N/A	$8,551,520
23	Planned Parenthood	L	501(c)(4)	$2,501,058	30.28	3.41	$8,259,427
24	Republican Governors Association	C	Political Party	$134,000	1.65	0.02	$8,135,353
25	The 2016 Committee	C	Super PAC (Carson)	$831,474	11.92	1.18	$6,973,555

the total amount on digital was $15.2 million and the second most of any outside group in 2012.

Another prominent conservative Super PAC, Ending Spending Action Fund, which was founded by TD Ameritrade's founder Joe Ricketts, allocated just under 10 percent of all their expenditures to digital media. Restore Our Future, which supported Republican nominee Mitt Romney's campaign and was the second-largest Super PAC in 2012, allocated only 2 percent of their expenditures to digital media.

The ranking of four out of the eight liberal groups among the top 10 suggests that while Democrats were overwhelmed by the Republicans in outside money, their largest groups were invested significantly in digital media in the 2012 presidential campaign. It also appears that white-collar labor unions embraced digital media sooner than blue-collar unions. On the GOP side, the two groups most invested in digital media were those created to support a single presidential candidate. Interestingly but perhaps not surprisingly, the two candidates—Newt Gingrich and Ron Paul—were two of the early adopters of the Internet for governing and campaigning. Former Speaker Gingrich had espoused the promise of technology early in this career and pushed development of the World Wide Web in the House after he became Speaker in 1995.[33] Rep. Paul's libertarian roots and following among younger people also suggest his campaign would have been particularly well suited for a communication strategy that embraced digital media.

The prevalence and use of digital media in the 2016 presidential campaigns seems to have been transformed significantly from four years earlier. As can be seen in Table 6.4, the pro-Trump Get our Jobs Back Super PAC not only spent the most on digital media, but also was the highest ranked among all Super PACs in terms of the proportion of expenditures that was spent on digital media. Get Our Jobs Back spent a little over $50 million on digital media, which represented a full 100 percent of its total independent expenditures. Another pro-Trump Super PAC, Great America PAC, allocated 15 percent to digital media. Two other pro-Trump Super PACs, 45 Committee and Rebuilding America Now, did not allot any of their nearly $50 million in independent expenditures to digital media. This suggests both a possible specialization and division of labor among the outside groups and perhaps even among the Republican National Committee and the Trump campaign itself.

An anti-Trump Super PAC, Lift Leading Illinois for Tomorrow, allocated 91 percent of its independent expenditures to digital media but was unable to match Get Our Jobs Back since it spent only $9.9 million overall. Similarly, Emily's List's Women Vote! allocated 61 percent of its independent expenditures to digital media but spent only $12.6 million in total on behalf of Hillary Clinton. Planned Parenthood again was among the top

Table 6.3. Digital Media Expenditures Ranked by Proportion of Digital Media Expenditures of Total Independent Expenditures for 25 Most Active Outside-Groups, 2012 Presidential Election

Rank	Group	View	Type	Digital Media Expenditures	Percentage Digital	Ratio Digital/ Traditional	Total Independent Expenditures
1	American Fed. of State, County & Muncip. Em.	L	501(c)(5)	$2,500,000	62.07	2.50	$4,027,831
2	Endorse Liberty	C	Super PAC (Paul)	$4,134,769	54.86	1.43	$7,537,217
3	Winning Our Future	C	Super PAC (Gingrich)	$22,583,926	44.61	0.88	$50,627,373
4	American Future Fund	C	501(c)(4)	$7,553,793	38.65	0.73	$19,545,002
5	Nation Rifle Association	C	501(c)(4)	$4,150,153	33.08	0.85	$12,546,577
6	Planned Parenthood Votes/Action Fund	L	501(c)(4)	$3,034,707	25.64	0.41	$11,835,848
7	Priorities USA Action	L	Super PAC	$7,552,392	11.65	0.13	$64,822,242
8	American Crossroads	C	501(c)(4)	$15,194,542	10.39	0.12	$146,181,859
9	Ending Spending Action Fund	C	501(c)(4)	$1,143,948	9.85	0.16	$11,608,200
10	Service Employees Int. Union	L	501(c)(5)	$1,508,250	9.26	0.49	$16,296,033
11	Americans For Prosperity	C	501(c)(4)	$5,183,670	9.03	0.10	$57,405,763
12	Americans For Job Security	C	501(c)(6)	$790,000	9.03	0.05	$15,223,067
13	Restore Our Future	C	Super PAC (Romney)	$2,513,035	5.19	0.02	$143,792,574
14	Republican Jewish Coalition	C	501(c)(4)	$65,000	1.75	0.01	$6,329,766
15	Red White And Blue Fund	C	Super PAC (Santorum)	$47,932	1.03	0.01	$9,154,751
16	Fair Share Alliance	L	501(c)(4)	$7,291	0.52	0.01	$2,555,899
17	The 60 Plus Association	C	501(c)(4)	$13,204	0.29	0.00	$6,128,784
18	Our Destiny PAC	C	Super PAC (Huntsman)	$5,473	0.22	0.00	$3,629,700
19	Workers' Voice	L	501(c)(5)	$2,880	0.15	N/A	$3,026,122
20	Republican National Committee	C	Political Party	$0	0.10	N/A	$50,294,711
21	Freedom Committee	L	Super PAC (Obama)	$0	—	N/A	$10,500,000
22	Americans For Resp. Leadership	C	501(c)(4)	$0	—	N/A	$10,044,989
23	Make Us Great Again	C	Super PAC (Trump)	$0	—	N/A	$4,126,124
24	Florida Freedom PAC	L	501(c)(4)	$0	—	N/A	$3,475,313
25	Conservative Majority Fund	C	501(c)(4)	$0	—	N/A	$4,027,831

Table 6.4. Digital Media Expenditures Ranked by Proportion of Digital Media Expenditures of Total Independent Expenditures for 25 Most Active Outside-Groups, 2016 Presidential Election

Rank	Group	View	Type	Digital Media Expenditures	Percentage Digital	Ratio Digital/ Traditional	Total Independent Expenditures
1	Get Our Jobs Back	C	Super PAC (Trump)	$50,019,666	100.00	N/A	$50,019,666
2	Lift Leading Illinois for Tomorrow	C	Super PAC (Anti-Trump)	$9,022,303	90.93	10.03	$9,922,028
3	Women Vote!	L	501(c)(4)	$7,711,792	61.15	1.60	$12,612,086
4	America Leads	C	Super PAC (Christie)	$8,026,850	40.87	0.72	$19,639,035
5	NextGen Action	L	501(c)(4)	$6,981,390	34.54	0.61	$20,212,709
6	Planned Parenthood	L	501(c)(4)	$2,501,058	30.28	3.41	$8,259,427
7	Priorities USA Action	L	Super PAC	$30,018,845	22.06	0.29	$136,096,232
8	Keep The Promise PAC	C	Super PAC (Cruz)	$2,141,621	17.84	0.23	$12,002,394
9	Great America PAC	C	Hybrid (Trump)	$3,582,505	15.05	0.15	$23,797,041
10	Stand For Truth	C	Super PAC (Cruz)	$1,434,093	13.97	0.16	$10,268,087
11	Club For Growth	C	501(c)(4)	$1,811,412	13.97	0.16	$12,970,866
12	The 2016 Committee	C	Super PAC (Carson)	$831,474	11.92	1.18	$6,973,555
13	Conservative Solutions PAC	C	Super PAC (Rubio)	$6,445,186	10.99	0.13	$58,668,654
14	League Of Conservation Voters	L	501(c)(4)	$741,928	8.35	0.74	$8,888,357
15	Our Principles PAC	L	Super PAC (Clinton)	$1,321,172	6.94	0.10	$19,039,614
16	National Rifle Association	C	501(c)(4)	$1,483,522	3.87	0.05	$38,288,778
17	New Day	L	Super PAC (Kasich)	$491,693	3.10	0.03	$16,507,440
18	United We Can	L	501(c)(5)	$275,847	2.03	N/A	$13,617,502
19	American Future Fund	C	501(c)(4)	$173,000	1.74	0.02	$9,916,281
20	Republican Governors Association	C	Political Party	$134,000	1.65	0.02	$8,135,353
21	Right to Rise USA	C	Super PAC (Bush)	$1,232,500	1.42	0.02	$87,089,454
22	45 Committee Inc.	C	Super PAC (Trump)	$0	—	N/A	$21,339,015
23	Rebuilding America Now	C	Super PAC (Trump)	$0	—	N/A	$26,591,734
24	Future45	C	Super PAC (Trump)	$0	—	N/A	$26,945,036
25	Democratic Cong. Campaign Comm.	L	Poitical Party	$0	—	N/A	$8,551,520

ten outside groups using digital media and supporting the Democratic nominee, increasing the proportion spent on digital from 26 percent in 2012 to 30 percent in 2016. Priorities USA Action again ranked seventh in terms of digital media and also increased their proportion spent on digital media from 12 percent to 20 percent. America Leads, which advocated for Gov. Chris Christie, was the fourth-highest Super PAC for spending on digital media, allocating 41 percent to digital for a sum of a little more than $8 million. Several other Super PACs dedicated solely to one of the Republicans who unsuccessfully competed for the presidential nomination also were significant users of digital media.

Sen. Ted Cruz had two prominent Super PACs advocate on his behalf, Keep the Promise and Stand for Truth, which allocated 18 percent and 14 percent, respectively. Ben Carson's The 2016 Committee allocated about 12 percent of their expenditures to digital media. Sen. Marco Rubio's Conservative Solutions PAC was not far behind, allocating about 11 percent of all expenditures to digital media. New Day for America, which supported Gov. John Kasich, allocated only 3 percent to digital media. This was much more than Gov. Jeb Bush's Right to Rise, however, which allocated only 1.4 percent of $87 million in independent expenditures to support their candidate's disappointing campaign.

Unlike in 2012, most established conservative outside groups focused more on congressional races and decreased their share of digital spending. The Club for Growth was one exception, allocating nearly 14 percent of their expenditures to digital media. The National Rifle Association, however, was the most generous outside group supporting the Republican nominee, but the share allocated to digital declined substantially from 33 percent in 2012 to 4 percent in 2016. American Future Fund declined from 39 percent to 2 percent, and American Crossroads was not even among the top 25 outside groups in the presidential race in terms of independent expenditures.

On the other hand, these data indicate that Mr. Trump's surrogates were quite active on his behalf over new media channels. Furthermore, viewers exposed to digital ads and viewers exposed to television ads could have been receiving different content, depending on their viewing behaviors. At the very least, messages came from different sources: established outside groups focused on traditional communication channels, while the largest single-candidate group focused exclusively on digital. Thus, within each medium, the content likely would be similar rather than contradictory in its messaging of the candidate. Across media this difference might have resulted in mixed messaging, although deconstructing ad content by medium is beyond the scope of our study.

DISCUSSION

We note first that outside group spending increased significantly from 2012 to 2016, indeed by a higher percentage than spending by the presidential candidates increased. Some of this increase can be attributed to a larger number of candidates contesting the nomination in both parties given there was no incumbent seeking reelection. More to the point of this chapter, outside group spending on digital ads increased more than did their spending in total or for traditional media. We further note that outside group spending on digital increased faster than candidate spending on digital.[34] Perhaps outside groups are in a better position than parties to experiment with new approaches and adjust their campaign strategy accordingly.

Our analysis also shows outside group spending on behalf of Republican candidates to be greater and to have increased by more than outside group spending on behalf of Democratic candidates. OpenSecrets reports the same trend, calculating that conservative groups comprised 55 percent of the total outside spending in the 2016 election cycle compared to 39 percent for liberal groups.[35] These results differ from Kreiss[36] who found that Democrats had an initial new technology adoption and investment advantage. As the out-party in 2016, Republicans may have recalibrated after their twin losses to Obama, embracing the newest digital advertising channels over television more quickly than their counterparts felt the need to do. Clearly, the Republican candidate himself favored new, and especially social media as a communication channel.

Finally, there is some evidence in the patterns we observe suggesting that at least on the Republican side, outside groups complemented rather than duplicated each other's media channel decisions. Established outside groups focused on traditional media, while the largest single-candidate group focused exclusively on digital. We also noted that some outside groups supporting Clinton did invest heavily in online ads even though her campaign favored television.

These findings have important implications for the conduct of democratic elections. First, we confirm the unsurprising and well-documented point that changes in campaign finance laws and court rulings about them have significant impacts on spending behavior. There continues to be a sizeable increase in the amount outside groups spend to support their favored candidates, and greater than the pace at which candidates themselves have increased their spending.[37] This leads to the conclusion that outside group spending is not replacing, but augmenting the money being spent to influence election outcomes. While outside groups represent additional players, they are also different in kind from candidates and parties.

We observe that outside groups do not have the same accountability as candidates because their names and affiliations are not readily identified by the public. For example, to the uninitiated, who does Winning Our Future or Americans for Job Security represent and support? More important, 501(c) groups do not disclose their donors' identities, precluding any accountability. As noted above, studies also show that negative ads from outside groups do not bring the same repercussions as those by the candidate's own campaign,[38] which may give these groups greater license to be aggressive in their attack ads. These groups not only speak independently of the candidate's campaign; there is evidence they are becoming more ideological as well.[39] That could fuel an already polarized electorate and policy discourse.

This chapter has explored the patterns and changes in outside group spending in the presidential elections of 2012 and 2016. This data set has certain limitations. First, two election cycles is not sufficient to establish a clear trend; differences could be the result of factors specific to those years and races. For example, 2012 involved an incumbent president whereas 2016 was an open contest with many more candidates vying for the nomination in both parties. There is also reason to expect spending patterns to differ for other levels of office. In 2016, some mainstream Republican donors and their outside group supporters seemed unwilling to embrace their party's nominee, and/or felt that retaining control of the Senate was a more important objective and directed their finances accordingly. Consistent with some prior research,[40] these groups may have responded to the lead taken by their nominee's campaign, with Republicans respecting Trump's preference for new media. As a result, we see a departure from their approach in 2012, and one that may turn out to be specific to his candidacy. As noted, a few groups took an offsetting, opposite approach that complemented rather than mirrored what the head of the ticket did. The data we have cannot address the reasons behind these allocation decisions.

Choosing among competing explanations for our findings raises additional questions and several avenues of future research that might be pursued. It will be important to learn from campaigns the strategies and goals they have when making decisions about how to allocate resources between digital and traditional advertising channels; outside groups are less likely to be forthcoming about that information. Microtargeting and narrowcasting have become common methods for reaching undecided and potentially persuadable voters with messages tailored to their interests.[41] Do digital ads increase how widely and finely campaigns and their supporters employ these tactics and with what consequences?

Other analyses could shed light on whether digital ads merely repackage what campaigns and these groups produce for television or their respective content differs, and if so, in what ways and why? Finally, there is an extensive literature on the effects of televised ads, especially negative ones, but we know relatively little about whether digital ads work in the same way or differently, and if their impact is less than, greater than, or equal to what has been observed for television ads. Researchers have studied and come to understand key differences between print and broadcast communications media and between radio and television, but are the attributes of digital media and the ads they host more similar to or more different from these?

The patterns we observe suggest not only opportunities and new directions for research, but also pose potential challenges in undertaking that work. Digital ads may prove more difficult for fact-checkers to monitor. Potentially, many more digital ads will be produced than televised ads, in part because they are cheaper and because they are not subject to the same saturation limits as the airwaves, particularly in battleground states. This also could mean they are more ephemeral than ads produced for television. In addition, it likely will be harder for researchers to isolate exposure to digital ads. For example, data about audience size and demographics can be obtained for television programs but are not typically public for websites. Nor are websites likely to provide the identities of all those who place political ads on their site. Controlled experiments and survey recall data will be able to give us some information about digital ad effects, but there will be new hurdles to surmount. We view this chapter and the data it analyzes as a starting point for understanding the changes legislation and court rulings have brought to campaign finance in the digital age.

NOTES

1. Dennis W. Johnson, *Campaigning in the Twenty-First Century: Activism, Big Data, and Dark Money* (New York: Routledge, 2016), chapter 7.

2. Wesleyan Media Project and The Center for Responsive Politics. "WMP/ CRP Special Report: Outside Group Activity, 2000–2016," (August 24, 2016), http://mediaproject.wesleyan.edu/wp-content/uploads/2016/08/Disclo-sureReport_FINAL-5.pdf.

3. Statista, "Outside Group Spending in United States Political Cycles from 1990 to 2016 (in U.S. dollars)," https://www.statista.com/statistics/611303/ outside-spending-in-us-political-cycles/.

4. Wesleyan Media Project and The Center for Responsive Politics. "WMP/ CRP Special Report: Outside Group Activity, 2000–2016," (August 24, 2016), http://mediaproject.wesleyan.edu/wp-content/uploads/2016/08/Disclo-sureReport_FINAL-5.pdf.

5. Statista, "Outside Group Spending in United States Political Cycles from 1990 to 2016 (in U.S. dollars)," https://www.statista.com/statistics/611303/ outside-spending-in-us-political-cycles/.

6. Statista, "Outside Spending for and against Major Parties in the 2016 U.S. Presidential Election (in U.S. Dollars)," https://www.statista.com/statistics/611844/outside-spending-for-and-against-parties-2016-us-presidential-election/.

7. The Nielsen Company, "The Nielsen Total Audience Report Q2 2016," (December 12, 2016).

8. Erika Franklin Fowler and Travis N. Ridout, "Negative, Angry, and Ubiquitous: Political Advertising in 2012," *The Forum*, 10, no. 4 (2013): 51–61.

9. Michael M. Franz, "Interest Groups in Electoral Politics: 2012 in Context," *The Forum*, 10, no. 4 (2013): 62–79.

10. eMarketer, "Digital Ad Spending to Surpass TV Next Year," (March 8, 2016), https://www.emarketer.com/Article/Digital-Ad-Spending-Surpass-TV-Next-Year/1013671.

11. Issie Lapowsky, "Political Ad Spending Online Is About to Explode, *Wired* (August 18, 2015), http://www.wired.com/2015/08/digital-politcal-ads-2016/.

12. Patrick O'Connor, "TV Remains King in Political Ad Spending," *The Wall Street Journal* (August 30, 2015), http://www.wsj.com/articles/tv-remains-king-in-political-ad-spending-1440978256.

13. Zachary Mider and Bill Allison, "Donald Trump Bets Big on Online Advertising," *Bloomberg Politics* (August 21, 2016), https://www.bloomberg.com/politics/articles/2016-08-21/donald-trump-bets-big-on-online-advertising.

14. *Associated Press*, "Here's How Much Less than Hillary Clinton Donald Trump Spent on the Election," *Fortune* (December 9, 2016), http://fortune.com/2016/12/09/hillary-clinton-donald-trump-campaign-spending/.

15. Eric M. Appleman, "Interest Group/Indep. Expenditure Ads—General Election," *Democray in Action* (2016), http://www.p2016.org/igads/igadsgeneral.html.

16. Open Secrets, https://www.opensecrets.org/outsidespending/detail.php?cmte=C00495861&cycle=2012.

17. B. J. Lutz, "Obama Nearly Doubles Romney in Online Ad Spending," NBC 5 Chicago (November 5, 2012), http://www.nbcchicago.com/blogs/ward-room/obama-romney-2012-election-online-advertising-money-spent-177306601.html.

18. Dino P. Christenson and Corwin D. Smidt, "Following the Money: Super PACs and the 2012 Presidential Nomination," *Presidential Studies Quarterly* 44, no. 3 (2014): 410–430; Michael S. Kang, "The Year of the Super PAC," *The George Washington Law Review* 81, no. 6 (2013): 1902–1927.

19. Dino P. Christenson and Corwin D. Smidt, "Following the Money: Super PACs and the 2012 Presidential Nomination," *Presidential Studies Quarterly* 44, no. 3 (2014): 410–430.

20. For a review, see Michael M. Franz and Travis N. Ridout, "Political Advertising and Persuasion in the 2004 and 2008 Presidential Elections," *American Politics Research* 38, no. 2 (2010): 303–329.

21. Michael M. Franz and Travis N. Ridout, "Political Advertising and Persuasion in the 2004 and 2008 Presidential Elections," *American Politics Research* 38, no. 2 (2010): 303–329.

22. Deborah Jordan Brooks and Michael Murov, "Assessing Accountability in a Post-Citizens United Era: The Effects of Attack Ad Sponsorship by Unknown

Independent Groups," *American Politics Research* 40, no. 3 (2012): 383–418; Christopher Weber, Johanna Dunaway, and Tyler Johnson, "It's All in the Name: Source Cue Ambiguity and the Persuasive Appeal of Campaign Ads," *Political Behavior* 34, no. 3 (2012): 561–584.

23. Erika Franklin Fowler and Travis N. Ridout. "Negative, Angry, and Ubiquitous: Political Advertising in 2012," *The Forum*, 10, no. 4 (2013): 51–61.

24. Victoria A. Farrar-Myers and Richard Skinner, "Super PACs and the 2012 Elections," *The Forum*, 10, no. 4 (2012): 105–118.

25. Victoria A. Farrar-Myers and Richard Skinner, "Super PACs and the 2012 Elections," *The Forum*, 10, no. 4 (2012): 105–118.

26. Michael M. Franz, "Interest Groups in Electoral Politics: 2012 in Context," *The Forum*, 10, no. 4 (2013): 62–79; Michael S. Kang, "The Year of the Super PAC," *The George Washington Law Review* 81, no. 6 (2013): 1902–1927.

27. Paul S. Herrnson, "The Roles of Party Organizations, Party-connected Committees, and Party Allies in Elections," *The Journal of Politics* 71, no. 4 (2009): 1207–1224.

28. Michael S. Kang, "The Year of the Super PAC," *The George Washington Law Review* 81, no. 6 (2013): 1902–1927.

29. Conor M. Dowling and Amber Wichowsky, "Attacks Without Consequence? Candidates, Parties, Groups, and the Changing Face of Negative Advertising," *American Journal of Political Science* 59, no. 1 (2015): 19–36; Travis N. Ridout, Michael M. Franz, and Erika Franklin Fowler, "Sponsorship, Disclosure, and Donors: Limiting the Impact of Outside Group Ads," *Political Research Quarterly* 68, no. 1 (2015): 154–166.

30. Dino P. Christenson and Corwin D. Smidt, "Following the Money: Super PACs and the 2012 Presidential Nomination," *Presidential Studies Quarterly* 44, no. 3 (2014): 410–430.

31. These are not final data. The FEC updates on an ongoing basis as campaigns amend their reports.

32. Bruce Bimber, "Digital Media in the Obama Campaigns of 2008 and 2012: Adaptation to the Personalized Political Communication Environment," *Journal of Informational Technology & Politics* 11, no. 2 (2014): 130–50; Dennis Johnson, *Campaigning in the Twenty-First Century: Activism, Big Data, and Dark Money* (New York: Routledge, 2016); Jennifer Stromer-Galley, *Presidential Campaigning in the Internet Age* (New York: Oxford University Press, 2014).

33. Girish J. Gulati, "Members of Congress and Presentation of Self on the World Wide Web," *The Harvard International Journal of Press/Politics* 9, no. 1 (2004): 22–40.

34. Williams and Gulati, forthcoming.

35. https://www.opensecrets.org/outsidespending/summ.php?cycle=2016&disp=O&type=A&chrt=V.

36. Daniel Kreiss, *Prototype Politics: Technology-Intensive Campaigning and the Data of Democracy* (Oxford University Press, 2016).

37. See, e.g., Ian Vandewalker, "Election Spending 2014: Outside Spending in Senate Races Since 'Citizens United,'" Brennan Center for Justice Analysis (2015) and Niv Sultan, "Outside Groups Spent More Than Candidates in 27 Races, Often by Huge Amounts," OpenSecrets Blog (February 14, 2017), https://www.

opensecrets.org/news/2017/02/outside groups-spent-more-than-candidates-in-27-races-often-by-huge-amounts/.

38. Conor M. Dowling and Amber Wichowsky, "Attacks Without Consequence? Candidates, Parties, Groups, and the Changing Face of Negative Advertising," *American Journal of Political Science* 59, no. 1 (2015): 19–36; Travis N. Ridout, Michael M. Franz, and Erika Franklin Fowler, "Sponsorship, Disclosure, and Donors: Limiting the Impact of Outside Group Ads," *Political Research Quarterly* 68, no. 1 (2015): 154–166.

39. Michael S. Kang, "The Year of the Super PAC," *The George Washington Law Review* 81, no. 6 (2013): 1902–1927.

40. Dino P. Christenson and Corwin D. Smidt, "Following the Money: Super PACs and the 2012 Presidential Nomination," *Presidential Studies Quarterly* 44, no. 3 (2014): 410–430.

41. Bruce I. Newman, *The Marketing Revolution in Politics: What Recent US Presidential Campaigns Can Teach Us about Effective Marketing* (University of Toronto Press, 2016).

II

POLITICAL MESSAGES: PRODUCTION, CONSUMPTION, AND EFFECTS

7

Tipping the Balance of Power in Elections?

Voters' Engagement in the Digital Campaign

Diana Owen

The extent to which digital media contribute to an active democracy and stimulate a civically responsible electorate has been a subject of debate. Digital technology potentially can reshape the political media ecology by influencing who controls, consumes, and distributes information.[1] Some scholars argue that the low barriers to entry into the social media marketplace render campaign communications more democratic and less filtered,[2] and go so far as to contend that campaigns in the social media era have become voter driven.[3] Voters have expanded opportunities for campaign engagement, many of which are more readily accessible and require less effort than offline activities. Information can be disseminated readily and widely by those with the requisite access and skills across a diverse range of platforms, including interactive websites, social media, apps, and virtual communities. These affordances contribute to a participatory culture that allows users to create their own content and engage more fully in the political and social sphere.[4] At the same time, some researchers argue that ever-expanding social media affordances reinforce existing power relationships and hierarchies.[5] Thus, the question arises: Has the distribution of political power begun to shift in favor of the voter, as opposed to political and media elites, as digital media are more fully integrated in campaigns?

The number of voters consulting social media during elections has been rapidly growing. Users increasingly encounter political information in their social media feeds posted by their contacts and political professionals.[6] Candidates' use of microtargeting techniques puts information in front of voters even if they are not actively seeking it. As a result, voters' awareness of candidates and campaign events may be increasing.[7] However, evidence suggests that few people prior to the 2016 presidential contest have taken advantage of the affordances that allow them to engage actively, such as participating in discussions, creating and disseminating campaign content through their networks, recruiting volunteers, or raising funds.[8] Social media use can have substantial consequences for voters'

151

influence in campaigns, as users who embrace more sophisticated applications that shape campaign discourse and facilitate active engagement
have a greater opportunity to make an impact. Voters can take on roles
that are more typically reserved for campaign and media elites, such as
creating and disseminating candidate videos online.

This study examines empirically the extent to which voters used social
media to gain a stronger political voice, play a more integral role in the
construction of political discourse, and become more active participants in
the 2016 presidential election. I begin by examining basic political and demographic characteristics of voters who used social media during the election to provide some context for the subsequent analysis. The core research
questions I address are: How did voters use social media to experience
and engage in the 2016 presidential campaign? What is the relationship
between social media use and offline campaign engagement? Additionally,
how much influence did social media have on voters' electoral decision
making compared to other sources? The study then examines how voters perceived social media affected their campaign knowledge, attitudes,
behavior, and influence by addressing the research question: Do voters feel
that their electoral role has changed as a result of social media?

Voters' use of social media in campaigns has continued to evolve since
its inception in the 2008 presidential election. A greater amount of campaign discourse was facilitated by social media platforms in 2016 than
in the past.[9] Much of the discussion in 2016 focused on how candidates
and journalists relied heavily on social media.[10] This study contributes
to the emerging literature on campaign social media—which has hardly
reached consensus about its effects—by identifying the types and levels
of voters' social media engagement during the 2016 election. It employs
data from three original national surveys of adults' digital media use over
the course of the campaign. The study finds that voters were tuned in to
social media throughout the presidential campaign, but their engagement
was heavily orientated toward seeking information rather than more active forms of engagement. In keeping with prior research, the findings
suggest a correspondence between online and offline campaign engagement. Voters reported that they were less influenced by social media than
some other sources of campaign information, such as candidate messages
and news reports. One-third of voters online feel that social media has
had a positive effect on their electoral role.

THE DYNAMICS OF SOCIAL MEDIA IN ELECTIONS

Social media are digital applications that facilitate the production, dissemination, and exchange of content within networks that accommodate

interaction and collaboration. Platforms, such as Facebook, Twitter, Instagram, and YouTube, are used by voters in campaigns to seek, access, develop, and share information. Some scholars and political observers contend that social media have fundamentally transformed the strategies that underpin political campaigns and changed the ways in which elections are covered by the press.[11] Social media also have altered the relationship between voters and candidates, political organizations, and the media. Candidates reach out directly to voters via social media, bypassing established press and party gatekeepers. Social media offer voters tools that can facilitate engagement in established and novel ways. They have the potential to move voters from bystanders to playmakers in elections. However, it appears that the possibility for more voter engagement increasingly is being foreclosed, especially as candidates have exerted greater control over the social media system.

Social Media's Evolving Electoral Role

Social media have been a staple of U.S. elections since their advent in the 2008 presidential contest.[12] With each election, digital media applications have become more sophisticated and the candidates' strategies more complex.[13] Democratic candidate Barack Obama's campaign revolutionized the way that presidential candidates run for office by reaching out to voters using social media. The Obama campaign encouraged voters' independent social media endeavors and harnessed their enthusiasm without entirely co-opting their efforts.[14] According to Michael Slaby, the Obama campaign's technology officer in 2008, his team members were primarily "opportunistic consumers of technology" who were entering uncharted territory.[15] The public's use of emerging technological tools served as a laboratory for the development of a more rigorous and controlled digital media strategy for future campaigns.[16] The Obama campaign used social media to target messages to particular groups of voters, recruit volunteers, advertise campaign rallies, and raise funds. At the same time, voters actively engaged social media outside the context of formal campaign and party organizations. They made and distributed videos to promote candidates, and used their social networks to get their friends involved in the campaign. Social media were especially important to young people who were at the forefront of innovation.[17]

Sifry[18] identifies notable moments when voter-generated content on social media changed the momentum of the 2008 campaign. The popular "Million Strong for Barack" and "Million Strong Against Hillary Clinton" Facebook groups connected voters from across demographic and social boundaries during the nominating phase to reinforce their support for Obama. Hillary Clinton's campaign was sidetracked by the "Vote Different" YouTube video, created on a home computer by a political activist, in which Clinton was portrayed as an Orwellian figure. A wounded Iraq War veteran produced the "Dear Mr. Obama" video in support of Republican candidate John McCain which was viewed over 14 million times.[19] This homemade video was rated the top campaign ad of 2008 by the BBC.

Since 2008, the pendulum has swung in the direction of candidates and media exerting greater control over campaign social media while voters have assumed a more reactive, even passive, role. Voters were less likely to create and disseminate their own material as they were more inclined to monitor social media without comment or to respond to material posted by campaign and media elites.[20] Obama's reelection team expanded their new media tactics in 2012, and managed their social media more tightly than in the previous election. This campaign strategy was successful for a number of reasons. The public's propensity for innovation and engagement through social media had waned. User-generated social media initiatives were less apparent, as voters had less enthusiasm for the candidates than they had for Barack Obama in 2008. Even more consequential was the fact that the presidential campaigns invested heavily in developing strategies that exerted greater control over messaging and voters' social media engagement. Campaigns had learned how to leverage social media to their advantage. As a result, voters felt less empowered to influence the campaign through their social media use.[21]

Slaby noted a shift in the Obama campaign's 2012 election social media strategy, arguing that campaigns had become "strategic integrators of technology." Campaign organizations incorporated social media comprehensively into their communication, programming, and fundraising operations.[22] Candidates were quick to hop on the latest social media bandwagons in an effort to maximize their outreach to voters. The number of links to social media accounts on their websites proliferated.[23] The campaigns posted thousands of messages, videos, and ads to their candidates' social media sites and YouTube channels. Still, in many ways campaigns treated social media like an extension of broadcast technology by seeking to control the agenda and get their message across by attracting mainstream media attention.[24]

The Obama and Romney campaigns did little to exploit the affordances of social media that might invest voters more solidly in the campaign. Instead, social media became "a new form of passing entertainment."[25] The Obama and Romney campaigns found ways to co-opt supporters' social media activation. They encouraged voters to channel their social media engagement through utilities on campaign websites and social media platforms. The campaigns would repurpose material posted by supporters on social media as part of their strategy. A photo taken by a supporter at an election rally might be reposted with a campaign-supplied caption that tied into the candidate's messaging.[26] Campaigns and the press used metrics, such as the number of Facebook "likes" and Twitter followers, as indicators of candidates' popularity as well as the public's engagement in the social media campaign. However, as Micah Sifry observes, "Not one of these things had any real effect on the course of the election or caused the campaigns to engage the voters in any but the most superficial ways."[27]

The trend toward increasing campaign and press control of social media continued in the 2016 presidential contest, coinciding with a narrowing of the voter's digital role. Candidate websites were tightly managed platforms that offered few opportunities for voter input or expression. Hillary Clinton's site was heavily populated with campaign-produced content, and had few links or posts related to outside news stories. Donald Trump's campaign site aggregated news stories that praised him and attacked his opponent. None of the major candidate websites offered users the opportunity to comment on site content, establish personal fundraising pages on behalf of the candidates, or organize volunteers through their own networks. Activities, such as volunteering, fundraising, and phone-banking, were orchestrated by the campaigns. Outreach to specific social and demographic groups, such as young people, the LGBT community, and veterans, which has been a staple of candidate campaign sites, was missing.[28]

The voices of the voting public were used to augment candidate messages and media stories as opposed to standing on their own. Voters posted a tremendous amount of content on Facebook and Twitter; however, much of the material was derived from candidates' campaign communication and news media articles to which posters would react. A Pew Research Center study concluded that the candidates' campaigns were active on social media, but their messages were greatly controlled, "leaving few ways overall for most voters to engage and take part."[29] The presidential campaigns "flooded the social media zone" with their own content, eclipsing the ability of voter-generated material to gain traction. These efforts were rewarded by news organizations, such as CNN, MSNBC, and Fox News. A single inflammatory tweet by a candidate and a rebuttal would dominate news cycles. Trump's colloquial social media messages left voters with the impression that he was speaking directly to them. This approach, along with the outrageous content of many of his messages, made Trump the most retweeted of all the candidates during the nominating campaign.[30] The candidates rarely tweeted out messages from voters, and most were superficial supportive notes.[31] Clinton encouraged supporters to retweet content furnished by the campaign as opposed to their own messages. Further, the number of social media platforms that were used by campaigns diminished markedly after 2012,[32] marginalizing users in some of the more innovative spaces, such as the short-form video site Vine (which shut down in January 2017). In 2012, the Obama campaign reached out to over 5 million supporters on fifteen different social network sites.[33] Presidential candidates in 2016 focused most of their efforts on Facebook, Twitter, and YouTube. Some candidates also had a presence on Instagram, Snapchat, and Reddit, but their activity on these platforms was limited.[34]

The highly contentious social media environment that characterized the 2016 presidential contest curbed the public's appetite for political discourse and engagement via these platforms. An October 2016 Pew Research Center study revealed that 9 percent of social media users posted frequently about government and politics and 23 percent posted sometimes. Users who exhibited high levels of political interest and engagement could be energized by discussions that take place on social media. However, the Pew report suggests that the majority were frustrated by the lack of civility, although research indicates that incivility can be a mobilizing force for political change.[35] Users became "worn out" by the amount of political content they encountered in their feeds. Some users found it stressful to deal with polarizing comments from family and friends, and took measures to block or avoid political messages. The study found that 83 percent of users ignored political content with which they disagree; 15 percent posted a response at least sometimes. Forty percent of the public believed that the nasty tone of political discussion in social media reflects the wider political reality where the tenor is set by politicians and the news media.[36]

Types of Social Media Engagement

Scholars distinguish between low and high threshold social media activities. Social media use can be viewed as serving "as a passive source of information" or "as an interactive environment for self-expression."[37] While there is some debate about how exactly to categorize particular forms of engagement,[38] social media use can be conceptualized as falling along a rough continuum. Low threshold activities involve less time, effort, skill, and commitment. They encompass using social media to monitor, seek, and consume information. Medium threshold engagement involves users interacting with content that is posted by others—politicians, news sources, political organizations, and other users. High threshold social media activities require the user to move beyond information monitoring and management to more active forms of participation, many of which have offline counterparts. They range from engaging in political discussion to contacting officials, organizing events, donating to a campaign, and establishing and joining online political groups.[39] Low threshold activities can be a precursor to higher threshold activities, and are related to positive outcomes, such as increased political knowledge and offline political engagement.[40] This study employs three categories of social media use: 1) information-seeking (low threshold); 2) interactive expression (medium threshold); and 3) campaign engagement (high threshold).

Low threshold campaign social media use is on the rise. More voters accessed campaign information through social media, either as a result of their direct efforts or incidentally through their networks, in the 2016 contest than in the past.[41] Social media platforms themselves promote political content targeted at voters based on information they have collected about users. Political news and advocacy pages made specifically for Facebook and other social media are designed to reach audiences within the digital sphere exclusively. Users see this information as an alternative to the mainstream media and are inclined to trust it despite the fact that much of the content originates with the press or political organizations. The public increasingly is inclined to share political material, including memes and videos, and to proliferate campaign messages within their networks.[42] This type of activity bridges low and high threshold social media use. The move to social media activities that require high levels of commitment appears to be a bigger jump.

HYPOTHESES

As the foregoing discussion indicates, studies have shown that low threshold social media use has increased in successive presidential election campaigns even as social media information seeking has been linked to greater online participation.[43] Still, social media users are highly inclined toward monitoring information and much less likely to actively engage in the digital campaign. I expect that this trend will hold for the 2016 election, especially as many voters were not excited about the campaign and lacked enthusiasm for the candidates,[44] and may have been less likely to actively engage in the election. Thus, I test empirically the following hypothesis:

H_1: People were more likely to use social media for low threshold campaign activities than high threshold activities during the 2016 presidential election.

Studies of previous elections demonstrate that low threshold social media activities can be a precursor to higher threshold activities.[45] I test the following hypothesis to determine if this pattern holds for the 2016 election:

H_2: Use of social media for low threshold social media campaign activities is correlated with social media use for higher threshold activities.

Prior research has established that people who engage in elections online will also take part offline. I test to see if there is a positive relationship between social media use and offline campaign engagement in 2016:

H_3: Use of social media for campaign engagement is correlated with offline engagement. Specifically, people who engage in higher threshold social media campaign activities are more likely to engage in offline campaign activities than those who use social media for lower-threshold campaign activities.

In addition to testing these three hypotheses, this study will provide some descriptive information about the characteristics of social media users in the 2016 campaign. It also will examine how much influence users report social media has on their vote choice compared to other factors, such as candidates' messages and campaign ads. Finally, it will look at voters' perceptions of whether or not social media affects their political interest, knowledge, attitudes, engagement, and influence on the political process.

DATA

This study employs data from three original online surveys of adult U. S. citizens who were eligible voters in the 2016 presidential election. Respondents were recruited through Mechanical Turk (MTurk), and accessed the survey on the SurveyMonkey platform. Respondents received a stipend for taking the surveys. The cross-sectional studies were conducted at different points in the 2016 presidential race. The first survey (n=1,125) was conducted April 15–22, 2015, during the pre-primary phase of the campaign when prospective contenders were forming exploratory committees while others were announcing their intention to run. The second survey (n=869) was administered April 1–5, 2016, in the heat of the nominating campaign. The Republican and Democratic candidates had engaged in numerous debates, and the field of candidates had been narrowing. Data for the final survey (n=1,631) were collected during the post-convention period August 8–15, 2016. This time frame coincided with a period when Donald Trump made several highly publicized missteps that dominated news coverage.

The limitations of using MTurk for survey data collection have been documented.[46] Huff and Tingley[47] suggest a method for building a survey pool by recontacting respondents with particular characteristics relevant for the study who have taken part in prior research using MTurk. This method was employed to recruit female, Republican, and conservative respondents who initially were underrepresented in the surveys.

The demographic profile of the participants in each survey is generally reflective of the U.S. population online with one exception—political ideology. Table 7.1 compares the study samples to an analysis of data from a 2016 Pew Research Center study using the question: "Do you use the Internet or email at least occasionally?" The samples used in this analysis skew slightly younger than the online population. Whites are slightly overrepresented and Blacks/African Americans are slightly underrepresented. As tends to be the case for MTurk samples, a higher percentage of liberals participated in the three studies than is present in the population online. However, the political party identification of the study participants is similar to that of online users.

The respondents to each of the surveys were generally interested in and attentive to the 2016 presidential election. The level of interest

Table 7.1. Comparison of Online Users in Study Samples to Pew Research Center National Sample

	Pew[1]	Pre-Primary	Nominating Campaign	Post-Convention
Men	50.5%	50.1%	52.0%	50.6%
Women	49.5%	49.9%	48.0%	49.4%
18–29	34.0%	37.7%	39.0%	36.3%
30–39	30.5%	32.7%	35.5%	36.1%
40–49	14.3%	14.3%	13.2%	14.3%
50–59	16.0%	11.1%	8.3%	8.4%
60+	5.2%	4.2%	3.9%	4.9%
High School or Less	14.9%	13.9%	14.0%	14.3%
Some College	21.4%	24.4%	26.8%	22.0%
Associate's Degree	13.1%	7.4%	11.6%	11.1%
Bachelor's Degree	37.3%	37.8%	36.8%	37.1%
Graduate Degree	13.3%	16.5%	10.8%	15.4%
White	72.6%	76.3%	74.8%	75.1%
Black/African American	13.1%	10.7%	10.9%	10.6%
Asian	4.9%	4.7%	5.2%	4.7%
Latino	6.3%	5.0%	6.2%	6.4%
Other	3.1%	3.3%	2.9%	3.0%
Republican	21.8%	19.0%	20.0%	23.0%
Democrat	38.6%	42.6%	40.6%	39.6%
Independent	39.6%	38.4%	39.4%	37.4%
Conservative	31.8%	27.9%	28.6%	28.3%
Moderate	32.7%	29.2%	31.3%	30.4%
Liberal	29.0%	42.9%	40.1%	41.3%

[1]Analysis of Pew March 7–April 4, 2016, Library Data Set question: "Do you use the Internet or email at least occasionally?"

increased as the campaign progressed. Twenty-five percent of the pre-primary survey participants were "very interested" in the election" and 54 percent were "somewhat interested." The percentage of respondents who claimed to be "very interested" in the campaign had increased to 55 percent in the post-convention survey, with 35 percent responding that they were "somewhat interested," suggesting that 88 percent of the public was at least somewhat interested. The high level of interest in the 2016 campaign is reflected in other studies. A July Pew Research Center study found that 85 percent of voters reported that they were following news about the election "very" or "fairly" closely, and 60 percent indicated that they were more interested in the 2016 presidential contest than they were in 2012.[48]

MEASURES

The questionnaires include items about the respondents' interest in and attention to the 2016 presidential election as well as their use of social media for politics, perceptions of social media's influence on their political orientations, their offline political engagement, and their political identifications and preferences.

A single item asked survey participants on all three studies how often they used social media to follow the 2016 election campaign (range 0 "never" to 4 "frequently"). Respondents were asked a battery of items about their election-related use of social media. The pre-primary survey asked respondents to indicate if they had *ever* done any of the activities during election campaigns. The nominating campaign and post-convention surveys asked more specifically if the respondents had done these things on social media *during the 2016 presidential election campaign*. Three categories of identically worded dichotomous media use items were included on each survey, and range from lower to higher threshold activities—information-seeking, interactive expression, and campaign engagement. The five information-seeking items ask respondents if they used social media to follow news about the campaign, learn about candidates and issues, look for information about a candidate, watch campaign ads, and follow those with opposing political views to your own. Interactive expression items tap whether or not people used social media to express an opinion about a candidate or issue knowing others might disagree, "like" or "favorite" campaign-related content, participate in election-related discussions, try to convince others to vote for or against a candidate, share campaign-related content, and encourage others to take action on behalf of a candidate. Finally, campaign engagement consists of respondents' use of social media to join a campaign-related group, accept a friend request from a candidate, political party, or political organization, donate to a campaign, create campaign-related content, and organize a campaign-related event. Additive indexes of information seeking (range 0–5; Cronbach's α=.773), interactive expression (range 0–6; Cronbach's α=.851), and campaign engagement (range 0–5; Cronbach's α=.745) were constructed for the post–convention period survey only.

A series of questions related to offline campaign activation were included in the surveys. A single item taps information seeking, and asked if the respondent had researched a candidate, campaign event, or issue. Offline interactive expression is measured by five items indicating if a person had talked about the election with family, friends, or colleagues; tried to convince others to vote for or against a candidate; encouraged others to turn out to vote; and wrote a letter to the editor. Campaign engagement offline consists of displaying a yard sign, bumper sticker, or button for a candidate; donating to a candidate, political party, or political organization; attending a political rally; volunteering for a candidate's campaign; recruiting volunteers to work for a candidates; and going door-to-door for a political campaign. Indexes of offline interactive expression (range 0–4; Cronbach's α=.528) and campaign engagement (range 0–5; Cronbach's α=.771) were constructed for the post-convention data.

To gauge how social media stacked up relative to other factors, respondents were asked on the post-convention survey to rate how much influence news reports, family and friends, social media, campaign advertisements, celebrities, and candidates' messages have on their vote choice. The response options ranged from 1 "no influence" to 4 "a lot of influence."

The post-convention survey includes seven items that tap users' perceptions of whether social media have had a positive, negative, or no effect on their political interest, knowledge, attitudes, and engagement. Respondents were asked if social media influenced their interest in politics and elections; knowledge of politics and elections; knowledge of candidates; and attitudes toward candidates. The study also takes into account whether or not people feel that social media have affected their active engagement. Respondents were asked how social media have influenced their offline political engagement; ability to take an active role in politics and elections; and ability to influence politics and elections. The items are scored so that 1 represents "negative effect," 2 "no effect," and 3 "positive effect." Additive indexes combined the knowledge of politics/elections and candidates items (range 1–5; Cronbach's α=.825) and the ability to take an active role in politics/elections and to influence politics/elections (range 1–5; Cronbach's α=.834) on the post-convention data set.

FINDINGS

I begin this section by providing some basic information about the demographic characteristics and political orientations of social media users in the 2016 election. Next, I examine how voters used social media in the campaign, including how often they engaged in low and high threshold activities. I then analyze the correspondence between online and offline campaign engagement. I determine the extent to which users feel that social media influences their electoral decisions compared to other factors, such as candidate messages and campaign ads. Finally, I assess whether or not voters feel that social media has changed their electoral role.

Political and Demographic Profile of Social Media Users

To provide some context for the subsequent analyses, I examined the basic political and demographic profile of people who used social media during the 2016 presidential contest. I ran a series of ordinary least squares (OLS) regression analyses with campaign interest, political identifications, candidate preference, and demographic variables as predictors of social media use during the 2016 elections. The dependent variables are frequency of social media use and the social media information seeking, interactive expression, and campaign engagement indexes. Party identification, political ideology, and candidate preference are highly correlated. I chose not to include them in the same equation due to the multicollinearity issue. Instead I ran three separate sets of regression analyses for party identification, ideology, and candidate preference. The first set of equations which included party identification incorporated dummy variables for Republican and Democratic party identification (Table 7.2). The reference group consisted of independents. Dummy variables for liberal and conservative ideology were used for the second set of equations that took into account political ideology; moderates were the baseline (Table 7.3). Finally, respondents' preferences for Republican candidate Donald Trump, Democratic candidate Hillary Clinton, or a third party candidate (Gary Johnson, Jill Stein, another candidate) were accounted for in the third model. The reference category was "undecided" (Table 7.4).

Independent variables for interest in the presidential election as well as gender, age, and education were entered in all of the regression equations. The amount of interest in the 2016 presidential election was expected to be a strong predictor of social media use in the campaign. Gender, age, and education were the demographic indicators in the analysis. Women traditionally have been more active on social media than men, although the gap has been closing.[49] It has been well-established that young people use social media more than older people, including for politics.[50] Social media use in general is not strongly related to education.[51] However, I expected that people with higher levels of education would be more inclined to use social media for election-related purposes than those with less formal education, especially for higher threshold activities that require more skills. Race was not a statistically significant predictor of social media use in this study, and I excluded it from the models estimated here.

Findings for only the post-convention survey are presented here because they best represent trends that are consistent across the three surveys.[52] The findings for the nominating campaign closely reflected the post-convention survey trends. The questions in the pre-primary surveys asked if respondents had *ever* used social media in these ways during campaigns, and they did not pertain specifically to the 2016 election. The pattern of responses was similar to results for the nominating campaign and post-convention surveys, although the magnitude of the findings was smaller.

The results of the OLS regression analysis confirm that interest in the election was a strong predictor of frequency of social media use, information seeking, and interactive expression. The relationship was greatest for frequency of election social media use, and was nearly identical for information seeking and interactive expression. The association between election interest and campaign engagement through social media was much smaller than for the other dependent variables. In fact, age—with younger people more likely to engage via social media—was a slightly stronger predictor of campaign engagement than was interest.

The findings for political party, ideology, and candidate preference were substantially weaker than for political interest, but there were some intriguing trends. As Table 7.2 depicts, party identification was not related to frequency of social media use or information seeking. However,

Table 7.2. OLS Regression of Campaign Interest, Party Identification, and Demographics on Campaign Social Media Use (Post-Convention Survey)

	Frequency of Social Media Use	Social Media Information Seeking	Social Media Interactive Expression	Social Media Campaign Engagement
Interest	.451*	.328*	.327*	.141*
Republican	.036	.032	.063*	.050
Democrat	.028*	.015	.055*	.049
Gender	.063*	.009	.029	−.012
Age	−.132*	−.158*	−.133*	−.148*
Education	.065*	.049*	−.052*	.026
R^2	.225*	.124*	.117*	.041*
n	1,601	1,595	1,593	1,597

*$p \leq .05$

there was a small, statistically significant positive relationship between Republican and Democratic party affiliation for interactive expression and campaign engagement. Similarly, as shown in Table 7.3, there was no association between ideology and frequency of social media use or information seeking. However, both liberals and conservatives were more inclined than moderates to use social media for interactive expression. Conservative ideology was positively associated with social media engagement, but liberal ideology was nonsignificant.

As Table 7.4 indicates, the relationship between candidate preference and campaign social media use was more pronounced than for political party identification and ideology. Supporters of Clinton, Trump, and third party candidates were more inclined to use social media to follow the campaign than those who were undecided. Candidate preference was a stronger predictor of interactive expression on social media than any of the other dependent measures; the relationship was statistically significant for Trump, Clinton, and third party candidates. Trump supporters were the most likely to use social media to actively express themselves about the campaign followed by backers of third party candidates. Clinton voters were the least inclined to engage in interactive expression via social media. The coefficient for Trump voters in the campaign engagement equation was notably larger than for Clinton or third party supporters, and was the only statistically significant relationship. There was no association between candidate preference and information seeking.

Among the demographic variables, age was the best predictor in all of the equations. Younger people were substantially more inclined to use social media during the campaign than older people. The coefficients were slightly higher in the information seeking and campaign engagement equations than for following the campaign on social media and

Table 7.3. OLS Regression of Campaign Interest, Political Ideology, and Demographics on Campaign Social Media Use (Post-Convention Survey)

	Frequency of Social Media Use	Social Media Information Seeking	Social Media Interactive Expression	Social Media Campaign Engagement
Interest	.457*	.331*	.332*	.147*
Conservative	.021	.032	.089*	.064*
Liberal	.006	.017	.087*	.027
Gender	.067*	−.009	.030	−.009
Age	−.133*	−.158*	−.131*	−.151*
Education	.067*	.051*	−.046	.033
R^2	.224*	.124*	.121*	.041*
n	1,601	1,597	1,597	1,597

*$p \leq .05$

Table 7.4. OLS Regression of Campaign Interest, Candidate Preference, and Demographics on Campaign Social Media Use (Post-Convention Survey)

	Frequency of Social Media Use	Social Media Information Seeking	Social Media Interactive Expression	Social Media Campaign Engagement
Interest	.447*	.328*	.325*	.138*
Trump	.086*	.047	.117*	.112*
Clinton	.061*	.037	.071*	.040
Third Party	.072*	.034	.093*	.035
Gender	.072*	−.007	.037	−.003
Age	−.132*	−.158*	−.135*	−.153*
Education	.069*	.050*	−.044	.038
R^2	.228*	.125*	.118*	.045*
n	1,601	1,597	1,597	1,597

*$p \leq .05$

interactive expression. There was a weak, positive relationship between education and frequency of social media use and information seeking. Those with lower levels of education were slightly more inclined to use social media for interactive expression than those with more education. The only significant gender relationship was that women used social media to follow the campaign slightly more than men.

Campaign Social Media Use

This section addresses the research question: How did voters use social media to experience and engage in the 2016 presidential campaign? The visibility and influence of social media in campaigns have increased dramatically with each election cycle along with the number of users. Over 200 million Americans use Facebook each month,[53] and 40 percent of them get their news from the platform.[54] According to the Pew Research Center, the number of voters who tracked election news through social media (28%) and followed candidates (16%) during the 2014 midterm campaigns had more than doubled since the 2010 elections. This trend marked a notable increase over the 17 percent of voters who used social media in any way during the 2012 presidential contest where voter interest was significantly higher.[55] There also has been a substantial climb in the number of people who follow political figures, including candidates, on digital media.[56] Donald Trump's official Twitter feed was followed by over 16 million people, compared to 11 million who followed Hillary Clinton. Twenty percent of voters regularly learned about the 2016 campaign from candidate or campaign groups' websites, apps, or emails.[57]

The evidence from the surveys analyzed here corroborated these trends, and indicated that the online public was strongly inclined to follow the 2016 election via social media. A majority of people online used social media at least sometimes to track the election (70% pre-primary, 68 percent nominating campaign, 70 percent post-convention). A little over a quarter reported frequent use during each phase of the study. Only around 10 percent of participants in each survey responded that they never follow the campaign through social media. The answers to this question were almost identical in the pre-primary and post-convention surveys that were fielded sixteen months apart. These findings are similar to those reported by the Pew Research Center,[58] which found that 65 percent of the public learned about the presidential election from digital media in February 2016.

As posited by the first hypothesis, the use of social media in the 2016 election was greatest for low threshold activities that involve less time, effort, skill, and commitment than high threshold activities that require more intensive levels of engagement. Thus, trends established in prior elections carry over to the 2016 contest. As Table 7.5 demonstrates, the online public was highly inclined to use social media for information seeking, especially following election news and gaining information about candidates and issues. A majority used social media to watch campaign ads. Approximately 40 percent followed other users with opposing viewpoints. The online public was moderately disposed to using social media for interactive expression related to elections. Around half of respondents reported using social media to voice their opinions about the campaign. Users were more likely to express opinions and participate in discussions than they were to use social media to convince others to take actions, such as voting for or against a candidate, or to share campaign-related content. Far fewer used social media to engage in the campaign beyond information seeking and expression. A majority (73%) of respondents engaged in none of the activities included in the social media campaign engagement index. Twenty percent or less joined a campaign-related group or accepted an election-specific "friend" request. Less than 15 percent of respondents used social media to donate to a campaign. A small percentage of study participants created their own campaign content via social media. Respondents were least likely to organize a campaign-related event.

There was a high level of consistency in the trends across the three surveys for most of the measures. The percentage of respondents using social media for each of the information-seeking items was similar for the three periods. By the post-convention period there was a slight, but statistically significant, drop in the percentage of respondents who used social media to learn about and look for information about the candidates. At this point, some voters may have felt that they had acquired sufficient in-

Table 7.5. Election Social Media Use

	(1) Pre-Primary	*(2) Nominating Campaign*	*(3) Post-Convention*	χ^2 $p \le .05$
Information Seeking				
Followed news about the campaign	72%	74%	76%	1,3
Learned about candidates and issues	76%	78%	73%	1,2; 1,3; 2,3
Looked for information about a candidate	68%	73%	66%	1,2; 2,3
Watched campaign ads	59%	59%	56%	
Followed those with opposing political views	40%	43%	43%	
Interactive Expression				
Expressed an opinion / others disagree	52%	62%	49%	1,2; 2,3
"Like" or "favorite" campaign-related content	49%	53%	49%	1,2; 2,3
Participated in election-related discussions	44%	55%	42%	1,2; 2,3
Convince others to vote for candidate	36%	39%	34%	2,3
Shared campaign-related content	41%	39%	33%	1,3; 2,3
Encouraged action on behalf candidate	33%	32%	26%	1,3; 2,3
Campaign Engagement				
Joined a campaign-related group	19%	17%	17%	
Accepted a "friend" request	20%	14%	14%	1,2; 1,3
Donated to a campaign	14%	11%	10%	1,3
Created campaign-related content	12%	13%	10%	
Organized a campaign-related event	9%	6%	6%	
n	1,125	869	1,631	

formation about candidates to make a decision. The trend was somewhat different for interactive expression. A higher percentage of respondents used social media to express opinions, "like" campaign-related content, participate in discussions, and convince people to vote for or against a candidate during the nominating campaign than during the pre-primary or post-convention periods. This difference was statistically significant. It may be the case that users perceived that the people in their networks were of the same partisan persuasion, and that the need to influence their

Table 7.6. Bivariate Correlations (Pearson's R) between Social Media Use Measures (Post-Convention Survey)

	Follow Election	Information Seeking	Interactive Expression
Follow Election	—		
Information Seeking	.627	—	
Interactive Expression	.518	.592	—
Campaign Engagement	.268	.335	.539

n = 1,609

All coefficients are statistically significant at p ≤ .01

"friends" was greater during the nominating campaign than the general election.

The second hypothesis tests whether lower threshold digital engagement led to users' embracing higher threshold activities during the 2016 election. Using social media to get information and for self-expression can prepare users to participate in more demanding activities.[59] The bivariate correlations (Pearson's R) between the four social media use measures—how often the respondent followed the campaign on social media and the three election social media engagement indices—presented in Table 7.6 lend support to this hypothesis. There were strong correlations between the frequency of using social media for following the election, information seeking, and interactive expression—activities that are at the lower to middle range of the digital engagement threshold. Importantly, the size of the association between the campaign engagement—our high threshold indicator—and the other social media measures increased with the threshold level of the activity. The correlation was lowest for following the campaign (.268), moderate for information seeking (.335), and highest for interactive expression (.539).

Offline Campaign Engagement

This section examines the research question: What is the relationship between social media use and offline campaign engagement? I test the third hypothesis that the use of social media for campaign engagement is correlated with offline engagement. I expect that people who engage in higher threshold social media campaign activities, such as organizing a campaign event, are more likely to engage in offline campaign activities than those who use social media for lower-threshold campaign activities, such as seeking information about the election.

The general trends for offline campaign engagement were similar to the patterns for social media use. Table 7.7 depicts the percentage of people

Table 7.7.   Offline Campaign Engagement (Post-Convention Survey)

Information Seeking	
Researched a candidate, campaign event, or issue	72%
Interactive Expression	
Talked about the election with family/friends/colleagues	93%
Tried to convince others to vote for or against a candidate	45%
Encouraged others to turn out to vote	56%
Wrote a letter to the editor	5%
Campaign Engagement	
Displayed a yard sign, bumper sticker, button for a candidate	16%
Donated money to a candidate, political party, or political organization	14%
Attended a political rally	12%
Volunteered for a candidate's campaign	7%
Recruited volunteers to work for a candidate	5%
Gone door-to-door for a political campaign	4%

n = 1,631

engaging in information seeking, interactive expression, and campaign engagement offline. Findings are reported for the post-convention survey only as they are similar to those for the pre-primary and nominating campaign phases. Respondents were more inclined to engage in information seeking and interactive expression than to participate actively in the campaign. However, there were some notable differences. Some forms of interactive expression are perhaps easier accomplished offline. Ninety-three percent of respondents reported talking about the election with family, friends, and colleagues. This was the most popular form of interactive expression either online or offline. At the same time, communicating opinions to a wider audience involves more effort offline than through social media. Only 5 percent of respondents had written a letter to the editor. The percentage of people who took part in campaign activities offline is comparable to the findings for social media engagement. The most prevalent activities were displaying a yard sign, bumper sticker, or campaign button (16%), donating money (14%), and attending a rally (12%). Only a small number of people volunteered themselves (7%), recruited others as volunteers (5%), or door-knocked for a campaign (4%).

To test the third hypothesis, I assessed the strength of the relationship between online and offline campaign engagement. I computed the bivariate correlations (Pearson's R) between the social media and offline campaign information seeking, interactive expression, and campaign engagement composite measures for the post-convention data for social media users. In general, the hypothesis is supported, although the strength of the correlation between online and offline activities varied widely across pairs of measures. The most robust support for the hypothesis was evidenced by the strong association between social media campaign

Table 7.8. Bivariate Correlations (Pearson's R) between Social Media and Offline Information Seeking, Interactive Expression, and Campaign Engagement (Post-Convention Survey)

	SM Information Seeking	SM Interactive Expression	SM Campaign Engagement
Information Seeking	.254	.186	.087
Interactive Expression	.364	.519	.309
Campaign Engagement	.205	.390	.613

n = 1,564
All coefficients are statistically significant at p ≤ .01

engagement—our indicator of high threshold social media involve-ment—and offline campaign engagement.

As Table 7.8 demonstrates, the highest association for offline information seeking was with social media information seeking, although the relationship is moderate (.254). The correlations between offline information seeking and interactive expression (.186) and campaign engagement (.087) via social media were the weakest. There was a strong correspondence between interactive expression on social media and offline (.519). The offline interactive expression measure was more highly correlated with social media information seeking (.364) and campaign engagement (.309) than was the case for offline information seeking. Offline campaign engagement had the weakest association with social media information seeking (.205). The relationship between offline and social media campaign engagement was the strongest in the study (.613). People who took part in elections offline also were likely to express themselves on social media (.390).

Sources of Influence on Voting Decisions

In this section I address the research question: How much influence did social media have on voters' electoral decision making compared to other sources? I compared how much influence respondents felt social media, candidate messages, news reports, family and friends, campaign ads, and celebrities had on their vote choice. The question was asked only in the post-election survey. As Table 7.9 indicates, a majority of respondents reported that social media had very little or no influence on their voting decision. Only 11 percent indicate that social media had a lot of influence, with 35 percent reporting some influence. This finding may upend the assumption that people trust information in their social networks more than from other sources because they have personal familiarity with the source. Candidate messages were the most influential source, with over

Table 7.9. Influence on Voting Decision (Post-Convention Survey)

	A Lot	Some	Very Little/None
Social Media	11%	35%	54%
Candidate Messages	44%	37%	19%
News Reports	22%	50%	28%
Family and Friends	14%	44%	42%
Campaign Ads	6%	24%	70%
Celebrities	3%	10%	87%

n = 1,631

80 percent of study participants noting that they had a lot (44%) or some (37%) impact on their voting decision. News reports were less influential, with 22 percent of respondents stating that they had a lot of influence and 50 percent indicating some influence. However, news reports rank higher than social media. Family and friends were somewhat influential in voter decision-making. However, the vast majority of respondents suggested that campaign ads held very little to no sway over their vote choice (70%). Eight-seven percent of respondents reported that celebrity endorsements had little to no influence on their voting decisions.

User Perceptions of Social Media's Effects

Finally, I examine the research question: Do voters feel that their electoral role has changed as a result of social media? Post-convention survey respondents who used social media were asked to evaluate whether they felt social media had a positive, negative, or no effect on their political interest, attitudes, engagement, and influence. As Table 7.10 indicates, perceptions differed notably across these political orientations. A majority of users believed that social media had a positive effect on their knowledge of candidates (60%) as well as politics and elections in general (53%). Users were split in their perception that social media had a positive or no effect on their interest in politics and elections, with 42 percent of respondents in each category. Fewer respondents felt that social media had a positive effect on their attitudes towards candidates (35%). The 29 percent of respondents reporting that social media negatively influenced their views of candidates was the highest percentage in the negative response category, while 36 percent indicated "no effect." This finding was in keeping with the trend reported above that social media does not influence people's vote choice. The highly vitriolic and combative social media messaging that characterized the 2016 presidential contest may have contributed to the negative effect on attitudes towards candidates. Positive perceptions were lowest for social media's effect on users' offline

Table 7.10.   Users' Perceptions of Social Media's Effect on Their Political Interest, Knowledge, Attitudes, Engagement, and Influence (Post-Convention Survey)

	Positive	Negative	No Effect
Interest in Politics/Elections	42%	16%	42%
Knowledge of Politics/Elections	53%	9%	38%
Knowledge of Candidates	60%	13%	28%
Attitudes toward Candidates	35%	29%	36%
Offline Political Engagement	31%	11%	58%
Ability to Take an Active Role	33%	8%	59%
Ability to Influence Politics/Elections	26%	9%	65%

n = 1,631

political engagement (31%), ability to take an active role in politics and elections (33%), and ability to influence politics and elections (26%). Still, the perception that social media positively impacted their electoral engagement and influence was held by approximately one-third of users. A majority of users indicated that social media had no effect on their offline political engagement (58%), ability to take an active political role (59%), and ability to influence politics (65%). With the exception of attitudes toward candidates, the percentage of respondents indicating that social media negatively influence their political orientations was relatively small.

CONCLUSION

The evolving role of social media in presidential campaigns highlights the shifting influence of candidates, political elites, the press, and the public in elections in the digital era. Social media in the 2008 contest opened new avenues of opportunity for voters seeking to become invested in the electoral process on their own terms. The 2012 election witnessed the incorporation, if not co-optation, of the public's social media engagement. In the 2016 campaign, outsider candidate Donald Trump and longtime political insider Hillary Clinton adopted somewhat different social media strategies, including the extent to which they embraced users' social media contributions. The general trend, however, is for campaigns and the press to exert greater control over social media, especially the higher threshold uses of social media by voters. Voters are inundated by campaign information from official campaign and media sources while their own voices are muffled. Campaigns actively seek to coordinate social media users' political engagement through their organizations rather than having users take the initiative, as occurred in 2008.

Yet there are trends signaling that social media have facilitated voters' engagement in elections. Social media, especially Facebook, have centralized online news consumption for users, making it easier to find information.[60] The present research reinforces the findings of other studies indicating that a substantial proportion of the online public is monitoring and seeking campaign information through social media. Voters also are using social networks to express themselves and share campaign messages, although engaging in real-life dialogue with family and friends remains the most prominent form of campaign discussion. Further, there is a synergy between social media and offline campaign engagement, especially among users who participate in higher threshold social media activities. Finally, users perceive that social media use has a positive influence on their knowledge of politics, elections, and candidates. One-third of the respondents in the study felt that their engagement and influence in campaigns has been enhanced by social media. Very few considered social media to have a negative impact on their campaign knowledge, engagement, or influence.

It may be the case that election campaigns are not conducive to sustaining user-driven initiatives, as political operatives discover how to appropriate social media in a way that overshadows, even precludes, some forms of voter engagement. However, effective citizen innovations and engagement via social media are happening outside the campaign context, as issue- and cause-focused groups develop movements for change.[61] Lessons from these initiatives may make their way into the electoral arena. Thus, the next phase of the evolution of campaign social media may see the pendulum swing back in the direction of the voter.

NOTES

1. Jason Gainous and Kevin M. Wagner, *Tweeting to Power* (New York: Oxford University Press, 2013).

2. Victoria A. Farrar-Meyers and Justin S. Vaughn, *Controlling the Message* (New York: NYU Press, 2015).

3. Richard Semiatin, ed., *Campaigns on the Cutting Edge*, 2nd ed. (Washington, D.C.: CQ Press, 2013).

4. Henry Jenkins, Sam Ford, and Joshua Green, *Spreadable Media* (New York: New York University Press, 2013).

5. Matthew Hindman, *The Myth of Digital Democracy* (Princeton: Princeton University Press, 2009).

6. John Herrman, "Inside Facebook's (Totally Insane, Unintentionally Gigantic, Hyperpartisan) Political-Media Machine," *The New York Times Magazine*, August 25, 2016: 1–14. http://www.nytimes.com/2016/08/28/magazine/inside-facebooks-totally-insane-unintentionally-gigantic-hyperpartisan-political-media-machine.html?_r=1.

7. Burkhard C. Schipper and Hee Yuel Woo, "Political Awareness, Microtargeting of Voters, and Negative Electoral Campaigning." Research Paper (Davis, CA:

University of California, Davis, 2016). http://faculty.econ.ucdavis.edu/faculty/schipper/polaw.pdf.

8. Aaron Smith, "Cell Phones, Social Media, and Campaign 2014," Research Report (Washington, D.C.: Pew Research Center, November 3, 2014). http://www.pewinternet.org/2014/11/03/cell-phones-social-media-and-campaign-2014/; Diana Owen, "The Campaign and the Media," in *The American Elections of 2012*, Janet M. Box-Steffensmeier and Steven E. Schier, eds. (New York: Routledge, 2013: 21–47); Diana Owen, "New Media and Political Campaigns," in *The Oxford Handbook of Political Communication Theories*, Kate Kenski and Kathleen Hall Jamieson, eds. (New York: Oxford University Press, 2015: Chapter 53).

9. Pew Research Center, *Election 2016: Campaigns as a Direct Source of News*, Research Report (Washington, D.C., July 18, 2016).

10. See, for example, David McCabe, "Welcome to the Social Media Election," *The Hill*, August 17, 2015, http://thehill.com/policy/technology/251185-welcome-to-the-social-media-election; Marissa Lang, "2016 Election Circus: Is Social Media the Cause?" *San Francisco Chronicle*, April 5, 2016.

11. Diana Owen, "The Political Culture of American Elections," in Georgiana Banita and Sascha Pohlmann, eds. *Electoral Cultures: American Democracy and Choice* (Heidelberg: Universitatsverlag, Publications of the Bavarian American Academy, 2015: 205–224); Robert Denton, Jr., ed., *Studies of Communication in the 2012 Presidential Election* (New York: Lexington Books, 2014); Farrar-Meyers and Vaughn, *Controlling the Message*, 2015.

12. Kate Kenski, Bruce W. Hardy, and Kathleen Hall Jamieson, *The Obama Victory* (New York: Oxford University Press, 2010); Terri L. Towner and David A. Dulio, "New Media and Political Marketing in the United States: 2012 and Beyond," *The Journal of Political Marketing*, 11, no. 1–2 (2012): 95–119.

13. Jennifer Stromer-Galley, *Presidential Campaigning in the Internet Age* (New York: Oxford University Press, 2014).

14. David Plouffe, *The Audacity to Win* (New York: Penguin, 2009).

15. Michael Slaby, "From Politics to Public Policy: Part 3: How Campaign Lessons Can Amplify Your Work: Embrace the Change," *Stanford Innovation Review*, April 9, 2013.

16. Laurence Cruz, "2012—The Social Media Election?" *The Network*, September 3, 2012. https://newsroom.cisco.com/feature-content?type=webcontent&articleId=1006785.

17. Plouffe, *The Audacity to Win*, 2009; Diana Owen, "The Campaign and the Media," in Janet M. Box-Steffensmeier and Steven E. Schier, eds., *The American Elections of 2008* (New York: Routledge, 2009: 9–32).

18. Micah Sifry, "The Rise and Fall of Social Media in American Politics (And How It May Rise Again)," *TechPresident*, November 6, 2012. http://techpresident.com/news/23103/rise-and-fall-social-media-american-politics-and-how-it-may-rise-again.

19. Michael Brown, "Dear Mr. Obama," YouTube video, duration 1:55. Posted August 27, 2008. https://www.youtube.com/watch?v=TG4fe9GlWS8.

20. Owen, "The Campaign and the Media," 2013; Sifry, "The Rise and Fall of Social Media in American Politics (And How It May Rise Again)," 2012.

21. Sifry, "The Rise and Fall of Social Media in American Politics (And How It May Rise Again)," 2012.

22. Slaby, "From Politics to Public Policy," 2013.

23. Pew Research Center, *2016 Campaign: Strong Interest, Widespread Dissatisfaction*. Research Report. (Washington, D.C., July 7, 2016).

24. Caroline Higgins, "The 2012 Presidential Campaign and Social Media: A New Age?," *Flip the Media*, August 31, 2012. http://flipthemedia.com/2012/08/the-2012-presidential-campaign-and-social-media-a-new-age/.

25. Sifry, "The Rise and Fall of Social Media in American Politics (And How It May Rise Again)," 2012 (online).

26. Owen, "The Political Culture of American Elections," 2015.

27. Sifry, "The Rise and Fall of Social Media in American Politics (And How It May Rise Again)," 2012 (online).

28. Pew Research Center, *The 2016 Presidential Campaign: A News Event That's Hard to Miss*. Research Report. (Washington, D.C., February 4, 2016).

29. Pew Research Center, *Election 2016: Campaigns as a Direct Source of News*, 2016.

30. Dan Patterson, "Election Tech: Why 2016 Is the First Made-for-Social Media Campaign," *Tech Republic*, March 26, 2016. http://www.techrepublic.com/article/election-tech-why-2016-is-the-first-made-for-social-media-campaign/.

31. Pew Research Center, *Election 2016: Campaigns as a Direct Source of News*, 2016.

32. Pew Research Center, *The Political Environment on Social Media*, Research Report (Washington, D.C., October 25, 2016).

33. Andy Smith and Jennifer Aker, *The Dragonfly Effect* (San Francisco: Jossey-Bass, 2010).

34. Ry Crist and Caitlin Petrakovitz, "How the 2016 Presidential Candidates Measure Up on Social Media," *NET*, February 8, 2016. https://www.cnet.com/news/2016-elections-comparing-presidential-candidates-on-social-media/.

35. Kathleen Hall Jamieson, Allyson Volinsky, Ilana Weitz, and Kate Kenski, "The Political Uses and Abuses of Civility and Incivility," in Kate Kenski and Kathleen Hall Jamieson, *The Oxford Handbook of Political Communication* (New York: Oxford University Press, 2015: online). http://www.oxfordhandbooks.com/view/10.1093/oxfordhb/9780199793471.001.0001/oxfordhb-9780199793471-e-79#oxfordhb-9780199793471-e-79-bibItem-28.

36. Pew Research Center, *The Political Environment on Social Media*, 2016.

37. Cristian Vaccari et al., "Political Expression and Action on Social Media: Exploring the Relationship Between Lower- and Higher-Threshold Political Activities Among Twitter Users in Italy," *Journal of Computer-Mediated Communication*, 20 (2015): 222.

38. Krueger, Brian S., "Assessing the Potential of Internet Political Participation in the United States: A Resource Approach," *American Politics Research*, 40, no. 5 (2002): 476–498; Rachel Gibson and Marta Cantijoch, "Conceptualizing and Measuring Participation in the Age of the Internet: Is Online Political Engagement Really Different to Offline?" *Journal of Politics*, 75, no. 3 (2013): 701–716.

39. Vaccari et al., "Political Expression and Action on Social Media: Exploring the Relationship Between Lower- and Higher-Threshold Political Activities Among Twitter Users in Italy," 2015.

40. Michael Xenos and Patricia Moy, "Direct and Differential Effects of the Internet on Political and Civic Engagement," *Journal of Communication*, 57, no. 4

(2007): 704–718; Homero Gil de Zuniga, Eulalia Puig-i-Abril, and Hernando Rojas, "Weblogs, Traditional Sources Online and Political Participation: An Assessment of How the Internet Is Changing the Political Environment," *New Media & Society*, 11, no. 4 (2009): 553–574; Homero Gil de Zuniga and Sebastian Valenzuela, "The Mediating Path to a Stronger Citizenship: Online and Offline Networks, Weak Ties, and Civic Engagement," *Communication Research*, 38, no. 3 (2011): 397–421.

41. John Herrman, "Inside Facebook's (Totally Insane, Unintentionally Gigantic, Hyperpartisan) Political-Media Machine," *The New York Times Magazine*, August 25, 2016: 1–14. http://www.nytimes.com/2016/08/28/magazine/inside-facebooks-totally-insane-unintentionally-gigantic-hyperpartisan-political-media-machine.html?_r=1.

42. Lee Rainie, Aaron Smith, Kay Lehman Schlozman, Henry Brady, and Sidney Verba, "Social Media and Political Engagement," Research Report (Washington, D.C., October 19, 2012).

43. Terri L. Towner, "All Political Participation Is Socially Networked? New Media and the 2012 Election," *Social Science Computer Review*, 31, no. 5 (2013). http://journals.sagepub.com/doi/full/10.1177/0894439313489656.

44. NORC Center for Public Affairs Research, *The Frustrated Public: Views of the 2016 Campaign, the Parties, and the Electoral Process*. Issue Brief. (Chicago, 2016). http://www.apnorc.org/projects/Pages/HTML%20Reports/the-frustrated-public-americans-views-of-the-election-issue-brief.aspx.

45. Xenos and Moy, "Direct and Differential Effects of the Internet on Political and Civic Engagement," 2007; Gil de Zuniga et al., "Weblogs, Traditional Sources Online and Political Participation: An Assessment of How the Internet Is Changing the Political Environment," 2009; Gil de Zuniga and Valenzuela, "The Mediating Path To a Stronger Citizenship: Online and Offline Networks, Weak Ties, and Civic Engagement," 2011; Towner, "All Political Participation Is Socially Networked? New Media and the 2012 Election," 2013.

46. Adam J. Berinsky, Gregory A. Huber, and Gabriel S. Lenz, "Evaluating Online Labor Markets for Experimental Research: Amazon.com's Mechanical Turk," *Political Analysis*, 20 (2012): 351–368; Jesse Chandler, Pam Mueller, and Gabriele Paolacci, "Nonnaïveté Among Amazon Mechanical Turk Workers: Consequences and Solutions for Behavioral Researchers," *Behavior Research Methods*, 46 (2014): 112–130.

47. Connor Huff and Dustin Tingley, "'Who Are These People?' Evaluating the Demographic Characteristics and Political Preferences of MTurk Survey Respondents," *Research and Politics*, July–September 2015: 1–12.

48. Pew Research Center, *2016 Campaign: Strong Interest, Widespread Dissatisfaction*, 2016.

49. Pew Research Center, *Cell Phones, Social Media and Campaign 2014*, Research Report. (Washington, D.C., November 3, 2014).

50. Tom P. Baker and Claes de Vreese, "Good News for the Future? Young People, Internet Use, and Political Participation," *Communication Research*, 30, no. 4 (2011): 451–470; Matthew James Kushkin and Masahiro Yamamato, "Did Social Media Really Matter? College Students' Use of Online Media and Political Decision-Making in the 2008 Elections," *Mass Communication and Society*, 13 (2012): 608–630.

51. Maeve Duggan, "The Demographics of Social Media Users," *Mobile Messaging and Social Media 2015*. Research Report. (Washington, D.C.: Pew Research Center, 2015). http://www.pewinternet.org/2015/08/19/the-demographics-of-social-media-users/.

52. Results of the analysis for all of the surveys may be obtained from the author (email: owend@georgetown.edu).

53. Herrman, "Inside Facebook's (Totally Insane, Unintentionally Gigantic, Hyperpartisan) Political-Media Machine," 2016.

54. Pew Research Center, *2016 Campaign: Strong Interest, Widespread Dissatisfaction*, 2016.

55. Pew Research Center, *The Political Environment on Social Media*, 2016; Pew Research Center, *Cell Phones, Social Media and Campaign 2014*, 2014.

56. Lang, "2016 Election Circus: Is Social Media the Cause?" 2016.

57. Diana Owen. 2017. "Twitter Rants, Press Bashing, and Fake News: The Shameful Legacy of Media in the 2016 Election," in *Trumped: The 2016 Election that Broke All the Rules*, Larry J. Sabato, Kyle Konkik, and Geoffrey Skelley, eds. (Lanham, MD: Rowman and Littlefield, 2017), 167–180.

58. Pew Research Center, *The 2016 Presidential Campaign: A News Event That's Hard to Miss*. Research Report (Washington, D.C., February 4, 2016).

59. Homero Gil de Zuniga, Logan Molyneux, and Pei Zheng, "Social Media, Political Expression, and Political Participation: Panel Analysis of Lagged and Concurrent Relationships," *Journal of Communication*, 64, no. 4 (2014): 612–634; Vaccari, "Political Expression and Action on Social Media: Exploring the Relationship Between Lower- and Higher-Threshold Political Activities Among Twitter Users in Italy," 2015.

60. Herrman, "Inside Facebook's (Totally Insane, Unintentionally Gigantic, Hyperpartisan) Political-Media Machine," 2016.

61. Sifry, "The Rise and Fall of Social Media in American Politics (And How It May Rise Again)," 2012 (online).

8

Campaign Messaging During the 2016 U.S. Presidential Election

How Twitter Compares to the Traditional Media

David S. Morris

The race for president of the United States between Hillary Clinton and Donald Trump was a national event and a global curiosity with never before seen levels of media coverage. Pew Research Center has referred to the 2016 U.S. presidential election as "a news event that's hard to miss,"[1] and *Showtime* aired a documentary series depicting the events surrounding the election entitled "The Circus." And Americans were paying attention to this spectacle. According to Pew, 90 percent of Americans learned about the election in a given week from a variety of media platforms, including the traditional media and social media platforms.[2]

Both the mediated traditional media that filters campaign information and unmediated social media outlets that allow campaigns to directly communicate with citizens—such as Twitter—were critical in the campaigns' attempts to influence voters and for voters to learn about the candidates. Prior to the 2016 presidential election there was an assumption that campaign messages sent through the traditional media are more influential, believable, and persuasive than messages sent via social media outlets like Twitter.[3] This is partly due to the fact that the traditional media ideally functions as mediated media and acts as an institutionalized gatekeeper of information and, consequently, evaluates and filters what potential voters see and hear while dictating the political conversation.[4] However, in a time when political polarization threatens to erode trust in traditional media outlets[5] and after a candidate called the "Master of Twitter" by *The New York Times* successfully deployed that unmediated communication platform to communicate directly with voters on his way to winning the 2016 election,[6] there is now a sense that things may have changed. In this new era of American politics, do campaign messages sent through the traditional media and those sent through Twitter resonate equally with voters? Or does the institutionalized and mediated traditional media still dominate campaign message effectiveness?

I make use of a survey experiment administered through Mechanical Turk (MTurk) to test whether potential voters regard campaign messages sent via *USA Today* to be more agreeable, believable, and persuasive than messages sent via Twitter, or whether potential voters regard messages sent via *USA Today* and Twitter to be similarly effectual. Next, I analyze a variety of key factors that might moderate the effect of a campaign message sent through Twitter and a campaign message sent through a *USA Today* headline, including political party affiliation, candidate favorability, educational attainment, income, and social media use. The results suggest that campaign messages about Hillary Clinton and Donald Trump sent via Twitter resonate just as strongly with potential voters as those sent via the traditional media. One exception to this pattern appears to be among people who do not use social media very often. These individuals appear to still find campaign messages sent via the traditional media to be more effectual. The findings presented and discussed here provide a potential partial explanation for the stunning rise of Donald Trump's political fortunes and adds insight into the role of Twitter and other non-traditional media platforms in future presidential campaigns.

THE TRUMP AND CLINTON CAMPAIGNS' USE OF TWITTER IN THE 2016 PRESIDENTIAL ELECTION

The 2016 presidential campaign was highly emotional and contentious with high levels of media coverage. People were paying close attention to the campaigns, with 90 percent of Americans keeping up with the election in a given week.[7] An essential tool in disseminating and gathering campaign information in this political environment was Twitter. On the day of the election Hillary Clinton had 10.4 million followers on Twitter and had sent nearly 10,000 tweets up to that point. However, she was bested in the "twitterverse" by Donald Trump who had 13.2 million followers on the day of the election and had sent over 30,000 tweets.[8]

In fact, it was Trump and his campaign that were renowned for truly embracing this form of campaign communication in an attempt to sway voters and dictate the national conversation. *The New York Times*—a left-leaning media outlet—went so far as to say that Trump had mastered Twitter in a way no other candidate ever had,[9] and Trump himself referred to his Twitter account as comparable to owning his own newspaper.[10] Candidate Trump was so prolific and inflammatory with his Twitter account that reports surfaced just days before the 2016 presidential election that his campaign had suspended his Twitter privileges.[11]

AMERICA'S USE OF MEDIA
IN THE 2016 PRESIDENTIAL CAMPAIGN

Internet use is near ubiquity in the United States, where almost 9 of 10 adults report using the Internet.[12] Use of Twitter and other social networking websites has steadily increased over the last five years to the point that 16 percent of Americans use Twitter, 19 percent use Instagram, and nearly 70 percent use Facebook. Of online Americans, 1 in 4 use Twitter, 1 in 3 use Instagram, and 4 of 5 report using Facebook. We have arrived at a point in history where social media use is now commonplace for Americans.[13]

The Internet and social media platforms like Twitter are also used to gather campaign information. Nearly 60 percent of Twitter users report getting news via Twitter[14] and nearly 10 percent of Twitter users reported getting information about the 2016 U.S. presidential election within a given week.[15] Not only is social media use now commonplace, but so is the use of such media platforms to gather information about politics and political candidates.

Nevertheless, getting information about the presidential race was done through traditional media outlets as well. Most Americans still view traditional media outlets—television news, online and print newspapers, and radio—as the most useful and effective avenues through which to receive information on the presidential race. For example, almost 50 percent of Americans said they received information about the election from online news websites alone within a given week—slightly more than the number of people reporting that they learned about the election from social media within the last week.[16] Taken as a whole, what this all indicates is that the traditional media is still essential when it comes to the public learning about politics and presidential campaigns, but platforms such as Twitter have become fundamental in the process as well. This begs the question of whether candidate information communicated via the traditional media is more effectual than candidate information communicated via Twitter—a social media platform that received much attention in the 2016 U.S. presidential campaign. Two different theoretical models help frame potential explanations to this research question.

FRAMING THE 2016 CAMPAIGN
USING A TRADITIONAL MEDIA MODEL

The mediated traditional media, made up of news organizations that produce online and print newspapers, television news, and radio programs, has long been assumed to be central to political campaign success.[17] Effective use of the traditional media allows candidates and their teams to broadcast their policy positions, convince people to support them, and motivate those who already support them to persuade others to back them. The traditional media also allows candidates and their campaigns to establish legitimacy by creating a narrative around the candidate and by discussing their policy positions and behaviors on the campaign trail.[18]

Because of the traditional media's established record of presenting information reliably over time and its perceived role as a truth-seeking institution, the traditional media has been viewed as more credible than social media platforms in their presentation of political information.[19] Social media outlets, blogs, YouTube videos, and other digital-based news are new entrants into the world of political messaging,[20] and they are often controlled by people who are not professional journalists, political insiders, or proclaimed unbiased observers. Messages delivered from and through Twitter, Facebook, and other social media platforms are unmediated and, therefore, can come from anyone and anywhere. Moreover, these platforms were not designed with news dissemination in mind and have typically been used for social and entertainment purposes. To many they are seen as the dwelling place for unserious individuals looking to spread unsubstantiated information, play pranks, and gather inconsequential information, and are playthings more than anything else.[21] Consequently, information gathered from traditional media sources has been seen as more serious, reliable, and believable than information gathered from sources like Twitter. For example, research examining college students found that increased attention to traditional media sources was associated with increased interest in and awareness of the political landscape while increased attention to social media was not.[22]

Using this logic, it stands to reason that information about a political candidate delivered through the traditional media will resonate more with the public. Therefore, from a traditional media model perspective one would expect that information gathered about a candidate from a *USA Today* headline would be more persuasive, believable, and motivating than information gathered from Twitter.

FRAMING THE 2016 CAMPAIGN USING A HYBRID MEDIA MODEL

One prominent scholar criticizes the traditional media model perspective, arguing that a dichotomy between "old media" and "new media" is inaccurate and misleading.[23] Instead, he argues that the dissemination of information through media outlets is better characterized as a continual crossbreeding between media platforms that have been used in the past and those that are currently being developed. According to Chadwick, many of the strategies and practices of the established media are adopted by recently developed media platforms, and the established media adopt many of the strategies and practices of the more recently developed media platforms. The result is the fusion of media platforms into a hybrid media system where clearly defined boundaries between media types are no longer apparent.

From a hybrid media perspective, clear boundaries between Twitter and the traditional media are not necessarily evident. Subsequently, campaign messages sent and received through social media differ little from campaign messages sent and received from a media source like *USA Today*. Why would they when they are part of the same interlaced system? By extension, the hybrid media model maintains that issues of credibility and persuasiveness of campaign information sent and gathered via online platforms like Twitter are not as relevant as some believe since the use of social media and other digital platforms is now heavily integrated into political campaigns.[24]

Indeed, research indicates that political campaigns are effectively deploying Twitter and other social media tools in unison with traditional media outlets in order to interact with voters and win elections.[25] As has been widely discussed, effective use of such tools by the Obama campaign had a direct impact on his ability to win the 2008 and 2012 U.S. presidential elections. Some even argue that social media platforms like Twitter in politics have effectively taken their place alongside traditional media, fundamentally shifting how citizens make decisions about who will get their vote and win the election.[26]

From the hybrid media model perspective, then, campaign messages sent and received from Twitter are likely to be no less compelling than information gathered from traditional media sources. Accordingly, the hybrid media model predicts that people will react similarly to tweets and *USA Today* headlines containing candidate information.

DATA AND METHODS

Data

Data were collected as part of the *Tweets and Headlines in the 2016 U.S. Presidential Election Survey Experiment* conducted between November 2 and November 6, 2016, just days before the United States presidential election. The survey was designed in Qualtrics and administered using Amazon's Mechanical Turk (MTurk). Respondents who completed the survey were compensated $.50 for their participation. Only people living in the United States and aged 18 or older were able to participate. Survey experiments combine the benefits of survey research, which can reach thousands of respondents, with the benefits of experimental designs, which have high internal validity making them valuable for uncovering causal relationships.[27]

MTurk is an Internet marketplace that provides access to a pool of individuals who can respond to social science surveys and other tasks of their choosing. Although MTurk is used for a variety of purposes, it has become a widely used resource for social science data collection.[28] Samples drawn using the service are more likely to be white, younger, more liberal, and more educated than population-based random samples.[29] This is to be expected, given that all respondents must be Internet users to access MTurk.

Studies have shown, however, that MTurk samples are often more representative of the United States' population than convenience samples, are at least as reliable as data obtained using traditional methods,[30] and are an excellent source for inexpensive and quality data.[31] Additionally, research comparing the social and political ideologies of liberals and conservatives in an MTurk sample to those of two nationally-representative samples found little difference between the three samples, indicating that political ideology divisions in MTurk mirror those in representative samples.[32] Because of the advantages offered by online labor markets like MTurk, use of such platforms has resulted in many high-quality studies in leading academic journals. A few examples include research on the effect of numeracy on managing numbers-based political policy appeals,[33] the role of racial bias in enrolling children in school,[34] and attitudes about redistributive economic policies in the U.S.[35]

The Survey Experiment

The *Tweets and Headlines Survey* was started by 1,011 respondents in MTurk, but 10 respondents failed to complete the majority of the survey so were excluded from the study. Of the remaining 1,001 respondents, 3 did not have information for all three dependent variables so these respondents were dropped from the analysis, resulting in a final sample size of 998.

The *Tweets and Headlines Survey* used experimental manipulation to investigate how people respond to political campaign information. By randomly manipulating experimental conditions the study is, ideally, controlling for all other potential explanatory factors except the manipulated condition. Controls are only added to the regressions to account for any demographic imbalance in the samples that may make them dissimilar on some key factors. Therefore, this approach allows for the interpretation that any effects were *caused* by the differences in treatment: a tweet or a news headline.[36] This is regardless of the use of a pretest-posttest design, or a posttest design only.[37] Candidate messages were presented in the form of a tweet or *USA Today* digital headline, with half of all respondents receiving a message via Twitter and the other half receiving a message via *USA Today*. Twitter was chosen as the social media communication platform due to Trump and his campaign's heavy reliance on it to communicate with potential voters, while *USA Today* was chosen because it has the widest U.S. circulation of all daily newspapers[38] and its readership tends to be ideologically similar to the average American.[39] For ease of discussion, the tweet treatment serves as the treatment effect while the *USA Today* headline treatment serves as the control (although in practice both are treatments and the study includes no control since each sample received a manipulation of media condition). The messages were randomly alternated so that the message focused on either Hillary Clinton or Donald Trump. Half of all respondents received a scenario with a message advocating for candidate Trump while the other half received a scenario with a message advocating for candidate Clinton. This was done so that attitudes toward a specific candidate and their use of different media outlets would not confound the results, and so that conclusions could be drawn about the treatment effect regardless of which campaign sent the message. Accordingly, each respondent was first presented with the following hypothetical scenario:

- "The economy is consistently one of the most important issues in determining who is elected President of the United States and this year looks to be no different. Imagine that tomorrow evening while you are online . . . "

And along with the hypothetical scenario each respondent received one of the following four treatments:

- " . . . you come across the following *USA Today* headline about Hillary Clinton written by a nationally-known Clinton political supporter: 'Hillary Clinton has clear vision to boost America's economy, restore jobs, and increase wages, has know-how to get it done.'"
- " . . . you come across the following tweet about Hillary Clinton from a nationally-known Clinton political supporter: '@HillaryClinton has clear vision to boost America's economy, restore jobs, and increase wages, has know-how to get it done #I'mWithHer.'"
- " . . . you come across the following *USA Today* headline about Donald Trump written by a nationally-known Trump political supporter: 'Donald Trump has clear vision to boost America's economy, restore jobs, and increase wages, has know-how to get it done.'"

- " . . . you come across the following tweet about Donald Trump from a nationally-known Trump political supporter: '@realDonaldTrump has clear vision to boost America's economy, restore jobs, and increase wages, has know-how to get it done #MakeAmericaGreat.'"

Again, treatments were distributed randomly and evenly so that approximately half of the sample (500 respondents) read a scenario that included a campaign message via Twitter and half of the sample read a campaign message via a *USA Today* headline.

Dependent Variables

Following each hypothetical scenario, respondents were asked three questions (with candidate name and media source altered based on the treatment), which serve as the three dependent variables under analysis. The first dependent variable (*agreement*) asked respondents, "How likely are you to agree with the above *USA Today* headline/tweet about Hillary Clinton/Donald Trump?: (1) extremely unlikely (2) moderately unlikely (3) somewhat unlikely (4) neither likely nor unlikely (5) somewhat likely (6) moderately likely (7) extremely likely."

The second dependent variable (*believability*) asked respondents, "On a scale of 1 to 10 (with 1 being 'not at all believable' and 10 being 'very believable') how believable is the above *USA Today* headline/tweet about Hillary Clinton/Donald Trump?"

The third dependent variable (*increased support*) asked respondents, "From your point of view, does the above *USA Today* headline/tweet make you more or less likely to support Hillary Clinton/Donald Trump? (1) more or somewhat more likely (0) equally, somewhat, or less likely."

Independent Variables

The treatment effects of reading a campaign message sent through Twitter and reading a campaign message sent through the traditional media in the form of a *USA Today* headline serves as the key independent variable in the analysis (1=Twitter treatment, 0=*USA Today* headline treatment). Additional independent variables are also included as controls and as moderating variables that are used to subdivide the sample. *Regular social media (SM) user* measures how often the person uses websites like Twitter, Facebook, or Instagram (1) regularly (0) not regularly. This variable captures a broader audience of several social media platforms rather than isolating the much more specific Twitter universe, which is a specific set of social media users.[40] *Favorable opinion of Trump* and *favorable opinion of Clinton* measure how respondents view each candidate (1) favorable

(0) unfavorable. *Political party identification* was dummied into three variables: Democrat (which serves as the referent category), Republican, and independent. *Liberal politically* is a five-point scale measuring political ideology (1) very conservative (2) conservative (3) moderate (4) liberal (5) very liberal. *Age* is a continuous measure of respondent age, *female* is a dummy variable indicating gender, *college degree* is a dummy variable indicating if the respondent has earned a 4-year college degree, and *racial/ethnic minority* is a dummy variable indicating whether a person is (1) racial/ethnic minority (0) white. *Income (in thousands)* is a quasi-continuous variable where categories of income ranges (e.g., $10,000 to under $20,000; $20,000 to under $30,000; $30,000 to under $40,000) were recoded to the midpoint of each income category and put in units of thousands ranging from $0 to $250,000.

Missing Data

If not addressed, the analyses would see a nearly 8 percent reduction in sample size through listwise deletion. To address this, multiple imputation (MI) in Stata was used to multiply impute missing values on independent variables that included missing information. MI generates more precise coefficients and standard errors than what is provided from single imputation or by relying on listwise deletion.[41] Nearly half of all independent variables had no missing information, while five others (regular SM user, age, female, favorable view of Clinton, and favorable view of Trump) had less than six cases each with missing information. However, racial/ethnic minority, income, and liberal politically had 13, 33, and 36 cases, respectively, with missing values. This may be due to some respondents viewing questions about race/ethnicity, income, and political ideology as sensitive and private information, increasing nonresponse. All variables in the full model were used to create the imputation model.[42] Based on recommendations from prior studies using simulations to assess the appropriate number of imputations for accurate estimates, 20 imputations and corresponding datasets were completed.[43] The results were then averaged across the 20 datasets. This allowed for the retention of all cases, except those with missing values on the dependent variables.

RESULTS OF THE SURVEY EXPERIMENT

Table 8.1 presents summary statistics for the sample and all variables used in the analysis. As noted earlier, sample members randomly received the Twitter treatment effect, with the exclusion criteria discussed earlier resulting in slightly less than 50 percent receiving the tweet treat-

Table 8.1.   Summary Statistics

Dependent Variables	Mean	SD	Min	Max
Agreement	3.336	2.212	1	7
Believability	4.524	3.165	1	10
Increased support	.182	.386	0	1
Tweet treatment	.498	.500	0	1
Regular SM user	.644	.479	0	1
Age	36.7	12.2	18	77
Female	.515	.500	0	1
Racial/ethnic minority	.274	.446	0	1
Income (in thousands)	57.6	43.5	0	250
College degree	.506	.500	0	1
Democrat (referent)	.544	.498	0	1
Republican	.308	.462	0	1
Independent	.148	.356	0	1
Liberal politically	3.36	1.15	1	5
Favorable opinion of Trump	.278	.448	0	1
Favorable opinion of Clinton	.453	.498	0	1

Sample Size = 998

ment. When looking at the dependent variables, the typical respondent is in the midrange for agreement and believability of campaign messages, while 18 percent of respondents reported that the messages increased their support for the candidate. What also stands out is the fact that the standard deviations for each of the dependent variables is large compared to the mean. This shows that there is a large amount of variability in each of the dependent variables, indicating that respondents provided an array of responses on these measures and were not clustered around the mean. Lastly, and typical of MTurk samples,[44] the current study's sample is whiter, more educated, more liberal, and more financially well-off than the overall U.S. population, although the differences are not dramatic.

Next, the analysis moves to examining the effect of reading a tweet advocating for one of the two 2016 U.S. presidential candidates compared to reading a *USA Today* headline advocating for one of the candidates. Looking at Table 8.2, the point estimates for agreement (-.077), believability (-.074), and increased support (-.058) are all close to zero. More importantly, the coefficients are not statistically significant. These findings suggest that people do not evaluate campaign messages about a candidate received via Twitter any differently than messages received via *USA Today*, which is one of the most consumed and ideologically centric traditional media outlets in the U.S. mass media market.[45]

Table 8.2.   Regressions Comparing Tweet Treatment Effect to Headline Treatment Effect for the Full Sample

	Agreement		Believability		Increased Support	
	B	SE	B	SE	B	SE
Tweet Treatment	−.077	(.137)	−074	(.194)	−.058	(.171)
R²/Pseudo R²	.068		.082		.072	
N	998		998		998	

The reference category is "*USA Today* headline." OLS regression is used to analyze agreement with state-ment about candidate *and* believability of statement about candidate. Logistic regression is used to analyze increased support for the candidate. All models include all control variables (age, gender, race, political party identification, income, educational attainment, social media use, political ideology, and favorability of Trump and Clinton).

It is important to consider, though, whether these results differ based on important demographic factors such as party identification, candidate support, income, and educational attainment. It is possible that affluent individuals compared to their less well-off counterparts are more likely to trust campaign messages sent through the traditional media, or that those without a college degree are more likely to trust campaign messages that come from unconventional digital media outlets like Twitter. The next section examines these possibilities along with an array of other important demographic factors that may impact the relationship between the treatment effect and each of the outcome variables.

Party Identification

A key factor that is important to consider when examining how people evaluate candidate messages via tweet and traditional media is political party affiliation. Since Donald Trump was more exuberant and vociferous with his use of Twitter than Hillary Clinton, it is possible that Republicans would find campaign messages sent via Twitter to be more effectual than Democrats. Table 8.3 displays the results of this analysis. When looking at Democrats only, the coefficient for tweet treatment is not statistically significant in each model measuring agreement, believability, and in-creased support. The same is true when looking at Republicans only and independents only. This indicates that the tweet treatment effect does not differ across political party, and suggests that Democrats, Republicans, and independents all evaluate candidate messages sent via Twitter in a similar manner as candidate messages sent via traditional media.

Candidate Favorability

The 2016 U.S. presidential campaign was unique in that it saw people who historically supported Democratic presidential candidates cross the

Table 8.3. Regressions Comparing Tweet Treatment Effect to Headline Treatment Effect by Party Identification

	Democrat					
	Agreement		Believability		Increased Support	
	B	SE	B	SE	Log odds	SE
Tweet Treatment	−.091	(.185)	−.064	(.263)	−.219	(.235)
Intercept	3.188	(.664)	4.729	(.943)	−2.631	(.902)
R^2/Pseudo R^2	.067		.078		.071	
N	543		543		543	

	Republican					
	Agreement		Believability		Increased Support	
	B	SE	B	SE	Log odds	SE
Tweet Treatment	−.095	(.265)	−.133	(.377)	.167	(.287)
Intercept	3.105	(.756)	4.289	(1.073)	−3.334	(.861)
R^2/Pseudo R^2	.064		.083		.069	
N	307		307		307	

	Independent					
	Agreement		Believability		Increased Support	
	B	SE	B	SE	Log odds	SE
Tweet Treatment	−.167	(.317)	−.105	(.453)	−.576	(.737)
Intercept	2.138	(1.107)	1.860	(1.580)	−9.036	(3.773)
R^2/Pseudo R^2	.187		.174		.350	
N	148		148		148	

The reference category is "*USA Today* headline." OLS regression is used to analyze agreement with statement about candidate and believability of statement about candidate. Logistic regression is used to analyze increased support for the candidate. All models include all control variables (age, gender, race, political party identification, income, educational attainment, social media use, political ideology, and favorability of Trump and Clinton).

aisle and support Trump, and conversely many people who historically supported Republican candidates backed Clinton.[46] Perhaps, then, it is more important to consider how opinions of each candidate moderate the Twitter treatment effect rather than political party identification. Table 8.4 displays the results of subdividing the sample based on favorable views of Trump and Clinton. Like the previous analysis based on party identification, the coefficient for tweet treatment is not statistically significant in each model measuring agreement, believability, and increased support for both those who have a favorable view of Trump and those who have a favorable view of Clinton. This indicates that those who have a favorable view of Trump regard campaign messages sent via tweet as effectual as messages sent via *USA Today*, and the same holds true for those who have a favorable view of Clinton.

Table 8.4. Regressions Comparing Tweet Treatment Effect to Headline Treatment Effect by Candidate Favorability

	Favorable View of Trump					
	Agreement		*Believability*		*Increased Support*	
	B	*SE*	*B*	*SE*	*Log Odds*	*SE*
Tweet Treatment	−.026	(.295)	.068	(.424)	.309	(.282)
Intercept	4.592	(1.063)	6.655	(1.526)	−1.584	(1.019)
R²/Pseudo R²	.067		.047		.040	
N	277		277		277	

	Favorable View of Clinton					
	Agreement		*Believability*		*Increased Support*	
	B	*SE*	*B*	*SE*	*Log Odds*	*SE*
Tweet Treatment	.138	(.216)	.110	(.306)	−.121	(.234)
Intercept	4.527	(.758)	7.185	(1.073)	−.881	(.817)
R²/Pseudo R²	.028		.035		.021	
N	452		452		452	

The reference category is "*USA Today* headline." OLS regression is used to analyze agreement with statement about candidate and believability of statement about candidate. Logistic regression is used to analyze increased support for the candidate. All models include all control variables (age, gender, race, political party identification, income, educational attainment, social media use, political ideology, and favorability of Trump and Clinton). Sample size does not total 998 since not all respondents had a favorable view of either candidate, while others had a favorable view of both candidates.

4-Year College Degree Attainment

Educational attainment is an important moderating factor to consider when analyzing the way people evaluate the effectiveness of a campaign tweet compared to a campaign headline in the traditional media. First, as was pointed out in the months leading up to the election and in its aftermath, Trump's campaign messages, often sent via Twitter, resonated with Americans who did not hold a 4-year college degree, potentially making those without a 4-year degree more open to a message sent via Twitter. Second, those who do hold a college degree may be more likely to trust information that comes from long-established sources such as *USA Today*. According to the results from Table 8.5, however, there appears to be no difference between how college-educated and non-college-educated people evaluate the effectiveness of tweets and *USA Today* headlines that promote a particular presidential candidate. Although the point estimates differ between college-educated and non-college-educated respondents. Those who hold a 4-year college degree, on average, report tweets as less effective than a headline while those without a degree report tweets as slightly more effective than a headline. However, here the coefficients are statistically insignificant.

Table 8.5. Regressions Comparing Tweet Treatment Effect to Headline Treatment Effect by 4-Year College Degree Attainment

	No 4-Year College Degree					
	Agreement		Believability		Increased Support	
	B	SE	B	SE	Log Odds	SE
Tweet Treatment	.075	(.193)	.092	(.278)	.127	(.253)
Intercept	2.824	(.711)	4.208	(1.024)	−3.615	(.992)
R²/Pseudo R²	.071		.077		.111	
N	493		493		493	

	4-Year College Degree					
	Agreement		Believability		Increased Support	
	B	SE	B	SE	Log Odds	SE
Tweet Treatment	−.214	(.197)	−.221	(.275)	−.204	(.238)
Intercept	3.422	(.752)	4.564	(1.052)	−2.722	(.929)
R²/Pseudo R²	.075		.101		.078	
N	505		505		505	

The reference category is "*USA Today* headline." OLS regression is used to analyze agreement with statement about candidate and believability of statement about candidate. Logistic regression is used to analyze increased support for the candidate. All models include all control variables (age, gender, race, political party identification, income, educational attainment, social media use, political ideology, and favorability of Trump and Clinton).

Income

Part of what led to Trump's victory in the 2016 presidential election was his success with working-class voters.[47] Consequently, it stands to reason that those lower on the income ladder might find candidate information sent through a method more frequently used by Trump's campaign to be more believable and persuasive compared to those who are more affluent. Although, it is also possible that higher-income individuals, with increased access to the Internet and digital devices due to their affluence, may regard campaign messages sent via Twitter to be more effectual than their lower-income counterparts.

Table 8.6 displays the results of the analyses breaking down the Twitter treatment effect by income tertile. Based on statistical significance, these findings suggest that income largely does not moderate how individuals evaluate the effectiveness of campaign messages sent via tweet and the traditional media. However, the point estimates across income categories do differ noticeably. And, at the .10 level of statistical significance, those in the middle-income category ($35K–<$63K) report campaign messages sent via tweet to be less effective in increasing candidate support. These findings suggest that middle-income Americans may find campaign messages sent via Twitter to be less effectual than those in the highest

Table 8.6. Regressions Comparing Tweet Treatment Effect to Headline Treatment Effect by Income Tertiles

	Lowest Income Tertile ($0–< $35K)					
	Agreement		Believability		Increased Support	
	B	SE	B	SE	Log Odds	SE
Tweet Treatment	−.150	(.257)	−.167	(.375)	.202	(.329)
Intercept	3.799	(.886)	4.705	(1.287)	−2.446	(1.199)
R²/Pseudo R²	.111		.137		.093	
N	287		287		287	

	Middle Income Tertile ($35K–< $63K)					
	Agreement		Believability		Increased Support	
	B	SE	B	SE	Log Odds	SE
Tweet Treatment	−.162	(.204)	−.128	(.291)	−.497+	(.263)
Intercept	3.566	(.749)	5.181	(1.066)	−2.615	(.972)
R²/Pseudo R²	.075		.074		.095	
N	452		452		452	

	Highest Income Tertile ($63K–$250K)					
	Agreement		Believability		Increased Support	
	B	SE	B	SE	Log Odds	SE
Tweet Treatment	.236	(.285)	.210	(.396)	.387	(.354)
Intercept	1.375	(1.156)	2.184	(1.594)	−6.069	(1.580)
R²/Pseudo R²	.068		.079		.122	
N	259		259		259	

The reference category is "*USA Today headline.*" OLS regression is used to analyze agreement with statement about candidate and believability of statement about candidate. Logistic regression is used to analyze increased support for the candidate. All models include all control variables (age, gender, race, political party identification, income, educational attainment, social media use, political ideology, and favorability of Trump and Clinton).
+p <.10 (two-tailed)

and lowest income segments, although only when it comes to increased support for the candidate. But the statistical evidence for this is rather thin (it is worth noting that ancillary models were also run using income quartiles and quintiles with very little change to the overall conclusions).

Social Media Use

The last set of models examining potential moderating factors for the tweet treatment effect looks at social media use. It stands to reason that those who do not regularly use social media outlets, like Twitter, will find campaign messages sent via Twitter to be less effectual than those who regularly use social media. Indeed, the results presented in Table 8.7

Table 8.7. Regressions Comparing Tweet Treatment Effect to Headline Treatment Effect by Social Media Use

	Not a Regular Social Media User					
	Agreement		Believability		Increased Support	
	B	SE	B	SE	Log Odds	SE
Tweet Treatment	−.393[+]	(.214)	−.577[+]	(.313)	−.561[+]	(.328)
Intercept	3.411	(.748)	5.129	(1.094)	−3.008	(1.162)
R²/Pseudo R²	.134		.132		.134	
N	356		356		356	

	Regular Social Media User					
	Agreement		Believability		Increased Support	
	B	SE	B	SE	Log Odds	SE
Tweet Treatment	.128	(.179)	.237	(.251)	.169	(.206)
Intercept	2.894	(.666)	3.925	(.936)	−3.372	(.801)
R²/Pseudo R²	.045		.066		.058	
N	642		642		642	

The reference category is "*USA Today* headline." OLS regression is used to analyze agreement with state-ment about candidate and believability of statement about candidate. Logistic regression is used to analyze increased support for the candidate. All models include all control variables (age, gender, race, political party identification, income, educational attainment, social media use, political ideology, and favorability of Trump and Clinton).
+p <.10 (two-tailed)

bear this out. For those who are not regular social media users, campaign messages sent via tweet compared to the traditional media are less agree-able (-.393), believable (-.577), and less likely to increase support for a candidate (-.561). However, the results suggest that regular social media users do not perceive campaign messages sent via tweet to be any more or less effectual than campaign messages sent via the traditional media. In fact, for this group the point estimates for the tweet treatment effect for each outcome variable are positive, indicating that regular social media users find campaign information sent via tweet to be more effectual, but they are not statistically significant. These models demonstrate a clear pattern in which people who do not regularly use social media are more influenced by campaign messages that are sent via the traditional media, but those who do use social media regularly are influenced to the same degree by campaign messages sent via tweet and the traditional media.

CONCLUSIONS

After the rise of Donald Trump in the political realm and his stunning election to the office of president of the United States, it is important to examine what may have led to his victory. The changing role of the mediated traditional media and social media platforms that allow for direct communication between campaigns and voters, like Twitter, in campaign messaging is one such factor. To explore this issue, I used a survey experiment administered through Mechanical Turk (MTurk) to compare how people perceived campaign messages received via the mediated traditional media in the form of a *USA Today* headline to campaign messages received via Twitter, which allows for immediate and direct campaign communication with voters. I then analyzed key demographic factors that have the potential to moderate people's perceptions of messages received via Twitter and the traditional media and further explain any potential media source effects.

The results of the experiment suggest that campaign messages about candidates sent via Twitter are deemed just as effectual by potential voters as those sent via the traditional media. When viewed from a hybrid media model perspective put forth by Chadwick,[48] these findings are not terribly surprising and fit a media world in which older and newer media platforms are fused with no clear boundaries between the two and media source effects are largely rendered moot. Furthermore, this effect holds even when the sample is subdivided by key demographic factors—political party identification, candidate favorability ratings, educational attainment, and income. The only factor that appears to moderate the Twitter versus traditional media effect is regular social media use, suggesting that as social media use increases the power of the traditional media in campaigns will continue to wane. The findings presented here buttress recent literature by Gainous and Wagner as well as Parmelee and Bichard, among others, that see social media, especially Twitter, as a political campaign game-changer in how it shapes voter perceptions and, ultimately, voters' decisions at the polls.[49] Moreover, these findings are especially relevant in the context of the 2016 U.S. presidential election where a man referred to by the media as the Master of Twitter eventually won the election.

Although the results of this survey experiment are interesting and potentially insightful, the study has limitations. First, in the experimental portion of the survey that provided a hypothetical message promoting Trump or Clinton, the tweets did not originate from the candidates themselves. Rather, they were sent by campaign supporters. This was done to standardize the treatment effects since campaign messages cannot really be sent directly from a candidate in a mediated media environment like that of *USA Today*. Consequently, in a scenario where the tweet comes directly from the candidate the results might have differed, and future studies should pursue this avenue of inquiry. Future studies could also examine other social media platforms that behave similarly to Twitter in their ability to connect directly with voters, such as Facebook—by far the most popular social network site—and Instagram. Second, the use of a survey experimental design creates benefits but also detractions. Although survey experiments are a powerful tool for causal inference, they often must simulate scenarios to create treatment effects. In this case, respondents did not actually come across a *USA Today* headline or a tweet. Rather, they received a hypothetical scenario to which they had to respond. This may have influenced how people responded to both forms of campaign messages.

Limitations aside, the results of this study provide new insight into how Americans are responding to campaign messages advocating for a particular candidate in a hybrid media model environment. Campaign messages sent through social media platforms like Twitter appear to have more resonance than previously thought and do not differ from those sent through the traditional media. That is unless an individual does not regularly use social media, in which case the traditional media is still regarded as more effectual than Twitter when it comes to campaign messaging. This provides a small explanatory piece to the puzzle that is Donald Trump's unexpected political success, and may be an indicator for the ascendency of Twitter and other non-traditional media platforms in future presidential campaigns.

NOTES

1. Jeffrey Gottfried, Michael Barthel, Elisa Shearer, and Amy Mitchell. "The 2016 Presidential Campaign: A News Event That's Hard to Miss." Pew Research Center, 2016.

2. Gottried et al., "A News Event That's Hard to Miss."

3. Thomas J. Johnson and Barbara K. Kaye. "Credibility of Social Network Sites for Political Information Among Politically Interested Internet Users." *Journal of Computer-Mediated Communication* 19, no. 4 (2014): 957–74; Jennifer Stromer-Galley. *Presidential Campaigning in the Internet Age.* (New York: Oxford University Press, 2014).

4. W. Lance Bennett and Robert M. Entman. *Mediated Politics.* (New York: Cambridge University Press, 2001).

5. Amy Mitchell and Rachel Weisel. "Political Polarization and Media Habits." Pew Research Center, 2014.

6. Michael Barbaro. "Pithy, Mean and Powerful: How Donald Trump Mastered Twitter for 2016." *The New York Times*, October 5, 2015.

7. Gottfried et al., "A News Event That's Hard to Miss."

8. Twitter Counter: Check Your Own Twitter Stats. http://twittercounter.com (retrieved November 9, 2016).

9. Barbaro. "How Donald Trump Mastered Twitter for 2016."

10. Rebecca Savransky. "Trump Compares Twitter to Owning His Own Newspaper." *The Hill*, April 3, 2016.

    11. Schultheis, 2016.
    12. Shannon Greenwood, Andrew Perrin, and Maeve Duggan. "Social Media Update 2016." Pew Research Center, 2016.
    13. Jeffrey Gottfried and Elisa Shearer. "News Use Across Social Media Platforms 2016." Pew Research Center, 2016.
    14. Gottfried and Shearer. "News Use Across Social Media Platforms 2016."
    15. Gottfried et al. "A News Event That's Hard to Miss."
    16. Ibid.
    17. Bennett and Entman, *Mediated Politics.*; Michael John Burton, William J. Miller, and Daniel M. Shea. *Campaign Craft: The Strategies, Tactics, and Art of Political Campaign Management, 5th Edition: The Strategies, Tactics, and Art of Political Campaign Management.* (Denver, CO: ABC-CLIO, 2015).; Gunn Enli and Hallvard Moe. "Social Media and Election Campaigns: Key Tendencies and Ways Forward." *Information, Communication & Society* 16, no. 5 (2013): 637–45.; Doris A. Graber. *Processing Politics: Learning from Television in the Internet Age.* (Chicago: University of Chicago Press, 2001).; Stromer-Galley, *Presidential Campaigning in the Internet Age.*; Darrell M. West. *Air Wars: Television Advertising and Social Media in Election Campaigns, 1952–2012.* (Thousand Oaks, CA: SAGE, 2014).
    18. Stromer-Galley. *Presidential Campaigning in the Internet Age.*
    19. Johnson and Kaye. "Credibility of Social Network Sites."; Andrew J. Flanagin and Miriam J. Metzger. "The Role of Site Features, User Attributes, and Information Verification Behaviors on the Perceived Credibility of Web-Based Information." *New Media & Society* 9, no. 2 (2007): 319–342.; Mike Schmierbach and Anne Oeldorf-Hirsch. "A Little Bird Told Me, So I Didn't Believe It: Twitter, Credibility, and Issue Perceptions." *Communication Quarterly* 60, no. 3 (2012): 317–37.
    20. Stromer-Galley. *Presidential Campaigning in the Internet Age.*
    21. Andrew Chadwick. *The Hybrid Media System: Politics and Power.* (New York: Oxford University Press, 2013).
    22. Matthew James Kushin and Masahiro Yamamoto. "Did Social Media Really Matter? College Students' Use of Online Media and Political Decision Making in the 2008 Election." *Mass Communication and Society* 13, no. 5 (2010): 608–30.
    23. Chadwick. *The Hybrid Media System.*
    24. Enli and Moe. "Social Media and Election Campaigns."
    25. Daniel Kreiss. "Seizing the Moment: The Presidential Campaigns' Use of Twitter During the 2012 Electoral Cycle." *New Media & Society*, 2014.; John H. Parmelee and Shannon L. Bichard. *Politics and the Twitter Revolution: How Tweets Influence the Relationship between Political Leaders and the Public.* (New York: Lexington Books, 2012).
    26. Jason Gainous and Kevin M. Wagner. *Tweeting to Power: The Social Media Revolution in American Politics.* (New York: Oxford University Press, 2014).
    27. Katrin Auspurg and Thomas Hinz. *Factorial Survey Experiments.* (Thousand Oaks, CA: Sage, 2015); Alan S. Gerber and Donald P. Green. *Field Experiments.* (New York: Norton, 2012).
    28. Adam J. Berinsky, Gregory A. Huber, and Gabriel S. Lenz. "Evaluating Online Labor Markets for Experimental Research: Amazon.com's Mechanical Turk." *Political Analysis* 20, no. 3 (2012): 351–68.
    29. Ibid.

30. Berinsky et al. "Evaluating Online Labor Markets for Experimental Research."; Michael Buhrmester, Tracy Kwang, and Samuel D. Gosling. "Amazon's Mechanical Turk a New Source of Inexpensive, yet High-Quality, Data?" *Perspectives on Psychological Science* 6, no. 1 (2011): 3–5.

31. Buhrmester et al. "Amazon's Mechanical Turk a New Source of Inexpensive, yet High-Quality, Data?"; Winter Mason and Siddharth Suri. "Conducting Behavioral Research on Amazon's Mechanical Turk." *Behavior Research Methods* 44, no. 1 (2013): 1–23.

32. Scott Clifford, Ryan M. Jewell, and Philip D. Waggoner. "Are Samples Drawn from Mechanical Turk Valid for Research on Political Ideology?" *Research & Politics* 2, no. 4 (2015).

33. Vittorio Mérola and Matthew P. Hitt. "Numeracy and the Persuasive Effect of Policy Information and Party Cues." *Public Opinion Quarterly* 80, no. 2 (2016): 554–62.

34. Chase M. Billingham and Matthew O. Hunt. "School Racial Composition and Parental Choice New Evidence on the Preferences of White Parents in the United States." *Sociology of Education* 89, no. 2 (2016): 99–117.

35. Ilyana Kuziemko, Michael I. Norton, Emmanuel Saez, and Stefanie Stantcheva. "How Elastic Are Preferences for Redistribution? Evidence from Randomized Survey Experiments." *The American Economic Review* 105, no. 4 (2015): 1478–1508.

36. Auspurg and Hinz. *Factorial Survey Experiments.*; Gerber and Green. *Field Experiments.*

37. Ibid.

38. Cision. "Top 10 US Daily Newspapers Updated 2016." http://www.cision.com/us/2014/06/top-10-us-daily-newspapers/.

39. Mitchell and Weisel. "Political Polarization and Media Habits."

40. Greenwood et al. "Social Media Update 2016."

41. Patrick Royston. "Multiple Imputation of Missing Values: Update of Ice." *Stata Journal* 5, no. 4 (2005): 527.

42. Royston, "Multiple Imputation of Missing Values."; Paul T. von Hippel. "Regression with Missing Ys: An Improved Strategy for Analyzing Multiply Imputed Data." *Sociological Methodology* 37, no. 1 (2007).

43. Craig K. Enders. *Applied Missing Data Analysis.* (New York: Guilford Press, 2010).; Ian R. White, Patrick Royston, and Angela M. Wood. "Multiple Imputation Using Chained Equations: Issues and Guidance for Practice." *Statistics in Medicine* 30, no. 4 (2011): 377–99.

44. Berinsky et al. "Evaluating Online Labor Markets for Experimental Research."

45. Cision. "Top Newspapers."; Mitchell and Weisel. "Political Polarization and Media Habits."

46. Lai et al. "How Trump Won the Election According to Exit Polls." *The New York Times,* November 8, 2016.

47. Ibid.

48. Chadwick. *The Hybrid Media System.*

49. Gainous and Wagner. *Tweeting to Power.*; Parmelee and Bichard. *Politics and the Twitter Revolution.*

9

"Going Public" in the Age of Twitter and Mistrust of the Media

Donald Trump's 2016 Presidential Campaign

Peter L. Francia

Real-estate mogul and billionaire celebrity Donald Trump announced his entry into the 2016 presidential election on June 16, 2015, from Trump Tower on Fifth Avenue in New York City. At the time of this announcement, few political commentators gave Trump, a candidate with no previous elected political experience and a reputation for generating controversy for making inflammatory comments, much chance of winning the presidency. As one early account of his presidential campaign concluded, "Donald Trump isn't really running for president; he's running to make more money and enhance a brand that's bigger than his real-estate holdings and golf courses."[1]

Months later, after Trump upended conventional wisdom by capturing the Republican Party's presidential nomination, most experts continued to doubt whether he could win the presidency by defeating the Democratic Party's presidential nominee, Hillary Clinton, in the general election. A headline from *Slate* confidently predicted, "Donald Trump Isn't Going to Be President."[2] An article in *Salon* went further, boldly proclaiming that Trump was "more likely to lose [to Clinton] in a historic rout than he is to win the White House."[3]

However, on November 8, 2016, Trump's presidential campaign stunned its many critics and doubters by winning the key battleground states of Florida, Wisconsin, Michigan, and Pennsylvania—all states that then-president, Democrat Barack Obama, had won four years earlier. When members of the Electoral College cast their votes a month later in December, Trump's presidential victory was official with 304 votes to Clinton's 227. This surprising result, or what *The Washington Post* called a "cataclysmic, history-making upset,"[4] forced many political observers to theorize afterward about what happened.[5]

The purpose of this chapter is to shed some light on how Trump was able to defy the odds. To be clear from the outset, this chapter's intent is *not* to make any definitive causal claims, but rather to offer a descriptive account and summary of events that may have contributed to Trump's victory. Specifically, this chapter focuses on Trump's unconventional public outreach and campaign communication efforts. As the pages that follow will discuss, the Trump campaign did not follow the usual approach of reaching a mass audience through thirty-second campaign spots. Instead, the Trump campaign opted to "go public"—an effort that political scientist Samuel Kernell explained as a "strategy whereby a president promotes himself and his policies . . . by appealing to the American public for support."[6] Although Kernell applied his theory to governing, this chapter borrows some of the underlying concepts from "going public" to Trump's presidential campaign.

Notably, the central thesis presented in this chapter is that Trump was able to wage a surprisingly effective presidential campaign through a two-fold approach that relied on (1) generating controversy, especially through the 140-character social network, Twitter, and (2) attacking journalists, the media, and independent fact-checking reports. To provide some support for this two-part argument, this chapter first confirms empirically that Trump indeed generated extensive free media coverage that reached a mass audience. Next, using polling data, it shows further that Trump supporters were untrusting of mainstream media outlets, including conservative-leaning newspapers such as *The Wall Street Journal*, and even fact-checking itself from journalists. Taken together, this chapter concludes that Trump could "go public" and reach a mass audience with his message virtually cost free—both in terms of actual money and in terms of any impact that negative media reports might have had on his support from voters.

GOING PUBLIC, TRUMP STYLE

As previously noted, political scientist Samuel Kernell first used the phrase "going public" to describe a president who made direct appeals to voters as part of a larger effort to pressure members of Congress to pass legislation that the administration favored.[7] Kernell argued that, under divided government, a president often could not bargain effectively with leaders in the opposition party, and was thereby forced into making direct appeals to the public to generate momentum for the administration's legislative agenda and priorities. This theory contrasted with previous ones, such as Richard Neustadt's "bargaining president" in which the president plays the "insider game" by working cooperatively with key leaders in Congress to advance the administration's policy interests.[8] On the surface, Kernell's theoretical model is directly relevant to governing; however, campaigning for presidential office can involve insider bargaining and outsider strategies much like battles over legislation.

In the case of Trump, his outsider status, combined with his impolitic temperament, made him an exceptionally risky candidate for elected officials and party leaders to support, making it difficult for Trump to negotiate any traditional insider bargaining deals (e.g., endorsements and campaign assistance from a prominent politician in a key state in exchange for a cabinet position in the administration). Indeed, early endorsements from key Republican officials did not go to Trump (see Table 9.1). In the so-called "endorsement derby," typically a strong predictor of the candidate who will ultimately emerge from the presidential nomination process,[9] Trump trailed all of his top opponents.

In addition, Trump also fell behind his Republican rivals in early fundraising totals. Including funds raised by the candidate's campaign and allied Super PACs, Jeb Bush, the former governor of Florida and brother of former president George W. Bush, topped the Republican field, followed by Senators Ted Cruz of Texas and Marco Rubio of Florida. Trump ranked ninth. Bush further shattered fundraising records for the first quarter of the 2015 reporting period, amassing a total of $114 million from his principal campaign organization and his allied Super PAC.[10] Perhaps not surprisingly, political prediction markets in August of 2015 had Bush as the favorite to win the Republican presidential nomination. Predict-Wise, which aggregates the probabilities from various political prediction markets, had Bush leading all Republicans with a 40 percent chance of winning the nomination compared to only a 14 percent probability of victory for Trump.[11]

Table 9.1. The Invisible Primary and the Initial Long Odds of the Trump Campaign

Candidate	Rank: National Endorsements	Rank: Money Raised
Jeb Bush	1	1
Marco Rubio	2	3
Ted Cruz	3	2
Rand Paul	4	6
Chris Christie	5	8
Carly Fiorina	8	5
John Kasich	7	7
Ben Carson	10	4
Mike Huckabee	5	10
Donald Trump	10	9

Note: Rankings above reflect where candidates stood before the first votes were cast in the 2016 primary season.
Source: The New York Times, "Who's Winning the Presidential Campaign," http://www.nytimes.com/interactive/2016/us/elections/presidential-candidates-dashboard.html.

Unable to find leverage in the "insider game," Trump, much like a new president who lacks strong Capitol Hill connections to bargain behind closed doors on legislation, was forced to play the "outsider game." In this outsider game, direct appeals to the public become necessary to harness political power.

However, for a typical presidential candidate, especially one without strong institutional support, "going public" is unlikely to garner much attention from the press given that other more prominent "insider" candidates are also competing for press coverage.[12] Trump, however, was different in an important respect—he had unusually high name recognition for an outsider seeking the presidency. Many Americans were already well familiar with Trump, who gained fame decades earlier as a flamboyant real-estate and casino mogul, and later as an outspoken critic of President Barack Obama. Trump was also known to most Americans as the fiery host of two nationally televised programs, *The Apprentice* and *The Celebrity Apprentice* (which aired with Trump from 2004 to 2015). Indeed, a Gallup tracking poll in July of 2015 showed Trump leading all of his rivals for the Republican presidential nomination, with a name recognition rate of 92 percent compared to 81 percent for Bush, 66 percent for Cruz, and 64 percent for Rubio.[13]

Trump also succeeded in attracting free news coverage by making public comments that were often deliberately designed to entice journalists with controversial statements. In no less than Trump's very first speech announcing his presidential candidacy, he drew widespread criticism for comments he made concerning illegal Mexican immigration into the United States:

> When Mexico sends its people, they're not sending their best. They're not sending you. They're not sending you. They're sending people that have lots of problems, and they're bringing those problems with us. They're bringing drugs. They're bringing crime. They're rapists. And some, I assume, are good people."[14]

Not long after making those comments, Trump was embroiled in controversy again for statements that he made about Senator John McCain, a former Republican presidential nominee and military veteran who endured torture as a prisoner of war in North Vietnam. After an earlier give-and-take exchange in which McCain had criticized Trump publicly, Trump responded by telling an audience at the Family Leadership Summit in Ames, Iowa, "He [McCain] is not a war hero. He was a war hero because he was captured. I like people who weren't captured."[15]

Trump even managed to generate significant controversy during the first televised Republican presidential debate. In the debate's opening minutes, Megyn Kelly of Fox News brought up comments that Trump had made in his past in which he had referred to some women as "fat pigs, dogs, slobs, and disgusting animals."[16] Trump angrily dismissed the question at the debate, and then later commented in an interview with Don Lemon of CNN about Kelly, "You could see there was blood coming out of her eyes. Blood coming out of her wherever."[17] Erick Erickson, editor of the conservative website RedState.com, quickly condemned Trump's comments and disinvited him to a RedState event. Not to be outdone, Trump fired back at Erickson, calling him "a total loser" with a "history of supporting establishment losers in failed campaigns."[18]

Trump's coarse language and penchant for generating controversy received considerable criticism. The editorial board of *USA Today* referred to Trump's public statements and tweets as "unpresidential" outbursts.[19] Steve Schmidt, a senior adviser to the McCain presidential campaign in 2008, called Trump "a cancer on the Republican Party and the conservative movement."[20] Likewise, conservative commentator Charles Krauthammer dismissed Trump as a "rodeo clown."[21] Fellow conservative columnist George Will offered perhaps the bluntest assessment, commenting that Trump often sounded like "the guy nursing his sixth beer at the end of a bar in Duluth."[22]

Yet, despite the criticism, Trump's words were generating considerable media attention, and his poll numbers eventually rose to the top of the Republican field. Trump also experienced significant gains in Twitter followers. In January of 2016, Trump commanded a Twitter following (@realDonaldTrump) of 5.5 million people that he saw gradually increase during the months of the Republican nomination contest all the way to

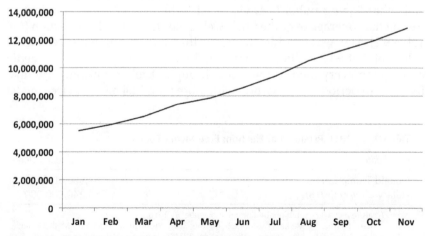

Figure 9.1.   Donald Trump's Twitter Followers, 2016
Source: MediaQuant, https://www.mediaquant.net.

13 million followers by the time of the November general election (see Figure 9.1).

Through Twitter, Trump seemed to relish in mocking his opponents. In one memorable tweet in February 2016, Trump attacked Jeb Bush: "Wow, Jeb Bush, whose campaign is a total disaster, had to bring in mommy to take a slap at me."[23] This comment came shortly after Bush's mother, former First Lady Barbara Bush, told CNN in an interview that she was "sick of" Trump. After Trump's tweet, a *USA Today* headline read, "Trump: Jeb Bush 'had to bring in mommy to take a slap at me.'"[24]

Trump ultimately defeated Bush and all of the Republicans vying for the nomination. In May of 2016, he surpassed the 1,237 delegate threshold required to win the Republican presidential nomination. Yet, while candidates often moderate themselves when the general election phase begins,[25] Trump continued to press forward in much the same manner that helped him win the Republican nomination. On Cinco de Mayo, Trump's controversial "taco bowl" tweet created considerable discussion. In the tweet, Trump posted a picture of himself eating a taco bowl at his Trump Tower desk with a posting that read, "Happy #CincoDeMayo! The best taco bowls are made in Trump Tower Grill. I love Hispanics!"[26]

The tweet not only reached Trump supporters, but also drew the attention of many of his sharpest critics, including a re-tweet from comedian Samantha Bee: "The best taco bowls are made by immigrants who resent a rich p---k calling them rapists. Love inauthentic Mexican!"[27] Over the course of the month, the controversy would help Trump generate nearly $195 million in free media attention from Twitter.[28]

Overall, Trump's tweets, numerous controversial public statements, and other "going public" activities led to an estimated $4.96 billion in free media coverage over the final twelve months of the 2016 election (see Table 9.2). This was considerably more than Hillary Clinton's free media value total at $3.24 billion. Moreover, Trump led Clinton in free media coverage in every month from June through October, finishing the final five-month period of the election with more than $2.4 billion in free media

Table 9.2.   2016 Presidential Election: Free Media Totals

Candidate	Free Media Value
Donald Trump (2016)	$4,960,000,000
Hillary Clinton (2016)	$3,240,000,000

Note: Totals reflect a 12-month period through November 1, 2016.
Source: Mary Harris, "A Media Post-Mortem on the 2016 Presidential Election," MediaQuant, November 14, 2016, http://www.mediaquant.net/2016/11/a-media-post-mortem-on-the-2016-presidential-election.

value compared to just over $2 billion in media value for Clinton.[29] Trump was also the most Googled candidate in the 2016 presidential election and received the most mentions of any candidate on Facebook.[30]

This undoubtedly helped Trump offset some of the advantages that Clinton possessed that had made her such a strong favorite to win the general election. Of note, Clinton raised considerably more money than Trump and had built what most observers saw as the superior ground organization. Clinton and her allied super PACs raised $1.2 billion compared to Trump's $647 million.[31] Clinton also used her funds to spend considerably more than Trump did on ads for the so-called "air war" in battleground states during the closing weeks of the election.[32] Ground war totals heavily favored Clinton as well. Democrats had 5,138 staffers in 15 battleground states for Clinton compared to the Republicans' 1,409 staffers in 16 battleground states for Trump.[33]

Indeed, forecasting models made Clinton the overwhelming favorite (although a handful of political scientists did favor Trump).[34] *The Huffington Post's* polling team gave Clinton a 98 percent probability of defeating Trump,[35] whereas Nate Silver's vaunted FiveThirtyEight.com website pegged Clinton with a 71.6 percent probability of defeating Trump at 9 a.m. on Election Day.[36] These forecasts were also in line with the dominant media narrative that Clinton would defeat Trump with relative ease due to changing demographics. Clinton's likely coalition of minorities, college-educated white professionals, suburban women, and young voters were expected to make it all but impossible for Trump to win in states where Mitt Romney, the 2012 Republican presidential nominee, had lost.[37] Most analysts agreed that Trump would need to come close to "running the table" in the competitive, "swing" states that ultimately determine the winner of the presidential election.[38] In the words of one commentator, "Barring a historic failure of polling . . . Hillary Clinton will be elected the 45th president of the United States."[39]

Of course, those predictions proved to be incorrect. Clinton's traditional advantages were ultimately outweighed by Trump's ability to dominate news coverage. As one political observer summarized, "[Trump] ran his campaign like a soap opera, deliberately creating new controversies with his uncouth comments. Just as media interest in one Trumpism crested, he'd supply a new Trumpism to replace it, riding it through the press storm until it was depleted and was in need of replacement itself."[40] Another added, "The medium made the man—much as radio won the presidency for Franklin Roosevelt and television boosted John Kennedy, social media allowed Trump and his allies to drive the narrative."[41]

Yet, while Trump attracted considerable news coverage by "going public" with his controversial tweets and public statements, his free media exposure suffered from one noticeable problem: reports about

Trump were more likely to be negative than positive in tone.[42] To deal with the negative reports, there was a second critically important aspect to Trump's larger strategy. He aggressively attacked the media. On the campaign trail and on Twitter, Trump routinely lashed out at reporters and journalists as "sleazy," "extremely dishonest," "unfair," "not good people," and "dopes."[43]

Indeed, as the next section discusses, Trump made clear throughout his campaign that the media were the opposition. Under this frame, Trump reduced any negative press stories against him as proof of the very media bias he claimed was deliberately designed to help elect Clinton. In Trump's own words, "The reporters collaborate and conspire directly with the Clinton campaign on helping her win the election."[44] As one columnist summarized, "Trump . . . established the ground rules: He and the media were enemies. 'Reporting' wasn't any different from an attack ad."[45]

TRUMP SUPPORTERS AND THE "CROOKED" MEDIA

Perhaps the best illustration of Trump's anti-media attack message came with just a month before Election Day when the campaign had been left reeling from a major scandal. On October 7, 2016, *The Washington Post* released a hot-microphone recording of Trump in 2005 speaking off-air to *Access Hollywood* host Billy Bush in which Trump describes making sexual advances towards women. On the recording, Trump says to Bush, "And when you're a star, they [women] let you do it. You can do anything. . . . Grab them by the p---y. You can do anything."[46]

Following the release of this story, several high-profile Republicans, including Senator John Thune of South Dakota, former Secretary of State Condoleezza Rice, and former Utah governor Jon Huntsman, made the unprecedented call for Trump, their own party's presidential nominee, to withdraw in the final weeks of the presidential race.[47] Even Trump's running mate, Mike Pence, released a statement highly critical of Trump's comments, which read, "As a husband and father, I was offended by the words and actions described by Donald Trump in the eleven-year-old video released yesterday. I do not condone his remarks and cannot defend them."[48]

Trump, however, was undeterred by the criticism, and responded by ripping into the news media on Twitter: "This election is being rigged by the media pushing false and unsubstantiated charges, and outright lies in order to elect Crooked Hillary!"[49] Trump continued the attacks at a campaign rally in Greensboro, North Carolina, "Our media is indeed sick, and it's making our country sick, and we're going to stop it."[50]

Similar attacks from Trump against the media were commonplace throughout the election. At one gathering in St. Augustine, Florida, Trump riled up the crowd by exclaiming that the media were "almost as crooked as Hillary" and then added, "They may be more crooked than Hillary, because without the media, she would be nothing. They're disgraceful."[51] Trump even attacked polls showing Clinton ahead as "phony" and fact-checking reports in the media as "crooked as hell."[52] At his campaign rallies, Trump's most ardent supporters applauded his attacks against the credibility of the press. Within these crowds, it was not uncommon to hear chants like "Tell the truth," and insults like "presstitutes" directed at members of Trump's traveling press corps.[53]

Yet, whether Trump's attacks against the media extended to a wider and more electorally meaningful audience requires deeper and more systematic examination. A poll from *The Economist* and YouGov conducted in mid-October 2016 allows for a broader assessment of public opinion. It asked Trump and Clinton supporters the following question: "How trustworthy do you rate the following news organizations: *The New York Times, The Washington Post, The Wall Street Journal, CNN, Fox News, MS-NBC, The Huffington Post,* and *Breitbart?*"

As the results in Table 9.3 reveal, significant differences separated Trump and Clinton supporters on this question. With respect to the trustworthiness of *The New York Times*, 79 percent of Clinton supporters rated the newspaper as trustworthy or very trustworthy compared to a mere 9 percent of Trump supporters. These patterns were similar for *The Washington Post*: 67 percent of Clinton supporters rated the newspaper as trustworthy or very trustworthy compared to just 10 percent of Trump supporters.

Given the liberal leanings of both newspapers' editorial boards, greater support from Clinton voters is hardly surprising. However, the intense lack of trust from Trump supporters warrants some attention. Some 70 percent of Trump voters reported *The New York Times* to be untrustworthy or very untrustworthy. For *The Washington Post*, 65 percent of Trump voters reported that they believed the newspaper to be untrustworthy or very untrustworthy. During the election, both newspapers did investigative pieces critical of Trump's handling of the Trump Foundation and his refusal to release his income tax filings, to name just two issues. Yet, despite the reporting, these investigations into Trump never had a significant impact on public opinion. Trump routinely hammered away at the legitimacy of *The New York Times* and *The Washington Post*, and in the end, his supporters remained dubious of reporting from both major newspapers.

Table 9.3 also shows a low level of trust among Trump voters towards the conservative-leaning *Wall Street Journal* (*WSJ*). Just 23 percent of

Table 9.3.   Public Opinion: Trustworthiness of News Organizations

News Organization	Trump Voters	Clinton Voters
The New York Times		
Very trustworthy/trustworthy	9%	79%
Neither	21%	16%
Very untrustworthy/untrustworthy	70%	5%
N	336	471
The Washington Post		
Very trustworthy/trustworthy	10%	67%
Neither	26%	25%
Very untrustworthy/untrustworthy	65%	8%
N	335	472
The Wall Street Journal		
Very trustworthy/trustworthy	23%	63%
Neither	35%	28%
Very untrustworthy/untrustworthy	43%	9%
N	337	470
CNN		
Very trustworthy/trustworthy	10%	69%
Neither	14%	22%
Very untrustworthy/untrustworthy	75%	10%
N	337	472
Fox News		
Very trustworthy/trustworthy	59%	21%
Neither	23%	15%
Very untrustworthy/untrustworthy	19%	64%
N	338	470
MSNBC		
Very trustworthy/trustworthy	10%	61%
Neither	17%	30%
Very untrustworthy/untrustworthy	73%	10%
N	339	474
Huffington Post		
Very trustworthy/trustworthy	9%	56%
Neither	33%	37%
Very untrustworthy/untrustworthy	58%	7%
N	340	469
Breitbart		
Very trustworthy/trustworthy	34%	7%
Neither	44%	48%
Very untrustworthy/untrustworthy	22%	44%
N	339	470

Source: The Economist/YouGov Poll, October 15–18, 2016
Note: Differences between Trump and Clinton voters are statistically significant at $p < .01$ using chi-squared tests.

Trump supporters report that they found the reporting in the *WSJ* to be trustworthy or very trustworthy compared to a significantly higher 63 percent of Clinton voters. These numbers are somewhat surprising given that the *WSJ* received some criticism for its "soft approach" in covering Trump.[54]

Among the cable news networks, Trump supporters were most trusting of Fox News (59%) when compared to CNN (10%) and MSNBC (10%). Given that Trump frequently clashed with CNN and given MSNBC's nightly lineup of anti-Trump hosts, these results certainly comport with expectations. However, the Fox News numbers bear closer scrutiny. While Fox News rates highest in trust among Trump supporters, a healthy segment, roughly two in five of Trump supporters, is either neutral or does not trust the reporting from Fox News—a source long regarded as "fair and balanced" to conservatives.[55]

Nonetheless, Fox News was the dominant information vehicle for Trump supporters. A separate poll from the Pew Research Center showed that 40 percent of Trump voters named Fox News as their main source for information about the 2016 campaign. This was followed by just 8 percent who named CNN, 7 percent who named Facebook, 6 percent who named NBC, and 5 percent who named local television.[56] By comparison, the top five sources for Clinton voters were CNN (18%), MSNBC (9%), Facebook (8%), local television (8%), and NPR (7%).[57]

Finally, Trump supporters report little trust in the left-leaning *Huffington Post* (9%), but some trust (34%) in the right-wing website *Breitbart*. The Breitbart results are noteworthy only because of the controversy that has surrounded its news reporting. *Breitbart*, for example, has run such headlines as "Birth control makes women unattractive and crazy" and "Science proves it: Fat-shaming works."[58] Despite its tabloid-style reputation, *Breitbart* ranked ahead of every source in the poll, with the exception of Fox News, among Trump supporters. Of course, it bears mentioning that Trump did hire Steve Bannon, who served as executive chair of *Breitbart News*, in August of 2016 to be the campaign's chief executive. (Bannon now serves President Trump as White House chief strategist.) Results from the Pew Research Center also show that a healthy 11 percent of Trump voters reported *Breitbart* as a source from which they regularly relied upon for their campaign news during the 2016 election.[59]

Trump voters were also significantly less trusting of fact-checking by journalists and experts (see Table 9.4). A mere 1 percent of Trump voters expressed a "great deal" of trust in fact-checking by journalists and experts compared to 39 percent for Clinton voters. Likewise, an exceptionally high percentage of Trump supporters, 77 percent, expressed "not much" trust in fact-checking or "none at all" compared to just 11 percent of Clinton voters. These numbers provide good reason to believe that

Table 9.4. Public Opinion: Trustworthiness of Fact-Checking by Journalists and Experts

	Trump Voters	Clinton Voters
A great deal	1%	39%
A moderate amount	22%	50%
Not much	54%	8%
Not at all	23%	3%
N	342	476

Source: The Economist/YouGov Poll, October 15–18, 2016
Note: Differences between Trump and Clinton voters are statistically significant at p < .01 using chi-squared tests.

Trump supporters were very likely to dismiss any negative news coverage about Trump. In such an environment, the old saying—"not all buzz is good buzz"—may not have applied to the Trump campaign.

The results in Tables 9.5 and 9.6 further show that Trump voters perceived the national press as unfair and the quality of the media's news coverage as having gotten worse in its coverage of the 2016 election. As the results in Table 9.5 reveal, a majority of Trump voters believed the national press was "very fair" to Hillary Clinton (56%), whereas 66 percent claimed that the national press was "not at all" fair to Donald Trump. The percentages were radically different among Clinton supporters: 17 percent claimed that the national press was "very fair" to Hillary

Table 9.5. Public Opinion: Fairness of the National Press in Its Treatment of Trump and Clinton

	Trump Voters	Clinton Voters
Fair treatment of Hillary Clinton		
Very fair	56%	17%
More fair than unfair	31	23
About equal	9	31
More unfair than fair	1	23
Very unfair	3	5
N	341	474
Fair treatment of Donald Trump		
Very fair	1%	29%
More fair than unfair	–	36
About equal	4	28
More unfair than fair	30	5
Very unfair	66	1
N	340	471

Source: The Economist/YouGov Poll, October 15–18, 2016
Note: Differences between Trump and Clinton voters are statistically significant at p < .01 using chi-squared tests.

Table 9.6.   Public Opinion of News Media: Better or Worse Than Usual in 2016?

	Trump Voters	Clinton Voters
Better than usual	3%	18%
About the same as usual	21	39
Worse than usual	75	39
Don't Know	1	5
N	415	495

Source: The Economist/YouGov Poll, October 7–8, 2016
Note: Differences between Trump and Clinton voters are statistically significant at p < .01 using chi-squared tests.

Clinton; just 1 percent claimed that the national press was "not at all" fair to Donald Trump. Similarly, a remarkably high percentage of Trump supporters (75%) believed that the news media was "worse than usual" in its coverage of the 2016 election compared to 39% of Clinton supporters (see Table 9.6).

Taken together, the results in each of the tables make one overriding point clear: Trump supporters were far less trusting of media sources and fact-checking. They also believed strongly, as Trump argued throughout the campaign, that the national press was unfairly biased in favor of Hillary Clinton. This dynamic may explain, at least to some degree, how Trump was able to survive what appeared to be several fatal scandals during his campaign. Absent the ability of the media to serve as an effective check on Trump's often controversial statements and claims, both on Twitter and in his public speeches, the Trump campaign could effectively "go public" without any fear of reprisals for saying almost anything.

CONCLUSION: A REVOLUTIONARY CAMPAIGN?

Donald Trump's campaign undeniably defied the odds and upended conventional wisdom about what it takes to wage a winning presidential campaign. The old way of playing the game, which involved insider bargaining to win endorsements from prominent officials, raising large sums of money, saturating the airwaves with advertisements, and organizing a ground game gave way to a new style of campaigning for president that involved "going public" through Twitter, generating controversy and free media with inflammatory comments, and then discrediting the media to mitigate any negative stories.

While Trump's victory would suggest that this was an effective strategy, it is not entirely clear if Trump was trying to drum up coverage deliberately through controversial statements, or if his controversial statements and tweets were simply an extension of his contentious personality.

Whether a deliberate strategy or not, Trump found a receptive audience in his attacks against news organizations, fact-checkers, and the media as a whole. These attacks certainly played to a conservative audience that has long been skeptical of the media.[60] A Gallup poll also showed trust in the mass media reaching an all-time low during the heart of the 2016 election, hinting that Trump's persistent attacks against the media may have had some impact.[61] This allowed Trump to not only reach a large audience through Twitter and through the free media coverage that his tweets often generated, but also to make statements and claims that effectively could go unchallenged among his supporters, and perhaps among some undecided voters as well.

Of course, this is only one of several explanations that might have contributed to Trump's surprising victory. Some post-election analysis[62] points to the final days of the campaign when FBI Director James Comey announced on October 28 that he was re-opening the FBI's investigation into Hillary Clinton's use of handling classified documents over a private e-mail server while she served as the nation's Secretary of State—a case that Comey had previously closed in August. Although Comey would close the case again on November 6 without any criminal charges against Clinton, the Trump campaign experienced some late gains in the polls.[63]

Still, Trump's hostile approach to press relations cannot be ignored. Indeed, this approach has extended into the first weeks of the Trump presidency. Just days after taking office, Trump claimed that he drew the largest inauguration crowd in history, that three to five million illegal votes were cast in the 2016 election, that the U.S. murder rate was the highest in 47 years, and that the press had "covered up" terrorist attacks. When the press correctly reported that none of these claims were true or supported by evidence, Trump returned to denigrating the media, calling them "among the most dishonest human beings on earth" and tweeting that they are "the enemy of the American people."[64] With no signs of Trump's attacks on the media likely to abate, it seems fair to conclude that a Trump re-election campaign in 2020 could look very similar, with controversial tweets and attacks on the media playing a central role in any communications and outreach strategy.

NOTES

1. Charles Gasparino, "Trump's Running—But the Joke's on You," *The Daily Beast*, June 22, 2015, http://www.thedailybeast.com/articles/2015/06/22/how-much-is-trump-is-really-worth.html.

2. Jamelle Bouie, "Donald Trump Isn't Going to Be President," *Slate*, May 4, 2016, http://www.slate.com/articles/news_and_politics/politics/2016/05/donald_trump_isn_t_going_to_be_president.html.

3. Anthony J. Gaughan, "Donald Trump Will Not Be President: History, Polling Data and Demographics All Point to a Single Result," *Salon*, May 5, 2016, http://www.salon.com/2016/05/05/donald_trump_will_not_be_president_history_polling_data_and_demographics_all_point_to_a_single_result_partner/.

4. Chris Cillizza, "President-Elect Donald Trump's Cataclysmic, History-Making Upset," *The Washington Post*, November 9, 2016, https://www.washingtonpost.com/news/the-fix/wp/2016/11/09/how-donald-trump-pulled-off-an-upset-of-cataclysmic-historic-proportions/.

5. For example, see Don Hazen, Kali Holloway, Jenny Pierson, Jan Friel, Les Leopold, Steve Rosenfeld, Michael Arria, Ilana Novick, and Janet Allon, "Why Donald Trump Won—and How Hillary Clinton Lost: 13 Theories Explain the Stunning Election," *Salon*, December 26, 2016, http://www.salon.com/2016/12/26/13-theories-on-why-trump-won-and-how-clinton-lost_partner/.

6. Samuel Kernell, *Going Public: New Strategies of Presidential Leadership*, 3rd edition (Washington, DC: CQ Press, 1997), 2.

7. Samuel Kernell, *Going Public: New Strategies of Presidential Leadership* (Washington, DC: CQ Press, 1986).

8. Richard E. Neustadt, *Presidential Power: The Politics of Leadership from FDR to Carter* (New York: John Wiley and Sons, 1980).

9. Marty Cohen, David Karol, Hans Noel, and John Zaller, *The Party Decides: Presidential Nominations Before and After Reform* (Chicago: University of Chicago Press, 2008); see also Lynn Vavrek, "2016 Endorsements: How and Why They Matter," *The New York Times*, July 29, 2015, http://www.nytimes.com/2015/07/30/upshot/2016-endorsements-how-and-why-they-matter.html.

10. Ed O'Keefe and Matea Gold, "Jeb Bush and Allied Super PAC Raise an Unprecedented $114 Million War Chest," *The Washington Post*, July 9, 2015, https://www.washingtonpost.com/politics/jeb-bush-and-allied-super-pac-raise-an-unprecedented-114-million-war-chest/2015/07/09/652e1206–2651–11e5-b72c-2b7d516e1e0e_story.html.

11. *Reuters*, "Prediction Markets: Jeb Bush Likely to Beat Donald Trump for 2016 Republican Nomination," *Newsweek*, August 26, 2015, http://www.newsweek.com/jeb-bush-donald-trump-prediction-markets-polls-366122.

12. Christopher F. Arterton, *Media Politics: The News Strategies of Presidential Campaigns* (Lexington, MA: Heath, 1984). See also Audrey A. Haynes, Julianne F. Flowers, and Paul-Henri Gurian, "Getting the Message Out Early: Candidate Strategy and the Invisible Primary," *Political Research Quarterly*, 55 (2002): 633–52.

13. Andrew Dugan, "Among Republicans, GOP Candidates Better Known Than Liked," Gallup, July 24, 2015, http://www.gallup.com/poll/184337/among-republicans-gop-candidates-better-known-liked.aspx.

14. Michelle Ye Hee Lee, "Donald Trump's False Comments Connecting Mexican Immigrants and Crime," *The Washington Post*, July 8, 2015, https://www.washingtonpost.com/news/fact-checker/wp/2015/07/08/donald-trumps-false-comments-connecting-mexican-immigrants-and-crime.

15. Ben Schreckinger, "Trump Attacks McCain: 'I Like People Who Weren't Captured,'" *Politico*, July 18, 2015, http://www.politico.com/story/2015/07/trump-attacks-mccain-i-like-people-who-werent-captured-120317.

16. Karen Tumulty and Philip Rucker, "Trump Roils First Debate Among GOP Contenders," *The Washington Post*, August 6, 2015, https://www.washingtonpost.com/politics/donald-trump-dominates-raucous-republican-debate/2015/08/06/b8a5f0e6–3c79–11e5–8e98–115a3cf7d7ae_story.html.

17. Holly Yan, "Donald Trump's 'Blood' Comment about Megyn Kelly Draws Outrage," *CNN*, August 8, 2015, http://www.cnn.com/2015/08/08/politics/donald-trump-cnn-megyn-kelly-comment/.

18. Ibid.

19. *USA Today*, "Donald Trump's Unpresidential Campaign: Our View," August 31, 2015, http://www.usatoday.com/story/opinion/2015/08/31/donald-trump-megyn-kelly-jorge-ramos-attacks-editorials-debates/71429356/.

20. Dan Balz, "Trump's Attack on McCain Marks a Turning Point for Him—and the GOP," *The Washington Post*, July 19, 2015, https://www.washingtonpost.com/politics/trumps-attack-on-mccain-marks-a-turning-point-for-him--and-the-gop/2015/07/19/92759254–2e51–11e5–97ae-30a30cca95d7_story.html.

21. Al Weaver, "'Not Serious Politics': Krauthammer Dismisses 'Rodeo Clown' Donald Trump," *The Daily Caller*, July 6, 2015, http://dailycaller.com/2015/07/06/not-serious-politics-krauthammer-dismisses-rodeo-clown-donald-trump/.

22. Ibid.

23. Cooper Allen, "Trump: Jeb Bush 'Had to Bring in Mommy to Take a Slap at Me,'" *USA Today*, February 6, 2015, http://www.usatoday.com/story/news/politics/onpolitics/2016/02/06/jeb-bush-donald-trump/79922352/.

24. Ibid.

25. George C. Edwards and Stephen J. Wayne, *Presidential Leadership: Politics and Policymaking*, 9th ed. (Stamford, CT: Cengage, 2014).

26. Sophie Tatum, "Pictured with Taco Bowl, Trump Proclaims, 'I Love Hispanics!'" *CNN*, May 6, 2016, http://www.cnn.com/2016/05/05/politics/donald-trump-taco-bowl-cinco-de-mayo/.

27. Ed Mazza, "Donald Trump's Taco Bowl Hilariously Backfires," *The Huffington Post*, May 6, 2016, http://www.huffingtonpost.com/entry/donald-trump-taco-bowl_us_572bf20be4b096e9f090e1c5.

28. Emily Stewart, "Donald Trump Rode $5 Billion in Free Media to the White House," *The Street*, November 20, 2016, https://www.thestreet.com/story/13896916/1/donald-trump-rode-5-billion-in-free-media-to-the-white-house.html.

29. Peter L. Francia, "Free Media and Twitter in the 2016 Presidential Election: The Unconventional Campaign of Donald Trump," *Social Science Computer Review*, forthcoming.

30. Laeeq Khan, "Trump Won Thanks to Social Media," *The Hill*, November 15, 2016, http://thehill.com/blogs/pundits-blog/technology/306175-trump-won-thanks-to-social-media.

31. Bill Allison, Mira Rojanasakul, Brittany Harris, and Cedric Sam, "Tracking the 2016 Presidential Money Race," *Bloomberg*, December 9, 2016, https://www.bloomberg.com/politics/graphics/2016-presidential-campaign-fundraising/.

32. Ken Goldstein, John McCormick, and Andre Tartar, "Candidates Make Last Ditch Ad Spending Push Across 14-State Electoral Map," *Bloomberg*, Novem-

ber 2, 2016, https://www.bloomberg.com/politics/graphics/2016-presidential-campaign-tv-ads/.

33. Reid Wilson and Joe Disipio, "Clinton Holds Huge Ground Game Advantage Over Team Trump," *The Hill,* October 22, 2016, http://thehill.com/campaign/302231-clinton-holds-huge-ground-game-advantage-over-team-trump.

34. Helmut Norpoth, "Primary Model Predicts Trump Victory," *PS: Political Science & Politics,* 49 (2016): 655–58. See also Alan I. Abramowitz, "Will Time for Change Mean Time for Trump?" *PS: Political Science & Politics,* 49 (2016): 659–60.

35. Natalie Jackson, "HuffPost Forecasts Hillary Clinton Will Win 323 Electoral Votes," *Huffington Post,* November 7, 2016, http://www.huffingtonpost.com/entry/polls-hillary-clinton-win_us_5821074ce4b0e80b02cc2a94.

36. FiveThirtyEight.com, "Who Will Win the Presidency?" November 8, 2016, https://projects.fivethirtyeight.com/2016-election-forecast/.

37. Philip Bump, "With Nearly Every Demographic, Hillary Clinton is Outperforming Barack Obama in 2012," *The Washington Post,* July 7, 2016, https://www.washingtonpost.com/news/the-fix/wp/2016/07/07/with-nearly-every-demographic-hillary-clinton-is-outperforming-barack-obama-in-2012/. See also David Byler, "Will Demographics Sink Donald Trump?" *RealClearPolitics,* March 28, 2016, http://www.realclearpolitics.com/articles/2016/03/28/will_demographics_sink_donald_trump_130095.html; and Peter Fenn, "Why Trump Won't Win," *U.S. News & World Report,* March 21, 2016, http://www.usnews.com/opinion/blogs/peter-fenn/articles/2016-03-21/trump-has-deep-demographic-problems-come-the-2016-general-election.

38. Alex Seitz-Wald, "Donald Trump's Ugly Electoral Map," *MSNBC,* May 5, 2016, http://www.msnbc.com/msnbc/donald-trumps-ugly-electoral-map. See also David Catanese, "Donald Trump's Electoral Map to Victory," *U.S. News & World Report,* September 15, 2016, http://www.usnews.com/news/articles/2016-09-15/donald-trumps-electoral-map-to-victory.

39. Robert Schlesinger, "Done Deal," *U.S. News & World Report,* October 28, 2016, http://www.usnews.com/opinion/thomas-jefferson-street/articles/2016-10-28/7-reasons-why-hillary-clintons-win-over-donald-trump-is-a-done-deal.

40. Jack Shafer, "How Trump Took Over the Media by Fighting It," *Politico,* November 5, 2016, http://www.politico.com/magazine/story/2016/11/2016-election-trump-media-takeover-coverage-214419.

41. Gregory Krieg, "How Did Trump Win? Here Are 24 Theories," *CNN,* November 10, 2016, http://www.cnn.com/2016/11/10/politics/why-donald-trump-won/.

42. Thomas E. Patterson, "News Coverage of the 2016 National Conventions: Negative News, Lacking Context," *Harvard Kennedy School Shorenstein Center on Media, Politics, and Public Policy,* July 11, 2016, https://shorensteincenter.org/news-coverage-2016-national-conventions/.

43. Shafer, "How Trump Took Over the Media by Fighting It."

44. Donald J. Trump, "Remarks on the Clinton Campaign of Destruction," Press release, October 13, 2016, https://www.donaldjtrump.com/press-releases/remarks-on-the-clinton-campaign-of-destruction.

45. Shafer, "How Trump Took Over the Media by Fighting It."

46. David A. Fahrenthold, "Trump Recorded Having Extremely Lewd Conversation About Women in 2005," *The Washington Post*, October 8, 2016, https://www.washingtonpost.com/politics/trump-recorded-having-extremely-lewd-conversation-about-women-in-2005/2016/10/07/3b9ce776–8cb4–11e6-bf8a-3d26847eeed4_story.html.

47. Jonathan Martin, Maggie Haberman, and Alexander Burns, "Lewd Donald Trump Tape Is a Breaking Point for Many in the G.O.P." *The New York Times*, October 8, 2016, https://www.nytimes.com/2016/10/09/us/politics/donald-trump-campaign.html.

48. Matthew Nussbaum, "Pence Says He Was 'Offended' by Trump's Remarks About Groping Women," *Politico*, October 8, 2016, http://www.politico.com/story/2016/10/pence-says-he-was-offended-by-trumps-remarks-about-groping-women-229355.

49. Jeremy Diamond and Eugene Scott, "Trump Ratchets Up 'Rigged Election' Claims, Which Pence Downplays," *CNN*, October 17, 2016, http://www.cnn.com/2016/10/15/politics/donald-trump-rigged-election-hillary-clinton/.

50. Jim Morrill and Bryan Anderson, "In NC, Trump Mocks Accuser: 'She's a Liar,'" *The Charlotte Observer*, October 14, 2016, http://www.charlotteobserver.com/news/politics-government/campaign-tracker-blog/article108260817.html.

51. Asma Khalid and Scott Detrow, "How Trump and Clinton Are Framing Their Closing Arguments," *NPR*, October 26, 2016, http://www.npr.org/2016/10/26/499321154/clinton-and-trump-the-final-sprint.

52. Ibid.

53. Shafer, "How Trump Took Over the Media by Fighting It."

54. Joe Pompeo, "*Wall Street Journal* Editor to Face Critics," *Politico*, February 8, 2017, http://www.politico.com/media/story/2017/02/gerry-baker-wall-street-journal-trump-newsroom-tensions-004928.

55. Kevin Coe, David Tewksbury, Bradley J. Bond, Kristin L. Drogos, Robert W. Porter, Ashley Yahn, and Yuanyuan Zhang, "Hostile News: Partisan Use and Perceptions of Cable News Programming," *Journal of Communication*, 58 (2008): 201–219.

56. Jeffrey Gottfried and Michael Barthel, "Trump, Clinton Voters Divided in Their Main Source for Election News," Pew Research Center, January 18, 2017, http://www.journalism.org/2017/01/18/trump-clinton-voters-divided-in-their-main-source-for-election-news/.

57. Ibid.

58. Jill Disis, "10 of Breitbart's Most Incendiary Headlines," *CNN*, November 15, 2016, http://money.cnn.com/2016/11/14/media/breitbart-incendiary-headlines/.

59. Gottfried and Barthel, "Trump, Clinton Voters Divided in Their Main Source for Election News."

60. David A. Jones, "Why Americans Don't Trust the Media: A Preliminary Analysis," *The Harvard International Journal of Press/Politics* 9 (2004): 60–75.

61. Art Swift, "Americans' Trust in Mass Media Sinks to New Low," Gallup, September 14, 2016, http://www.gallup.com/poll/195542/americans-trust-mass-media-sinks-new-low.aspx.

62. Sam Wang, "The Comey Effect," *Princeton Election Consortium*, December 10, 2016, http://election.princeton.edu/2016/12/10/the-comey-effect/.

63. Ibid. See also *RealClearPolitics*, "General Election: Trump vs. Clinton," November 7, 2016, http://www.realclearpolitics.com/epolls/2016/president/us/general_election_trump_vs_clinton-5491.html.

64. Julie Hirschfeld Davis and Matthew Rosenberg, "With False Claims, Trump Attacks Media on Turnout and Intelligence Rift," *The New York Times*, January 21, 2017, https://www.nytimes.com/2017/01/21/us/politics/trump-white-house-briefing-inauguration-crowd-size.html.

10

Late Night Talk Moves Online

Political Humor, YouTube, and the 2016 Presidential Election

Jody C Baumgartner

The Internet has played host to a wealth of political humor since its mass popularization and penetration. This is perhaps most apparent during presidential campaigns, when there seems to be an embarrassment of comedic riches centered around the race to the White House. However, the election of 2016 was a watershed election for political humor and the Internet. Many of the familiar Internet political humor names were still represented during the campaign, as were several new players. But importantly, by the summer of 2015, virtually all of the late-night television talk show hosts and comedians had a YouTube channel on which they posted short clips and vignettes. Because these men (and one woman) are the central players in the contemporary political humor environment, this had the effect of making clips from all late-night talk shows on the Internet accessible at no cost.

This development is explored in some detail in this chapter. I first provide a short overview of the evolution of the Internet as a source of political humor throughout the 2000s, focusing on the major sources of political, and in particular, campaign humor. The discussion then shifts to the campaign of 2016, where I focus on the video clips that late night television talk shows (broadcast network and cable) presented on YouTube. How political were these programs in the context of the 2016 campaign? How popular was this political content, both in general and in comparison with other content? Were either of the presidential candidates targeted more than the other? I conclude the chapter by discussing the implications of the migration of televised late night talk to YouTube in light of what we know about how political humor helps shape individuals' political understanding and engagement.

POLITICAL HUMOR ON THE INTERNET:
A BRIEF (SELECTIVE) HISTORY

It is hardly surprising to learn that political humor has long been an integral part of Internet content. Numerous articles discuss the merits and de-merits of the Internet in terms of its contribution to democratic deliberation and discourse.[1] One of the foremost theorists of humor included a chapter on online humor in a recent book, much of which dealt with political humor (in particular, jokes targeted at former president Clinton). The chapter examined content, the nature of the sites the jokes were contained on, and who seemed to be reading them.[2] Another study that drew on a sample of 400 jokes found that online joke content mirrored that of jokes not found online. They further found that approximately ten percent of the jokes studied were political (specifically, anti–George W. Bush).[3] There are a few studies examining the emergence and development of Internet memes,[4] however, none specifically examine political memes. There are also a few analyses of Internet disaster jokes, two of which focus specifically on 9/11 and its aftermath, which could probably be considered political humor.[5] Similarly, a recent book chapter focuses on the subversive role of online humor on the crisis in Zimbabwe.[6] However, in general, searching the academic literature for accounts or a theoretical review of online political humor is at best a frustrating exercise.[7]

A partial exception to the general neglect of online political humor in academic literature can be found in research which focuses on the effects of viewing online political humor on viewers' attitudes. One experimental study of college students found that an animated Flash cartoon depicting President George W. Bush singing about his second term was associated with more positive opinions of him.[8] A subsequent experiment found that animated clips by editorial cartoonist Walt Handelsman targeting various presidential candidates in 2008 lowered opinions of them.[9] Still another experimental study showed that not only did the viewing of online political cartoons lower evaluations of the target of the humor, but this negative effect had a "spillover effect" on evaluations of the political system as a whole.[10] In all cases findings regarding the effects of viewing online political humor were consistent with research on the effects of viewing televised political humor.[11]

As early as 1987, political jokes were being shared on the Internet by way of postings to the *rec.humor.funny* group on USENET.[12] The mass popularization of the World Wide Web by the mid-1990s opened the door to even more online political humor. The satirical magazine *The Onion*, for example, started in 1988 by students at the University of Wisconsin, had an online presence as early as 1996.[13] The campaign of 1996 saw the first "spoof" or parody campaign websites. For example, Republican presidential candidate Bob Dole was targeted by several sites, one of which was titled "Bob Dole for President" and linked "the candidate with Dole pineapples and other information on 'fruits and vegetables.'"[14] In 1999, the George W. Bush campaign made headlines by (unsuccessfully) attempting to have the spoof website "gwbush.com" taken down.[15] One analysis of the 2000 election season found that a certain "carnival" aspect of the online campaign, including spoof and parody sites, was becoming fairly common.[16] In addition to spoof websites, some candidates themselves got into the act during the campaign of 2000 by adding humorous games to their campaign websites or producing web-based humorous campaign ads.[17]

It is probably fair to say that it was during the 2004 election that Internet-based political humor began to receive widespread attention. One academic report focused on "independently-produced political videos" during the campaign, several of which were humorous in nature.[18] Many of these videos, produced on several websites (e.g., bushflash.com, toostupidtobepresident.com, whitehouse.org), targeted the incumbent President Bush, but this is not to say that Bush's challenger, Senator John Kerry, was immune to humorous attacks. For example, the Republican National Committee released a campaign ad modeled after a movie trailer titled "John Kerry, International Man of Mystery," making fun of his relationship with world leaders. They also had an online game making fun of Kerry's wealth called "Kerryopoly."[19] But there is no evidence that any of these examples of political humor were viewed by much more than a few hundred thousand people.

This was not the case with JibJab.com's "This Land" animated Flash cartoon. Released on July 9, 2004, the short, digital video lampooned the campaigns of both Bush and Kerry and immediately went viral. By the end of the month, the online clip had been seen by more than 10 million viewers (far more than visitors to the Bush and Kerry websites combined) and been featured on numerous television talk and news programs.[20] Similarly, the progressive, political action group "America Coming Together" produced a web video featuring comedian Will Ferrell as George Bush in a *faux* political ad that was seen by millions.[21] Internet-based political humor had come of age: One study claimed that "sending and receiving political jokes was the most popular political activity online during the 2004 presidential election."[22]

By the campaign of 2008, 19 percent of all adult respondents reported viewing online humor on sites like *The Onion* and Comedy Central's *The Daily Show*; of those under the age of 30, the percentage was 27 percent.[23] *The Onion*, for example, had numerous fake news and political commentary clips on its site that targeted the candidates (both Obama and McCain), parties, voters, the media, and more. The various *Saturday Night*

Live (SNL) clips featuring Tina Fey as Sarah Palin were seen several millions of times on NBC's official website, Hulu, and numerous other sites.

In the summer of 2008, John McCain released an online ad, featuring footage of Paris Hilton and Britney Spears, which attacked Obama for being "the biggest celebrity in the world." The comedy website "Funny or Die," which had by then established itself (by way of content) as a left-leaning outlet, responded to the "celebrity" ad by producing a humorous online ad of their own titled "Paris Hilton Responds to McCain Ad."[24] In fall 2008, writer-producer David Morgasen produced the "mashup" (previously recorded audio and video re-mixed and re-combined) video "Obama and McCain — Dance-Off!" in which the two candidates decide the election by way of a dance contest.[25] Both the Paris Hilton and the "dance-off" clips immediately went viral. Another class of online political videos that gained popularity were parodies of a scene from the film *Downfall* in which Hitler furiously reacts when told World War II has been lost by the Germans. Producers of these clips, virtually all ordinary citizens, replace the original soundtrack and subtitles with their own content.[26] While not all of these parodies are political, many are.

The campaign of 2012 saw another viral video featuring the two presidential candidates. Similar to the 2008 "dance-off" ad, "Barack Obama vs Mitt Romney: Epic Rap Battles Of History" saw Obama and Romney imitators competing against each other in a rap music contest.[27] As of January 2017, this video had attracted more than 130 million views. Another YouTube (YT) channel, "Bad Lip Reading," which overlays various video clips with nonsensical audio tracks, released a number of videos poking fun at Republican presidential candidates during the 2012 nomination process. In the fall, their "Eye Of The Sparrow — A Bad Lip Reading of the First 2012 Presidential Debate" attracted millions of online views.[28] Of course, there was also a slew of political cartoons, short clips, memes, and jokes circulated by way of email, Facebook postings, Twitter, Instagram, and other social media. In 2012, 55 percent of registered voters (who were online) reported having watched online political videos; of these, 37 percent reported watching "humorous or parody videos dealing with political issues."[29]

The preceding discussion of the history of online political humor is admittedly brief, and more to the point, quite selective. The plain fact is that the universe of Internet-based political humor is enormous. The focus of this chapter is specifically on the political humor of late night television talk show hosts' YT channels. Even more to the point, I propose the following research questions:

> *RQ#1*: How "political" were late night talk shows as represented on YouTube? In context of the 2016 election, how focused were they on the presidential campaign?

RQ#2: How popular was their campaign-related content, both in general and in comparison with other content?

RQ#3: Were either of the presidential candidates—Trump or Clinton—favored or targeted in the clips?

LATE NIGHT TALK SHOWS ON YOUTUBE

The late night talk show landscape in 2016 was dramatically different than the one that prevailed just two or three years earlier. On the broadcast networks, David Letterman and Jay Leno had been dominating ratings at 11:35 p.m. for better than two decades. At 12:35 a.m., Craig Ferguson and Jimmy Fallon had enjoyed respectable followings for several years.[30] On cable, Comedy Central's *The Daily Show with Jon Stewart* and *The Colbert Report* were extraordinarily popular among youth and the politically interested.[31] By September 2015, the late night television lineup had almost completely changed. Leno and Letterman had both retired, to be replaced by Fallon and Stephen Colbert, respectively; Ferguson left, replaced by newcomer James Corden; SNL alum Seth Meyers replaced Fallon; Trevor Noah took over *The Daily Show* (*TDS*) from the departed Stewart. Comedy Central replaced *The Colbert Report* with *The Nightly Show with Larry Wilmore* (this program was cancelled after 20 months). In addition, the number of late night comedy choices increased. John Oliver (formerly of *TDS*) joined Bill Maher with a weekly program on cable's Home Box Office (HBO); Samantha Bee (also of *TDS*) was given a weekly program by Turner Broadcasting System (TBS), joining Conan O'Brien who had been a nightly staple since 2010. By 2015, there were 11 late night choices, of which 7 aired four or five nights per week.

Importantly, for our purposes, this changing of the guard was also accompanied by another development. Content from most late night television talk shows (broadcast network and cable) had already been online for a few years, either on a television network website, Hulu, iTunes, Yahoo Screen, or other platforms. However, by the summer of 2015, virtually all late night talk shows had their own YT channel.[32] This had the effect of making clips from all late-night talk shows to the Internet accessible at no cost. Table 10.1 lists the late night shows examined in this chapter, with their television and YT channel start dates.

In the following pages, I present various data which, taken together, paint a portrait of the landscape of these late night talk shows on YT. Of course, as noted, there are any number of websites devoted to political humor on the Internet, and more political humor on other websites.

Table 10.1. Late Night Television: Program and YouTube Channel Start Dates

Program	Date Started	YouTube Channel Started
Full Frontal with Samantha Bee	March 2015	Oct. 12, 2015
The Late Show with Stephen Colbert	Sept. 2015	May 5, 2015
The Late Late Show with James Corden	March 2015	Nov. 21, 2006*
The Tonight Show Starring Jimmy Fallon	Feb. 2014	Jan. 8, 2006*
Jimmy Kimmel Live	Jan. 2003**	Sept. 9, 2006
Real Time with Bill Maher	Feb. 2003	Jan. 18, 2006
Late Night with Seth Meyers	Feb. 2014	May 10, 2013
The Daily Show with Trevor Noah	Sept. 2015	May 26, 2015
Conan	Nov. 2010	June 22, 2008
Last Week Tonight With John Oliver	April 2014	March 18, 2014
Saturday Night Live	Oct. 1975	July 23, 2013

*YouTube channel started for the program under the previous host.
**"Jimmy Kimmel Live" aired at 12:05 a.m. from 2003 until January 2013, when it moved to 11:35 p.m.
Source: See program name on http://www.imdb.com/, or channel name on http://socialblade.com/youtube/.

However, because YT is consistently either the second or third most visited website in the world and in the U.S.,[33] it seems reasonable to restrict attention to this site alone. Moreover, many of these late night television talk show channels are among the most popular on YT itself. Although the politically humorous content on these channels may vary in important respects from political humor on other websites (for example, it is professionally produced and scripted, and much of it is censored), it can be thought of as being representative of what many people turn to when viewing political humor online, if only by virtue of its popularity.

Data were gathered from two main sources. The first, Social Blade, is a website devoted to social media analytics, "track[ing] user statistics for YT, Twitch, Instagram, and Twitter."[34] The site, which makes its data available to the public, posts various viewing and subscriber statistics, as well as rankings for accounts on these social media venues. These data were gathered for all of the YT channel programs on November 15, 2016. The second source was YT, more specifically, the various channels associated with the programs themselves. I extracted data from these channels on November 15, 2016, as well. Tables 10.2 and 10.3 present an overview of the YT channels dedicated to both broadcast and cable network (respectively) late night television talk shows.

The focus of Table 10.2 is on the broadcast network talk shows. These include the three programs that air Monday through Friday at 11:35 p.m. (hosted by Colbert, Fallon, and Kimmel), two that follow at 12:35 a.m. on CBS and NBC (hosted by Corden and Meyers), and SNL. The first thing apparent in examining the "Channel" category is that there is, not surprisingly, wide variation in the popularity of these programs. The total, or

Table 10.2. Late Night Television Talk Show YouTube Channels: Broadcast Networks

	Colbert	Corden	Fallon	Kimmel	Meyers	SNL
YouTube Channel						
Date Started	5/27/2015	11/21/2006*	1/8/2006*	9/19/2006	5/10/2013	7/23/2013
Number Subscribers	1,708,457	8,039,741	12,376,293	8,632,700	758,476	3,047,365
Subscriber Rank	1,409	122	47	106	3,907	575
Number Videos	1,761	1,457	2,794	3,319	1,005	5,659
Total Video Views	830,039,945	1,927,768,544	6,123,906,395	3,898,108,209	290,257,271	1,649,437,418
Video View Rank	820	277	37	90	2,922	332
Videos (July 18–Nov. 7)						
Number Total Videos (July 18–Nov. 7)	510	214	324	359	183	57
Number Campaign Videos (July 18–Nov. 7)	156	24	29	91	79	15
Percent Campaign Videos (July 18–Nov. 7)	30.6%	11.2%	9.0%	25.3%	43.2%	26.3%
Videos (Sept. 15–Oct. 15)						
Number Total Videos (Sept. 15–Oct. 15)	132	155	113	154	63	17
Number Campaign Videos (Sept. 15–Oct. 15)	35	12	17	30	28	5
Percent Campaign Videos (Sept. 15–Oct. 15)	26.5%	7.7%	15.0%	19.5%	44.4%	29.4%
Video Views (Sept. 15–Oct. 15)						
Average Views, Camp. Videos (Sept. 15–Oct. 15)	925,880	271,403	1,668,347	231,683	985,315	7,188,818
Fewest Views, Camp. Videos (Sept. 15–Oct. 15)	74,606	68,045	139,932	17,473	51,697	1,816,831
Most Views, Camp. Videos (Sept. 15–Oct. 15)	3,032,650	910,916	9,827,019	2,297,218	3,126,310	22,093,815
Political Videos in 100 Most Popular	52	1	3	0	47	20
Video Targets						
Videos Attacking Trump (July 18–Nov. 7)	41.0%	41.7%	44.8%	34.1%	45.6%	13.3%
Videos Attacking Clinton (July 18–Nov. 7)	17.9%	12.5%	17.2%	18.7%	22.8%	—

*Includes some videos from show's previous host.
Source: http://socialblade.com/youtube/ (November 15, 2016).

overall number of subscribers and video views gives a general picture of
how popular late night television content is on YouTube.

However, because these channels were started at different times we
cannot use these figures to gauge the popularity of a given program.
For this we can look to subscriber rank, which varies from a high of 47
for Fallon to a low of 3,907 for Meyers. Fallon's YT popularity, in other
words, mirrors that of his television popularity, inasmuch as until fairly
recently he consistently topped late night ratings.[35] It is probably unfair
to come to a similar conclusion about Meyers' lack of popularity because
his program airs at 12:35 a.m. Subscriber rankings among these hosts do
correspond to the video view rank. Notable is the fact that Colbert comes
in last in subscriber rankings among the 11:35 p.m. broadcast network
programs. This may be a reflection of the fact that his is a more politically
oriented program than that of either Fallon or Kimmel. This orientation
may not be consistent with the preferences of late night broadcast television audiences. This said, Colbert's "video views last 30 days" number,
while lower than all but Meyers', seems more consistent with the other
programs' than his subscriber rank.

To address RQ#1, the "Video" category of Table 10.2 is a direct measure of how much campaign content appeared on these channels during
the presidential campaign. The table contains different measures of how
many total videos were posted to the channel and how many contained
campaign-related content. Two measurement periods were used: From
July 18 (the start of the Republican National Convention) through November 8 (Election Day), and a one-month period during the height of the
campaign, September 15 through October 15. On average, these programs
posted 274.5 video clips during the longer period and 105.7 in the one-
month period beginning September 15.

Within each period, I also counted "campaign videos." A video clip
was classified as campaign-related if it was clear from either the title or
the image associated with the clip that it was somehow related to the
campaign of 2016. During both periods measured, Meyers had the highest percentage of campaign-related videos (43.2% during the longer,
44.4% for the one-month period). Colbert and *SNL* traded second and
third place for the two periods, while Corden and Fallon brought up
the rear, so to speak, in terms of campaign-related content. Campaign
videos during the one-month period averaged 4:17 in length, from a
minimum of 24 seconds (Colbert) to a maximum of 9:46 (*SNL*). Generally, Colbert, Meyers, and *SNL* clips were longer than those of Corden,
Fallon, and Kimmel.

To get at RQ#2, I recorded the number of times each campaign video
during the shorter one-month (Sept. 15 to Oct. 15) period was viewed.
Here, we see a clear separation in terms of popularity. *SNL* had an aver-

age of over seven million views recorded for its 17 campaign-related videos during this period, making it by far the most popular of the late night broadcast network channels. Its most popular video ("Donald Trump vs. Hillary Clinton Debate Cold Open," posted 10/1/2016) attracted over 22 million views, while its least popular ("Trump vs. Clinton," 9/28/2016) garnered almost two million. To put this into perspective, *SNL*'s least popular campaign-related video had more views than any of the other programs' most popular clip. This most certainly is a product of the hype that surrounds *SNL*'s campaign skits. Fallon places second in this category, followed by Colbert and Meyers. On the other end of the scale, both Corden (68,045 views) and Kimmel's (17,473 views) campaign-related videos during this period seem to have garnered the fewest views.

Another measure of how political each program's YouTube channel was during the campaign is how many of the channel's 100 most popular videos were related to the campaign (see "Political Videos in 100 Most Popular"). Because jockeying for the presidency begins shortly after the mid-term elections, I used January 2014 as a start date to count a video as campaign-related. There is an obvious separation to be seen here. A high percentage of the most popular content for both Colbert and Meyers was campaign related (52% and 47%, respectively). On the other hand, of the 300 most popular videos on Corden's, Fallon's, and Kimmel's channels, a total of only four were campaign related. Clearly, viewers wanting political content turn to certain hosts and not others.

Finally, RQ#3 asks if any of the YouTube channels favored either of the two candidates. It may come as no surprise that in all but one case (Kimmel), Trump was targeted more than twice as often as Clinton by these late night hosts in their humorous clips (see final row, Table 10.2) However, before coming to the conclusion that this was a product of the 2016 election generally, and of Trump's candidacy in particular, one should remember that research has shown that late night talk shows demonstrate a liberal bias during presidential campaigns.[36] The partisan bias uncovered in Table 10.2 is completely consistent with that seen in previous election cycles.

Table 10.3 presents results for YT channels for the five cable network programs. Of these five, three (Bee, Maher, and Oliver) are weekly broadcasts, while two (Noah and O'Brien) air Monday through Thursday. There was noticeably less activity on these channels than on those associated with broadcast network programs. There was an average of only 127.6 videos posted for these five channels from convention through Election Day and 35.4 during the one-month period starting on September 15. There are other disparities between cable and network YT channels as well. For example, the campaign-related videos on the channels associated with cable networks were longer than those for broadcast network programming, ranging from a minimum of 56 seconds to a maximum of

Table 10.3.   Late Night Television Talk Show YouTube Channels: Cable Networks

	Bee	Maher	Noah	O'Brien	Oliver
YouTube Channel					
Date Started	10/12/2015	1/18/2006	5/26/2015	6/22/2008	3/18/2014
Number Subscribers	447,716	789,993	968,808	4,455,452	4,280,097
Subscriber Rank	7,116	3,742	2,909	330	350
Number Videos	322	1,140	96	4,775	186
Total Video Views	107,780,663	227,779,444	195,102,334	2,871,158,766	930,825,825
Video View Rank	8,751	3,876	4,593	153	708
Videos (July 18–Nov. 7)					
Number Total Videos (July 18–Nov. 7)	110	68	70	370	20
Number Campaign Videos (July 18–Nov. 7)	65	28	47	14	6
Percent Campaign Videos (July 18–Nov. 7)	59.1%	41.2%	67.1%	3.8%	30.0%
Videos (Sept. 15–Oct. 15)					
Number Total Videos (Sept. 15–Oct. 15)	9	27	20	116	5
Number Campaign Videos (Sept. 15–Oct. 15)	5	15	12	5	2
Percent Campaign Videos (Sept. 15–Oct. 15)	55.6%	55.6%	60.0%	4.3%	40.0%
Video Views (Sept. 15–Oct. 15)					
Average Views, Camp. Videos (Sept. 15–Oct. 15)	589,230	812,363	1,674,691	151,638	9,682,163
Fewest Views, Camp. Videos (Sept. 15–Oct. 15)	81,078	201,942	633,681	55,152	7,799,162
Most Views, Camp. Videos (Sept. 15–Oct. 15)	851,032	3,623,317	3,830,748	306,248	11,565,164
Number Political Videos in 100 Most Popular	55	27	61	0	8
Video Targets					
Videos Attacking Trump (July 18–Nov. 7)	27.7%	28.6%	29.8%	35.7%	16.7%
Videos Attacking Clinton (July 18–Nov. 7)	28.5%	7.1%	10.6%	21.4%	16.7%

Source: http://socialblade.com/youtube/ (November 15, 2016).

21:16. On average, these campaign-related clips were a full three minutes longer (7:22) than those from the broadcast networks.

Subscriber rankings show that both O'Brien (330) and Oliver (350) are more popular than the other three channels. The next closest is Noah, with 2,909 subscribers. A similar pattern emerges when looking at total video views. While O'Brien has almost three billion views (an astonishing number), Oliver has almost one billion; the other three lag far behind. The same hierarchy prevails with respect to video view rank.

On the other hand, the data show that while O'Brien was by far the most popular, he was the least political of the five. In neither period measured did his campaign-related videos represent even five percent of the total number posted. And while Noah ranks first in this respect during both periods, there is less of a difference between the channels of the overtly political programs of Bee, Maher, Noah, and Oliver.

In terms of campaign-related video views, there is again clear separation (RQ#2). Oliver's five campaign-related videos drew an average of almost 10 million views, with one ("Scandals," 9/25/2016) garnering close to 12 million. O'Brien's channel again clearly lags behind the others, while there is some relative parity between the remaining three. Finally, looking at the 100 most popular videos of these channels we can see that Bee and Noah focused a great deal on the campaign, with 55 and 61 percent of their top 100 videos devoted to 2016 campaign-related content. On the other end of the scale, O'Brien had no campaign-related videos in his 100 most popular.

Interestingly, there seems to be more parity among the cable network talk show hosts in terms of which presidential candidate was targeted in their humor (RQ#3). Bee and Oliver, for example, seemed to spread their ire equally among the two candidates, although in the case of Oliver this may be the result of the fact that he had far fewer videos posted.

Table 10.4 is another look at RQ#2, the popularity of campaign-related content on these channels. It tracks the three most popular campaign-related videos from both broadcast and cable network talk shows, by channel. Excluded from the table are the channels (3) which did not have three campaign-related videos in their top 100 most popular videos. Previous data suggests that these three are among the least politically oriented in terms of their content. Corden's "The Tale of Election 2016 w/ Benedict Cumberbatch" (posted 11/7/2016) ranked 97th, with an average of 301,218 views per day from the day it was posted through November 15. Corden had no other campaign-related videos in his top 100. Kimmel's "Does President Obama Wish He Were Running Against Trump?" (posted 10/25/2016) ranked 150th on his channel with an average of 175,353 views per day. Finally, O'Brien's "Louis C.K. Is All In For Hillary" (posted 11/1/2016) ranked 289th, with average daily views of 163,982.

Table 10.4. Most Popular Campaign-Related Videos, by YouTube Channel

Channel	Video	Date Posted	Rank	Views per Day
Bee	"The Morning After"	Nov. 9, 2016	2	479,340
	"A Totally Real, 100% Valid Theory"	Oct. 31, 2016	3	188,206
	"RIGGED!!!"	Oct. 5, 2016	5	56,112
Colbert	"Melania Trump Did Not Plagiarize Her RNC Speech"	July 19, 2016	2	74,865
	"Donald Trump Has Nothing To Apologize For"	Sept. 23, 2015	3	20,829
	"This Diagram Explains Trump's Response To Orlando"	June 15, 2016	4	53,568
Fallon	"Donald Trump Interviews Himself in the Mirror"	Sept. 11, 2015	49	39,063
	"Obama Calls Donald Trump with Debate Advice"	Aug. 3, 2015	56	33,847
	"Donald Trump's Phone Call with Hillary Clinton"	Sept. 16, 2015	59	36,669
Maher	"Bill Maher Spars with Trump Campaign Manager Kellyanne Conway"	Sept. 16, 2016	2	59,723
	"Bernie Sets the Record Straight on Socialism"	Oct. 16, 2015	5	4,936
	"The Notorious HRC"	July 29, 2016	8	13,625
Meyers	"A Closer Look: First Presidential Debate"	Sept. 26, 2016	8	62,526
	"New Bombshell Allegations Against Trump: A Closer Look"	Oct. 13, 2016	9	93,502
	"Trump Lies about His Birther Past: A Closer Look"	Sept. 19, 2016	10	53,880
Noah	"Donald Trump: America's African President"	Oct. 3, 2015	2	9,762
	"Sparks Fly at the First Trump–Clinton Presidential Debate"	Sept. 26, 2016	3	76,615
	"Not So Pro-Life After All"	Oct. 6, 2015	4	8,671
Oliver	"Donald Trump"	Feb. 28, 2016	1	117,353
	"Border Wall"	March 20, 2016	7	53,707
	"Scandals"	Sept. 25, 2016	12	224,329
SNL	"Donald Trump v. Hillary Clinton Debate Cold Open"	Oct. 1, 2016	1	490,974
	"Donald Trump v. Hillary Clinton Third Debate Cold Open"	Oct. 23, 2016	5	765,526
	"Democratic Debate Cold Open"	Oct. 18, 2015	12	30,809

Data for Fallon also point to the idea that his content is less political. His most popular campaign-related video was 49th of 100, and all his top three most popular campaign-related videos were short skits of Fallon imitating Trump. In other words, each was more comedic as opposed to political.

The remaining seven channels in Table 10.4 appear to have been relatively popular destinations for viewers of campaign-related video. The three most popular campaign-related videos for five of the seven (Bee, Colbert, Maher, Meyers, and Noah) were in the top ten most popular videos on their channel. The remaining two (Oliver and *SNL*) had two campaign-related videos on their top ten, and their third most popular campaign-related video was ranked at number 12. An average of the views-per-day of the three top campaign-related videos of these seven channels suggests that *SNL* was by far the most popular for campaign videos, with 429,103, easily surpassing Bee's 241,219, who was second-most popular according to this metric. Both *SNL*'s "Donald Trump vs. Hillary Clinton Debate Cold Open" (10/1/2016) and Bee's "The Morning After," posted the day after the election, averaged almost one-half million views per day from the date they were posted through November 15. Oliver's average views-per-day of 131,796 places him third, with the remaining channels (Colbert, Maher, Meyers, and Noah) clustered at the bottom.

Table 10.5 is a final examination of how political each of these programs were (RQ#1). It shows the total number of times presidential candidates appeared on late night television and how many clips of these appearances were posted to their YT channel. A few things are immediately evident from a cursory examination of these data. First, neither Corden nor O'Brien hosted any candidates throughout the campaign. This is consistent with other data suggesting that these two hosts are less political than others.

Second, not all candidates made late night appearances. This is perhaps not surprising, given that the Republican field was so crowded. In fact, Republicans Jim Gilmore, Bobby Jindal, George Pataki, Rick Perry, and Rick Santorum, all lower-tier candidates to be sure, appeared to be completely absent from late night television, as was Democrat Jim Webb. Other lower-tier candidates had only one appearance, including Republican Mike Huckabee and Democrat Martin O'Malley. Somewhat surprisingly, given his initial popularity among Christian conservatives, Ben Carson appeared only once as well (on *TDS*). This may have been a result of his relative unpopularity, but may also have been a decision on the part of hosts to not book a guest who was perceived as somewhat less dynamic. Similarly, the initially popular Marco Rubio made only two appearances. Also surprising was the fact that Republican Ted Cruz, who contested the nomination until the bitter end, only made four appearances on late night television. Democrat Bernie Sanders, who stayed

Table 10.5. Presidential Candidates on Late Night TV: Total Appearances (YouTube Clips), 2015–2016

	Fallon	Kimmel	Colbert	Meyers	TDS	SNL	TOTAL
Bush	1(2)	0	1(3)	0	0	0	2(5)
Carson	0	0	0	0	1(1)	0	1(1)
Christie	2(5)	0	0	0	1(0)	0	3(5)
Clinton	3(14)	3(20)	2(4)	1(3)	0	1(1)	10(42)
Cruz	1(2)	1(4)	1(1)	1(1)	0	0	4(8)
Fiorina	1(0*)	0	0	1(1)	0	0	2(1)
Graham	0	0	0	1(1)	2(2)	0	3(3)
Huckabee	0	0	0	0	1(0)	0	1(0)
Kasich	0	0	1(3)	2(2)	0	0	3(5)
O'Malley	0	0	0	1(0)	0	0	1(0)
Paul	0	0	1(1)	0	2(1)	0	3(2)
Rubio	1(1)	0	0	0	1(0)	0	2(1)
Sanders	1(2)	3(15)	2(11)	2(4)	0	1(1)	9(33)
Trump	3(11)	2(14)	1(2)	0	0	1(3)	7(30)
TOTAL	13(37)	9(53)	9(25)	9(12)	8(4)	3(5)	51(136)

*One or more clips of this appearance were uploaded by and made available from other YouTube users. This may have also been the case with other candidate appearances on other shows, but these were not recorded because "official" clips were available for each appearance

in the race until the end, was a guest on late night talk shows nine times, only one less than Hillary Clinton and two more than Donald Trump.

The data also reveal a few surprises. For example, Fallon, who according to much of the data included in this chapter is not extremely political in terms of his YT content, hosted candidates the most times (13) and had the most clips (37) associated with these visits. Tied for second place were three hosts: Colbert, Kimmel, and Meyers. Kimmel stands out because like Fallon, his YT content was on the whole not very political.

Perhaps the most interesting aspect of these data is the fact that 51 candidate appearances generated 136 YT clips. Candidates appear on talk shows for strategic reasons. First, the old adage that any exposure is good exposure applies. Second, lighthearted conversation with hosts humanizes candidates to some extent, making it easier for viewers to relate to them. Relatedly, it gives candidates an opportunity to show they can take a joke. This further humanizes them in the eyes of viewers, and in the end, makes them more likable.[37] Third, although policy discussion on these programs is typically kept to a minimum, candidates can and do talk policy without fear of the type of aggressive follow-up questions they might expect from hard news journalists.[38] The fact that video clips of candidate appearances are made available on hosts' YT channels means that there is a multiplier effect at work. Not only does the availability of the clips on YT make it possible for people who did not watch the televised broadcast to see the candidates' appearances, each appearance generates an average of greater than 2.5 clips.

DISCUSSION

There is no question that the Internet has, in a sense, democratized political humor. Greater numbers of people are able to share their politically comedic messages by way of various websites and social media. Moreover, these messages can in turn be consumed by greater numbers of people, accessing these websites any time of day on various computer and telephonic devices.

This can be clearly seen in the political humor of late night television talk shows. Videos posted to YT channels associated with these programs have had the effect of multiplying the message. In other words, people who may not have tuned in to the original telecast are now able to view these videos. There is some evidence, in fact, that online-only viewing of late night television programs may be an important part of the future of this type of programming. Some people (e.g., the present author) "watch" late night television exclusively on YT, not bothering to tune in to the original televised version of the program at all. It is certainly the case that "late-night success is" to some extent "unmoored from TV," as one recent article suggests.[39] James Corden, for example, claims he does not look at his TV ratings, but rather his YT numbers.[40] Corden's and Meyers' popularity on YT are higher than one would expect from a program that airs at 12:35 a.m. This is probably also the case for Oliver, inasmuch as not everyone subscribes to HBO.

In addition to making late night talk shows more accessible to more people, YT has had a multiplier effect on viewership of these programs. Relying only on YT views tells part of this story, but does not account for news sites, Facebook, blogs, and other social media which link to YT videos. This can be seen as good news for politicians appearing on these programs who are hoping for a boost in their favorability ratings, or bad news for those who are being lampooned. This is because a decade of scholarship has demonstrated that viewing political humor has a deleterious effect on opinions of the targets of the humor. Conversely, self-deprecating humor, the type that politicians typically engage in when appearing on these programs, serves to boost opinion of the politician in question.[41] We might therefore be able to assume that the multiplier effect on viewership applies also to the *effects* of viewership.

The YT clips surveyed for this study mirrored public discourse throughout the campaign. Clinton was frequently targeted about the email scandal and to a lesser extent, her health. Trump jokes, on the other hand, focused on his use of Twitter, his tax returns, building a wall between the Southern US and Mexico, and his relationship with Black voters.

The data in this chapter confirm what any casual viewer might already understand about the late night talk show landscape, namely, that there is a clear separation among hosts in terms of both their popularity and how political they are. However, on the whole, the data here suggest that there is a negative correlation between how political and how popular a show is. Corden, Fallon, Kimmel, and O'Brien clearly constitute a lower tier among the YT channels under consideration in this chapter in terms of the amount of their political content. Whether deliberate or not, this is likely the product of the fact that all but O'Brien are hosts on broadcast network programs (and, O'Brien's previous program was also on broadcast network television). As such, they try to appeal to a wider (i.e., not necessarily politically interested) audience. Not coincidentally, they also seem to be in the top tier in terms of their popularity.

On the other hand, Bee, Colbert, Maher, Meyers, and Noah are all more political but less popular. All but Colbert are cable hosts who cater to a narrower audience and therefore can afford to be more political. Colbert, a broadcast network host, is the exception, but his previous program (*The Colbert Report* on Comedy Central) was on cable and his persona on that program was extremely political. There seems to be something of a trade-off between how political and how popular a late night talk program is.

The exceptions to this rule seem to be *SNL* and Oliver. *SNL*, of course, has made a name for itself with campaign humor over the past several decades, so it is hardly surprising that they can be both popular and political. Oliver too seems to have found a formula for political humor programming that is both political and popular.

This chapter has certain limitations that should be acknowledged. First, it has completely ignored most sources of political humor on the Internet, focusing only on late night TV hosts on YT. The rationale for this was that this strategy would capture a good deal of online political humor. However, there is a wealth of political humor both not on YT and from sources other than late night hosts. Second, the YT metrics employed leave something to be desired in terms of capturing popularity. For example, the number associated with YT "views" is not the same as the number of viewers. In other words, one person can watch a clip multiple times, inflating this face value popularity measure. Another deficiency is the fact that many YT videos are linked to and viewed on any number of other websites. While it might be exceedingly difficult to identify all of the Internet sites and pages that a YT video is linked to, it must be acknowledged that YT views is a conservative measure of a clip's popularity in many cases.

This said, the chapter has gone a long way toward presenting a snapshot of the online political humor landscape from the 2016 presidential election. There was a veritable wealth of material—an embarrassment of riches—for aficionados of political humor during this cycle. This situation will certainly prevail in the future, at least assuming the continued existence of YT.

NOTES

1. See the excellent review in Todd Steven Graham, "What's Wife Swap Got to Do with It? Talking Politics in the Net-Based Public Sphere," *University of Amsterdam Digital Academic Repository (UvA-DARE)*, (2009), https://pure.uva.nl/ws/files/812355/68836_thesis.pdf.

2. Elliott Oring, *Engaging Humor* (Illinois: University of Illinois Press, 2003), Chapter 10.

3. Limor Shifman, "Humor in the Age of Digital Reproduction: Continuity and Change in Internet-Based Comic Texts," *International Journal of Communication* 1 (2007): 187–209.

4. Linda K. Börzsei, "Makes a Meme Instead: A Concise History of Internet Memes," *New Media Studies* 7 (2013): 152–188.

5. Giselinde Kuipers, "Media Culture and Internet Disaster Jokes: Bin Laden and the Attack on the World Trade Center," *European Journal of Cultural Studies* 5 (2002): 450–470; Giselinde Kuipers, "Where Was King Kong When We Needed Him? Public Discourse, Digital Disaster, Jokes, and the Functions of Laughter After 9/11," *The Journal of American Culture* 28 (2005): 70–84.

6. Jennifer Musangi, "'A Zimbabwean Joke Is No Laughing Matter': E-Humour and Versions of Subversion," 161–175, in Sarah Chiumbu and Muchaparara Musemwa, eds., *Crisis! What Crisis? The Multiple Dimensions of the Zimbabwean Crisis* (Human Sciences Research Council, 2012), 3–286.

7. See Jody Baumgartner, "Humor on the Next Frontier: Online Political Humor and Its Effects on Youth," *Social Science Computer Review* 29 (2007): 319–38, for a brief—yet incomplete—account of Internet political humor.

8. Baumgartner, "Humor on the Next Frontier."

9. Jody C Baumgartner, "Editorial Cartoons 2.0: The Effects of Digital Political Satire on Presidential Candidate Evaluations," *Presidential Studies Quarterly* 38 (2008): 735–58.

10. Jody C Baumgartner, "No Laughing Matter? Young Adults and the 'Spillover Effect' of Candidate-centered Political Humor," *HUMOR: International Journal of Humor Research* 26 (2013): 23–43; see also Heather L. LaMarre, Kristen D. Landreville, Dannagal Young, and Nathan Gilkerson, "Humor Works in Funny Ways: Examining Satirical Tone as a Key Determinant in Political Humor Message Processing," *Mass Communication and Society* 17 (2014): 400–23, for an examination of how differing types of satire, including online video, may result in differential message processing.

11. For a comprehensive review, see Jody C Baumgartner, "Political Humor and its Effects: A Review Essay," in Camilo Cuéllar, ed., *Los Efectos Del Humor: Una Perspectiva Transdisciplinar* [*The Effects of Humor: A Trans-Disciplinary Perspective*], (Bogota, Colombia: Ediciones Universidad Cooperativa de Colombia, forthcoming 2017).

12. See "Brad Templeton's Rec.Humor.Funny," at http://www.netfunny.com/rhf/.

13. Mike Tanner, "A Funny Thing Didn't Happen on the Way to the Web," *Wired*, November 13, 1997, http://archive.wired.com/culture/lifestyle/news/1997/11/8518.

14. Edmund Andrews, "The '96 Race on the Internet: Surfer Beware," *The New York Times*, October 23, 1995, http://www.nytimes.com/1995/10/23/us/the-96-race-on-the-internet-surfer-beware.html?pagewanted=all.

15. Michael Cornfield, *Politics Moves Online: Campaigning and the Internet* (New York: The Century Foundation, 2004), 60.

16. Kirsten A. Foot and Steven M. Schneider, "Online Action in Campaign 2000: An Exploratory Analysis of the U.S. Political Web Sphere," *Journal of Broadcasting and Electronic Media* 46 (2002): 222–244, 232–235.

17. Ibid.

18. Carol Darr and Julie Barko, "Under the Radar and Over the Top: Independently-Produced Political Videos in the 2004 Presidential Election" (Washington, DC: Institute for Politics, Democracy & the Internet, 2004).

19. Lynda Lee Kaid, "Political Web Wars: The Use of the Internet for Political Advertising" in *The Internet Election: Perspectives on the Web Campaign in 2004*, ed. Andrew P. Williams and John C. Tedesco (Lanham, MD: Rowman & Littlefield, 2006), 67–82.

20. Baumgartner, "Humor on the Next Frontier."

21. Cornfield, *Politics Moves Online*

22. Shifman, "Humor in the Age of Digital Reproduction," 187.

23. Aaron Smith, "The Internet's Role in Campaign 2008," *Pew Research Center*, April 15, 2009, http://www.pewinternet.org/~/media//Files/Reports/2009/The_Internets_Role_in_Campaign_2008.pdf.

24. See http://www.funnyordie.com/videos/64ad536a6d/paris-hilton-responds-to-mccain-ad-from-paris-hilton-adam-ghost-panther-mckay-and-chris-henchy.

25. See https://www.youtube.com/watch?v=wzyT9–9lUyE.

26. *Sydney Morning Herald*, "YouTube Hitler Parodies Go Viral," *Stuff*, last modified September 30, 2008, http://www.stuff.co.nz/technology/651645.

27. See https://www.youtube.com/watch?v=dX_1B0w7Hzc.

28. See https://www.youtube.com/watch?v=QlwilbVYvUg.

29. Aaron Smith and Maeve Duggan, "Online Political Videos and Campaign 2012," *Pew Research Center*, November 2, 2012, http://www.pewinternet.org/files/old-media/Files/Reports/2012/PIP_State_of_the_2012_race_online_video_final.pdf.

30. S. Robert Lichter, Jody C Baumgartner, and Jonathan Morris, *Politics Is a Joke!: How TV Comedians Are Remaking Political Life* (Boulder, CO: Westview, 2014).

31. Jody C Baumgartner and Jonathan S. Morris, "Stoned Slackers or Super-citizens? 'Daily Show' Viewing and Political Engagement of Young Adults," quoted in Amarnath Amarasingam, ed., *The Stewart / Colbert Effect: Essays on the Real Impacts of Fake News* (Jefferson, NC: McFarland & Co., 2011).

32. Each of the channels discussed in this chapter can be found by simply searching within YouTube for the program's full name.

33. See rankings at http://www.alexa.com/topsites or https://www.quant-cast.com, among others.

34. See http://socialblade.com/.

35. Bill Carter, "Bill Carter: How Jimmy Fallon Crushed Stephen Colbert (and Everyone Else in Late Night)," *Hollywood Reporter*, last modified December 16, 2015, https://www.hollywoodreporter.com/news/bill-carter-how-jimmy-fallon-848851.

36. Lichter, Baumgartner, and Morris, *Politics Is a Joke!*, 69.

37. Jody C Baumgartner, Jonathan S. Morris, and Jeffrey Michael Coleman, "Does the 'Road to the White House Run Through' Letterman? Chris Christie, Letterman, and Attack v. Self-Depreciating Humor," *Journal of Political Marketing* (forthcoming).

38. Michael Parkin, *Talk Show Campaigns* (New York: Routledge, 2014).

39. Dave Itzkoff, "As Letterman Moves On, Late-Night Success Is Unmoored From TV," *The New York Times*, last modified May 10, 2015, https://www.ny-times.com/2015/05/11/arts/television/as-letterman-retires-late-night-tv-faces-a-changing-landscape.html; see also David Sims, "What Conan O'Brien Means to Late-Night's Weekly Future," *The Atlantic*, last modified January 10, 2017, https://www.theatlantic.com/entertainment/archive/2017/01/what-conan-ob-rien-means-to-late-nights-future/512633/, and Nick Bilton, "The Battle for Late Night Viewers on Screens of All Sizes," *The New York Times*, last modified April 14, 2014, https://bits.blogs.nytimes.com/2014/04/10/the-battle-for-late-night-eyeballs-on-screens-of-all-sizes/?_r=0.

40. Nathan McAlone, "James Corden Never Looks at His Ratings, Only His YouTube Numbers," *Business Insider*, last modified October 14, 2016, http://www.businessinsider.com/james-corden-only-cares-about-youtube-2016–10.

41. Jody C Baumgartner, "Political Humor and Its Effects: A Review Essay," in *Los Efectos Del Humor: Una Perspectiva Transdisciplinar* [*The Effects Of Humor: A Trans-Disciplinary Perspective*], Ediciones Universidad Cooperativa de Colombia.

III

POLITICAL ISSUES ON TWITTER AND INSTAGRAM

11

Issue Emphasis and Agenda Building on Twitter During the 2016 Presidential Primary Season

Bethany A. Conway-Silva, Christine R. Filer,
Kate Kenski, and Eric Tsetsi

Every day millions of people access Twitter for up-to-date political information.[1] Knowing this, candidates and parties use Twitter as a direct conduit to voters. It allows them to bypass traditional media gatekeepers, lets them post free messages in lieu of expensive advertisements, and, as an express line to journalists, serves an agenda-building function. President Donald J. Trump appeared to be keenly aware of mainstream media's Twitter obsession; recent findings suggest that he used it to his advantage in the 2016 presidential election.[2]

In the changing media environment, "the Internet allows campaigns to engage in the traditional activities of campaigns with new tools."[3] Such traditional activities include emphasizing the important issues of the day, building perceptions of candidate character, and general campaign activity (e.g., fundraising, advertising campaign events). Given the importance of issues in a campaign and the allowance for pithy, 140-character messages on Twitter, we ask: What issues might U.S. presidential candidates and their parties choose to make salient in Twitter feeds?[4]

Some research suggests candidates and parties would be wise to make salient issues that resonate with party members.[5] Others suggest there are benefits to focusing on issues of major concern to the public, regardless of party affiliation.[6] In a previous study, we found that 2012 presidential candidates focused on similar issues in tweets.[7] This initial study, however, needs replication in order to determine whether the findings were incidental or representative of presidential campaign communication on social media beyond 2012. It is possible that as Republican and Democratic voter bases become increasingly polarized, such emphasis may change across elections.[8] Additionally, candidates tend to gain more footing with the press when they focus on issues "owned" by their parties.[9]

This chapter examines the issues emphasized on Twitter by Republican and Democratic candidates and the two major parties during the 2016 presidential primary season. Further, it investigates the extent to which these issues were picked up by the nation's top newspapers. The new media environment raises questions about the agenda-setting power of traditional news media.[10] Though our previous study of the 2012 primaries found a symbiotic relationship between newspapers and candidate/campaign Twitter feeds, it also found that politicians still rely on national newspapers for legitimacy. Was this the case in 2016? Further, is the power of candidate Twitter feeds in predicting the news media agenda on the rise? Findings suggest that, compared to the 2012 primary season, issue emphasis moved toward greater differentiation as demonstrated by their focus on dissimilar and party-owned issues. Further, candidate and party issue emphasis on Twitter may result in mainstream press attention, though this was not confined to owned issues as demonstrated by 2016 primary data.

ISSUE EMPHASIS

Issue emphasis is often explored through the theory of issue ownership, which suggests that parties acquire a reputation for handling certain issues due to marked concern (by affiliated politicians and voters) and policy success.[11] Over time, voters have come to associate each party with particular issues and expect issue emphasis within campaign media with these expectations.[12] For example, Democratic politicians are often associated with issues of social welfare (e.g., health care and education). Republicans, however, are often associated with budgetary issues related to small government, as well as terrorism and national defense. Survey research and experimental research support these associations and suggest that emphasizing owned issues influences voter attitudes (more so than emphasizing non-owned issues).[13] A content analysis by Benoit also suggests owned-issue emphasis is associated with positive election outcomes.[14]

Given the above literature, it may seem surprising to find that the issue ownership hypothesis lacks support in recent research. Evidence shows that parties deviate from owned issues and even focus or "trespass" on issues owned by the other party.[15] Reasons for this include (1) high levels of competition, (2) success (or failure) on certain issues by past administrations, and (3) the benefits that come with stressing issues of public importance.[16] Democrats may be forced to trespass more often than Republicans because certain issues traditionally considered in the Republican purview are practically unavoidable, such as defense spending when global conflict arises.[17] Though straying from owned issues and trespassing is currently the norm, it may be counterintuitive in that these practices do not resonate with voters due to the stability of party characteristics.[18]

We suggest that social media encourage both issue convergence and trespassing. Even within traditional media, such as advertisements, blogs, and press releases, congruence in issue emphasis and trespassing occur, and social media are not beholden to the same constraints as traditional platforms.[19] Unlike campaign ad spending, which reached $350 million in the 2016 election, Twitter messaging allows nearly free publicity.[20] Thus, social media come with the possibility for experimentation. In 2012, this resulted in the floating of "trial balloons" on Twitter—messages meant to test the waters and, ideally, attract public attention.[21] If a message does not work, campaigns can quickly and cheaply try another angle. This likely results in varied issue emphasis. Supporting this assertion, our analysis of issue emphasis during the 2012 presidential primaries found that issue convergence across parties, not issue ownership, took precedence on Twitter, with both parties trespassing on some issues.[22]

These findings not only have to do with Twitter's low cost, but also the nearly limitless nature of Twitter messaging. Newsworthy information makes its way to and circulates through the Twittersphere quickly. Indeed, research shows that message output patterns on Twitter somewhat mirror those of traditional news.[23] Therefore, some messaging on Twitter by candidates and parties is event-driven. In 2016, Trump did this regularly, picking up on issues and tweeting in a way that facilitated further news coverage.[24] Due to the above, we expected to see similar issue emphasis and at least some trespassing on Twitter by campaigns and parties during the 2016 presidential primaries.

ISSUE OWNERSHIP AND THE PRESS AGENDA

The issues candidates focus on are consequential for the press agenda. After discovering that news media set the public's issue agenda, researchers later turned their attention to who/what sets the news media agenda.[25] Agenda-building theory examines the precursors to issue emphasis by the press, one consequential antecedent being candidate and campaign messaging.[26] Here, we focus on the intermedia agenda-setting component of agenda building, which stresses the level of influence across different media (e.g., ads, blogs, websites, news articles, etc.).[27] Specifically, we focus on the Twitter-to-news-media relationship (and vice versa). As with other campaign media, journalists report actively using Twitter to gather leads on breaking news and to follow politicians.[28] Candidates, campaigns, and parties can use the platform to build the press agenda when it comes to important issues.

Previous research testing the relationship between overall issue emphasis on Twitter and mainstream news suggests that Twitter's ability to set the news agenda is limited.[29] In other words, when focusing on messaging across the Twittersphere, news media can set the Twitter agenda to a greater extent than the reverse. This does not, however, mean that social media messaging cannot or does not set the news media agenda, especially when it comes to campaign messaging.[30] The bulk of research on traditional campaign media indicates that "the electoral context makes it more difficult for the media to set the political agenda and to focus autonomously on issues that are not brought forward by parties or candidates."[31]

Even if campaigns and parties hold the power in the agenda-building relationship during election season, social media messaging comes with an added layer of difficulty. In particular, candidates and campaigns must grapple with the potential loss of message control in social media as messages are misinterpreted and parodied by other media users.[32] In our former research on Twitter, we suggested that following the news media agenda would allow campaigns to play it safe.[33] In other words, by following and even citing news media content, candidates could increase their credibility. Overall, our previous findings support this assertion. During the 2012 primaries, newspapers set candidate/campaign agendas on Twitter to a greater extent than the reverse. But, we also found that candidates/parties use Twitter to communicate unique agendas in that candidate and party issue emphasis preceded that of the nation's top newspapers on some issues. In the end, these relationships are likely issue specific and symbiotic (both campaigns/parties and mainstream media have some power).

On which issues might we expect candidates, campaigns, and parties to successfully predict/influence the news media agenda? Research indicates that news media may report on candidates in a partisan fashion, such that Republicans see more media coverage when it comes to defense, taxes, and spending, and Democrats receive more coverage on issues of social welfare.[34] Even when candidates choose to trespass, news media may still link candidates to party-owned issues, thus resulting in discrepancies between campaign agendas and media agendas.[35] Our study testing the impact of 2012 presidential primary Twitter feeds, however, found that this was not the case with Twitter.[36] During the 2012 primaries, both parties predicted newspaper emphasis on employment, energy, foreign policy, health care, and taxes. That the Obama campaign led on taxes and Republican candidates led on health care suggests that owned-party emphasis on Twitter does not necessarily result in elevated levels of news coverage. Once again, this may be candidate or election specific. Here, we explore on which issues the candidates and their parties set the newspaper agenda to capture dynamics in agenda building on Twitter across elections.

EXAMINING ISSUE EMPHASIS AND AGENDA BUILDING IN 2016

This study used computer-assisted content analysis to determine issue emphasis within Twitter feeds of the 2016 U.S. presidential primary candidates, their campaigns, and the two major parties, as well as the nation's top newspapers. To examine issue emphasis across the two parties and test the issue ownership hypothesis, the Twitter feeds of the Democratic contenders and the Republican contenders were combined to create two indices. We kept feeds for the Democratic National Committee (DNC) and the Republican National Committee (RNC) separate to investigate whether the issue agendas aligned between candidates and their parties.

Newspapers examined in this study were *The Wall Street Journal, The New York Times, USA Today, The Los Angeles Times,* and *The Washington Post.* The first four were chosen as the largest circulation newspapers in the country.[37] *The Los Angeles Times* also gives us a West Coast perspective. *The Washington Post,* the eighth-largest circulation newspaper in the US, was chosen due to its emphasis on national politics. All articles published from January 1 through June 7 were collected using LexisNexis and ProQuest. January 1 marked one month prior to the Iowa Caucus. On June 6, Hillary Clinton officially garnered enough delegates to secure the nomination.[38] Articles were retrieved using the term "president*" in combination with "Republican Primar*," "Republican Caucus*," "Republican nomination," "Democratic Primar*," "Democratic Caucus*," "Democratic nomination," or any of the names of the primary candidates. All news articles and editorials that mentioned any of the candidates were included, resulting in a population of articles. If any of the returned articles did not reference one of the primary candidates, they were discarded, resulting in a total of 6,434 relevant articles (*The New York Times* = 1,775, *The Wall Street Journal* = 1,623, *USA Today* = 593, *The Los Angeles Times* = 818, and *The Washington Post* = 1,625).[39]

All tweets posted on the feeds of major party candidates and their campaigns from January 1 through June 7 were gathered weekly using R to query Twitter's REST API. The REST API allows researchers to "query Twitter's databases for data corresponding to specific parameters," including tweets posted by specific users.[40] These data included the tweet, user name, and date posted. Rarely, retweets were cut off because the original poster's Twitter handle was included, and this resulted in tweet text longer than 140 characters. As such lengthy tweets typically ended in a hyperlink directing readers to another site or a general hashtag (e.g., #GOPDebate), this limitation should minimally influence analyses focused on issue content.

For the purposes of this study, if a candidate also had an individual feed that was not necessarily linked to their campaign (e.g., Chris Christie had both a feed representing his presidential candidacy, @ChrisChristie, and a feed representing his role as governor of New Jersey, @GovChristie), both were included. In the final dataset, candidate and campaign tweets were included up to the day an individual dropped out of the race (e.g., the last tweet included for John Kasich occurred on May 4, which was the day he dropped out of the race) (N = 30,232). Twitter feeds and the total number of tweets are displayed in Table 11.1.

Table 11.1.   List of Included Twitter Feeds

Twitter Handle	Total Tweets
Democratic Candidate Index	
@BernieSanders	3,423
@HFA	600
@HillaryClinton	2,663
@MartinOMalley	193
@SenSanders	1,170
@TheBriefing2016	1,301
Total	9,350
Republican Candidate Index	
@CarlyFiorina	192
@ChrisChristie	546
@GovChristie	176
@gov_gilmore	389
@GovMikeHuckabee	360
@JebBush	742
@JohnKasich	2,607
@marcorubio	1,207
@RandPaul	1,248
@RealBenCarson	647
@RealDonaldTrump	2,131
@RickSantorum	128
@SenTedCruz	165
@TeamJohnKasich	627
@TeamMarco	1,828
@TeamSantorum	885
@TeamTedCruz	412
@TedCruz	4,205
Total	18,495
Official Party Feeds	
@The Democrats	1,333
@GOP	1,054

Coding for Issues

The coding program QDA Miner and its companion program WordStat were used to analyze issue frequencies within Twitter feeds and newspapers. While QDA Miner is used for qualitative coding, its quantitative component WordStat allows researchers to examine the frequency of words and phrases. For newspapers, the unit of analysis was all published news content concerning the primary candidates on a given day. For Twitter indices and the RNC and DNC feeds, the unit of analysis was all tweets posted on a given day.

Coding employed a combination of automated and manual analysis to ensure that the former was coded as intended by the researcher.[41] We created a list of national political issues examined in previous studies.[42] Based on these topics, thousands of words that appeared in news articles and tweets were analyzed in WordStat to detect additional categories and to fully develop previously established categories fully. This resulted in a total of 26 issues.[43] Words were included if they appeared 10 times or more, including hashtags, which were placed in the appropriate category based on their original intent. For example, in our dataset, #FixtheDebt was placed in the budget category. Following our previous study, after adding these words and categories to the dictionary, we searched leftover words that were not included in the dictionary to make sure no relevant words were excluded. If the placement of a word was unclear, it was investigated in context to determine its use. In some cases, rules were created based on corresponding words or phrases to ensure proper coding.

Due to the nature of issue emphasis over time, not all issues included in previous studies were included in the current analysis. Although there are some specific differences in issues analyzed between key agenda-setting studies, overall, similarities are dominant.[44] For example, prior studies also focused on abortion, affirmative action, agriculture, health care, economy, and immigration. Differences arise primarily due to narrow, emergent issues that are often election-specific. In this study, for example, Clinton's email scandal was included in the list of issues due to the focus on Clinton's use of a private email server. Zika was also included. In other words, the issues that dominate public consciousness and political rhetoric can change slightly year to year and from campaign to campaign depending on historical events. Therefore, agenda-setting studies will include slightly different lists of issues especially when compared across large periods of time.

Analyzing Issue Emphasis and Agenda Building

First, we identified the top five issues that appeared within the Republican candidate index, the Democratic candidate index, and the feeds of the DNC and RNC. This resulted in 12 issues (see Table 11.2). Descriptive statistics and correlation analyses were used to examine owned-issue emphasis within the four Twitter sources. Next, time series analysis was used to determine whether the Twitter agendas of the Democratic candidate index, the Republican candidate index, and the feeds of the two parties predicted the agenda of the nation's top newspapers and, if so, on which issue(s). We continued using the two indices to further test whether news media reported on candidate issues in a partisan fashion, as previous literature suggests. The time series analysis also allowed us to examine whether issue emphasis on Twitter was predicted by the nation's top newspapers.

Table 11.2.   Total Case Occurrences by Issue between January 1, 2016, and June 7, 2016

		Democratic Index	Republican Index	DNC	RNC
Affirmative Action	Total (%)	304 (3.72)	114 (0.58)	57 (4.28)	7 (0.66)
	Rank	2	17	4	10
Banking	Total (%)	292 (3.57)	154 (0.78)	2 (0.15)	11 (1.04)
	Rank	4	13	19	8
Education	Total (%)	228 (2.79)	207 (1.05)	15 (1.13)	4 (0.38)
	Rank	5	9	13	13
Email Scandal	Total (%)	6 (0.07)	16 (0.08)	0 (-)	71 (6.74)
	Rank	24	23	22	1
Employment	Total (%)	296 (3.62)	441 (2.24)	67 (5.03)	5 (0.47)
	Rank	3	3	1	11
Gun Control	Total (%)	195 (2.38)	188 (0.96)	54 (4.05)	15 (1.42)
	Rank	7	10	5	6
Health Care	Total (%)	320 (3.91)	292 (1.48)	63 (4.73)	19 (1.80)
	Rank	1	6	3	5
Foreign Policy	Total (%)	154 (1.88)	515 (2.62)	21 (1.58)	34 (3.23)
	Rank	10	2	10	2
Military Spending	Total (%)	94 (1.15)	395 (2.01)	16 (1.20)	14 (1.33)
	Rank	18	5	12	7
National Security	Total (%)	130 (1.59)	575 (2.92)	13 (0.98)	29 (2.75)
	Rank	14	1	14	3
Supreme Court	Total (%)	55 (0.67)	56 (0.28)	67 (5.03)	24 (2.28)
	Rank	21	20	2	4
Taxes	Total (%)	159 (1.94)	395 (2.01)	18 (1.35)	3 (0.28)
	Rank	9	4	11	18

Note: The Republican Candidate Index is comprised of @CarlyFiorina, @ChrisChristie, @GovChristie, @gov_gilmore, @GovMikeHuckabee, @JebBush, @JohnKasich, @marcorubio, @RandPaul, @Real-BenCarson, @RealDonaldTrump, @RickSantorum, @SenTedCruz, @TeamJohnKasich, @TeamMarco, @TeamSantorum, @TeamTedCruz, and @TedCruz, who together had 18,495 tweets during the primary. The Democratic Candidate Index is comprised of @BernieSanders, @HFA, @HillaryClinton, @MartinOMalley, @SenSanders, and @TheBriefing2016, who together had 9,350 tweets during the primary.

To perform the time series, we first inspected the data for linear and quadratic trends. Newspaper indices, Twitter indices, and the tweets of the two parties were then de-trended if the linear or quadratic trends were statistically significant so that the relationship between the days could be analyzed without concerns about autocorrelation.[45] Then, the cross-lagged correlations between the de-trended time series were calculated to evaluate the strength of the relationships among the sources of interest.

Issue Emphasis within Twitter Feeds

Top issues for the Democratic candidate index were health care, affirmative action, employment, banking, and education. Top issues for the DNC were employment, the Supreme Court nomination, health care, affirmative action, and gun control. Top issues for the Republican candidate index were national security/terrorism, foreign policy/relations, employment, taxes, and military spending/veterans. Top issues for the RNC were Clinton's email scandal, foreign policy/relations, national security/terrorism, the Supreme Court nomination, and health care. Specific frequencies for these are displayed in Table 11.2 (a total of 12 issues).

Qualitatively, the rankings indicate dissimilar issue emphasis across the aisle and, to a certain extent, a focus on owned issues. They also suggest somewhat similar emphasis between the candidates and their chosen party. To test these relationships, we computed Spearman's rank correlation coefficients across the four sources on the 12 issues in question. Correlation results suggest that issue ownership and divergence in issue emphasis were supported in the 2016 election. No significant relationships were found in terms of issue emphasis between the Republican candidate index and the Democratic candidate index. Surprisingly, however, no significant relationships were found between the Democratic candidate index and the DNC or the Republican candidate index and the RNC. The candidates and their parties were not emphasizing the same issues on Twitter during the primary.

Success Influencing the Newspaper Agenda

Next, we ran time series analyses to examine whether the four Twitter sources predicted the newspaper agenda (or vice versa) and, if so, on which issues. First, the daily frequencies for the four Twitter indices as well as the newspaper index were examined for linear and quadratic trends within each series. Trends were detected in newspaper indices for affirmative action (quadratic function with $R^2 = .06$, $p < .01$), banking (quadratic function with $R^2 = .07$, $p < .01$), education (quadratic function with

$R^2 = .08$, $p < .01$), employment (quadratic function with $R^2 = .13$, $p < .01$), gun control (linear function with $R^2 = .23$, $p < .01$), health care (linear function with $R^2 = .09$, $p < .01$), foreign policy/relations (quadratic function with $R^2 = .10$, $p < .01$), national security/terrorism (linear function with $R^2 = .13$, $p < .01$), and the Supreme Court nomination (quadratic function with $R^2 = .07$, $p < .01$).

Trends were detected in the Democratic candidate Twitter index for affirmative action (quadratic function with $R^2 = .06$, $p < .01$), banking (linear function with $R^2 = .09$, $p < .01$), education (linear function with $R^2 = .06$, $p < .05$), gun control (linear function with $R^2 = .11$, $p < .01$), and health care (linear function with $R^2 = .15$, $p < .01$). Trends were detected in the DNC tweets for affirmative action (linear function with $R^2 = .04$, $p < .05$), gun control (linear function with $R^2 = .08$, $p < .01$), foreign policy/relations (linear function with $R^2 = .05$, $p < .01$), and national security/terrorism (linear function with $R^2 = .03$, $p < .05$). The DNC did not mention Clinton's email scandal; therefore, this issue was excluded from the DNC analysis.

Trends were detected in the Republican Candidate Twitter index for affirmative action (linear function with $R^2 = .03$, $p < .05$), banking (linear function with $R^2 = .08$, $p < .01$), education (linear function with $R^2 = .21$, $p < .01$), Clinton's email scandal (linear function with $R^2 = .09$, $p < .01$), employment (linear function with $R^2 = .08$, $p < .05$), gun control (linear function with $R^2 = .13$, $p < .01$), health care (linear function with $R^2 = .13$, $p < .01$), foreign policy/relations (linear function with $R^2 = .16$, $p < .01$), military spending/vets (linear function with $R^2 = .21$, $p < .01$), national security/terrorism (linear function with $R^2 = .20$, $p < .01$), the Supreme Court (linear function with $R^2 = .03$, $p < .05$), and taxes (linear function with $R^2 = .09$, $p < .01$). Trends were detected in the RNC tweets for military spending/vets (linear function with $R^2 = .03$, $p < .05$) and the Supreme Court (quadratic function with $R^2 = .09$, $p < .01$). To prevent autocorrelation, trends for newspapers and the four Twitter sources were removed prior to analysis.

Finding of time series suggest two things: (1) rather than predicting the newspaper index on owned issues, candidates and parties led newspapers on a variety of issues, including those specific to the current election (the Supreme Court nomination and Clinton's email scandal) and (2) newspapers were still more successful at predicting Twitter issue emphasis than Twitter feeds were at predicting newspaper issue emphasis, especially on event-driven issues. Results of the time series findings are in Tables 11.3a and 11.3b, with leads showing those instances in which newspaper issue emphasis predicted that of Twitter and lags indicating those instances when Twitter predicted newspapers.

The feeds of Democratic candidates and their campaigns preceded newspapers on six issues: education, Clinton's email scandal, gun rights,

Table 11.3a. Results of Time Series: Significant Cross-Correlations between the Newspaper Index and the Primary Candidate/Campaign/ Party Twitter Index

	Affirmative Action	Banking	Education	Clinton's Email Scandal	Employment	Foreign Policy/Relations
Democratic Candidate Index		Lag 0: 0.19	Lead 6: 0.15 Lag 2: 0.18	Lead 7: 0.21 Lead 4: 0.17 Lag 1: 0.17	Lead 2: 0.31 Lead 1: 0.17 Lag 0: 0.28	Lead 7: 0.21 Lag 0: 0.29
Republican Candidate Index		Lead 6: 0.16 Lead 2: 0.19 Lag 0: 0.17	Lead 7: 0.22 Lead 5: 0.18 Lead 2: 0.15 Lead 1: 0.19	Lead 7: 0.20 Lead 6: 0.26 Lead 3: 0.22	Lag 0: 0.25 Lag 1: 0.23	Lag 0: 0.16 Lag 1: 0.21
DNC	Lag 0: −0.18	Lead 1: −0.18 Lag 7: 0.16	Lead 2: 0.16	N/A	Lead 5: 0.20	
RNC	Lag 0: −0.18	Lead 7: 0.16 Lead 3: −0.20 Lead 1: 0.16 Lag 2: 0.20 Lag 3: 0.18	Lead 3: 0.30 Lag 7: 0.16	Lead 7: 0.25 Lead 6: 0.16 Lead 2: 0.16 Lead 1: 0.26 Lag 0: 0.35 Lag 1: 0.18 Lag 6: 0.18 Lag 7: 0.18		Lead 4: −0.17

Note: All cross-lagged correlations shown here are significant, $p < .05$. Leads shown indicate that newspapers predicted tweet emphasis a given number of days prior to the contemporary frequencies. Lags indicate that tweets predicted newspaper mentions a given number of days prior to the contemporary frequencies. Lag 0 indicates a contemporaneous relationship. Negative correlations indicate low incidence on Twitter.

Table 11.3b. Results of Time Series: Significant Cross-Correlations between the Newspaper Index and the Primary Candidate/Campaign/ Party Twitter Index (cont.)

	Gun Control	Health Care	Military Spending	National Security	Supreme Court	Taxes
Democratic Candidate Index	Lead 2: 0.22 Lag 0: 0.28 Lag 6: 0.17	Lag 0: 0.21 Lag 1: 0.16	Lag 1: 0.17		Lead 1: 0.30 Lag 0: 0.17	Lag 0: 0.18 Lag 5: 0.23 Lag 6: 0.17 Lag 7: 0.16
Republican Candidate Index	Lead 6: 0.18 Lead 3: 0.32 Lead 2: 0.26 Lag 0: 0.33	Lead 6: 0.21 Lead 5: 0.16 Lag 0: 0.18	Lag 0: 0.22 Lag 2: 0.21	Lag 0: 0.20	Lead 5: 0.17 Lead 4: 0.15 Lead 3: 0.23 Lead 2: 0.37 Lead 1: 0.44 Lag 0: 0.31 Lag 1: 0.19 Lag 2: 0.20	Lag 2: 0.20
DNC	Lead 7: 0.19 Lead 1: 0.16 Lag 0: 0.27	Lag 2: 0.15 Lag 5: −0.17	Lag 0: 0.21 Lag 7: 0.18	Lead 3: −0.18 Lag 2: 0.17	Lead 2: 0.32 Lead 1: 0.57	Lag 2: 0.30 Lag 3: 0.18
RNC	Lead 3: 0.16 Lead 1: 0.18 Lag 0: 0.37 Lag 4: −0.17		Lead 2: 0.25 Lead 1: 0.21	Lag 0: 0.23 Lag 6: 0.19	Lead 1: 0.30 Lag 1: 0.15	

Note: All cross-lagged correlations shown here are significant, $p < .05$. Leads shown indicate that newspapers predicted tweet emphasis a given number of days prior to the contemporary frequencies. Lags indicate that tweets predicted newspaper mentions a given number of days prior to the contemporary frequencies. Lag 0 indicates a contemporaneous relationship. Negative correlations indicate low incidence on Twitter.

health care, military spending, and taxes, anywhere from 1 to 7 days prior. Thus, these were made salient within the Democratic candidate index and subsequently covered by newspapers. While education and health care can be considered Democratic-owned issues, military spending and taxes are not. The DNC agenda also preceded the newspaper agenda, predicting newspaper emphasis on banking, health care, military spending/vets, national security/terrorism, and taxes, anywhere from 2 to 7 days prior. While financial regulation and health care can be interpreted as issues owned by the left, military spending, taxes, and national security are traditionally conservative issues, undermining support for an assertion that parties are more successful on owned issues.

The Republican candidate index predicted the newspaper agenda on five issues. Once again, this was not necessarily on owned issues. The issue agenda of Republicans candidates and their campaigns preceded issue emphasis by newspapers 1 to 2 days prior on employment, foreign policy, military spending, the Supreme Court, and taxes. Military spending and taxes can be considered issues owned by Republicans, while employment and foreign policy can be considered pressing issues owned by neither party, although foreign policy may be perceived as closely aligned with defense, which is a Republican-owned issue. The latter two are also issues on which Republicans may have been trying to attack the Obama administration and, by association, the Clinton campaign. The RNC agenda preceded that of newspapers on four issues: banking, Clinton's email scandal, national security, and the Supreme Court nomination (1 to 7 days prior). While national security can be considered an owned issue, the Supreme Court nomination and the email scandal are timely issues for which both parties have much at stake. Overall, then, we see success on both sides of the aisle on a variety of issues, some owned, some not, and some specific to the current election.

An important addition to the above findings is the success newspapers exhibited in predicting the agenda of the four Twitter sources. Newspapers led at least one of the four Twitter sources on every issue except affirmative action, national security, and taxes. Further, newspapers saw their greatest success at predicting the Twitter agenda on timely issues that were specific to the current election (Clinton's email scandal and the Supreme Court nomination). On Clinton's email scandal, the newspaper agenda preceded that of Democrats, Republicans, and the RNC anywhere from 1 to 7 days prior, with the largest number of leads appearing for the RNC. Newspapers led all four Twitter sources on the Supreme Court nomination anywhere from 1 to 5 days prior. This was especially true for the DNC ($r = 0.57$) and the Republican candidate index ($r = 0.44$) where we saw two of the largest cross-lagged correlations across issues. Along with the email scandal and the Supreme Court, newspapers led both

Republicans and Democrats on gun control. Traditionally a Republican issue, this can also be considered timely due to increased levels of violence in Chicago and recent mass shootings in America during the past two years (e.g., San Bernardino, Orlando, and Charleston).

Along with leads by newspapers, contemporaneous relationships were found on several issues, including affirmative action, banking, Clinton's email scandal, employment, gun control, health care, foreign policy/relations, military spending/veterans, national security, the Supreme Court, and taxes. On most issues newspapers, candidates, campaigns, and parties commented on the day's concerns simultaneously.

EVALUATING ISSUE EMPHASIS AND AGENDA BUILDING IN 2016

This study presents three important findings. First, issue emphasis on Twitter during the 2016 election supported the owned-issue hypothesis, as well as dissimilar issue emphasis across parties. Issue emphasis on Twitter was more differentiated than in the 2012 election. Second, candidates, campaigns, and parties put forth a unique agenda on Twitter, thus predicting issue emphasis in newspapers; however, such emphasis was not necessarily confined to party-owned issues. Third, the power in the agenda-building relationship, at least when examining candidate/campaign indices and the feeds of the DNC and the RNC, lies with newspapers, especially on timely, controversial issues. While the current findings on issue ownership diverge from our study on agenda building during the 2012 primary elections, findings on the Twitter-newspaper relationship reveal consistent patterns across elections.[46]

More distinctive issue emphasis in 2016 may be attributed to candidates and parties attempting to appeal to an increasingly polarized voter base.[47] Negotiations in Congress also became more polarized in recent years, and such a divide may have influenced election issue emphasis.[48] In other words, party politics are invading all aspects of political life. Results of the 2016 election revealed "one of the most polarizing in recent history," suggesting that candidates, especially Trump, largely benefitted from such owned-issue emphasis.[49]

A closer look at issue emphasis across the candidates and parties reveals further nuances and strategic emphasis on timely issues. In terms of owned-issue emphasis, both the Democratic candidates and the DNC focused heavily on affirmative action, mainly stressing issues of race and gender equality. This emphasis was undoubtedly meant to draw in minority voters and women, two voter bases that were expected to spurn Republicans in 2016. The emphasis on affirmative action, employment, and banking was also likely intended to target an important voter base:

those facing economic hardships. While affirmative action and employment focused a great deal on income inequality and wages, banking focused to a large extent on Wall Street corruption and the need for financial regulation, partly driven by Bernie Sanders. The lack of emphasis on the Clinton email scandal (which was low on the list of Democrats and was never mentioned by the DNC) also indicates selective avoidance on behalf of Democrats.

On the other side, Republicans focused on several issues meant to appeal to their voter base, as well as two timely issues. Owned issues emphasized heavily by the right include national security/terrorism and taxes. National security was a top issue for Republicans in 2016, often emphasized to poke holes in Obama administration policies and to inspire fear in the Republican voter base.[50] Along with undermining the Obama administration (and, by default, a future Clinton administration) on national security, the emphasis on foreign relations was also a key topic for Republicans, who focused largely on trade, relations with China, the 2012 Benghazi attack, and U.S. standing around the world. Republicans also focused heavily on two timely issues: the Clinton email scandal and the Supreme Court nomination. The emphasis on Clinton's email scandal echoes exemplary attacks by the Trump campaign, including the infamous "Lock her up!" chant that regularly occurred at his campaign rallies.[51]

Lack of support for the issue ownership hypothesis in recent years has caused some to question the validity of this theory in general.[52] Our previous findings on 2012 Twitter use by candidates, campaigns, and parties further undermined this hypothesis on Twitter.[53] Yet, the results here suggest that we should not rush to disregard the issue ownership hypothesis. It has a place in modern campaigns and may continue to garner support in a polarized political environment. For example, within Democrat feeds and that of the DNC one important, generally considered liberal, issue was missing: the environment. Trump's victory is largely seen as a triumph for climate change deniers.[54] Should he pursue anti–climate change policies, as promised during his campaign, this issue may come to the fore among Democratic politicians. These findings are based on Twitter and newspaper indices and do not take into account the various other types of campaign media that can influence the press (ads, press releases, rallies, etc.). It is worth noting that previous research by Conway, Filer, and Kenski detected content overlap between candidate tweets and campaign ads in the 2012 presidential campaign.[55] Future research should examine whether issue ownership is becoming commonplace in other campaign media, as well as investigate relationships across campaign media (ads, websites, and social media feeds).

Moving to our time series investigation of agenda building on behalf of campaigns and parties, similar to the 2012 study, we again see the newspaper agenda predicted that of Twitter to a greater extent than the reverse. Across the two studies there is also limited support, at least with Twitter, that candidate and party agendas are more likely to predict media coverage when it comes to owned issues. Both sides saw success on non-owned and timely issues. It is noteworthy that the two sides had similar success in predicting the newspaper agenda. This finding does not support a possible Trump effect.[56] This study is limited, of course, in that it only focused on issues and Trump's campaign was not issue laden. Further, issue emphasis is theorized to be lower during primary campaigns than in the several months leading up to the general election.[57] Still, issue emphasis in this study was not insignificant. We would argue further that, regardless of lower number, political issue emphasis (as opposed to entertainment-laden content) begs future research, especially as we contemplate the ramifications of new media for democratic outcomes.[58] Future studies should explore agendas other than those of issues. This study is also limited in that it relied on dictionary work, which is not without certain flaws.[59] We are confident, however, in the rigorous nature of our coding and analysis.

It is important to note that the relationships between Twitter sources and the newspaper index should not be equated with causality. Such patterns, especially consistent patterns over time, do suggest a nonrandom relationship, but cannot be interpreted as Twitter feeds directly influencing the news agenda.[60] What we can say is that, when combined with our previous study, two studies suggest that newspapers are, if not responding to Twitter feeds, paying attention to candidate issue emphasis in social media. Future studies should also investigate the relationship between public opinion and candidate social media.

A main takeaway here is the apparent reliance on traditional news media by our Twitter sources when it comes to timely and controversial issues. Newspapers predicted Twitter emphasis to the greatest extent when it came to the Clinton email scandal and the next Supreme Court appointee. Thus, campaigns and parties, especially the RNC in this case, continue to look to mainstream media for credibility on high-profile issues. This finding, combined with the overall finding that newspapers were better able to predict the Twitter agenda, indicates that even in the fragmented media environment, mainstream newspapers still hold the power in the agenda-building/agenda-setting relationship.

NOTES

1. Maeve Duggan and Aaron Smith, "The Political Environment on Social Media," *Pew Research Center*, October 25, 2016; Shannon Greenwood, Andrew

Perrin, and Maeve Duggan, "Social Media Update 2016," Pew Research Center, November 11, 2016.

2. Michael M. Grynbaum and Sydney Ember, "If Trump Tweets It, Is It News? A Quandary for the News Media," *New York Times*, November 29, 2016.

3. Terri L. Towner and David A. Dulio, "New Media and Political Marketing in the United States: 2012 and Beyond," *Journal of Political Marketing* 11 (2012): 97.

4. For information on the importance of issues in campaign media, see John R. Petrocik, "Issue Ownership in Presidential Elections, with a 1980 Case Study," *American Journal of Political Science* 40 (1996): 825–50; and Owen G. Abbe et al., "Agenda Setting in Congressional Elections: The Impact of Issues and Campaigns on Voting Behavior," *Political Research Quarterly* 56 (2003): 419–30.

5. Abbe et al., "Agenda Setting in Congressional Elections," 419–30; William L. Benoit, "Own Party Issue Ownership Emphasis in Presidential Television Spots," *Communication Reports* 20 (2007): 42–50.

6. John Sides, "The Consequences of Campaign Agendas," *American Politics Research* 35 (2007): 465–88.

7. Bethany A. Conway, Kate Kenski, and Di Wang, "The Rise of Twitter in the Political Campaign: Searching for Intermedia Agenda-Setting Effects in the Presidential Primary," *Journal of Computer Mediated Communication* 20 (2015): 363–80.

8. Carroll Doherty, "7 Things to Know About Polarization in America," Pew Research Center, June 12, 2014.

9. Danny Hayes, "Party Reputation, Journalistic Expectations: How Issue Ownership Influences Election News," *Political Communication* 25 (2008): 377–400.

10. W. Lance Bennett and Shanto Iyengar, "A New Era of Minimal Effects? The Changing Foundations of Political Communication," *Journal of Communication* 58 (2008): 707–731.

11. Petrocik, "Issue Ownership in Presidential Elections," 825–50.

12. Kathleen Hall Jamieson, *Packaging the Presidency: A History and Criticism of Presidential Campaign Advertising*, 3rd ed. (New York: Oxford University Press, 1996).

13. For experimental research on issue ownership, see Abbe et al., "Agenda Setting in Congressional Elections," 419–30; For survey research on issue ownership, see Pew, "Wide Partisan Differences Over the Issues That Matter in 2014," Pew Research Center, September 12, 2014.

14. William L. Benoit, "Own Party Issue Ownership Emphasis in Presidential Television Spots," *Communication Reports* 20 (2007): 42–50.

15. David F. Damore, "The Dynamics of Issue Ownership in Presidential Campaigns," *Political Research Quarterly* 57 (2004): 391–97; David F. Damore, "Issue Convergence in Presidential Campaigns," *Political Behavior* 27 (2005): 71–97.

16. For examples of competition, success/failure with issues, and public importance, see Sides, "The Consequences of Campaign Agendas," 465–88; Lee Sigelman and Emmett H. Buell, "Avoidance or Engagement? Issue Coverage in U. S. Presidential Campaigns, 1960–2000," *American Journal of Political Science* 48 (2004): 650–61; and Noah Kaplan, David K. Park, and Travis N. Ridout, "Dialogue in American Political Campaigns? An Examination of Issue Convergence in Candidate Television Advertising," *American Journal of Political Science* 50 (2006): 724–36.

17. William L. Benoit and Glenn J. Hansen, "Issue Ownership in Primary and General Presidential Debates," *Argumentation and Advocacy* 40 (2004): 143–54.

18. Shanto Iyengar and Nicholas A. Valentino, "Who Says What? Source Credibility as a Mediator of Campaign Advertising," in *Elements of Reason: Cognition, Choice, and the Bounds of Rationality*, ed. Arthur Lupia, Mathew D. McCubbins, and Samuel L. Popkin (New York: Cambridge University Press, 2000), 108–29; Anke Tresch, Jonas Lefevere, and Stefaan Walgrave, "'Steal Me if You Can!' The Impact of Campaign Messages on Associative Issue Ownership," *Party Politics* 21 (2015): 198–208.

19. For examples of trespassing in traditional media, see William L. Benoit et al., "Staying 'on Message': Consistency in Content of Presidential Primary Campaign Messages Across Media," *American Behavioral Scientist* 55 (2011): 457–68; Damore, "The Dynamics of Issue Ownership in Presidential Campaigns," 391–97; Damore, "Issue Convergence in Presidential Campaigns," 71–97; Kaplan, Park, and Ridout, "Dialogue in American Political Campaigns?" 724–36; Sides, "The Consequences of Campaign Agendas," 465–88; and Sigelman and Buell, "Avoidance or Engagement?" 650–61.

20. For information on 2016 campaign ad spending, see AP, "Ad Spending: The Candidate Ad Spending Race," *AP*, November 16, 2016.

21. Emily Metzgar and Albert Maruggi, "Social Media and the 2008 U.S. Presidential Election," *Journal of New Communications Research* 4 (2009): 141–65.

22. Conway, Kenski, and Wang, "The Rise of Twitter in the Political Campaign," 363–80.

23. Andreas Jungherr, "The Logic of Political Coverage on Twitter: Temporal Dynamics and Content," *Journal of Communication* 64 (2014): 239–59.

24. Grynbaum and Ember, "If Trump Tweets It, Is It News?"

25. Maxwell E. McCombs, *Setting the Agenda: The Mass Media and Public Opinion* (Malden, MA: Blackwell Publishing Inc., 2004); Maxwell E. McCombs and Donald L. Shaw, "The Agenda-Setting Function of Mass Media," *Public Opinion Quarterly* 36 (1972): 176–87.

26. David H. Weaver and Jihyang Choi, "The Media Agenda: Who (or What) Sets It?" in *The Oxford Handbook of Political Communication*, ed. Kate Kenski and Kathleen Hall Jamieson (Oxford University Press, 2014): online edition.

27. Bryan E. Denham, "Toward Conceptual Consistency in Studies of Agenda-Building Processes: A Scholarly Review," *The Review of Communication*, 10 (2010): 306–23.

28. Paul Farhi, "The Twitter Explosion," *American Journalism Review*, April/May 2009; John H. Parmelee, "The Agenda-Building Function of Political Tweets," *New Media & Society* 16 (2013): 434–50; John H. Parmelee, "Political Journalists and Twitter: Influences on Norms and Practices," *Journal of Media Practice* 14 (2013): 291–305.

29. Andrea Ceron, Luigi Curini, and Stefano M. Iacus, "First- and Second-Level Agenda Building in the Twittersphere: An Application to the Italian Political Debate," *Journal of Information Technology & Politics* 13 (2016): 159–74; Ingrid Rogstad, "Is Twitter Just Rehashing? Intermedia Agenda Setting Between Twitter and Mainstream Media," *Journal of Information Technology & Politics* 13 (2016): 142–58; Chris J. Vargo, Ekaterina Basilaia, and Donald L. Shaw, "Event Versus Issue: Twit-

ter Reflections of Major News—A Case Study," in *Communication and Information Technologies Annual (Studies in Media and Communications, Volume 9)*, ed. Laura Robinson, Sheila R. Cotton, and Jeremy Schulz (Bingley, UK: Emerald Publishing Limited, 2015), 215–39.

30. Kate Kenski and Kathleen Hall Jamieson, "Political Communication: Looking Ahead," in *The Oxford Handbook of Political Communication*, ed. Kate Kenski and Kathleen Hall Jamieson (Oxford University Press, 2016), online version.

31. Stefan Walgrave and Peter Van Aelst, "The Contingency of the Mass Media's Political Agenda Setting Power: Toward a Preliminary Theory," *Journal of Communication* 56 (2006): 97.

32. Vassia Gueorguieva, "Voters, MySpace, and YouTube: The Impact of Alternative Communication Channels on the 2006 Election Cycle and Beyond," *Social Science Computer Review* 26 (2008): 288–300; Thomas J. Johnson and David D. Perlmutter, "Introduction: The Facebook Election," *Mass Communication & Society* 13 (2010): 554–59; Jennifer Stromer-Galley, "On-Line Interaction and Why Candidates Avoid It," *Journal of Communication* 50 (2000): 111–32.

33. Conway, Kenski, and Wang, "The Rise of Twitter in the Political Campaign," 363–80.

34. Hayes, "Party Reputation, Journalistic Expectations," 377–400.

35. John R. Petrocik, William L. Benoit, and Glenn L. Hansen, "Issue Ownership and Presidential Campaigning, 1952–2000," *Political Science Quarterly* 118 (2003): 599–626.

36. Conway, Kenski, and Wang, "The Rise of Twitter in the Political Campaign," 363–80.

37. Pew, "The State of the News Media 2013." Pew Research Center, 2013.

38. Amy Chozik and Patrick Healy, "Hillary Clinton Has Clinched Democratic Nomination, Survey Reports," *New York Times*, June 6, 2016.

39. In a revision to Conway, Kenski, and Wang's (2015) approach, we chose to include all articles and editorials that mentioned any of the candidates or the election, rather than only those that specifically focused on the election. This resulted in a higher number of articles compared to the 2012 study. Due to the number of candidate names included, several articles needed to be discarded. For example, many uses of "Bush" referenced former presidents, not 2016 candidate Jeb Bush, and "Cruz" resulted in articles that referenced "Santa Cruz" in *The Los Angeles Times*. Of the articles discarded, *The New York Times* had 473, *The Wall Street Journal* had 315, *USA Today* had 174, *The Los Angeles Times* had 1,146, and *The Washington Post* had 520.

40. Andreas Jungherr, "Twitter Use in Election Campaigns: A Systematic Literature Review," *Journal of Information Technology & Politics* 13 (2016): 82.

41. Linh Dang-Xuan et al., "An Investigation of Influentials and the Role of Sentiment in Political Communication on Twitter During Election Periods," *Information, Communication & Society* 16 (2013): 795–825.

42. Conway, Kenski, and Wang, "The Rise of Twitter in the Political Campaign," 363–80; John C. Tedesco, "Issue and strategy agenda-setting in the 2000 presidential primaries," *American Behavioral Scientist* 44 (2011): 2048–2067.

43. Final categories included abortion, affirmative action, agriculture, banking, budget, campaign finance reform, crime/criminal justice, the economy, educa-

tion, Clinton's email scandal, employment, energy, environment, First Amendment, Flint water crisis, foreign policy/relations, gun control, health care, immigration, military spending/veterans, national security/terrorism, social welfare, Supreme Court, taxes, the war on drugs, and the Zika virus. To test the validity of our dictionary work, 50 random tweets and 50 random articles were examined for each of 26 issues. This precautionary measure suggested limited error in coding.

44. Conway, Kenski, and Wang, "The Rise of Twitter in the Political Campaign," 363–80; Tedesco, "Issue and strategy agenda-setting in the 2000 presidential primaries," 2048–2067.

45. Daniel Romer, "Time Series Models," in *Capturing Campaign Dynamics 2000 & 2004*, ed. Daniel Romer et al. (Philadelphia, PA: University of Pennsylvania Press, 2006), 165–243.

46. Conway, Kenski, and Wang, "The Rise of Twitter in the Political Campaign," 363–80.

47. Carroll Doherty, "7 Things to Know About Polarization in America," Pew Research Center, June 12, 2014.

48. For information on congressional polarization, see Mark Z. Barabak and Lisa Mascaro, "Republicans Hold the House and Senate, but Will That End the Washington Gridlock Even with President Trump?" *Los Angeles Times*, November 9, 2016.

49. Shane Shifflet, "A Divided America: Election Results Reveal the 2016 Presidential Contest to Be One of the Most Polarizing in Recent History. Donald Trump Benefited as More Counties Voted Republican by Wider Margins Than in 2012," *Wall Street Journal*, November 10, 2016.

50. Molly Ball, "Donald Trump and the Politics of Fear," *The Atlantic*, September 2, 2016.

51. Peter W. Stevenson, "A Brief History of the 'Lock Her Up!' Chant by Trump Supporters Against Clinton," *Washington Post*, November 22, 2016.

52. Sides, "The Consequences of Campaign Agendas," 465–88.

53. Conway, Kenski, and Wang, "The Rise of Twitter in the Political Campaign," 363–80.

54. Clare Foran, "Donald Trump and the Triumph of Climate-Change Denial," *The Atlantic*, December 25, 2016.

55. Bethany Anne Conway, Christine R. Filer, and Kate Kenski, "Campaign Media Congruence: Issues in 2012 Presidential Election Tweets and Ads," Paper presented at the American Political Science Association, San Francisco, CA, September 2015.

56. Chris Wells et al., "How Trump Drove Coverage to the Nomination: Hybrid Media Campaigning," *Political Communication* 33 (2016): 669–76.

57. Kathleen E. Kendall, "Presidential Primaries and General Election Campaigns: A Comparison," in *Praeger Handbook of Political Campaigning in the United States*, ed. William L. Benoit (Santa Barbara: Praeger, 2016), 31–60.

58. Peter Van Aelst et al., "Political Communication in a High Choice Media Environment: A Challenge for Democracy?" *Annals of the International Communication Association* 41 (2017): 3–27.

59. Guo et al., "Big Social Data Analytics in Journalism and Mass Communication: Comparing Dictionary-Based Text Analysis and Unsupervised Topic Modeling," *Journalism & Mass Communication Quarterly* 93 (2016): 332–59.

60. Ben Sayre et al., "Agenda Setting in a Digital Age," *Policy & Internet* 2 (2010): 7–32.

12

Picture Perfect?

The Role of Instagram in Issue Agenda Setting during the 2016 Presidential Primary Campaign

Terri L. Towner and Caroline Lego Muñoz

The role of social media in political campaigning has been an ever-increasing trend since Barack Obama successfully employed Facebook to win the White House in 2008. Indeed, social media's importance and use in political campaigning is well-known and frequently studied, but newer forms of social media, such as Snapchat, Instagram, Tumblr, and Pinterest, have increased in usage since the 2012 presidential election.[1] Candidates now employ a wide variety of platforms, intelligently targeting citizens, challengers, and journalists with tailor-made comments, online videos, infographics, GIFs, and pictures. During the 2016 U.S. presidential primaries, every candidate employed the visual social networking site Instagram as a campaign tool, posting a variety of pictures, videos, and infographics.[2] Yet, as a newer digital platform, Instagram's role in political communications is largely unstudied. Therefore, we seek to examine if candidate Instagram posts influence campaign content in the mainstream media and if the mainstream media's agenda impacts candidate's Instagram posts during the presidential primary period.

This study focuses on the Instagram accounts from the top Democratic and Republican presidential nominees and articles from the nation's leading newspapers. To shed light on the agenda-setting effects between Instagram posts and the mainstream media, we coded the number of daily issue mentions in the candidate's Instagram images and captions as well as in newspaper articles. Consistent with previous studies examining social networking sites,[3] we expect to find a reciprocal relationship between Instagram posts and mainstream news by empirically testing whether Instagram posts are a predictor of newspaper coverage or if the relationship is reversed. Therefore, we expect an intermedia agenda-setting effect between Instagram and mainstream media.[4]

ORIGINS OF AGENDA SETTING

According to McCombs and Shaw,[5] the mainstream media—journalists, editors, and reporters—set the public agenda, telling citizens what to think about on any given day. Conducted during the 1968 U.S. presidential election, McCombs and Shaw's Chapel Hill study found that undecided voters' responses on the most important issue of the day was significantly correlated with issue mentions in newspapers, newsmagazines, and television news.[6] McCombs and Shaw grounded their work on the "need for orientation" theory, which asserts that citizens desire the familiar and rely, to varying degrees, on the media to become familiar with their surroundings.[7] If a citizen has low interest in politics and is unsure about a political campaign, he/she is more susceptible to agenda setting by the media.[8] Overall, the mainstream media plays a critical role in politics and campaigning, directly influencing citizens' attitudes about the campaign, candidates, and government issues.

Agenda setting is one of the most frequently studied media effects theories.[9] Given this, many studies have expanded on McCombs and Shaw's original work by employing a variety of methods—surveys, content analysis, and experimental designs—largely confirming that the media agenda impacts citizens' agendas.[10] Along the way, the theory has developed two different levels. The first level asserts that the media tell citizens "what to think about," whereas the second level argues that the media tell citizens "how to think about" issues or candidates.[11] Second-level agenda setting purports that the public develops opinions based on the type of coverage the media chooses to allocate to objects (i.e., attribute agenda setting). As McCombs states, an object "has numerous attributes, those characteristics and properties that fill out the picture of each object. Just as objects vary in salience, so do the attributes of each object".[12] Therefore, the media's focus on certain attributes over other attributes can influence a citizen's opinion and ultimately their perceptions of government, policy, and candidates.[13]

Agenda Setting in the Internet Age

Early work on agenda setting examined the empirical differences between print and television media.[14] The media landscape, however, has changed dramatically since the 1990s. The Internet's rise ushered in an era where citizens can communicate news and information via email, website, and blog.[15] As a result, it has been suggested that the mainstream media's agenda-setting power has been diminished.[16] In fact, McCombs acknowledges that digital media, particularly blogs, are now part of the media arena, but notes that "who is influencing who" is unclear.[17] The news agenda may now be shared among traditional and non-traditional media outlets (a phenomenon known as intermedia agenda setting). Mc-Combs likely correctly predicted: "Intermedia agenda setting at both the first and second levels is likely to remain high on the journalism research agenda for a very long time."[18]

Candidates and campaigns have readily adopted online tools, such as blogs and websites, to directly communicate with citizens. Previously, political candidates influenced the mainstream media agenda via press releases, brochures, and ads.[19] Now, candidate-controlled websites and blogs sidestep the mainstream media, allowing for the possibility of themselves influencing citizens and the media agenda. Some research supports this notion. Early research examining television news, newspapers, and candidate websites during the 2000 presidential election found that the agenda offered on candidate websites predicted the mainstream media agenda as well as the reverse, that the mainstream media agenda predicted candidate websites' agendas.[20] Research on the agenda-setting effects of blogs has also concluded that the mainstream media agenda is related to content in political blogs.[21] Indeed, bloggers seem to rely on the mainstream reports for information and sources while the mainstream media use blogs for "hot" topics and sources.[22] The relationship between traditional media and online media, however, is complex. One cannot assume that a correlation between the agendas in offline and online media indicates causation. It may be likely that both the mainstream media and websites are reacting to the same event, but further research is necessary.

AGENDA SETTING IN THE SOCIAL MEDIA ERA

Scholars have also explored the agenda-setting role of newer online sources, particularly social networking sites. Some studies confirm a reciprocal relationship between the agendas of social media, such as Facebook, Twitter, and YouTube, and the mainstream media. One study offers evidence that YouTube videos, Google News searches, and newspaper coverage of California's Proposition 8 on same-sex marriage were interrelated.[23] Another examined the relationship among political issue coverage in the traditional press and social media (e.g., Twitter, blogs, and forums), finding evidence of a shared or reciprocal Granger causality between mainstream and social media coverage on certain issues.[24] In one recent study on the Black Lives Matter movement the authors found that tweets predicted mainstream media coverage of the movement and ultimately elite discourse.[25] Other agenda-setting research is more skeptical, suggesting that social media only has a moderate influence on the mainstream media's agenda.[26] For example, one recent paper concluded that social networking sites' agendas are not dramatically altering mainstream media's agenda, as their ability to predict the agenda of traditional media is limited to only certain topics (e.g., cultural coverage).[27] When comparing Twitter's trending topics to CNN headlines and Google Trends, another team of researchers found that CNN was ahead of Twitter in reporting information the majority of the time. Thus there is some evidence that social networking sites can set the mainstream agenda, but this evidence is not dramatic and the issues/topics are not consistent.[28]

These mixed findings suggest additional research on social media's agenda-setting power is required, particularly regarding how candidates employ social media to set the media's agenda during a campaign. Acknowledging social media's ability to influence citizens[29] as well as the mainstream media,[30] every presidential candidate in recent elections has utilized a variety of social media platforms, including Facebook, Twitter, YouTube, Instagram, and more.[31] Candidates employ social media to directly communicate with citizens, solicit donations, and mobilize the electorate, all without the mainstream media filter.[32] Research suggests that attention to social media about the candidates and campaign is linked to candidate evaluations[33] as well as political participation.[34] Examining Obama's and Romney's Facebook walls during the 2012 presidential election, one study found a link between the public's "most important issue" and the issue agendas of Facebook commenters, hinting at a relationship between Facebook's agenda and the public agenda.[35]

While we do not presume that candidates' campaign content on social media has the same impact on news media as it does on citizens, it is plausible that the candidates' use of social media may predict the traditional media agenda. During the 2012 presidential election, for example, there is some evidence of a reciprocal relationship between the top political issues mentioned (e.g., the budget, economy, employment, energy, foreign policy, health care, and taxes) on the Twitter feeds of political candidates/parties and in newspapers.[36] In addition, a 2013 study reveals similarities between U.S. Congress members' issue tweets and newspaper issue coverage, particularly for the economy, immigration, health care, and marginalized groups, suggesting that journalists rely on Twitter for news content.[37] Existing research, however, focuses largely on Twitter's role in agenda setting during campaign periods, rarely considering newer social platforms, such as Instagram.

INSTAGRAM'S ROLE IN CAMPAIGNING

Instagram, started in 2010, is an online photo- and video-sharing social networking service that allows users to take and share pictures and videos. Users communicate largely with images that include a caption with no clickable links. The ease with which consumers can now capture images and videos on their smartphone has contributed to Instagram's growing popularity. In fact, Instagram has reportedly over 600 million monthly active users, growing faster in active users than both Twitter and Facebook.[38] In 2015, about 24 percent of adults used Instagram, largely used by non-whites, women, and young adults. In comparison, 20 percent of adults use Twitter and 62 percent use Facebook.[39]

Acknowledging Instagram's increasing popularity, candidates across the globe have begun to include Instagram in their social media toolkit. The limited research on Instagram finds that political parties (in the Swedish context) employed Instagram largely to broadcast information as a "visual pamphlet" or "virtual billboard" rather than for mobilization.[40] The Instagram images the political parties posted often presented the personal side of the top candidates, but in a political and professional setting. Similarly, another study, focusing on the 2015 Bahraini election, found the candidates used Instagram to self-promote and connect with citizens on a personal level.[41] In the case of the 2014 Scottish independence referendum (#IndyRef), three prominent themes were found in Instagram posts with the #IndyRef hashtag: the election, portrayal of the human side of the debate, and symbolism.[42] Compared to these international elections, candidates during the 2016 U.S. presidential nomination season used Instagram in a similar fashion, posting snapshots with family members, informative infographics, graphics of the latest polling, pictures from backstage moments at events and rallies, and videos of debates, events, and interviews. Overall, U.S. presidential nominees used Instagram to shape their image, humanize the campaign, foster a sense of unity, communicate with voters about issues, and engage with followers.

RESEARCH QUESTIONS AND HYPOTHESES

The 2016 presidential nominees employed Instagram as a campaign tool. Presently, however, it is unclear how presidential candidates' use of Instagram impacts the mainstream media agenda, if at all. Building on intermedia agenda-setting research, we expect that the issue agenda of candidates' Instagram posts will predict the mainstream media's issue agenda during the 2016 presidential nomination season. This expectation is in line with studies showing that blog content can predict traditional news media content. In fact, these studies note how traditional journalists rely on blogs for sources and topics, often referencing some of the top blogs in reports.[43] Our expectation is also consistent with research indicating that social media content on Twitter and YouTube predicts the mainstream media agenda.[44] One study, for example, demonstrated that the tweets from the Republican candidates, Barack Obama, and the Republican and Democratic parties significantly predicted issue mentions in newspapers during the 2012 presidential nomination season.[45] While we primarily build on blog and Twitter agenda-setting research, it is important to note that Instagram is a fundamentally different medium than blogs, based largely on visuals rather than text. Does a predominantly visual social network, such as Instagram, make it more or less powerful in terms of agenda setting? Drawing on psychology literature, which has long established that visuals have greater impact on memory and recall,[46] we expect visuals on Instagram to be powerful agenda setters. Moreover, social media is increasingly becoming more image dominated, with photos and online video receiving the most engagement on sites such as Facebook and Twitter.[47] In fact one scholar found that attention to photos and infographics about the 2016 presidential primary campaign posted on social networking sites were a stronger predictor of citizens' candidate evaluations than attention to textual content.[48] This growing importance of online, visual content is likely not ignored by mainstream journalists, especially visual content that is shared over and over—perhaps becoming trending issues or topics. Thus, we assert that professional journalists and reporters will turn to Instagram as a news and information source, just as journalists rely on blogs and Twitter for sources, leads, data, and topics.[49] We specifically posit that candidates' Instagram posts will predict the issue agenda in mainstream newspapers (H1).

Additionally, we anticipate that the mainstream media's issue agenda will predict the issue agenda of candidates' Instagram posts. Candidates and campaigns do not always seek to bypass the mainstream press on their digital platforms, as many include web links to outside news media articles or videos.[50] In addition to dissemination, some candidates employ social media platforms to complement mainstream press coverage by releasing press announcements and television ads on social media. Candidates also respond to national media reports that negatively or unfairly portray them or create headlining controversy. Most important, candidates and campaigns can quickly and easily respond to national media in real time by simply posting an image on Instagram—no text or lengthy speech needed. Thus, perhaps it should be anticipated that candidates' Instagram agenda is easily affected by the traditional media's agenda. Our expectation builds on prior work that finds that the mainstream press can predict social media's agenda.[51] Specifically, we are interested in how mainstream issue coverage predicts a political candidate's Instagram issue agenda. Some research found evidence that mainstream newspapers predicted the issue agenda in candidate and political parties' Twitter feeds in the 2012 primaries.[52] Therefore we hypothesize that mainstream newspapers will predict the issue agenda of candidates' Instagram posts (H2).

RESEARCH METHOD AND DATA

Candidate Instagram Posts

Largely adapting the methodology employed by Conway et al.,[53] this study examined the Instagram feeds of the leading six Republican and Democratic candidates during the 2016 presidential nomination season: Bernie Sanders, Hillary Clinton, Donald Trump, John Kasich, Marco Rubio, and Ted Cruz. To gather Instagram posts of these candidates a novel, visual intelligence platform, Beautifeye (www.Beautifeye.com), was contracted to scan and collect images, captions, and tags of individual candidate's Instagram feeds during the nomination period: January 1, 2016, through June 30, 2016. The logic for the starting point was that January 1, 2016, marked one month prior to the Iowa Caucuses held on February 1, 2016. Since the last presidential primary was held on June 14, 2016, in the District of Columbia, the June 30, 2016, end point was appropriate. The six candidates' verified Instagram accounts were scanned and documented by Beautifeye: BernieSanders (N = 286), HillaryClinton (N=307), RealDonaldTrump (N = 449), JohnKasich (N = 155), MarcoRubioFla (N = 122), SenTedCruz (N = 16), and CruzforPresident (N = 109).[54]

Mainstream Newspapers

To compare candidate Instagram posts to mainstream media content, we examined four of the highest-circulation national newspapers in the U.S.[55] The newspaper sample included *The New York Times, The Washington Post, USA Today,* and *The Los Angeles Times. The New York Times* and *The Washington Post* were selected because they are considered the national newspapers of record, read by political elites and highly engaged citizens. *USA Today* was included because it targets the more general reader who has some interest in politics. To include West Coast political perspectives, we also included the *Los Angeles Times.* Lexis Nexis and Pro-Quest were employed to gather all newspaper articles published in these newspapers during the primary period: January 1, 2016, through June 30, 2016. To search for relevant articles and editorials in each database, we used the key term "U.S. Presidential elections," in combination with "primaries" or "caucuses." The final sample includes 724 relevant articles. In our analysis, the four newspapers are examined as a "Newspaper Index" to measure the overall issue agenda in the mainstream press.

Content Analysis

For Instagram feeds, the unit of observation was daily posts, specifically the image and caption, on a candidate's account. For newspapers, the unit of observation was daily content about the presidential nomination season published in a newspaper. Coding of newspaper articles and Instagram images and captions was conducted by the lead author. To develop an initial coding sheet, we drew upon previous studies' content analyzing issue coverage during campaign periods.[56] Based on this prior work, we crafted a coding sheet including 23 issue categories: abortion, affirmative action, banking, budget, campaign finance, civil rights, crime/guns, corruption/ethics, drugs, economy, education, environment, equality racial, foreign policy, health care, immigration, income equality, military, minimum wage, religion, Social Security, tax, and welfare. To develop a list of issue categories, twenty newspaper articles and twenty Instagram posts were randomly selected for preliminary coding by the lead author. This preliminary coding produced a more detailed coding sheet, with subcategories, many unique to this election cycle, tied to each issue category.

Using the final coding sheet, the lead author coded the newspaper articles and Instagram posts and images for issue frequencies.[57] Each newspaper article and Instagram post was coded for how many times an issue (or issues) was mentioned, meaning that more than one issue could be coded per article or post. For example, one newspaper article may mention banking five times, the economy twice, and immigration ten times. A minimum threshold of 5 issue mentions for at least one newspaper or candidate Instagram feed was employed to identify the primary campaign's important issues. Considering this threshold, two issue categories were later removed from the analysis (affirmative action and religion) as they did not meet the threshold. To calculate intercoder agreement, a random subsample of 10 percent of all newspaper articles and Instagram images and captions (N = 228) were coded by a second coder. This second coder was a political science student trained in coding and content analysis. The intercoder agreement ranged from 100 percent to 77 percent agreement across all issues coded.

RESULTS

Table 12.1 reports the frequency of issue mentions for the Newspaper Index as well as the Instagram posts for Clinton, Sanders, and the Republican candidates. Although the Republican candidates frequently posted on Instagram, with Trump posting more than all other primary candidates, there were a limited number of issues mentioned by the GOP candidates. The latter was similar to earlier findings which showed that Republicans rarely tweeted about issues.[58] Therefore, following Conway et al.'s approach,[59] the Republican candidates' Instagram posts were summed to form an index (GOP Index).[60] Newspaper issue mentions (N = 4410) exceeded the number of issue mentions in all of the candidates' Instagram posts combined (N = 451; see Table 12.1). The latter finding reaffirms that mainstream newspapers have more carrying capacity for issue coverage than Instagram. Indeed, while Instagram has a generous character limit (2200 characters), candidates are brief when crafting their Instagram captions and images. A majority of the issue mentions appeared in the Instagrammed caption, with only about 18 percent of the issue mentions appearing in the Instagram images. Table 12.1 indicates that Hillary Clinton Instagrammed more about political issues (N = 212) than her Democratic challenger, Bernie Sanders (N = 156), and all of the Republican candidates combined (N = 83).

Table 12.1. Issue Frequencies and Rankings for Newspaper Index and Candidate Instagram Accounts for Twenty-One Issues

	Newspaper Index		Hillary Clinton		Bernie Sanders		GOP Index	
	N	rank	N	rank	N	rank	N	rank
Abortion	100	12	3	14	2	14	1	12
Bank	321	4	4	12	16	3	0	13
Budget	63	15	2	15.5	0	19	2	10.5
Campaign finance	324	3	1	18	23	2	2	10.5
Civil rights	77	14	18	5	0	21	0	14
Corruption/ethics	220	10	1	17	1	15	3	8.5
Crime	277	6	23	3	7	9	10	2.5
Drugs	63	16	2	15.5	1	16	0	15
Economy	584	2	41	1	29	1	9	4
Education	253	8	29	2	10	7	6	5
Equality race	87	13	22	4	14	4	3	8.5
Environment	54	17	15	7	4	11	0	16
Foreign policy	246	9	4	13	3	12	0	17
Health care	300	5	9	8	11	6	5	6
Immigration	906	1	7	10	6	10	4	7
Income equality	49	18	16	6	14	5	0	18
Military	258	7	9	9	10	8	28	1
Minimum wage	48	19	5	11	3	13	0	19
Social Security	22	20	0	20	1	17	0	20
Tax	144	11	1	19	1	18	10	2.5
Welfare	14	21	0	21	0	20	0	21
N = 21 issues	N = 4410		N = 212		N = 156		N = 83	

Table 12.1 also shows that newspapers and the candidates differed regarding which issues were at the top of their agenda. To more easily examine the issue agendas, the issue frequencies were ranked from 1 = the top issue mentioned to 21 = the least issue mentioned. For example, the Newspaper Index illustrates that the number one issue in the mainstream press was immigration (N = 900) followed by the economy (N = 584). Examining issue mentions between the Democratic candidates, the economy was the number one issue for both Clinton and Sanders. The second issue differed between Clinton and Sanders, with Clinton posting more about education and Sanders posting more about campaign finance. In contrast to the Democrats' top issue, Republican candidates only posted about the economy 9 times. Instead, the top Instagrammed issue topic among Republicans was the military, followed by crime and taxes.

Table 12.1 indicates that the mainstream press and the candidates' Instagram posts differed on which issues were primary in their campaigns, but is there an empirical relationship between their overall issue agendas? The relationship between the issue rankings (all 21 issues) in newspapers and in candidate Instagram posts were first compared by employing Spearman's p correlation. Table 12.2 reports the results, showing significant positive correlations between Sanders, the GOP Index, and the Newspaper Index, with the GOP Index more strongly correlated with the Newspaper Index than Sanders' Instagram posts. Interestingly, the relationship between Clinton's Instagram posts and the Newspaper Index was not statistically significant. Not surprisingly, Sanders' and Clinton's Instagram posts were significantly and positively correlated, suggesting that the Democratic candidates had similar issue priorities in their social media campaigns. There was no relationship between the Democratic candidates' posts and the GOP Instagram Index. In general, Table 12.2 suggests a relationship between the overall issue agendas of the mainstream media and candidates' Instagram posts.

To examine the most salient issues covered in the presidential primary campaign, the top six issues were identified by summing issue frequencies across the Newspaper Index and all candidate Instagram posts.

Table 12.2. Spearman's rho Rank-Order Correlations of 21 Issue Rankings

	Newspaper Index	Hillary Clinton	Bernie Sanders	GOP Instagram Index
Newspaper Index	1.00	—	—	—
HillaryClinton	n.s.	1.00	—	—
BernieSanders	.623**	.540*	1.00	—
GOP Instagram Index	.729**	n.s.	n.s.	1.00

$*p < .05, **p < .01$

The top six issues in rank order were immigration (N = 923 mentions), economy (N = 663), campaign finance (N = 350), banking (N = 341), health care (N = 325), and crime (N = 317). It is important to note that none of the Republican candidates mentioned the issue of banking on Instagram. In Table 12.3, the top six issue rankings for the Newspaper Index and candidate Instagram posts were compared by employing Spearman's *p* correlation. Unlike the results in Table 12.2, there are no significant relationships between the top six issue mentions in the Newspaper Index and candidate Instagram posts, with the exception of a positive and moderately significant correlation between Hillary Clinton's and the Republican candidates' Instagram posts. The results in Table 12.3 imply that there was little-to-no relationship between the top issue agendas between the mainstream media and candidate Instagram posts.

To further measure the inter-media relationships between the frequency of issue mentions in the mainstream media and Instagram, cross-correlations were estimated. In agenda-setting research, cross-correlations empirically test the association between two agendas over time.[61] We want to note, however, that cross-correlations do not prove real-world causality and only offer evidence for possible intermedia agenda-setting effects. When conducting cross-correlations, scholars often face the problem of stationarity in the time series. Therefore, each issue series was examined for linear and quadratic trends. This preprocessing step uncovered trends in newspaper indices for the issues of campaign finance (linear function with R_2 =.04, $p<.05$) and economy (linear function with R_2 =.02, $p<.05$). For Sanders' issue mentions on Instagram, trends were found for banking (linear function with R_2 =.04, $p<.01$), campaign finance (quadratic function R_2 =.04, $p<.01$), and the economy (quadratic function R_2 =.03, $p<.05$). There were no linear or quadratic trends uncovered for the issue series for the GOP Index and Clinton's issue mentions on Instagram. To remove linear and quadratic trends from the aforementioned series, detrending was employed to achieve stationarity.

Table 12.3. Spearman's rho Rank-Order Correlations of Top 6 Issue Rankings

	Newspaper Index	Hillary Clinton	Bernie Sanders	GOP Instagram Index
Newspaper Index	1.00	—	—	—
HillaryClinton	n.s.	1.00	—	—
BernieSanders	n.s.	n.s.	1.00	—
GOP Instagram Index	n.s.	.866*	n.s.	1.00

*p < .05, **p < .01

To test Hypotheses 1 and 2, cross-correlations were estimated to examine the direction of the frequency of issue mentions between the Newspaper Index and the candidate Instagram posts for the top-six issues (see Table 12.4). When examining the daily number of issue mentions in media content, particularly daily newspaper content, it is important to consider the lagged effects or control for the level of content seven days prior to the present value (seven lags back). In the Internet era, the time lag between mainstream media and online source is determined to be within days or within a weekly media cycle.[62] A reported lag suggests that candidate Instagram posts significantly predicted newspaper issue mentions 1 to 7 days before the issue mentions in the newspaper indices. A lead indicates that issue mentions in the newspaper indices significantly predicted issue mentions in the candidate Instagram posts 1 to 7 days prior to the "same day" issue frequencies. A reported lag of 0 indicates than any influence occurred on the same day.

Turning to Table 12.4, overall there are 20 significant lags for five of the top six issues, offering some evidence that candidate Instagram posts predicted newspaper mentions for immigration, economy, banking, health care, and crime. The latter offers moderate support for Hypothesis 1, asserting that candidate Instagram posts can predict mainstream newspapers' agenda on certain issues during the primary period. In addition, there are 13 significant leads for four of the top six issues, particularly immigration, economy, banking, and crime. The significant leads suggest that newspapers' issue mentions predicted candidate Instagram posts, providing support for Hypothesis 2. There are four, same-day correlations (lag 0) for three issues: immigration, economy, and crime. Taken as a whole, there are slightly more significant lags than leads, which implies that candidates' Instagram posts had a bit more predictive power on the newspapers' issue mentions than the reverse. The evidence here is not overwhelming, however, as only 20 lags out of the possible 126 lags were significant.

A closer examination of Table 12.4, particularly rows 1 and 2, reveals that both Clinton's and Sanders' Instagram posts significantly predicted newspaper mentions for four issues: immigration, economy, health care, and crime. However, the Democratic candidates differed on the issue of banking and health care. Bernie Sanders' Instagram posts about "banking" significantly predicted newspaper issue mentions as well as the reverse: newspapers predicted Sanders' Instagram posts. In contrast, there were no significant lags or leads between the Newspaper Index and Clinton's Instagram posts for "banking." Meanwhile, there were no significant leads or lags between the Newspaper Index and Sanders' Instagram posts on "health care." Examining row 1, eight (out of forty-two possible lags) of the lags for Clinton were significant, followed by 4 leads.

Table 12.4. Daily Lag and Lead Cross-Correlations for Newspaper Index and Candidate Instagram Posts

	Immigration	Economy	Campaign Finance	Bank	Health Care	Crime
Hillary Clinton	Lag 1: .17 Lag 0: .20 Lead 6: .13 Lead 7: .10	Lag 7: .16 Lag 1: –.12	N.S.	N.S.	Lag 6: .13 Lag 5: .18 Lag 2: .15 Lag 1: .20	Lag 3: .19 Lead 2: –.11 Lead 6: .31
Bernie Sanders	Lag 0: .12 Lead 6: .38 Lead 7: .10	Lag 1: –.10 Lag 0: .15 Lead 3: .10	N.S.	Lag 6: –.10 Lag 5: –.13 Lead 2: .16 Lead 3: –.16	N.S.	Lag 7: .13 Lead 7: .20
GOP Instagram Index	Lag 5: .11 Lead 1: .26 Lead 6: .17	Lag 7: .18 Lag 2: –.14 Lag 1: .15	N.S.	No output.	Lag 7: .40 Lag 6: .10 Lag 3: .65	Lag 7: .17 Lag 0: –.10 Lead 2: .28

Note: "N.S." indicates that there were no statistically significant lags or leads for that estimated cross-correlation. There is also no output for the cross-correlation for the "bank" issue between the newspaper index and GOP index, as there are no issue mentions for "bank" in the GOP index. All cross-lagged correlations shown here are significant, p < .05.

Clinton's lags not only outnumber leads but are also of higher magnitude (ranging from $r=.197$ to $r=.127$) than the leads. The latter findings suggest that Clinton's Instagram posts were somewhat better predictors of the newspapers' issue agenda than the reverse. Only on the issue of crime did the Newspaper Index have notable predictive power on Clinton's Instagram posts.

In contrast to Clinton, Sanders' Instagram posts tended to follow the mainstream newspaper agenda. As shown in row 2, newspaper issue mentions (6 leads) predicted slightly more Instagram posts by Sanders than Instagram posts predicted newspapers (4 lags). Moreover, the strength of Sanders' leads were higher than the lags, with the Newspaper Index having a robust impact on Sanders' Instagram posts on immigration and crime. Interestingly, the cross-correlations between the Newspaper Index and the Democrats' Instagram posts for "campaign finance" has no significant lags and leads. Overall, the Democratic candidates' Instagram posts predicted the issue mentions in newspapers just as much as the newspaper indices predicted the Instagram posts.

Moving to the Republican candidates' Instagram posts in Table 12.4 (row 3), 8 of the lags significantly predicted newspaper mentions for four issues: immigration, economy, health care, and crime. There was "no output" for the issue of "banking," as the Republican candidates did not Instagram about this issue. Lags for the GOP Index outnumbered the leads (only 3 leads), which suggests that the GOP Instagram posts were more predictive of the newspaper issue mentions than the reverse. The GOP Instagram index was linked to the newspaper indices on two issues: economy and health care. The number of lags on these two issues alone (6 lags) outnumbered the total leads (3 leads), indicating that the Republicans' Instagram posts had an important association with the newspapers' issue coverage during the primaries. In addition, the magnitude of the lags are high, with a notable range ($r=.652$ to $r=.396$) for the lags on health care. Regarding leads, the strength of the newspapers' issue agenda on the GOP's Instagram issue mentions for immigration and crime was slightly more pronounced, as the magnitude of the leads was higher than the lags. Similar to the Democratic candidates, there was no significant lags or leads between the Newspaper Index and the GOP Instagram index for "campaign finance."

DISCUSSION AND CONCLUSION

This research sought to extend our understanding of the agenda-setting effects that social media, specifically Instagram, played in the 2016 presidential primary. Similar to previous studies conducted on both traditional and new media, our research offers some early evidence of agenda setting between Instagram and mainstream media. We found that candidates' Instagram posts predicted the issue agenda in mainstream newspapers. Notably, Hillary Clinton's Instagram posts more readily predicted, as evidenced by slightly more time lags, newspaper issue agenda. Arguably, Clinton was the most established candidate in the field. As such, the mainstream media might have been more inclined to follow her and be influenced by her social media posts. The GOP Instagram Index was also predictive of the newspaper mentions of immigration, economy, health care, and crime issues. Our research suggests that, as journalists rely on other social media outlets, such as Twitter and Facebook, for news content,[63] Instagram may also be another potential political news source.

While candidates' Instagram posts moderately influenced newspaper mentions, we also find some evidence that mainstream newspapers predicted the issue agenda of candidates' Instagram posts. In particular, Bernie Sanders' Instagram posts followed the newspaper agenda more frequently for the topics of immigration and banking. On the whole, our research offers some modest evidence that intermedia agenda setting existed during the 2016 presidential primary period. The Democratic candidates' Instagram posts predicted the issue mentions in newspapers as much as the newspaper indices predicted the Instagram posts, whereas the GOP Instagram posts were more strongly linked to newspaper issue mentions. However, our results do not offer overwhelming evidence of intermedia agenda-setting effects between Instagram and mainstream media. As previously noted, only 20 lags out of the possible 126 lags were significant and only 13 of the leads out of 126 possible leads were significant. Moreover, only 4 out of the 6 top issues contained lags and leads between Instagram and mainstream media. Therefore, this study may suggest to some that there is little intermedia agenda setting occurring between Instagram and mainstream media.

Looking beyond our hypotheses, another interesting observation was the overall lack of issues that were communicated via Instagram (see Table 12.1). For instance, the Republican candidates rarely mentioned issues on Instagram, suggesting that there is likely not much issue agenda setting taking place. This raises a number of strategic marketing questions of the overall role of the Instagram platform in political marketing, and specifically, is Instagram an appropriate venue to communicate issue platforms? Are other social media platforms better venues? Do specific issue topics, such as the economy, lend themselves to be better communicated via Instagram's visual communication modality? Considering the competitiveness in the 2016 primary campaign, the absence of issues mentioned by the GOP candidates may be surprising. Although, the last two presidential elections demonstrated that the Democratic party had better implemented social media as a marketing and mobilization tool. Thus, a possible explanation to the lack of issues communicated by the GOP candidates may simply be attributed to the Democratic party having a stronger social media proficiency.[64]

Our research also found no relationship between the top mainstream media issues and that of the candidates' Instagram posts (see Table 12.3). While having Instagram issue consistency with the mainstream media is not necessarily a recipe for success, the level of disconnect suggests that there are opportunities for additional issue messaging on Instagram for candidates. It is apparent that both parties need to more critically consider implementing issue messaging in their social media planning. Furthermore, they should seek to include more issue mentions in their visual communication-opposed to sidelining it in the picture's accompanying text.

This analysis has several limitations that require note. First, we acknowledge that correlation is not causation. Indeed, we find significant intermedia agenda-setting effects, but this does not mean that mainstream media causes issue mentions on Instagram, and vice versa. There are other factors that may be influencing the frequency of issue mentions in the mainstream media and on Instagram: events, other media, or debates. In addition, we relied on manual content analysis of political issues. The latter method is frequently employed and considered reliable by scholars, but it is dependent on the issue list and coding of the author. Third, we only examined newspapers to represent the mainstream media. An analysis of television broadcasts and local and national news will likely produce different results.

Political research on Instagram is in its infancy. Political candidates and their campaigns are only beginning to understand how to integrate Instagram into their overall integrated marketing communication strategy. As such, we have much to learn in terms of how candidates market themselves (e.g., agenda setting, self-framing, etc.) on Instagram, what types of images generate higher levels of engagement, and the effects of visual communication on candidate evaluations and political participation. The 2016 presidential candidates' use of Instagram to set their issue agenda was not picture perfect, however, it is our hope that this research will help to sharpen the focus in our understanding of Instagram's role in political communication.

NOTES

1. Pew Research Center, "Election 2016: Campaign as a Direct Source of News," accessed on November 11, 2016, from http://assets.pewresearch.org/wp-con-

tent/uploads/sites/13/2016/07/PJ_2016.07.18_election-2016_FINAL.pdf, 2016; Shannon Greenwood, Andrew Perrin, and Maeve Duggan, "Social Media Update 2016." Pew Research Center. Accessed March 2, 2017, http://assets.pewresearch. org/wp-content/uploads/sites/14/2016/11/10132827/PI_2016.11.11_Social-Media-Update_FINAL.pdf, 2016.

2. Hootsuite, "The 2016 Presidential Candidates on Instagram, Ranked," Accessed on March 2, 2017, https://blog.hootsuite.com/the-2016-presidential-candidates-on-instagram-ranked/, 2015.

3. Bethany A. Conway, Kate Kenski, and Di Wang, "The Rise of Twitter in the Political Campaign: Searching for Intermedia Agenda-Setting Effects in the Presidential Primary," *Journal of Computer-Mediated Communication* 20, (2015): 363–380; Jacob Groshek and Megan Clough Groshek, "Agenda Trending: Reciprocity and the Predictive Capacity of Social Networking Sites in Intermedia Agenda Setting Across Topics over Time," *Media and Communication* 1, no. 1 (2013): 15–27.

4. Maxwell McCombs, "A Look at Agenda-Setting: Past, Present, and Future," *Journalism Studies* 6, no. 4 (2005): 543–557.

5. Maxwell McCombs and Donald L. Shaw, "The Agenda-Setting Function in the Mass Media," *The Public Opinion Quarterly* 36, no. 2 (1972): 176–187.

6. Ibid.

7. Ibid.

8. Jorg Matthes, "The Need for Orientation towards News Media: Revising and Validating a Classic Concept," *International Journal of Public Opinion Research* 18, no. 4 (2006): 422–444; Klaus Schoenbach and K. Weaver, "Finding the Unexpected: Cognitive Building in a Political Campaign," in *Mass Media and Political Thought: An Information-Processing Approach*, ed. Sidney Kraus and Richard M. Perloff (Beverly Hills, CA: Sage, 1985), 157–176; David H. Weaver, "Audience Need for Orientation and Media Effects," *Communication Research* 7, no. 3 (1980): 361–376.

9. McCombs, "A Look at Agenda-Setting: Past, Present, and Future"; Everett Rogers, James Dearing, and Dorine Bregman, "The Anatomy of Agenda-Setting Research," *Journal of Communication* 43, no. 2 (1993): 68–84; Wayne Wanta and Salma Ghanem, "Effects of Agenda Setting," in *Meta-Analysis of Media Effects*, ed. Jennings Bryant and Rodney Carveth (Mahwah, NJ: Erlbaum, 2000).

10. Salma Ghanem, "Filling in the Tapestry: The Second Level of Agenda Setting," in *Communication and Democracy*, ed. Maxwell McCombs, Donald L. Shaw, and David Weaver (Mahwah, NJ: Erlbaum, 1997); Spiro Kiousis, Philemon Bantimaroudis, and Hyun Ban, "Candidate Image Attributes: Experiments on the Substantive Dimension of Second Level Agenda Setting," *Communication Research* 26, no. 4 (1999): 414–428; Maxwell McCombs, *Setting the Agenda: The Mass Media and Public Opinion* (Cambridge, UK: Polity Press, 2004); Maxwell McCombs, Esteban Lopez-Escobar, and Juan Pablo Llamas, "Setting the Agenda of Attributes in the 1996 Spanish General Election," *Journal of Communication* 50, no. 2 (2000): 77–92; David H. Weaver, Maxwell McCombs, and Donald L. Shaw, "Agenda-Setting Research: Issues, Attributes, and Influences," in *Handbook of Political Communication Research*, ed. Lynda L. Kaid (Mahwah, NJ: Erlbaum, 2004), 257–282.

11. Meital Balmas and Tamir Sheafer, "Candidate Image in Election Campaigns: Attribute Agenda Setting, Affective Priming, and Voting Intentions," *International*

Journal of Public Opinion Research 22, no. 2 (2010): 204–229; Kihan Kim and Maxwell McCombs, "News Story Descriptions and the Public's Opinions of Political Candidates," *Journalism and Mass Communication Quarterly* 84, no. 2 (2007): 299–314; Maxwell McCombs, Juan Pablo Llamas, Esteban Lopez-Escobar, and Federico Rey, "Candidate Images in Spanish Elections: Second-Level Agenda-Setting Effects," *Journalism and Mass Communication Quarterly* 74, no. 4 (1998): 703–717.

12. McCombs, *Setting the Agenda*, 70.

13. Guy Golan and Wayne Wanta, "Second-Level Agenda Setting in the New Hampshire Primary: A Comparison of Coverage in Three Newspapers and Public Perceptions of Candidates," *Journalism and Mass Communication Quarterly* 78, no. 2 (2001): 247–259; Sei-Hill Kim, Dietram A. Scheufele, and James Shanahan, "Think about It This Way: Attribute Agenda-Setting Function of the Press and the Public's Evaluation of a Local Issue," *Journalism and Mass Communication Quarterly* 79 (2002): 7–25; Pu-tsung King, "The Press, Candidate Images, and Voter Perceptions," in *Communication and Democracy: Exploring the Intellectual Frontiers in Agenda-Setting Theory*, ed. Maxwell McCombs, Donald L. Shaw, and David Weaver (Mahwah, NJ: Erlbaum, 1997), 29–40; Spiro Kiousis, "Compelling Arguments and Attitude Strength: Exploring the Impact of Second-Level Agenda Setting on Public Opinion of Presidential Candidate Images," *Harvard International Journal of Press-Politics* 10, (2005): 3–27; Kiousis et al., "Candidate Image Attributes"; Wayne Wanta, Guy Golan, and Cheolhan Lee, "Agenda Setting and International News: Media Influence on Public Perceptions of Foreign Nations," *Journalism and Mass Communication Quarterly* 81, (2004): 364–377.

14. Shanto Iyengar and Donald R. Kinder, *News that Matters: Television and American Opinion* (Chicago: University of Chicago Press, 1987); Thomas Patterson and Robert McClure, *The Unseeing Eye* (New York: Putnam, 1976); Wayne Wanta, "The Messenger and the Message: Differences across News Media," in *Communication and Democracy: Exploring the Intellectual Frontiers of Agenda-Setting Theory*, ed. Maxwell McCombs, Donald L. Shaw, and David Weaver (Mahwah, NJ: Erlbaum, 1997), 137–151; David H. Weaver, Doris Graber, Maxwell E. McCombs, and Chaim H. Eyal, *Media Agenda Setting in a Presidential Election: Issues, Images, and Interest* (New York, NY: Praeger, 1981); Harold Zucker, "The Variable Nature of News Media Influence," in *Communication Yearbook* 2, ed. by Brent D. Ruben (New Brunswick, NJ: Transaction, 1978).

15. McCombs, "A Look at Agenda-Setting."

16. Bruce Williams and Michael X. Delli Carpini, "Monica and Bill All the Time and Everywhere: The Collapse of Gatekeeping in the New Media Environment," *American Behavioral Scientist* 47, no. 9 (2004): 1208–1230.

17. McCombs, "A Look at Agenda-Setting."

18. McCombs, "A Look at Agenda-Setting," 549.

19. Thomas P. Boyle, "Intermedia Agenda Setting in the 1996 Presidential Election," *Journalism and Mass Communication Quarterly* 78, no. 1 (2001): 26–44; Scott Dunn, "Candidate and Media Agenda Setting in the 2005 Virginia Gubernatorial Election," *Journal of Communication* 59, no. 3 (2009): 635–652; Guy Golan, Spiro Kiousis, and Misti McDaniel, "Second-Level Agenda Setting and Political Advertising: Investigating the Transfer of Issue and Attribute Saliency during the 2004 U.S. Presidential Election," *Journalism Studies* 8, no. 3 (2007): 432–443; Lynda L. Kaid, "Newspaper Treatment of a Candidate's News Releases," *Journalism Quarterly*

51, no. 1 (1976): 135–157; Marilyn Roberts and Maxwell E. McCombs, "Agenda Setting and Political Advertising: Origins of the News Agenda," *Political Communication* 11, no. 3 (1994): 249–262; John C. Tedesco, "Issue and Strategy Agenda Setting in the 2004 Presidential Election: Exploring the Candidate-Journalist Relationship," *Journalism Studies* 62, no. 2 (2005): 187–201; John C. Tedesco, "Issue and Strategy Agenda-Setting in the 2000 Presidential Primaries," *American Behavioral Scientist* 44, no. 12 (2001).

20. Gyotae Ku, Lynda L. Kaid, and Michael Pfau, "The Impact of Web Site Campaigning on Traditional News Media and Public Information Processing," *Journalism & Mass Communication* 80, no. 3 (2003): 528–547; See also Glenn J. Hansen and William L. Benoit, "The Role of Significant Policy Issues in the 2000 Presidential Primaries," *American Behavioral Scientist* 44, no. 12 (2001): 2082–2100.

21. Michael Cornfield, Jonathan Carson, Alison Kalis, and Emily Simon, "Buzz, Blogs, and Beyond." Accessed November 11, 2016, from http://www.michelemiller.blogs.com/Marketing_to_women/Files/Buzz_blogs_beyond.pdf, 2005; Kyle Heim, "Framing the 2008 Iowa Democratic Caucuses: Political Blogs and Second-Level Intermedia Agenda Setting," *Journalism and Mass Communication Quarterly* 90, no. 3 (2013): 500–519; Sharon Meraz, "Is There an Elite Hold? Traditional Media to Social Media Agenda Setting Influence in Blog Networks," *Journal of Computer Mediated Communication* 14, no. 3 (2009): 682–707; Kaye Sweetser, Guy J. Golan, and Wayne Wanta, "Intermedia Agenda Setting in Television, Advertising, and Blogs during the 2004 Election," *Mass Communication & Society* 11, no. 2 (2008): 197–216; Kevin Wallsten, "Agenda Setting and the Blogosphere: An Analysis of the Relationship between Mainstream Media and Political Blogs," *Review of Policy Research* 24, no. 6 (2007): 567–587; Williams and Delli Carpini, "Monica and Bill All the Time and Everywhere."

22. Marcus Messner and Marcia Watson Distaso, "The Source Cycle: How Traditional Media and Weblogs Use Each Other as Sources," *Journalism Studies* 9, no. 3 (2008): 447–463.

23. Ben Sayre, Leticia Bode, Dhavan Shah, Dave Wilcox, and Chirag Shah, "Agenda Setting in a Digital Age: Tracking Attention to California Proposition 8 in Social Media, Online News, and Conventional News," *Policy and Internet* 2, no. 2 (2010): 7–32.

24. W. Russell Neuman, Lauren Guggenheim, S. Mo Jang, and Soo Young Bae, "The Dynamics of Public Attention: Agenda-Setting Theory Meets Big Data," *Journal of Communication* 64, no. 2 (2014): 193–214.

25. Deen Freelon, Charlton D. McIlwain, and Meredith D. Clark, "Quantifying the Power and Consequences of Social Media Protest," *New Media & Society* (2016): 1–22.

26. Groshek and Groshek, "Agenda Trending"; Haewoon Kwak, Changhyun Lee, Hosung Park, and Sue Moon, "What is Twitter, a Social Network or News Media?" Paper presented at the Proceedings of the 19th International Conference on World Wide Web, Raleigh, NC, 2010; Chris J. Vargo, Ekaterina Basilaia, and Donald Lewis Shaw, "Event versus Issue: Twitter Reflections of Major News, Case Study," *Communication and Information Technologies Annual: Studies in Media and Communications* 9 (2015): 215–239.

27. Groshek and Groshek, "Agenda Trending."

28. Kwak, Lee, Park, and Moon, "What is Twitter, a Social Network or News Media?"

29. Terri L. Towner, "All Political Participation is Socially Networked?: New Media and the 2012 Election," *Social Science Computer Review* 31, no. 5 (2013): 527–541; Terri L. Towner, "The Influence of Twitter Posts on Candidate Perceptions: The 2014 Michigan Midterms," in *Media, Message, and Mobilization: Communication and Midterm Elections*, ed. John A. Hendricks and Daniel Schill (New York: Palgrave, 2016), 145–167; Terri L. Towner and David A. Dulio, "An Experiment of Campaign Effects during the YouTube Election," *New Media and Society* 13, no. 4 (2011): 626–644; Terri L. Towner and Caroline Lego Muñoz, "Baby Boom or Bust?: The New Media Effect on Political Participation," *The Journal of Political Marketing*, forthcoming, 2016; Terri L. Towner and Caroline Lego Muñoz, "Boomers versus Millennials: Online Media Influence on Political Perceptions and Media Performance," *Social Sciences* 5, no. 4 (2016): 56.

30. Conway, Kenski, and Wang, "The Rise of Twitter in the Political Campaign."; John H. Parmelee, "The Agenda-Building Function of Political Tweets," *New Media & Society* 16, no. 3 (2014): 434–450.

31. Pew Research Center, "Election 2016."

32. Terri L. Towner and David A. Dulio, "New Media and Political Marketing in the United States: 2012 and Beyond," *The Journal of Political Marketing* 11, no. 1–2 (2012), 95–119.

33. Towner, "The Influence of Twitter Posts on Candidate Perceptions."; Towner and Muñoz, "Baby Boom or Bust?"

34. Towner, "All Political Participation is Socially Networked?"; For a review, see Shelley Boulianne, "Social Media Use and Participation: A Meta-Analysis of Current Research," *Information, Communication, & Society* 18, no. 5 (2015): 524–538.

35. Arthur Santana and Lindita Camaj, "Facebook as a Campaign Tool during the 2012 Elections: A New Dimension to Agenda Setting Discourse," *Journal of Social Media in Society* 4, no. 2 (2015): 106–137.

36. Conway, Kenski, and Wang, "The Rise of Twitter in the Political Campaign."; Yoejin Kim, William Gonzenbach, Chris Vargo, and Youngju Kim, "First and Second Levels of Intermedia Agenda Setting: Political Advertising, Newspaper, and Twitter during the 2012 Presidential Election," *International Journal of Communication* 10, (2016): 4550–4569.

37. Matthew Shapiro and Libby Hemphill, "Politicians and the Policy Agenda: Does Use of Twitter by the U.S. Congress Direct *New York Times* Content?" *Policy and Internet* 9, no. 1 (2017): 109–132.

38. Instagram. 2016. "Press Page." Instagram. Accessed November 1, 2016, https://www.instagram.com/press/; Kate Knibbs, "Instagram Is Growing Faster than Twitter, Facebook, and Pinterest Combined." Accessed November 11, 2016, http://www.digitaltrends.com/social-media/instagram-is-growing-faster-than-twitter-facebook-and-pinterest-combined-in-2013/, 2014.

39. Maeve Duggan, "Mobile Messaging and Social Media 2015." Pew Research Study. Accessed November 11, 2016, from http://www.pewinternet.org/files/2015/08/Social-Media-Update-2015-FINAL2.pdf, 2015.

40. Kirill Filimonov, Uta Russmann, and Jakob Svensson, "Picturing the Party: Instagram and Party Campaigning in the 2014 Swedish Elections," *Social Media + Society* no. July-September (2016): 1–11.

41. Amira Karan Eldin, "Instagram Role in Influencing Youth Opinion in 2015 Election Campaign in Bahrain," *European Scientific Journal* 12, no. 2 (2016): 245–257.

42. Tom Feltwell, Jamie Mahoney, and Shaun Lawson, "'Aye, Have a Dream #IndyRef': Use of Instagram during the Scottish Referendum." Paper presented at the British HCI '15 Proceedings of the 2015 British HCI Conference, Lincoln, Lincolnshire, UK, July 13–17, 2015.

43. Cornfield et al., "Buzz, Blogs, and Beyond"; Meraz, "Is There an Elite Hold?"; Marcus Messner and Bruce Garrison, "Study Shows Some Blogs Affect Traditional News Media Agenda," *Newspaper Research Journal* 32, no. 3 (2011): 112–126; Sweetser, Golan, and Wanta, "Intermedia Agenda Setting in Television, Advertising, and Blogs during the 2004 Election"; Wallsten, "Agenda Setting and the Blogosphere."

44. Conway, Kenski, and Wang, "The Rise of Twitter in the Political Campaign."; Freelon, McIlwain, and Clark, "Quantifying the Power and Consequences of Social Media Protest"; Sayre et al., "Agenda Setting in a Digital Age."

45. Conway, Kenski, and Wang, "The Rise of Twitter in the Political Campaign."

46. Colin Berry and Hans-Bernd Brosius, "Multiple Effects of Visual Format on TV News Learning," *Applied Cognitive Psychology* 5, no. 6 (1991): 519–528; Janis L. Edwards, "Echoes of Camelot: How Images Construct Cultural Memory through Rhetorical Framing," in *Defining Visual Rhetorics*, ed. by Charles A. Hill and Marguerite Helmers (New York, NY: Routledge, 2004), 179–194; William E. Hockley, "The Picture Superiority Effect in Associative Recognition," *Memory & Cognition* 36, no. 7 (2008): 1351–1359; Allan Paivio, *Imagery and Verbal Processes* (Hillsdale, NJ: Erlbaum, 1979); Georg Stenberg, "Conceptual and Perceptual Factors in the Picture Superiority Effect," *European Journal of Cognitive Psychology*, 18, no. 6 (2006): 813–847.

47. Simon Rogers, "What Fuels a Tweet's Engagement?" Twitter. Accessed April 1, 2017, from https://blog.twitter.com/2014/what-fuels-a-tweets-engagement, 2014; Phillip Ross, "Photos Are Still King on Facebook," *SocialBakers*. Accessed April 1, 2017, from http://www.socialbakers.com/blog/2149-photos-are-still-king-on-facebook, 2014; Phillip Ross, "Photos Get the Most Engagement on Twitter," *SocialBakers*. Accessed April 1, 2017, from http://www.socialbakers.com/blog/2306-photos-get-the-most-engagement-on-twitter, 2014; Phillip Ross, "Three Trends that Dominated Social Video in . . . " *SocialBakers*. Accessed April 1, 2017, from http://www.socialbakers.com/blog/2489-three-trends-that-dominated-social-video-in-2015, 2016.

48. Terri L. Towner, "The Infographic Election: The Role of Visual Content on Social Media in the 2016 Presidential Campaign," in *The Presidency and Social Media: Discourse, Disruption, and Digital Democracy in the 2016 Presidential Election*, ed. by John Allen Hendricks and Dan Schill (New York, NY: Routledge, forthcoming).

49. John H. Parmelee, "Political Journalists and Twitter: Influences on Norms and Practices," *Journal of Media Practice* 14, no. 4 (2013): 291–305; Parmelee, "The Agenda-Building Function of Political Tweets."

50. Pew Research Center, "Election 2016: Campaign as a Direct Source of News."

51. Conway, Kenski, and Wang, "The Rise of Twitter in the Political Campaign."; Groshek and Groshek, "Agenda Trending."; Neuman et al., "The Dynamics of Public Attention."; Sayre et al., "Agenda Setting in a Digital Age."; Vargo, Basilaia, and Shaw, "Event versus Issue."

52. Conway, Kenski, and Wang, "The Rise of Twitter in the Political Campaign."

53. Ibid.

54. Ted Cruz had two verified Instagram accounts, which were both included in this analysis.

55. MediaMiser, "The Top 15 U.S. Newspapers by Circulation." Last modified on November 11, 2016, from https://www.mediamiser.com/resources/top-media-outlets/top-15-daily-american-newspapers/

56. Conway, Kenski, and Wang, "The Rise of Twitter in the Political Campaign."; Hansen and Benoit, "The Role of Significant Policy Issues in the 2000 Presidential Primaries."; Kim and McCombs, "News Story Descriptions and the Public's Opinions of Political Candidates"; Tedesco, "Issue and Strategy Agenda Setting in the 2004 Presidential Election."; Tedesco, "Issue and Strategy."

57. The coding sheet is available by request from the lead author.

58. Conway, Kenski, and Wang, "The Rise of Twitter in the Political Campaign."

59. Ibid.

60. Donald Trump Instagrammed more about political issues (N = 38) than any other Republican candidate. The frequency of issue mentions for the Republican candidates' Instagram posts are available by request.

61. Maxwell McCombs, Donald L. Shaw, and David H. Weaver, *Communication and Democracy: Exploring the Intellectual Frontiers in Agenda-Setting Theory* (New York: Routledge, 2013); Donald L. Shaw and Maxwell McCombs, *The Emergence of American Political Issues* (St. Paul, MN: West, 1977).

62. Marilyn Roberts, Wayne Wanta, and Tzong-Horng (Dustin) Dzwo, "Agenda Setting and Issue Salience Online," *Communication Research* 29, no. 4 (2002): 452–465.

63. Shapiro and Hemphill, "Politicians and the Policy Agenda."

64. For example, see Girish J. Gulati and Christine Williams, "Social Media and Campaign 2012: Developments and Trends for Facebook Adoption," *Social Science Computer Review* 31, no. 5 (2013): 577–588.

13

Getting the Picture

Issues and the 2016
Presidential Campaign on Instagram

Mark D. Ludwig

A picture paints a thousand words, or so the old saw goes. If that's the case, politicians are posting millions of words' worth on social media, particularly on the photo-sharing app Instagram, which became a force in the 2016 presidential election campaign. There are pictures and videos of candidates at events, of campaign supporters, of the scenery of America—and food, oh so many pictures of food, on the campaign trail. More than 4,000 Instagram posts were posted by the campaigns across the nomination and general election seasons. But exactly how did the candidates use it?

Social media have become a force in political communication to be reckoned with. Indeed, Barack Obama's 2008 campaign embraced this technology wholeheartedly with the creation of a social networking tool within its own website. External social media are another matter altogether. Campaigns can create their own pages on Facebook, maintain Twitter feeds, post photos on Instagram, and more. The genius of this is that followers of the pages and feeds can then forward them to friends and family, creating the potential for viral effects. However, that strength is also its weakness. Campaigns must cede control of the message to the users of these social networks. How these social platforms are used and their impact on campaigns continued to unfold during the 2016 presidential campaign. This study looks first at how much Instagram was used, in particular, how often was it used and who the most prolific posters were. It then focuses on a particular of aspect campaigning, the communication of issue positions. What issues did the candidate "own," or take responsibility for, during the 2016 campaign?

Instagram is a photo-sharing application developed by Kevin Systrom and Mike Krieger in 2010.[1] With its mobile phone app, users can easily post pictures and captions on the site, where followers can see these posts and comment. As of December 2016, about 600 million people worldwide had Instagram accounts. Such a tool has the potential for candidates for office to reach citizens they might not otherwise reach through other social media. It is also a player in a crowded field of social network applications. The most popular include Facebook, Twitter, Tumblr, LinkedIn, Pinterest, Google+, Flickr, Snapchat, and Meetup. Social media sites were so prominent that by 2016, 68 percent of adult Americans reported having a Facebook account; 21 percent used Twitter; and 28 percent used Instagram.[2]

The roots of social media can be traced to the 1997 launch of SixDegrees .com. This network allowed users to "create profiles, list their Friends and, beginning in 1998, surf the Friends lists."[3] The term "social media" is so broad that it has been categorized into four types: social networking sites; user-generated content, which includes Instagram; trading and marketing sites; and play and game sites. Social networking sites "primarily promote interpersonal contact, whether between individuals or groups; they forge personal, professional, or geographical connections and encourage weak ties."[4] Social networking sites are platforms for a culture of connectivity that can be capitalized on.[5]

In the early years of social media (2000–2005), users of social media were highly involved in the platforms, which they helped to create and manage.[6] As usage of these sites exploded, however, self-governance was dropped and corporate management of social network sites began to experiment with models of monetizing these platforms. This was largely done by "tapping into academics' celebratory rhetoric of a new public sphere of nonmarket collaboration, business managers and marketers glorified in the potential of mixed public-private entrepreneurship by absorbing Wikipedian-style peer-production into their for-profit business models."[7] Social media sites turned social relationships into commodities by developing programming to gather behavioral and profiling data; these sites turned connectedness into connectivity, a highly profitable business model.[8] Demographic and psychographic data are mined and sold to advertisers to better target an audience; these types of data can also be used in politics.

Social media have been around for nearly two decades, though some applications are younger than that, and the political communication literature about its use and usefulness in politics is still growing. An early assessment of YouTube and MySpace found that the platforms "affected election campaigns in simple, but significant, ways" and that social media posed new challenges for campaigns because they turn some control over the message to outsiders.[9] Hillary Clinton's use of YouTube during the 2008 nomination season floundered at first but evolved into uses of parody and polyphony to create interactivity with citizens.[10] Barack Obama's campaign included frequent posts on Twitter during the 2008 campaign, particularly to talk about campaign events, while John McCain's use was much more sparse and focused on introducing campaign ads and criticizing news media.

During the same campaign, Twitter posts by the public were "very close to trivial rants, personal, and random thoughts about the election or candidates."[11] Meanwhile, intense Facebook engagement among users during the same election facilitated public political participation.[12] In the 2008 and 2012 presidential elections, the Obama campaign focused on positive messages while those of McCain and Mitt Romney made appeals to fear.[13] Other research to date has focused on the effectiveness of organizing political action and transmitting political ideas.[14] A meta-analysis of 36 studies of social media found a positive relationship between their use and political participation.[15]

Social media in other countries have helped to organize citizen action against governments in countries like the Philippines, Spain, and Moldova, and the Catholic Church. Although the use of social media to organize political action is not always fruitful, they "have become coordinating tools for nearly all of the world's political movements, just as the world's most authoritarian governments (and, alarmingly, an increasing number of democratic ones) are trying to limit access to it."[16] Social media are seen as a way not only to organize political action, but also to aid in the transmission of political ideas.

There is some indication that new media use generally (as opposed to just social media) is positively correlated with voter turnout[17] and that nontraditional media use, or visiting sites other than those of legacy media, was on the rise during the 2008 election cycle.[18] A study of political engagement on Facebook during the 2008 presidential election concluded that although the network did provide a forum for political engagement, its use for that purpose was not as widespread as popularly believed:

> While many have considered whether the Internet can equalize access to information and politics, we find, as have others, that interest propels action. Those who are more interested are those who are more likely to be engaged and politically active.[19]

One function of social media, at least from the candidate's perspective, is to persuade citizens to support and to act—primarily by voting. One analyst, using traditional rhetorical analysis, found that candidate appeals on Facebook tended to be more emotional than rational.[20]

Other explorations of new media use have focused on college students' use of online media;[21] whether social media use was a predictor of political cynicism;[22] and the relationship between online media use and political disaffection.[23] But none of these studies single out how Instagram is being used nor its potential utility as a campaign tool. Indeed, a recent search of several databases of academic literature yielded nothing instructive about Instagram.

One potential use of social media for the campaigns is to communicate about the various issues confronting the country, thought to be important for effective political participation.[24] Theory suggests that when candidates do communicate issues, they will focus on those "owned" by their political party.[25] In its original formulation, Republicans "owned" foreign policy, defense, and matters of morality while Democrats "owned" social welfare issues. Handling of the economy was classified as a performance issue. In other words, ownership of handling the economy is dependent on current circumstances. This formulation was used to confirm issue ownership across presidential campaigns from 1948 to 2000.[26]

METHODOLOGY

Each morning beginning on July 1, 2015, and continuing through November 9, 2016, I created screen captures of all of the Instagram posts posted in the previous 24 hours by each of the major presidential candidates, as updated daily on the *New York Times* website. The candidates were:

- Former Florida Governor Jeb Bush
- Retired neurosurgeon Ben Carson
- Former U.S. Senator Lincoln Chafee
- New Jersey Governor Chris Christie
- Former Secretary of State Hillary Clinton
- U.S. Senator Ted Cruz
- U.S. Senator Lindsey Graham
- Louisiana Governor Bobby Jindal
- Ohio Governor John Kasich
- Former New York Governor George Pataki
- U.S. Senator Rand Paul
- Former Texas Governor Rick Perry
- U.S. Senator Marco Rubio
- U.S. Senator Bernie Sanders
- Former U.S. Senator Rick Santorum
- Businessman Donald Trump
- Wisconsin Governor Scott Walker
- Former U.S. Senator Jim Webb.[27]

In all, these candidates posted about 4,300 Instagram pictures during the 497 days studied. The data captured included the accompanying caption posted by the campaign, but not the subsequent comments of Instagram users.[28] The unit of analysis was a single post. Using a Google Form that fed data directly into a spreadsheet, two coders looked at the posted picture and text in concert to make coding determinations.

Because this chapter looked particularly at issues, the pictures unfortunately were not all that relevant. The coders noted whether the posts suggested any of the following:

- An image or video as opposed to text only;[29]
- An endorsement from someone;
- A request for a contribution;
- A mention of health or medical care, but not including the Affordable Care Act ("Obamacare");
- An explicit mention of the ACA.

In addition, I searched for references to another candidate, poverty, the elderly, labor or job creation, the environment or climate change, national security including the response to terrorism, reduction of government spending or the deficit, morality or religion, gay marriage, abortion rights or anti-abortion, Muslims, crime, traditional or alternative energy, foreign policy, the economy, immigration, Syrian refugees, and immigration.[30] The posts' captions were also copied into the coded data set.[31] For example, in mid-October around the time of a debate, the Clinton campaign posted an arty picture of a pensive candidate with the caption "Let's go. #Debate."

RESULTS

Instagram, a largely visual medium, offers a number of possible uses for a political campaign. These include but are not limited to mobilizing supporters, soliciting donations, telling followers about endorsements, communicating about issues, and informing people about campaign events. Indeed, an examination of the Instagram posts in this study found most of those uses. This section describes the nature of the Instagram posts more generally and then focuses more specifically on how and to what extent the Instagram posts communicated about issues.

The first impression that results from an informal review of the posts is that they are almost all tied to campaign events. Although I did not code for location, posts from Iowa and New Hampshire dominated the Instagram posts through the end of 2015: county and state fairs, town halls, and pictures from the road were typical during this period. For example, many of Scott Walker's posts involved food from wherever he happened to be. Some candidates created text-laden images for use on Instagram, frequently to report the latest favorable poll numbers (Donald Trump was particularly fixated with those). Almost all of the Instagram posts had accompanying captions, ranging from a few words to those which were quite verbose, particularly Clinton's.

The number of Instagram posts over time are illustrated in Figure 13.1, which plots the mean daily number of posts for each month. The highest monthly means were in August 2015 and January 2016, periods that correspond with the first televised debates and the Iowa caucuses and New Hampshire primary. The most Instagram posts in a single day across the period was 31, this on July 1, 2015, while there were a handful of days where just one candidate shared a photo. Interestingly, the mean daily postings each month did not vary that widely, despite the number of Republican candidates at the start of the campaign. The number of posts waxed and waned depending on events tied to the campaign. For example, the number of Republican posts surged around the debates and a few days in advance of a caucus or primary.

Variation was considerable, however, among the candidates of each party across the nomination period (Table 13.1). Not surprisingly, by virtue of their longevity in the race, Trump (954) and Clinton (772) posted the most Instagram posts across the nomination and general election period, followed by Bernie Sanders (380) and Ben Carson (320). Kasich, the last holdout of the Republican candidates, posted about 178 photos on Instagram. A few candidates appear to have not considered Instagram important. For example, Republican George Pataki posted just 5 times between July 1, 2015, and January 1, 2016. A breakdown of each candidate's posts appears in Table 13.2.

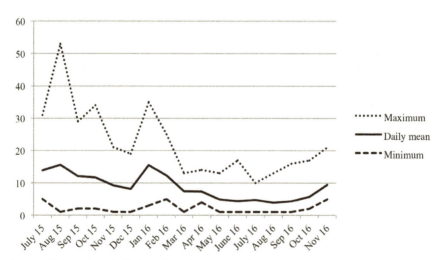

Figure 13.1. Mean Daily Number of Instagram Posts

Table 13.1. Total Number of Instagram
Posts per Candidate

Candidate Name	Posts
Trump	954
Clinton	772
Sanders	380
Carson	320
Rubio	280
Cruz	236
Christie	229
Paul	226
Kasich	178
Bush	150
Huckabee	137
Jindal	125
Santorum	76
Walker	69
O'Malley	58
Graham	53
Perry	51
Chafee	27
Webb	15
Pataki	5
Total	4,341

Most of the Instagram posts fit into the categories described in Table 13.3. Of the 4,341 posts analyzed, more than two-thirds were linked to a campaign event, 19.5 percent addressed an issue, nearly 10 percent were videos, nearly 9 percent named an opponent, 2 percent noted an endorsement, and less than 1 percent solicited donations. When the nomination periods are broken out, 70 percent of the Republicans' and nearly 62 percent of the Democrats' posts were tied to a campaign event. Democrats addressed issues more than Republicans did, with issues mentioned in 27 percent of the posts compared to about 14 percent of Republicans. Videos made up 9.6 percent of Republican posts and 7.9 percent of Democrats' (Table 13.4). The visual rather than textual emphasis of Instagram may explain the primary emphasis on campaign events.

During the general election period,[32] 67 percent of Trump's Instagram posts and 54 percent of Clinton's depicted a campaign event in some way (Table 13.5). Clinton addressed at least one issue in 36.62 percent of her posts, while Trump mentioned one or more in 27 percent of his posts ($\chi^2=11.75$, $p \leq 0.05$). Sixteen percent of Clinton's posts and 24 percent of Trump's named their opponent, either directly or indirectly ($\chi^2=0.47$,

Table 13.2. Instagram Use by Candidate, Full Election Cycle, as Percentage of Candidate's Total Posts

	Campaign Event	Addressed Issue(s)	Noted an Endorsement	Solicited Donation	Named an Opponent	Post Was a Video
Republicans						
Bush	66.67%	19.33%	0.67%	0.67%	7.33%	7.33%
Carson	35.94	26.25	0.31	0.31	8.75	3.12
Christie	85.59	3.93	1.75	0	0.44	5.24
Cruz	81.36	9.32	3.81	0	3.81	17.8
Graham	90.57	22.64	3.77	0	0	7.55
Huckabee	87.59	20.44	2.92	0	1.46	6.57
Jindal	84	6.4	0	0	2.4	1.6
Kasich	82.02	4.49	1.69	1.69	1.69	6.18
Pataki	58.62	20	0	0	40	0
Paul	68.14	26.99	0.44	0.88	5.75	23.45
Perry	72.55	11.76	1.96	0	1.96	3.92
Rubio	73.21	10	2.5	1.79	2.86	5.36
Santorum	52.63	7.89	1.32	0	0	3.95
Trump	68.13	19.29	2.31	0.1	17.61	12.57
Walker	53.62	8.7	0	1.45	2.9	18.84
Democrats						
Chafee	88.89	7.4	0	0	0	3.7
Clinton	55.31	30.05	2.46	0.52	15.03	11.66
O'Malley	58.62	22.41	3.45	0	1.72	6.9
Sanders	77.11	23.37	2.63	1.84	5.79	6.84
Webb	100	26.67	0	0	0	0
Pearson's χ^2	375.75*	210.61*	22.47	30.43*	230.87*	140.41*
N	4,341	4,341	4,341	4,341	4,341	4,341

*$p \leq 0.05$

Table 13.3. Instagram Posts by Category, Full Election Cycle

Category	Percentage
Campaign event	67.73
Addressed issue(s)	19.51
Noted an endorsement	2
Solicited donation	0.6
Named an opponent	8.98
Post was a video	9.86

n = 4,341

Table 13.4. Instagram Posts by Category, Nomination Period

Category	Republicans*	Democrats**
Campaign event	70.04	65.87
Addressed issue(s)	13.9	27.18
Noted an endorsement	1.98	2.28
Solicited donation	0.03	0.93
Named an opponent	5.48	6.64
Post was a video	9.6	7.88
	n = 2,626	n = 1,002

*July 1, 2015–May 26, 2016
**July 1, 2015–June 8, 2016

Table 13.5. Instagram Categories, General Election

Category	Percentage		Pearson's c^2
	Trump	Clinton	
Campaign event	66.97	54.26	11.75*
Addressed issue(s)	28.21	32.62	1.59
Noted an endorsement	0.92	3.19	4.98*
Solicited donation	0.23	0.71	0.95
Named an opponent	24.31	26.6	0.47
Post was a video	11.93	15.96	3.3
n = 718			

ns). Clinton noted an endorsement in 3 percent of her posts while Trump noted an endorsement in less than 1 percent of his posts ($\chi^2=4.98$, $p\leq0.05$). The other categories saw a negligible number of posts.

COMMUNICATION OF ISSUES

One of the common complaints about American political campaigns, as well as news coverage of the campaigns, is that there is too much focus on strategy (the "horse race" frame) and insufficient attention to issues facing the electorate.[33] The evolution of social media has provided campaigns the opportunity to bypass the news media filter[34] and communicate directly with voters. This development provides the opportunity for campaigns to directly tell voters about where they stand on issues and other matters of importance that legacy news media might ignore. Are they using Instagram to do so? The answer is, well, a little bit.

For the full election cycle, issues were addressed in about 19 percent percent of the posts, which means 81 percent of the posts did not. This study looked for mentions of 21 issues. The most frequent issue cited was national security at 4.2 percent of all Instagram posts, followed by education (3.2%) and religion/morality (2.33%).

One approach to examining candidates' communication about issues is through the lens of issue ownership, a theory that asserts that political candidates will tend to limit their discussions to those "owned" by their political party. For purposes of this paper, and following others,[35] I treated the following issues as owned by Democrats: education, health care, poverty, the elderly, labor, and the environment (and, by extension, climate change). Republican Party–owned issues were job creation, national security, government spending/deficit, morality/religion, crime, traditional energy, immigration (and, by extension, treatment of Muslims and Syrian immigrants). Performance issues, or those invoked by one party or the other depending on circumstances, were foreign policy and the economy. Finally, because some of the original issue categories are too broad to assign to one particular party, I broke out three sub-issues from the Republican-owned issues and designated them as more in tune Democratic ideology: abortion rights, alternative energy, and gay marriage, included because the 2015 Supreme Court ruling in *Obergefell v. Hodges* came early in the nomination process.

Democratic Issues

For the initial examination of issue communications I used a calculation of mentions of each issue as a percentage of each candidate's Instagram posts over the nomination and general election cycles (Tables 13.6 and 13.7). For the nomination period, the most-mentioned Democratic issue, as a percentage of each candidate's posts, was abortion rights by a Republican, Rick Santorum (he was opposed). The next most-mentioned in a Democratic category were also made by a Republican, Ben Carson, with 12.5 percent of his posts devoted in some way to education. It bears noting that appearances at schools and shows of support by student groups were coded as education; Carson had a period where a number of the posts were from Students for Carson at various college campuses. Most of the other Republicans made some passing reference to education. Among the Democrats, the most-mentioned issue was education by Clinton in 6.7 percent of her posts. Significant differences, as determined by calculating Pearson's χ^2, were found among the Republicans for mentions of education, the environment, climate change, and abortion rights. For the Democrats, the candidates' positions differed significantly for

Table 13.6. Democratic-owned Issues on Instagram, Nomination Period[†]

	Education	Health Care	Poverty	Elderly	Labor	Environment	Climate Change	Abortion Rights	Alternative Energy	Gay Marriage
Republicans										
Bush	4	0.67	0	0	0	0	0	0.67	0	0
Carson	12.54	0.63	0	0	0.31	0	0	0.31	0	0
Christie	0.44	0.44	0	0	0	0	0	0.42	0.44	0
Cruz	0	0.42	0	0	0	0	0	0	0	0
Graham	1.89	0	0	0	0	1.89	0	0	0	0
Huckabee	4.38	0	0	0	0	0	1.46	0.73	0.73	0.73
Jindal	0	0	0	0	0	0	0	0.8	0	0
Kasich	0.56	0	0	0	0	0	0	0	0	0
Pataki	0	0	0	0	0	0	0	0	0	0
Paul	3.54	0.8	0	0	0.44	0	0	0.44	0	0
Perry	0	0	0	0	0	0	0	0	0	0
Rubio	1.79	1.79	0.36	0	0	0	0	0.36	0	0
Santorum	1.32	0	0	0	1.32	0	0	13.16	0	0
Trump	0.2	0.61	0	0	0.41	0	0.2	0	0	0
Walker	1.45	0	0	0	1.45	0	0	1.45	0	0
Pearson's χ^2	153.19*	11.87	8.38	—	13	48.57*	24.36*	182.77*	13.33	18.17
n	2,626	2,626	2,626	2,626	2,626	2,626	2,626	2,626	2,626	2,626
Democrats										
Chafee	0	0	0	0	3.7	0	0	0	0	0
Clinton	6.73	2.65	0.82	0.2	5.92	0.82	1.02	2.04	1.02	1.02
O'Malley	5.17	1.72	0	0	0	0	0	1.72	0.53	1.72
Sanders	3.74	3.48	4.55	0.8	7.75	1.6	0	0.8	0.53	0.8
Webb	0	0	0	0.8	0	0	0	0	20	0
Pearson's χ^2	6.27	2.12	16.33*	2.3	6.81	2.45	4.86	2.94	49.06*	0.9
n	964	964	964	964	964	964	964	964	964	964

[†]Reported as a percentage of candidate's total Instagram posts.
*$p \leq 0.05$

Table 13.7. Democratic-owned Issues Addressed on Instagram, General Election Period†

	Education	Health Care	Poverty	Elderly	Labor	Environment	Climate Change	Abortion Rights	Alternative Energy	Gay Marriage
Clinton	6.03	6.03	0.71	0.35	7.45	0.35	0.35	1.42	0	0.35
Trump	0.69	1.61	0	0	3.21	0.23	0.34	0	0.23	0
Pearson's χ^2	18.04*	10.37*	3.1	1.55	6.63*	0.1	0.1	6.22*	0.65	10.99*
n	718	718	718	718	718	718	718	718	718	718

†Reported as a percentage of candidate's total Instagram posts
*p ≤ 0.05

just poverty and alternative energy, suggesting more of an adherence to Democratic-owned issues.

Table 13.6 breaks down the percentage of Instagram posts for Trump and Clinton during the general election period. Statistically significant differences were found for education (Clinton mentioned it more often), health care (again, Clinton took the lead), labor (again, Clinton), abortion rights (not addressed at all by Trump), and gay marriage, although the number of mentions there were minuscule.

Republican Issues

Tables 13.8 and 13.9 break down the Republican-owned issues for the nomination and general election periods, respectively. During the nomination period, it was a Democrat who had the most mentions of a Republican issue, with 8.62 percent of O'Malley's posts mentioning immigration. The next highest were religion/morality (6.9% for Carson), national security (6.6% for Paul), and reducing government (6.6% for Paul). Among all the Republicans, significant differences were found for national security, government reduction, religion/morality, treatment of Syrian refugees, immigration, and taxes. Immigration was the only issue with a significant difference among the Republican issues during the nomination season.

For the general election period, the most-addressed issue was national security, with 8.51 percent of Clinton's and 11.93 percent of Trump's posts addressing it in some way. The only issue where a significant difference existed was religion/morality (χ^2=5.81, p≤0.05).

Performance Issues

The performance issues for this study, issues in which voters judge the parties' performance, were foreign affairs and the economy (Tables 13.10 and 13.11). Graham addressed foreign affairs the most among both parties' candidates during the nomination season with 11.32 percent of posts devoted to the subject. For the economy, Sanders was the most frequent commenter with 4 percent of his posts mentioning that topic. Significant differences at the 95 percent confidence level existed among the Republican candidates for both issues, but not among the Democrats. During the general election period, Clinton addressed foreign affairs 6 percent of the time and Trump about 3 percent. For the economy, 1.8 percent of Clinton's posts and 1.83 percent of Trump's addressed that issue. Neither was statistically significant.

Table 13.8. Republican-owned Issues Addressed on Instagram, Nomination Period†

	Job Creation	National Security	Government Reduction	Religion Morality	Crime	Traditional Energy	Syrian Refugees	Immig.	Treatment Muslims	Taxes
Republican candidates										
Bush	2.67	6.67	0.67	2	0.67	0.67	0	0.67	0	3.33
Carson	0	3.45	0.63	6.9	0.31	0	1.88	0.31	0	0.63
Christie	0	0	0.44	0.87	0.87	0	0	0.44	0.31	0
Cruz	0.85	1.69	1.27	3.39	0.42	0	0	0	0.42	2.12
Graham	1.89	11.32	0	0	0	0	0	0	0	4.38
Huckabee	0.73	2.92	0	5.84	0	0	0	0	0.73	4.38
Jindal	0	0.8	0	4	0.8	0.8	0	0	0	0
Kasich	0.56	1.69	2.81	0	0	0	0	0	0	0
Pataki	0	0	0	0	0	0	0	20	0	0
Paul	0.88	6.64	6.64	1.77	0.88	0	0	0.44	0	4.87
Perry	0	3.92	0	1.96	0	0	0	3.92	0	0
Rubio	0.36	2.14	0	1.07	0.36	0	0	0	0	1.43
Santorum	1.32	0	0	2.63	0	0	0	1.32	0	0
Trump	0.61	4.67	0	1.42	1.42	0	0.41	2.44	1.02	0.41
Walker	0	1.45	0	1.45	0	0	0	0	1.45	1.45
Pearson's χ^2	18.27	45.59*	90.42*	47.49*	10.38	17.27	31.81*	59.61*	14.38	49.52*
n	2,626	2,626	2,626	2,626	2,626	2,626	2,626	2,626	2,625	2,626
Democratic candidates										
Chafee	0	0	0	0	0	0	0	0	0	0
Clinton	1.43	2.24	0	2.65	3.47	0.2	0.2	2.04	0.61	0.41
O'Malley	0	0	0	1.72	3.45	0	1.72	8.62	1.72	0
Sanders	1.6	2.14	0	2.14	1.07	1.07	0	2.41	0.53	0.27
Webb	0	0	0	0	0	0	0	0	0	0
Pearson's χ^2	1.57	2.26	—	1.4	6.56	3.66	7.31	10.47*	3.39	0.31
n	964	964	964	964	964	964	964	64	964	0.48

†Reported as a percentage of candidate's total Instagram posts
*$p < 0.05$

Table 13.9. Republican-owned Issues Addressed on Instagram, General Election Period†

	Job Creation	National Security	Govern Reduction	Religion Morality	Crime	Traditional Energy	Syrian Refugees	Immig.	Treatment Muslims	Taxes
Clinton	2.84	8.51	0	4.26	2.48	0	0	2.48	1.06	2.13
Trump	2.52	11.93	1.15	1.38	5.05	1.15	0.45	1.38	0.23	3.44
Pearson's χ^2	0.07	2.11	3.26	5.81*	2.9	3.26	1.3	1.18	2.35	1.04
n	718	718	718	718	718	718	718	718	718	718

†Reported as a percentage of candidate's total Instagram posts
*$p < 0.05$

Table 13.10. Performance Issues Addressed on Instagram, Nomination Period†

	Foreign affairs	Economy
Republican candidates		
Bush	2	2
Carson	0.63	0
Christie	0	0
Cruz	0.85	0.85
Graham	11.32	0
Huckabee	0	1.46
Jindal	0	0
Kasich	0	0
Pataki	0	0
Paul	3.98	0.44
Perry	1.96	1.96
Rubio	0.71	1.07
Santorum	2.63	0
Trump	1.83	0
Walker	2.9	0
Pearson's χ^2	62.15*	23.63*
n	2,626	2,626
Demoratic candidates		
Chafee	3.7	0
Clinton	1.22	2.04
O'Malley	0	0
Sanders	1.34	4.01
Webb	6.67	0
Pearson's χ^2	5.16	6.23
n	964	964

†Reported as a percentage of candidate's total Instagram posts
*$p \leq 0.05$

Table 13.11. Performance Issues Addressed on Instagram, General Election*

	Foreign affairs	Economy
Clinton	6.03	3.9
Trump	2.98	1.83
Pearson's χ^2	3.97*	2.84
n	718	718

*Reported as a percentage of candidate's total Instagram posts
*$p < 0.05$

DISCUSSION

That the candidates' Instagram posts were mostly devoted to depicting campaign events should not come as much of a surprise, given that Instagram is largely a visual medium. Many of the pictures could be categorized as routine. During the early campaign period, these mainly consisted of candidates making various stops in Iowa and New Hampshire. Many of Trump's posts depicted his rallies at arenas and airports. Some candidates were quite verbose, particularly Hillary Clinton, in their accompanying captions, as if they were unclear about the concept of a visual medium. Still, the text supplied in the captions helped to bring more meaning to the photographs as well as to tell Instagram followers where they could go to get more information.[36]

The number of Instagram posts that addressed issues was a fairly small percentage of the more than 4,300 pictures posted during the full campaign cycle. Still, there were enough to provide a glimpse of the campaigns' attention to issues and their willingness to trespass on the other party's owned issues.

Issue Ownership During the Primaries

For a more robust examination of issue ownership in Instagram posts, I conducted a comparison of each party on the issues separately for the nomination and the general election period. The results were calculated as a percentage of total posts about issues and are reported in Tables 13.12 and 13.13.

As Panel A of Table 13.12 shows, all of the issues "owned" by the Democratic Party were addressed more often by Democrats than Republicans. For eight of the issues, the finding was significant at the 95 percent confidence level: health care (χ^2=10.44); poverty (χ^2=28.4); labor (χ^2=73.95); environment (χ^2=11.73); climate change (χ^2=9.38); abortion rights (χ^2=21.56); alternative energy (χ^2=10.64); and gay marriage (χ^2=11.83). Additionally, Democrats trespassed on four Republican-owned issues: job creation (χ^2=0.22, n.s.), crime (χ^2=5.00, p≤0.05), traditional energy (χ^2=2.78, n.s.), and immigration (χ^2=2.57, n.s.). Of the remaining Republican issues, Republicans led Democrats, with five reaching significance at the 95 percent confidence level: national security (χ^2=33.34), government reduction (χ^2=19.34), religion/morality (χ^2=12.54), treatment of Muslims (χ^2=9.74), and taxes (χ^2=18.75). Of the performance issues, Democrats addressed the economy more often than Republicans (χ^2=10.73, p≤0.05), while Republicans emphasized foreign policy more frequently (χ^2=8.47, p<0.05).

During the general election season (Table 13.13), Clinton dominated in all the Democratic issues except for alternative energy, which received

Table 13.12. Comparison of Issue Mentions as a Percentage of Posts About Issues

Democratic Issues	Education	Health Care	Poverty	Elderly	Labor	Environ.	Climate Change	Abortion Rights	Alternative Energy	Gay Marriage
Democrats	20	10.8	8.4	1.6	23.2	4	2	5.6	4.4	3.2
Republicans	19.45	4.11	0.27	0	1.64	0.27	0.82	0.27	0.55	0
Pearson's χ^2	0.03	10.44*	28.4*	5.88	73.95*	11.73*	9.38*	21.56*	10.64*	11.83*
n	615	615	615	615	615	615	615	615	615	615

Republican Issues	Job Creation	Nat'l Security	Reduce Govt.	Religion Morality	Crime	Traditional Energy	Syrian Refugees	Immig.	Treat. Muslims	Taxes
Democrats	5.2	6	0	8	8.8	2	0.8	8.8	2	1.2
Republicans	4.38	23.56	7.4	18.08	4.38	0.55	2.19	5.48	2.47	9.86
Pearson's χ^2	0.22	33.34*	19.34*	12.54*	5.00*	2.78	1.8	2.57	9.74*	18.75*
N	615	615	615	615	615	615	615	615	615	615

Perform. Issues	Foreign Policy	Economy
Democrats	4	9.6
Republicans	10.41	3.29
Pearson's χ^2	8.47*	10.73*
n	615	615

*$p \leq 0.05$

Table 13.13. Comparison of Issue Mentions as Percentage of All Issue Mentions

Democratic Issues	Education	Health Care	Poverty	Elderly	Labor	Environ.	Climate Change	Abortion Rights	Alternative Energy	Gay Marriage
Clinton	18.48	18.48	2.17	1.09	22.83	1.09	1.09	4.35	0	1.09
Trump	2.44	5.69	0	0	11.38	0.81	0.81	0	0.81	0
Pearson's χ^2	16.05*	8.68*	2.7	1.34	5.06*	0.04	0.04	5.45*	0.75	9.59*
N	215	215	215	215	215	215	215	215	215	215

Republican Issues	Job Creation	National Security	Reduce Govt.	Religion Morality	Crime	Trad. Energy	Syrian Refugees	Immig.	Treatment Muslims	Taxes
Clinton	8.7	26.09	0	13.04	7.61	0	0	7.61	3.26	6.52
Trump	8.94	42.28	4.07	4.88	17.89	4.07	1.63	4.88	0.81	12.2
Pearson's χ^2	0	6.04*	0.05	4.57*	4.76*	3.83*	1.51	0.69	1.83	1.92
n	215	215	215	215	215	215	215	215	215	215

Performance Issues	Economy	Foreign Policy
Clinton	11.96	18.48
Trump	6.5	10.57
Pearson's χ^2	1.94	2.74
n	215	215

*$p \leq 0.05$

almost no attention by either candidate. Of the Democratic issues, a significant relationship exists for education (χ^2=16.05), health care (χ^2=8.68), labor (χ^2=5.06), abortion rights (χ^2=5.45), and gay marriage (χ^2=9.59). The Republican issues (Table 13.12) were mixed, however, with Clinton trespassing on religion/morality (χ^2=4.57, p≤0.05), immigration (χ^2=0.69, n.s.), treatment of Muslims (χ^2=1.83, n.s.), and, surprisingly, taxes, although that relationship was not significant (χ^2=1.92). Finally, for performance issues (Table 13.12), Clinton dominated in both foreign policy and economy mentions, although neither result was statistically significant.

Given the free-for-all that characterized much of the 2016 presidential campaign, it was possible that issue ownership in practice would be pushed aside. Surprisingly, this was not the case. Although the primary use of Instagram was not to communicate issues, when candidates did address an issue, it was usually in alignment with the theory of issue ownership. Combined with the feel-good-about-the-candidate nature of most of the pictures posted on Instagram, it appears that the campaigns' goals in their Instagram use were not to persuade citizens to switch sides but rather to activate or reinforce already held dispositions, and to remind supporters when it was time to vote.

CONCLUSION

This chapter focused on the general nature of the candidates' Instagram posts and explored to what extent the candidates communicated about issues facing the nation with these posts, given the importance of information in the functioning of pluralistic democracy. Other aspects of Instagram use need more examination. Additionally, because Instagram is primarily visual communication, what do the actual images communicate? What inferences can be drawn about character from the combination of the picture and its caption?

Other unanswered questions are beyond this data set: Who were the actual recipients of this campaign information? What were their motivations? Did they follow more than one candidate on Instagram, or do they choose to just follow their preferred candidate? What can be deduced from the comments that users can attach to an Instagram? Are they mostly from supporters, or is there substantial trolling involved? How is Instagram being used in down-ticket races?

While this study isolated Instagram from other numerous online tools that political candidates can now use to directly reach citizens, it should be considered to be part of a more complex social media strategy that reaches citizens in different ways. The interaction of the various Internet applications likely had a stronger influence on citizens than each application in isolation. It will be interesting to see what new tools will be used in 2020.

NOTES

1. Instagram is now a unit of Facebook, Inc.

2. Shannon Greenwood, Andrew Perrin, and Maeve Duggan, "Social Media Update," Pew Research Center, 2016.

3. Danah M. Boyd and Nicole B. Ellison, "Social Network Sites: Definition, History, and Scholarship," *Journal of Computer-Mediated Communication*, 13 (2007): 210–230.

4. Jose Van Dijck, *The Culture of Connectivity: A Critical History of Social Media.* (New York: Oxford University Press, 2013), 8.

5. Van Dijck, 4–5.

6. Van Dijck, 15.

7. Van Dijck, 15.

8. Van Dijck, 16

9. Vassia Gueorguieva, "Voters, MySpace, and YouTube: The Impact of Alternative Communication Channels," in *Politicking Online: The Transformation of Election Campaign Communications*, edited by Costas Panagopoulos. (New Brunswick, NJ: Rutgers University Press), 2008.

10. Amber Davisson, "'I'm In!': Hillary Clinton's 2008 Democratic Primary Campaign on YouTube," *Journal of Visual Literacy* 28 (2009): 70–91.

11. Monica Ancu, "Techno Politics in Presidential Campaigning: New Voices, New Technologies, and New Voters," in *From Soundbite to Textbite: Election 2008 Comments on Twitter* edited by John Allen Hendricks and Lynda Lee Kaid. (New York: Routledge, 2011). E-book.

12. Leticia Bode, "Facebooking It to the Polls: A Study in Online Social Networking and Political Behavior," *Journal of Information Technology and Politics* 9 (2012): 352–69.

13. Porismita Borah, "Poltical Facebook Use: Campaign Strategies Used in 2008 and 2012 Presidential Elections." *Journal of Information Technology and Politics* 13, no. 4 (2016): 326–38.

14. See Daniela V. Dimitrova and Dianne Bystrom, "The Effects of Social Media on Political Participation and Candidate Image Evaluations in the 2012 Iowa Caucuses," *American Behavioral Sciences* 57, no. 11 (2013): 1568–83; Daniela V. Dimitrova, Adam Shehata, Jesper Stromback, and Lars W. Nord, "The Effects of Digital Media on Political Knowledge in Election Campaigns: Evidence from Panel Data," *Communication Research* 41, no. 1 (2014): 95–118; Mauricio Avendaño, "Information Sources in the Spanish Social Media During the 'Three Days of March,'" *Revista Latina De Comunicación Social*, 13 no. 65 (2010): 1–15; Jody Baumgartner and Jonathan S. Morris, "MyFaceTube Politics: Social Networking Web Sites and Political Engagement of Young Adults," *Social Science Computer Review* 28, no. 1 (2010): 24–44; Manuel Castells, "Communication, Power, and Counter-Power in the Network Society," *International Journal of Communication*, 1

(2007): 238–266; Sharon Meraz, "The Fight For 'How To Think': Traditional Media, Social Networks, and Attribute Agenda Setting," *Conference Papers — International Communication Association*, 2009; Clay Shirky, "The Political Power of Social Media: Technology, the Public Sphere, and Political Change," *Foreign Affairs*, 90 (2011): 26–38.

15. Shelley Boulianne, "Social Media Use and Participation: A Meta-Analysis of Current Research," *Information, Community & Society* 18, no. 5 (2015): 524–38.

16. Shirky, "The Political Power of Social Media," 3.

17. Gang Han, "New Media Use, Sociodemographics, and Voter Turnout in the 2000 Presidential Election," *Mass Communication and Society*, 11 (2008): 62–81.

18. John H. Parmelee, John Davies, and Carolyn A. McMahan, "The Rise of Non-Traditional Site Use for Online Political Information," *Communication Quarterly* 59, no. 5 (2011): 625–40.

19. Juliet Carlisle and Robert C. Patton, "Is Social Media Changing How We Understand Political Engagement? An Analysis of Facebook and the 2008 Presidential Election," *Political Research Quarterly*, 66 no. 4 (2013): 883–895.

20. Jenny Bronstein, "Like Me! Analyzing the 2012 Presidential Candidates' Facebook Pages," *Online Information Review* 37, no. 2 (2013): 173–92.

21. See Matthew James Kushin and Masahiro Yamamoto, "Did Social Media Really Matter? College Students' Use of Online Media and Political Decision Making in the 2008 Election," *Mass Communication and Society*, 13 (2010): 608–630; Juliana Fernandes, Magda Giurcanu, Kevin W. Bowers, and Jeffrey C. Neely, "The Writing on the Wall: A Content Analysis of Students' Facebook Groups for the 2008 Presidential Election," *Mass Communication and Society*, 13 (2010): 653–675.

22. Gary L. Hanson, Paul M. Haridakis, Audrey Wagstaff Cunningham, Rekha Sharma, and J.D. Ponder, "The 2008 Presidential Campaign: Political Cynicism in the Age of Facebook, MySpace, and YouTube." *Mass Communication and Society*, 13 (2010): 584–607.

23. Masahiro Yamamoto and Matthew J. Kushin, "More Harm than Good? Online Media Use and Political Disaffection Among College Students in the 2008 Election," *Journal of Computer-Mediated Communication*, 19 (2014): 430–445.

24. Michael X. Delli Carpini and Scott Keeter, *What Americans Know About Politics and Why It Matters*. (New Haven: Yale University Press, 1996).

25. John R. Petrocik, "Issue Ownership in Presidential Elections, with a 1980 Case Study," *American Journal of Political Science* 40, no. 3 (1996): 825–850.

26. See John R. Petrocik, William L. Benoit, and Glenn J. Hansen, "Issue Ownership and Presidential Campaigning, 1952–2000," *Political Science Quarterly* 118, no. 4 (2003): 599–626; but for an alternate view, see Lee Sigelman and Emmett H. Buehl Jr., "Avoidance or Engagement? Issue Convergence in U.S. Presidential Campaigns," *American Journal of Political Science* 48, no. 4 (2004): 650–61, and David F. Damore, "The Dynamics of Issue Ownership in Presidential Campaigns," *Political Research Quarterly* 57, no. 3 (2004): 391–97.

27. The race for some of the candidates began later than July 1, 2015: Webb (July 3), Walker (July 13), Kasich (July 22). Jim Gilmore announced in early August but failed to establish an Instagram account. Due to either an oversight in data collection or a failure of her campaign to make any posts, Carly Fiorina is not included in this study.

28. The program used to archive Instagram videos did not capture any accompanying text, so the analysis of those is restricted to the accompanying audio.

29. Some posts contained no images but rather a graphic presentation of text.

30. An intercoder reliability test of 1,695 data points found 98.94 percent agreement ($k=0.57$; $p \leq 0.05$).

31. The coding sheet and instructions are available from the author.

32. For the purposes of this study, the general election period started June 8, 2016, after Clinton had enough delegates for the nomination.

33. Delli Carpini and Keeter, *What Americans Know About Politics and Why It Matters*.

34. See David Manning White, "The 'Gate-Keeper': A Case Study in the Selection of News," *Journalism Quarterly*, 27 (1950): 383–390; Maxwell E. McCombs and Donald L. Shaw, "The Agenda-Setting Function of Mass Media," *Public Opinion Quarterly* 36 (1972): 176–187; and Pamela J. Shoemaker and Tim P. Vos, *Gatekeeping Theory*. (New York: Routledge, 2009).

35. Petrocik, Benoit, and Hansen, "Issue Ownership and Presidential Campaigning, 1952–2000."

36. Instagram does not allow direct links in captions, so many times candidates referred followers to links in the candidates' Instagram "bios." Although beyond the scope of this study, it would be interesting to know how many followers actually went to the bios to click through.

Bibliography

Abbe, Owen G., Jay Goodliffe, Paul S. Herrnson, and Kelly D. Patterson. "Agenda Setting in Congressional Elections: The Impact of Issues and Campaigns on Voting Behavior." *Political Research Quarterly* 56 (2003): 419–30. doi:10.1177/106591290305600404.

Abramowitz, Alan I. "Will Time for Change Mean Time for Trump?" *PS: Political Science & Politics*, 49 (2016): 659–60.

Abramowitz, Alan I., and Kyle L. Saunders. "Ideological Realignment in the US Electorate." *Journal of Politics* 60 (1998): 634–652.

Abramowitz, Alan I., Brad Alexander, and Matthew Gunning. "Incumbency, Redistricting, and the Decline of Competition in U.S. House Elections." *Journal of Politics* 68 (2006): 75–88.

Adams, Amelia, and McCorkindale, Tina. "Dialogue and Transparency: A Content Analysis of How the 2012 Presidential Candidates Used Twitter." *Public Relations Review* 39:4 (2013) 357–359.

Aday, Sean, and John Devitt. "Style Over Substance: Newspaper Coverage of Elizabeth Dole's Presidential Bid." *The Harvard International Journal of Press/Politics* 6 (2001): 52–73.

Adler, E. Scott, Chariti E. Gent, and Cary B. Overmeyer. "The Home Style Homepage: Legislator Use of the World Wide Web for Constituency Contact." *Legislative Studies Quarterly* 23:4 (1998): 585–595.

Allen, Cooper. "Trump: Jeb Bush 'Had to Bring in Mommy to Take a Slap at Me.'" *USA Today*, February 6, 2015, http://www.usatoday.com/story/news/politics/onpolitics/2016/02/06/jeb-bush-donald-trump/79922352/.

Allison, Bill, Mira Rojanasakul, Brittany Harris, and Cedric Sam. "Tracking the 2016 Presidential Money Race." *Bloomberg*, December 9, 2016, https://www.bloomberg.com/politics/graphics/2016-presidential-campaign-fundraising/.

Ancu, Monica. "From Soundbite to TextBite: Election 2008 Comments on Twitter." In *Techno Politics in Presidential Campaigning: New Voices, New Technologies, and New Voters*, edited by John A. Hendricks and Lynda Lee Kaid, 11–21. New York: Routledge, 2011.

Ancu, Monica, and Raluca Cozma. "MySpace Politics: Uses and Gratifications of Befriending Candidates." *Journal of Broadcasting & Electronic Media* 53:4 (2009). doi http://dx.doi.org/10.1080/08838150903333064.

Anderson, Ashley A., Dominique Brossard, Dietram A. Scheufele, Michael A. Xenos, and Peter Ladwig. "The 'Nasty Effect': Online Incivility and Risk Perceptions of Emerging Technologies." *Journal of Computer-Mediated Communication* 19, no. 3 (2014): 373–387.

Anderson, Monica. 2015. "Men Catch Up with Women on Overall Social Media Use." *Fact Tank*. Pew Research Center, August 28. http://www.pewresearch.org/fact-tank/2015/08/28/men-catch-up-with-women-on-overall-social-media-use/.

Andrews, Edmund. "The '96 Race on the Internet: Surfer Beware." *New York Times*. October 23, 1995. http://www.nytimes.com/1995/10/23/us/the-96-race-on-the-internet-surfer-beware.html?pagewanted=all.

Ansolabehere, Stephen, and Shanto Iyengar. *Going Negative: How Political Advertisements Shrink and Polarize the Electorate*. New York: Free Press, 1995.

Ansolabehere, Stephen, and James M. Snyder. "Using Term Limits to Estimate Incumbency Advantages When Officeholders Retire Strategically." *Legislative Studies Quarterly* 29 (2004): 487–515.

Arterton, F. Christopher. *Media Politics: The News Strategies of Presidential Campaigns*. Lexington, MA: Heath, 1984.

Associated Press. "Ad Spending: The Candidate Ad Spending Race." *AP*, November 16, 2016. http://elections.ap.org/content/ad-spending.

Auspurg, Katrin, and Thomas Hinz. *Factorial Survey Experiments*. Thousand Oaks, CA: SAGE, 2014.

Ausserhofer, Julian, and Axel Maireder. "National Politics on Twitter." *Information, Communication & Society* 16:3 (2013): 291–314. doi:10.1080/1369118X.2012.756050.

Auter, Zachary J., and Jeffrey A. Fine. "Negative Campaigning in the Social Media Age: Attack Advertising on Facebook." *Political Behavior* 38, no. 4 (2016). 999–1020.

Auter, Zachary J., and Jeffrey A. Fine. "Social Media Campaigning: Mobilization and Fundraising on Facebook." *Social Science Quarterly* (Forthcoming).

Avendaño, Mauricio. "Information Sources in the Spanish Social Media During the 'Three Days of March.'" *Revista Latina De Comunicación Social*, 13 no. 65 (2010): 1–15.

Bafami, Joseph, and Robert Y. Shapiro. "A New Partisan Voter." *The Journal of Politics* 71 (2009): 1–24.

Baker, Tom P., and Claes de Vreese. 2011. "Good News for the Future? Young People, Internet Use, and Political Participation." *Communication Research*, 30 (4): 451–470.

Ball, Molly. "Donald Trump and the Politics of Fear." *The Atlantic*, September 2, 2016. http://www.theatlantic.com/politics/archive/2016/09/donald-trump-and-the-politics-of-fear/498116.

Balmas, Meital, and Tamir Sheafer. "Candidate Image in Election Campaigns: Attribute Agenda Setting, Affective Priming, and Voting Intentions." *International Journal of Public Opinion Research* 22, no. 2 (2010): 204–229.

Balz, Dan. "Trump's Attack on McCain Marks a Turning Point for Him—and the GOP." *The Washington Post*, July 19, 2015, https://www.washingtonpost.com/

politics / trumps-attack-on-mccain-marks-a-turning-point-for-him--and-the-go
p / 2015 / 07 / 19 / 92759254–2e51–11e5–97ae-30a30cca95d7_story.html.

Barabak, Mark Z., and Lisa Mascaro. "Republicans Hold the House and Senate, but Will That End the Washington Gridlock Even with President Trump?" *Los Angeles Times*, November 9, 2016. http:// www.latimes.com / politics / la-na-pol-election-congress-control-20161108-story.html.

Barbaro, Michael. "Pithy, Mean and Powerful: How Donald Trump Mastered Twitter for 2016." *The New York Times*, October 5, 2015.

Barbaro, Michael, Maggie Haberman, and Alan Rappeport. "As America Sleeps, Donald Trump Seethes on Twitter." *New York Times*. September 30, 2016. Available at: https:// www.nytimes.com / 2016 / 10 / 01 / us / politics / donald-trump-alicia-machado.html.

Baumgartner, Jody C. "Humor on the Next Frontier: Online Political Humor and Its Effects on Youth." *Social Science Computer Review* 29, (2007): 319–338.

Baumgartner, Jody C. "Editorial Cartoons 2.0: The Effects of Digital Political Satire on Presidential Candidate Evaluations." *Presidential Studies Quarterly* 38 (2008): 735–58.

Baumgartner, Jody C. "No Laughing Matter? Young Adults and the 'Spillover Effect' of Candidate-centered Political Humor." *HUMOR: International Journal of Humor Research* 26 (2013): 23–43.

Baumgartner, Jody C. "Political Humor and Its Effects: A Review Essay," in Camilo Cuéllar, ed., *Los Efectos Del Humor: Una Perspectiva Transdisciplinar [The Effects of Humor: A Trans-Disciplinary Perspective]*, (Bogota, Colombia: Ediciones Universidad Cooperativa de Colombia, forthcoming 2017).

Baumgartner, Jody C, and Jonathan S. Morris. "MyFaceTube Politics: Social Networking Web Sites and Political Engagement of Young Adults." *Social Science Computer Review*, 28 no. 1 (2010): 24–44.

Baumgartner, Jody C, and Jonathan S. Morris. "Stoned Slackers or Super-citizens? 'Daily Show' Viewing and Political Engagement of Young Adults." Quoted in Amarnath Amarasingam, ed., *The Stewart/Colbert Effect: Essays on the Real Impacts of Fake News* (Jefferson, NC: McFarland & Co., 2011).

Baumgartner, Jody C, Jonathan S. Morris, and Jeffrey Michael Coleman. "Does the 'Road to the White House Run Through' Letterman? Chris Christie, Letterman, and Attack v. Self-Depreciating Humor." *Journal of Political Marketing* (forthcoming).

Baumgartner, Jody C, Jenn Burleson Mackay, Jonathan S. Morris, Eric E. Otenyo, Larry Powell, Melissa M. Smith, Nancy Snow, Frederic I. Solop, and Brandon C. Waite. *Communicator-in-chief: How Barack Obama used new media technology to win the White House.* Edited by John Allen Hendricks and Robert E. Denton Jr. Lexington Books, 2010.

Bekafigo, Marija, and Allison Clark Pingley. "Do Campaigns 'Go Negative' on Twitter?" In *Politics, Protest, and Empowerment in Digital Spaces*, edited by Yasmin Ibrahim, 178–191. Hershey: IGI Global, 2017.

Bello, Jason, and Meredith Rolfe. "Is Influence Mightier than Selection? Forging Agreement in Political Discussion Networks During a Campaign." *Social Networks* 36 (2014): 134–146.

Bennett, W. Lance, and Robert M. Entman. *Mediated Politics: Communication in the Future of Democracy.* New York: Cambridge University Press, 2001.

Bennett, W. Lance, and Shanto Iyengar. "A New Era of Minimal Effects? The Changing Foundations of Political Communication." *Journal of Communication* 58 (2008): 707–731. doi:10.1111/j.1460–2466.2008. 00410.x.

Benoit, William L. "Beyond Genre Theory: The Genesis of Rhetorical Action." *Communications Monographs* 67, no. 2 (2000): 178–192.

Benoit, William L. "Election Outcome and Topic of Political Campaign Attacks." *Southern Journal of Communication* 69, no. 4 (2004): 348–355.

Benoit, William L. "Own Party Issue Ownership Emphasis in Presidential Television Spots." *Communication Reports* 20 (2007): 42–50. doi:10.1080/08934210601182818.

Benoit, William L., and Glenn J. Hansen. "Issue Ownership in Primary and General Presidential Debates." *Argumentation and Advocacy* 40 (2004): 143–54.

Benoit, William L., Mark J. Glantz, Anji L. Phillips, Leslie A. Rill, Corey B. Davis, Jayne R. Henson, and Leigh Anne Sudbrock. (2011). "Staying 'on Message': Consistency in Content of Presidential Primary Campaign Messages Across Media." *American Behavioral Scientist* 55 (2011): 457–68. doi:10.1177/0002764211398072.

Berinsky, Adam J., Gregory A. Huber, and Gabriel S. Lenz. "Evaluating Online Labor Markets for Experimental Research: Amazon.com's Mechanical Turk." *Political Analysis* 20, no. 3 (2012): 351–68.

Berland, Leslie. "#ThisHappened in 2016." Twitter Blog. Last modified December 6, 2016. Accessed February 2, 2017, https://blog.twitter.com/2016/thishappened-in-2016.

Berry, Colin, and Hans-Bernd Brosius. "Multiple Effects of Visual Format on TV News Learning." *Applied Cognitive Psychology* 5, no. 6 (1991): 519–528.

Bichard, Shannon L. "Building Blogs: A Multi-dimensional Analysis of the Distribution of Frames on the 2004 Presidential Candidate Websites." *Journalism & Mass Communication Quarterly* 83, no. 1 (2006): 329–345.

Billingham, Chase M., and Matthew O. Hunt. "School Racial Composition and Parental Choice: New Evidence on the Preferences of White Parents in the United States." *Sociology of Education* 89, no. 2 (2016): 99–117.

Bilton, Nick. "The Battle for Late Night Viewers on Screens of All Sizes." *The New York Times.* Last modified April 14, 2014. https://bits.blogs.nytimes.com/2014/04/10/the-battle-for-late-night-eyeballs-on-screens-of-all-sizes/?_r=0.

Bimber, Bruce. "Digital Media in the Obama Campaigns of 2008 and 2012: Adaption to the Personalized Political Communication Environment." *Journal of Information Technology and Politics* 11.2 (2014): 130–150.

Bimber, Bruce, and Richard Davis. *Campaigning Online: The Internet in U.S. Elections.* New York: Oxford University Press, 2003.

Black, Kate. "What We're Not Hearing from Republicans: Issues that Matter to Women and Families." 2016 Presidential Gender Watch, October 28, 2015. Available here: http://presidentialgenderwatch.org/issuesthatmatter/#more-4748.

Bode, Leticia. "Facebooking It to the Polls: A Study in Online Social Networking and Political Behavior." *Journal of Information Technology and Politics* 9 (2012): 352–369.

Bode, Leticia. "Political News in the News Feed: Learning Politics from Social Media." *Mass Communication and Society* 19 (2016): 24–48.

Borah, Porismita. "Political Facebook Use: Campaign Strategies Used in 2008 and 2012 Presidential Elections." *Journal of Information Technology & Politics* 13:4 (2016): 326–338. doi: 10.1080/19331681.2016.1163519.

Börzsei, Linda K. "Makes a Meme Instead: A Concise History of Internet Memes." *New Media Studies* 7, 2013.

Bouie, Jamelle. "Donald Trump Isn't Going to Be President." *Slate*, May 4, 2016, http://www.slate.com/articles/news_and_politics/politics/2016/05/donald_trump_isn_t_going_to_be_president.html.

Boulianne, Shelley. "Social Media Use and Participation: A Meta-Analysis of Current Research." *Information, Communication, & Society* 18, no. 5 (2015): 524–538.

Boulianne, Shelley. "Does Internet Use Affect Engagement? A Meta-Analysis of Research." *Political Communication* 26(2009): 193–211.

Boyd, Danah M., and Nicole B. Ellison. "Social Network Sites: Definition, History, and Scholarship." *Journal of Computer-Mediated Communication*, 13 (2007): 210–230.

Boyle, Thomas P. "Intermedia Agenda Setting in the 1996 Presidential Election." *Journalism and Mass Communication Quarterly* 78, no. 1 (2001): 26–44.

Brader, Ted. "Striking a Responsive Chord: How Political Ads Motivate and Persuade Voters by Appealing to Emotions." *American Journal of Political Science* 49, no. 2 (2005): 388–405.

Brader, Ted. *Campaigning for Hearts and Minds: How Emotional Appeals in Political Ads Work*. University of Chicago Press, 2006.

Brady, David W., Hahrie Han, and Jeremy C. Pope. "Primary Elections and Candidate Ideology: Out of Step With the Primary Electorate?" *Legislative Studies Quarterly* 32, no. 1 (2007): 79–105.

Bratton, Kathleen. A. "The Effect of Legislative Diversity on Agenda Setting: Evidence from Six State Legislatures." *American Politics Research*, 30 (2002): 115–142.

Broder, John M. "The 2000 Campaign: The Money Race; His Success in New Hampshire Brings McCain an Overnight Infusion of Cybercash," *The New York Times*, February 3, 2000, accessed March 1, 2017, http://www.nytimes.com/2000/02/03/us/2000-campaign-money-race-his-success-new-hampshire-brings-mccain-overnight.html.

Bronstein, Jenny. "Like Me! Analyzing the 2012 Presidential Candidates' Facebook Pages." *Online Information Review* 37, no. 2 (2013): 173–92.

Brooks, Deborah Jordan, and John G. Geer. "Beyond Negativity: The Effects of Incivility on the Electorate." *American Journal of Political Science* 51, no. 1 (2007): 1–16.

Brooks, Deborah Jordan, and Michael Murov. "Assessing Accountability in a Post-Citizens United Era: The Effects of Attack ad Sponsorship by Unknown Independent Groups." *American Politics Research* 40, no. 3 (2012): 383–418.

Brooks, Deborah Jordan. *He Runs, She Runs: Why Gender Stereotypes Do Not Harm Women Candidates*. Princeton, NJ: Princeton University Press, 2013.

Bucy, Erik P., and Kimberly S. Gregson. "Media Participation: A Legitimizing Mechanism of Mass Democracy." *New Media and Society* 3(2001): 357–380.

Brundidge, Jennifer, R. Kelly Garrett, Hernando Rojas, and Homero Gil de Zúñiga. "Political Participation and Ideological News Online: 'Differential Gains' and 'Differential Losses' in a Presidential Election Cycle." *Mass Communication and Society* 17, no. 4 (2014): 464–486.

Buhrmester, Michael, Tracy Kwang, and Samuel D. Gosling. "Amazon's Mechanical Turk a New Source of Inexpensive, yet High-Quality, Data?" *Perspectives on Psychological Science* 6, no. 1 (2011): 3–5.

Bump, Philip. "With Nearly Every Demographic, Hillary Clinton is Outperforming Barack Obama in 2012." *The Washington Post*, July 7, 2016, https://www.washingtonpost.com/news/the-fix/wp/2016/07/07/with-nearly-every-demographic-hillary-clinton-is-outperforming-barack-obama-in-2012/.

Burton, Michael John, William J. Miller, and Daniel M. Shea. *Campaign Craft: The Strategies, Tactics, and Art of Political Campaign Management*, 5th Edition. Denver, CO: ABC-CLIO, 2015.

Bycoffe, Aaron. "The Endorsement Primary," *Fivethirtyeight.com*, June 7, 2016 https://projects.fivethirtyeight.com/2016-endorsement-primary/.

Byler, David. "Will Demographics Sink Donald Trump?" *RealClear Politics*, March 28, 2016, http://www.realclearpolitics.com/articles/2016/03/28/will_demographics_sink_donald_trump_130095.html.

Bystrom, Dianne G., Mary C. Banwart, Lynda Lee Kaid, and Terry A. Robertson. *Gender and Candidate Communication: VideoStyle, WebStyle, NewsStyle*. New York: Routledge, 2004.

Campbell, Angus, Philip E. Converse, Warren E. Miller, and Donald E. Stokes. *The American Voter*. New York: Wiley, 1960.

Carlin, Diana B., and Kelly L. Winfrey. "Have You Come a Long Way, Baby? Hillary Clinton, Sarah Palin, and Sexism in 2008 Campaign Coverage." *Communication Studies* 60 (2009): 326–343.

Carlisle, Juliet E., and Robert C. Patton. "Is Social Media Changing How We Understand Political Engagement? An Analysis of Facebook and the 2008 Presidential Election." *Political Research Quarterly* 66, no. 4 (2013): 883–895.

Carney, Jordain. "Clinton Takes McConnell to Task for 'Gender Card' Comment." *The Hill*. July 7, 2015. Available at: http://thehill.com/blogs/ballot-box/presidential-races/248573-clinton-takes-mcconnell-to-task-for-gender-card-comment.

Carpenter, Cheris. "The Obamachine: Techno-politics 2.0." *Journal of Information Technology and Politics*, 7:1–2 (2010): 216–225.

Carter, Bill. "Bill Carter: How Jimmy Fallon Crushed Stephen Colbert (and Everyone Else in Late Night)." *Hollywood Reporter*. Last modified December 16, 2015. https://www.hollywoodreporter.com/news/bill-carter-how-jimmy-fallon-848851.

Castells, Manuel. "Communication, Power, and Counter-Power in the Network Society." *International Journal of Communication*, 1 (2007): 238–266.

Catanese, David. "Donald Trump's Electoral Map to Victory." *U.S. News & World Report*, September 15, 2016, http://www.usnews.com/news/articles/2016–09–15/donald-trumps-electoral-map-to-victory.

Ceron, Andrea, and Giovanna d'Adda. "E-campaigning on Twitter: The Effectiveness of Distributive Promises and Negative Campaign in the 2013 Italian Election." *New Media and Society* 18, no. 9 (2016). 1935–1955.

Ceron, Andrea, Luigi Curini, and Stefano M. Iacus. "First- and Second-Level Agenda Building in the Twittersphere: An Application to the Italian Political Debate." *Journal of Information Technology & Politics* 13 (2016): 159–74. doi:10.10 80/19331681.2016.1160266.

Chadwick, Andrew. *The Hybrid Media System: Politics and Power.* New York: Oxford University Press, 2013.

Chandler, Jesse, Pam Mueller, and Gabriele Paolacci. 2014. "Nonnaïveté Among Amazon Mechanical Turk Workers: Consequences and Solutions for Behavioral Researchers," *Behavior Research Methods,* 46: 112–130.

Chozik, Amy, and Patrick Healy. "Hillary Clinton has Clinched Democratic Nomination, Survey Reports." *New York Times,* June 6, 2016. http://www.nytimes.com/2016/06/07/us/politics/hillary-clinton-presidential-race.html.

Christenson, Dino P., and Corwin D. Smidt. "Following the money: Super PACs and the 2012 presidential nomination." *Presidential Studies Quarterly* 44, no. 3 (2014): 410–430.

Cillizza, Chris. "President-Elect Donald Trump's Cataclysmic, History-Making Upset." *The Washington Post,* November 9, 2016, https://www.washingtonpost.com/news/the-fix/wp/2016/11/09/how-donald-trump-pulled-off-an-upset-of-cataclysmic-historic-proportions/?utm_term=.253195490182.

Cision. "Top 10 Daily US Newspapers." Updated 2016, http://www.cision.com/us/2014/06/top-10-us-daily-newspapers/ (retrieved March 13, 2017).

Clifford, Scott, Ryan M. Jewell, and Philip D. Waggoner. "Are Samples Drawn from Mechanical Turk Valid for Research on Political Ideology?" *Research & Politics* 2, no. 4, 2015.

Coe, Kevin, David Tewksbury, Bradley J. Bond, Kristin L. Drogos, Robert W. Porter, Ashley Yahn, and Yuanyuan Zhang. "Hostile News: Partisan Use and Perceptions of Cable News Programming." *Journal of Communication,* 58 (2008): 201–219.

Cohen, Marty, David Karol, Hans Noel, and John Zaller. *The Party Decides: Presidential Nominations Before and After Reform.* Chicago: University of Chicago Press, 2008.

Colleoni, Elanor, Alessandro Rozza, and Adam Arvidsson. "Echo Chamber or Public Sphere? Predicting Political Orientation and Measuring Political Homophily in Twitter Using Big Data." *Journal of Communication* 64, no. 2 (2014): 317–332.

Collins, Randall. *The Sociology of Philosophies: A Global Theory of Intellectual Change.* Harvard University Press, 2000.

Commission on Presidential Debates. "The Commission on Presidential Debates: An Overview." 2016. Accessed December 30, 2016. http://debates.org/index.php?page=overview.

Conway, Bethany Anne, Kate Kenski, and Di Wang. "Twitter Use by Presidential Primary Candidates During the 2012 Campaign." *American Behavioral Scientist* 57, no. 11 (2013). 1596–1610.

Conway, Bethany A., Kate Kenski, and Di Wang. "The Rise of Twitter in the Political Campaign: Searching for Intermedia Agenda-Setting Effects in the Presidential Primary." *Journal of Computer-Mediated Communication* 20 (2015): 363–80. doi:10.1111/jcc4.12124.

Conway, Bethany Anne, Christine R. Filer, and Kate Kenski. "Campaign Media Congruence: Issues in 2012 Presidential Election Tweets and Ads." Paper presented at the American Political Science Association, San Francisco, CA, September 2015.

Cook, Tim. *Governing with the News: The News Media as a Political Institution.* Chicago: University of Chicago Press, 2005.

Cooper, Christopher A. "Internet Use in the State Legislature." *Social Science Computer Review* 22:3 (2004): 347–354.

Cornfield, Michael. *Politics Moves Online: Campaigning and the Internet.* New York: The Century Foundation, 2004.

Cornfield, Michael, Jonathan Carson, Alison Kalis, and Emily Simon. "Buzz, Blogs, and Beyond." Accessed November 11, 2016, http://www.michelemiller. blogs.com/Marketing_to_women/Files/Buzz_blogs_beyond.pdf, 2005.

Couper, Mick P. *Designing Effective Web Surveys.* New York: Cambridge University Press, 2008.

Coyne, Bridget. "How #Election2016 Was Tweeted So Far." Twitter Blog. Last modified November 7, 2016. Accessed February 20, 2017, https://blog.twitter. com/2016/how-election2016-was-tweeted-so-far.

Crist, Ry, and Caitlin Petrakovitz. "How the 2016 Presidential Candidates Measure Up on Social Media." CNET. February 8, 2016. Accessed March 27, 2017. https://www.cnet.com/news/2016-elections-comparing-presidential-candidates-on-social-media/.

Cruz, Laurence. 2012. "2012—The Social Media Election?" *The Network*, September 3. https://newsroom.cisco.com/feature-content?type=webcontent&articleId=1006785.

Dabelko, Kristen, and Paul Herrnson. "Women's and Men's Campaigns for the U.S. House of Representatives." *Political Research Quarterly* 50, no. 1 (1997): 121–135.

Damore, David F. "The Dynamics of Issue Ownership in Presidential Campaigns." *Political Research Quarterly* 57 (2004): 391–97.

Damore, David F. "Issue Convergence in Presidential Campaigns." *Political Behavior* 27 (2005): 71–97.

Dang-Xuan, Linh, Stefan Stieglitz, Jennifer Wladarsch, and Christoph Neuberger. "An Investigation of Influentials and the Role of Sentiment in Political Communication on Twitter During Election Periods." *Information, Communication & Society* 16 (2013): 795–825. doi:10.1080/1369118X.2013.783608.

Darr, Carol, and Julie Barko. "Under the Radar and Over the Top: Independently Produced Political Videos in the 2004 Presidential Election." Washington, DC: Institute for Politics, Democracy & the Internet (2004).

Davidson, Roger H., Walter J. Oleszek, Francis E. Lee, and Eric Schickler. *Congress and Its Members,* 15th ed. Los Angeles: CQ Press, 2016.

Davis, Julie Hirschfeld, and Matthew Rosenberg. "With False Claims, Trump Attacks Media on Turnout and Intelligence Rift." *The New York Times*, January

21, 2017, https://www.nytimes.com/2017/01/21/us/politics/trump-white-house-briefing-inauguration-crowd-size.html.

Davisson, Amber. "'I'm In!': Hillary Clinton's 2008 Democratic Primary Campaign on YouTube." *Journal of Visual Literacy* 28 (2009): 70–91.

Delli Carpini, Michael X., and Scott Keeter. *What Americans Know About Politics and Why It Matters*. New Haven: Yale University Press, 1996.

Denham, Bryan E. "Toward Conceptual Consistency in Studies of Agenda-Building Processes: A Scholarly Review." *The Review of Communication*, 10 (2010): 306–323. doi:10.1080/15358593.2010.502593.

Denton, Robert, Jr., ed. 2014. *Studies of Communication in the 2012 Presidential Election*. New York: Lexington Books.

Diamond, Jeremy, and Eugene Scott. "Trump Ratchets Up 'Rigged Election' Claims, Which Pence Downplays." *CNN*, October 17, 2016, http://www.cnn.com/2016/10/15/politics/donald-trump-rigged-election-hillary-clinton/.

Dimitrova, Daniela V., and Dianne Bystrom. "The Effects of Social Media on Political Participation and Candidate Image Evaluations in the 2012 Iowa Caucuses." *American Behavioral Sciences* 57, no. 11 (2013): 1568–1583.

Dimitrova, Daniela V., Adam Shehata, Jesper Stromback, and Lars W. Nord. "The Effects of Digital Media on Political Knowledge in Election Campaigns: Evidence from Panel Data." *Communication Research* 41, no. 1 (2014): 95–118.

Disis, Jill. "10 of Breitbart's Most Incendiary Headlines." *CNN*, November 15, 2016, http://money.cnn.com/2016/11/14/media/breitbart-incendiary-headlines/.

Dittmar, Kelly. "Trump's Gender Miscalculations." Presidential Gender Watch. April 28, 2016. Available at: http://presidentialgenderwatch.org/trumpsgendermiscalculations/#more-8007.

Dittmar, Kelly. "Everyone's Playing the Gender Card: The Question Is How?" Presidential Gender Watch. August 2, 2015. Available here: http://presidentialgenderwatch.org/everyones-playing-the-gender-card-the-question-is-how/

Dodson, Deborah L. *Reshaping the Agenda: Women in State Legislatures*. New Brunswick, NJ: Center for the American Woman and Politics, 1991.

Doherty, Carroll. "7 Things to Know About Polarization in America." Pew Research Center, June 12, 2014. http://www.pewresearch.org/fact-tank/2014/06/12/7-things-to-know-about-polarization-in-america.

Dolan, Kathleen. "Gender Stereotypes, Candidate Evaluations, and Voting for Women Candidates: What Really Matters?" *Political Research Quarterly* 67 (2014): 96–107.

Dowd, Maureen. "Vice in go-go boots?" *The New York Times*, August 31, 2008. Available at: http://www.nytimes.com/2008/08/31/opinion/31dowd.html?_r=1and.

Dowling, Conor M., and Amber Wichowsky. "Attacks Without Consequence? Candidates, Parties, Groups, and the Changing Face of Negative Advertising." *American Journal of Political Science* 59, no. 1 (2015): 19–36.

Downs, Anthony. "An Economic Theory of Political Action in a Democracy." *The Journal of Political Economy* 65, no. 2 (1957): 135–150.

Druckman, James N. "The Power of Television Images: The First Kennedy-Nixon Debate Revisited." *Journal of Politics* 65 (2003): 559–571.

Druckman, James N., and Rose McDermott. "Emotion and the Framing of Risky Choice." *Political Behavior* 30 (2008): 297–321.

Druckman, James N., Martin J. Kifer, and Parkin, Michael. "The Technological Development of Congressional Candidate Websites: How and Why Candidates Use Web Innovation." *Social Science Computer Review* 25:4 (2007): 425–442. doi: https://doi.org/10.1177/0894439307305623.

Druckman, James N., Martin J. Kifer, and Michael Parkin. "Campaign Communications in U.S. Congressional Elections." *American Political Science Review* 103.3 (2009): 343–366.

Druckman, James N., Martin J. Kifer, and Michael Parkin. "Timeless Strategy Meets New Medium: Going Negative on Congressional Campaign Websites, 2002–2006." *Political Communication* 27 (2010): 88–103.

Druckman, James N., Martin J. Kifer, and Michael Parkin. "Congressional Campaign Communications in an Internet Age." *Journal of Elections, Public Opinion, and Parties* 24 (2014): 20–44.

Druckman, James N., Martin J. Kifer, Michael Parkin, and Ivonne Montes. "An Inside View of Congressional Campaigning on the Web." *Journal of Political Marketing*, forthcoming.

Dugan, Andrew. "Among Republicans, GOP Candidates Better Known Than Liked." *Gallup*, July 24, 2015, http://www.gallup.com/poll/184337/among-republicans-gop-candidates-better-known-liked.aspx.

Duggan, Maeve. "Mobile Messaging and Social Media 2015." Pew Research Study. Accessed November 11, 2016, http://www.pewinternet.org/files/2015/08/Social-Media-Update-2015-FINAL2.pdf, 2015.

Duggan, Maeve. 2015. "The Demographics of Social Media Users," *Mobile Messaging and Social Media 2015*. Research Report. Washington, D.C.: Pew Research Center. http://www.pewinternet.org/2015/08/19/the-demographics-of-social-media-users/.

Duggan, Maeve, and Aaron Smith. "The Political Environment on Social Media." Pew Research Center, October 25, 2016. http://www.pewinternet.org/2016/10/25/the-political-environment-on-social-media.

Dunn, Scott. "Candidate and Media Agenda Setting in the 2005 Virginia Gubernatorial Election." *Journal of Communication* 59, no. 3 (2009): 635–652.

Edgerly, Stephanie, Emily K. Vraga, Kajsa E. Dalrymple, Timothy Macafee, and Timothy KF Fung. "Directing the Dialogue: The Relationship Between YouTube Videos and the Comments They Spur." *Journal of Information Technology & Politics* 10, no. 3 (2013): 276–292.

Edwards, George C., and Stephen J. Wayne. *Presidential Leadership: Politics and Policymaking*, 9th ed. Stanford, CT: Cengage, 2014.

Edwards, Janis L. "Echoes of Camelot: How Images Construct Cultural Memory through Rhetorical Framing." In *Defining Visual Rhetorics*, edited by Charles A. Hill and Marguerite Helmers, 179–194. New York, NY: Routledge, 2004.

Edwards, Janis L., and C. Austin McDonald. "Reading Hillary and Sarah: Contradictions of Feminism and Representation in 2008 Campaign Political Cartoons." *American Behavioral Scientist* 54 (2010): 313–329.

Eldin, Amira Karan. "Instagram Role in Influencing Youth Opinion in 2015 Election Campaign in Bahrain." *European Scientific Journal* 12, no. 2 (2016): 245–257.

Enders, Craig K. *Applied Missing Data Analysis*. New York: Guilford Press, 2010.

Enli, Gunn, and Hallvard Moe. "Social Media and Election Campaigns: Key Tendencies and Ways Forward." *Information, Communication & Society* 16, no. 5 (2013): 637–45.

Entman, Robert M. "Framing: Toward Clarification of a Fractured Paradigm." *Journal of Communication* 43, no. 4 (1993): 51–58.

Evans, Heather K. "Do Women Only Talk About 'Female Issues'? Gender and Issue Discussion on Twitter." *Online Information Review*, 40 (2016): 660–672.

Evans, Heather K., and Jennifer Hayes Clark. "'You Tweet like a Girl!': How Female Candidates Campaign on Twitter." *American Politics Research*, 44 (2016): 325–352.

Evans, Heather K., Victoria Cordova, and Savannah Sipole. "Twitter-Style: An Analysis of How House Candidates Used Twitter in Their 2012 Campaigns." *PS: Political Science and Politics* 47, no. 2 (2014). 454–462.

Evans, Heather K., Jocelyn Ovalle, and Stephen Green. "Rockin' Robins: Do Congresswomen Rule the Roost in the Twittersphere?" *Journal of the Association of Information Science and Technology*, 67 (2016): 268–275.

Fahrenthold, David A. "Trump Recorded Having Extremely Lewd Conversation About Women in 2005." *The Washington Post*, October 8, 2016, https://www.washingtonpost.com/politics/trump-recorded-having-extremely-lewd-conversation-about-women-in-2005/2016/10/07/3b9ce776–8cb4–11e6-bf8a-3d26847eeed4_story.html.

Falk, Erika. *Women for President: Media Bias in Nine Campaigns*. Urbana, IL: University of Illinois Press, 2008.

Farhi, Paul. "The Twitter Explosion." *American Journalism Review*, April/May 2009. http://www.ajr.org/Article.asp?id=4756.

Farrar-Myers, Victoria A., and Richard Skinner. "Super PACs and the 2012 Elections." *The Forum*, vol. 10, no. 4, pp. 105–118. 2012.

Farrar-Meyers, Victoria A., and Justin S. Vaughn. 2015. *Controlling the Message*. New York: NYU Press.

Feltwell, Tom, Jamie Mahoney, and Shaun Lawson. "'Aye, Have a Dream #IndyRef': Use of Instagram during the Scottish Referendum." Paper presented at the British HCI '15 Proceedings of the 2015 British HCI Conference, Lincoln, Lincolnshire, United Kingdom, July 13–17, 2015.

Fenn, Peter. "Why Trump Won't Win." *U.S. News & World Report*, March 21, 2016, http://www.usnews.com/opinion/blogs/peter-fenn/articles/2016–03–21/trump-has-deep-demographic-problems-come-the-2016-general-election.

Fernandes, Juliana, Magda Giurcanu, Kevin W. Bowers, and Jeffrey C. Neely. "The Writing on the Wall: A Content Analysis of College Students' Facebook Groups for the 2008 Presidential Election." *Mass Communication and Society* 13, no. 5 (2010): 653–675.

Festinger, Leon. *A Theory of Cognitive Dissonance*. Evanston, IL: Row, Peterson, 1957.

Filimonov, Kirill, Uta Russmann, and Jakob Svensson. "Picturing the Party: Instagram and Party Campaigning in the 2014 Swedish Elections." *Social Media + Society* July–September (2016): 1–11.

Fiorina, Morris P. *Congress: Keystone of the Washington Establishment,* 2nd ed. New Haven: Yale University Press, 1989.

FiveThirtyEight.com. "Who Will Win the Presidency?" November 8, 2016, https://projects.fivethirtyeight.com/2016-election-forecast/.

Flanagin, Andrew J., and Miriam J. Metzger. "The Role of Site Features, User Attributes, and Information Verification Behaviors on the Perceived Credibility of Web-Based Information." *New Media & Society* 9, no. 2 (2007): 319–342.

Foot, Kirsten A., and Steven M. Schneider. *Web Campaigning.* Cambridge, MA: MIT Press, 2006.

Foot, Kirsten A., and Steven M. Schneider. "Online Action in Campaign 2000: An Exploratory Analysis of the U.S. Political Web Sphere." *Journal of Broadcasting and Electronic Media* 46 (2002): 222–566.

Foran, Clare. "Donald Trump and the Triumph of Climate-Change Denial." *The Atlantic,* December 25, 2016. https://www.theatlantic.com/politics/archive/2016/12/donald-trump-climate-change-skeptic-denial/510359.

Fowler, Erika Franklin, and Travis N. Ridout. "Negative, Angry, and Ubiquitous: Political Advertising in 2012." *The Forum,* vol. 10, no. 4, pp. 51–61. 2013.

Fowler, Erika F., Michael M. Franz, and Travis N. Ridout. *Political Advertising in the United States.* Boulder, CO: Westview Press, 2016.

Fox, Richard L. *Gender Dynamics in Congressional Elections.* Thousand Oaks, CA: Sage, 1997.

Francia, Peter L. "Free Media and Twitter in the 2016 Presidential Election: The Unconventional Campaign of Donald Trump," *Social Science Computer Review,* forthcoming.

Franz, Michael M. "Interest Groups in Electoral Politics: 2012 in Context." *The Forum,* vol. 10, no. 4, pp. 62–79. 2013.

Franz, Michael M., and Travis N. Ridout. "Political Advertising and Persuasion in the 2004 and 2008 Presidential Elections." *American Politics Research* 38, no. 2 (2010): 303–329.

Freelon, Deen G. "ReCal: Intercoder Reliability Calculation as a Web Service." *International Journal of Internet Science* 5, no. 1 (2010): 20–33.

Freelon, Deen. "ReCal OIR: Ordinal, interval, and ratio intercoder reliability as a web service." *International Journal of Internet Science* 8, no. 1 (2013): 10–16.

Freelon, Deen, Charlton D. McIlwain, and Meredith D. Clark. "Quantifying the Power and Consequences of Social Media Protest." *New Media & Society* (2016): 1–22.

Fridkin, Kim L., and Patrick J. Kenney. "The Role of Gender Stereotypes in U.S. Senate Campaigns." *Politics and Gender* 5 (2009): 301–324.

Gainous, Jason, and Kevin M. Wagner. *Tweeting to Power: The Social Media Revolution in American Politics.* Oxford: Oxford University Press, 2013.

Gallup. "Congress and the Public." (2016). Accessed January 11, 2017, http://www.gallup.com/poll/1600/congress-public.aspx.

Garrett, R. Kelly. "Politically Motivated Reinforcement Seeking: Reframing the Selective Exposure Debate." *Journal of Communication* 59, no. 4 (2009): 676–699.

Gasparino, Charles. "Trump's Running—But the Joke's on You." *The Daily Beast,* June 22, 2015, http://www.thedailybeast.com/articles/2015/06/22/how-much-is-trump-is-really-worth.html.

Gaughan, Anthony J. "Donald Trump Will Not Be President: History, Polling Data and Demographics All Point to a Single Result." *Salon*, May 5, 2016, http://www.salon.com/2016/05/05/donald_trump_will_not_be_president_history_polling_data_and_demographics_all_point_to_a_single_result_partner/.

Geer, John G. *In Defense of Negativity: Attack Ads in Presidential Campaigns*. University of Chicago Press, 2008.

Gerber, Alan S., and Donald P. Green. *Field Experiments: Design, Analysis, and Interpretation*. Thousand Oaks, CA: Norton, 2012.

Ghanem, Salma. "Filling in the Tapestry: The Second Level of Agenda Setting." In *Communication and Democracy*, edited by Maxwell McCombs, Donald L. Shaw, and David Weaver. Mahwah, NJ: Erlbaum, 1997.

Gil de Zuniga, Homero, and Sebastian Valenzuela. 2011. "The Mediating Path to a Stronger Citizenship: Online and Offline Networks, Weak Ties, and Civic Engagement," *Communication Research*, 38 (3): 397–421.

Gibson, Rachel, and Marta Cantijoch. 2013. "Conceptualizing and Measuring Participation in the Age of the Internet: Is Online Political Engagement Really Different to Offline?" *Journal of Politics*, 75 (3): 701–716.

Gil de Zuniga, Homero, Eulalia Puig-i-Abril, and Hernando Rojas. 2009. "Weblogs, Traditional Sources Online and Political Participation: An Assessment of How the Internet Is Changing the Political Environment," *New Media & Society*, 11 (4): 553–74.

Gil de Zuniga, Homero, Logan Molyneux, and Pei Zheng. 2014. "Social Media, Political Expression, and Political Participation: Panel Analysis of Lagged and Concurrent Relationships," *Journal of Communication*, 64 (4): 612–634.

Gilmartin, Patricia. "Still the Angel in the Household: Political Cartoons of Elizabeth Dole's Presidential Campaign." *Women and Politics* 22 (2001): 51–63.

Glassman, Matthew Eric, Jacob R. Straus, and Colleen J. Shogan. "Social Networking and Constituent Communication: Member Use of Twitter During a Two-Week Period in the 111th Congress." *Congressional Research Service*. CRS Report for Congress (2009).

Golan, Guy, and Wayne Wanta. "Second-Level Agenda Setting in the New Hampshire Primary: A Comparison of Coverage in Three Newspapers and Public Perceptions of Candidates." *Journalism and Mass Communication Quarterly* 78, no. 2 (2001): 247–259.

Golan, Guy, Spiro Kiousis, and Misti McDaniel. "Second-Level Agenda Setting and Political Advertising: Investigating the Transfer of Issue and Attribute Saliency during the 2004 U.S. Presidential Election." *Journalism Studies* 8, no. 3 (2007): 432–443.

Golbeck, Jennifer, Justin Grimes, and Anthony Rogers. "Twitter Use by the U.S. Congress" *Journal for the American Society of Information Science and Technology* 61.8 (2010): 1612–1621.

Goldstein, Ken, John McCormick, and Andre Tartar. "Candidates Make Last Ditch Ad Spending Push Across 14-State Electoral Map." *Bloomberg*, November 2, 2016, https://www.bloomberg.com/politics/graphics/2016-presidential-campaign-tv-ads/.

Gottfried, Jeffrey, and Elisa Shearer. "News Use Across Social Media Platforms 2016." Pew Research Center, 2016.

Gottfried, Jeffrey, and Michael Barthel. "Trump, Clinton Voters Divided in Their Main Source for Election News." Pew Research Center, January 18, 2017, http://www.journalism.org/2017/01/18/trump-clinton-voters-divided-in-their-main-source-for-election-news/.

Gottfried, Jeffrey, Michael Barthel, Elisa Shearer, and Amy Mitchell. "The 2016 Presidential Campaign: A News Event That's Hard to Miss." Pew Research Center, 2016.

Graber, Doris A. *Processing Politics: Learning from Television in the Internet Age.* Chicago: University of Chicago Press, 2001.

Graham, Todd Steven. "What's Wife Swap Got to Do with It? Talking Politics in the Net-Based Public Sphere." *University of Amsterdam Digital Academic Repository (UvA-DARE).* (2009). https://pure.uva.nl/ws/files/812355/68836_thesis.pdf.

Greenwood, Sharon, Andrew Perrin, and Maeve Duggan. "Social Media Update 2016." Washington, D.C.: Pew Research Center, 2016.

Gronbeck, Bruce E. "Negative Political Ads and American Self Images." In *Presidential Campaigns and American Self Images*, edited by Arthur H. Miller and Bruce E. Gronbeck, 60–81. Oxford: Westview Press, 1994.

Gronke, Paul. *The Electorate, the Campaign, and the Office: A Unified Approach to Senate and House Elections.* Ann Arbor: University of Michigan Press, 2000.

Groshek, Jacob, and Megan Clough Groshek. "Agenda Trending: Reciprocity and the Predictive Capacity of Social Networking Sites in Intermedia Agenda Setting Across Topics over Time." *Media and Communication* 1, no. 1 (2013): 15–27.

Groshek, Jacob, and Daniela Dimitrova. "A Cross-section of Voter Learning, Campaign Interest and Intention to Vote in the 2008 American Election: Did Web 2.0 Matter?" *Studies in Communications* 9 (2011): 355–375.

Gross, Justin H., and Kaylee T. Johnson. "Twitter Taunts and Tirades: Negative Campaigning in the Age of Trump." *PS: Political Science & Politics* 49, no. 4 (2016): 748–754.

Gross, Justin H., and Kaylee T. Johnson. "Strafing, Spats, and Skirmishes: Social Dynamics of Negative Campaigning on Twitter." Political Networks Workshops & Conference (2016). Accessed from SSRN March 28, 2017.

Gruszczynski, Mike. "New and Traditional Media Reportage on Electoral Campaign Controversies." In *Controlling the Message: New Media in American Political Campaigns*, edited by Victoria A. Farrar-Myers and Justin S. Vaughn, 113–135. New York: New York University Press, 2015.

Grynbaum, Michael M., and Sydney Ember. "If Trump Tweets It, Is It News? A Quandary for the News Media." *New York Times*, November 29, 2016. http://www.nytimes.com/2016/11/29/business/media/if-trump-tweets-it-is-it-news-a-quandary-for-the-news-media.html.

Gueorguieva, Vassia. "Voters, MySpace, and YouTube: The Impact of Alternative Communication Channels on the 2006 Election Cycle and Beyond" *Social Science Computer Revew* 26.3 (2008): 288–300.

Gueorguieva, Vassia. "Voters, MySpace, and YouTube: The Impact of Alternative Communication Channels." In *Politicking Online: The Transformation of Election Campaign Communications*, edited by Costas Panagopoulos. New Brunswick, NJ: Rutgers University Press, 2009.

Gulati, Girish J., and Christine Williams. "Social Media and Campaign 2012: Developments and Trends for Facebook Adoption." *Social Science Computer Review* 31, no. 5 (2013): 577–588.

Guo, Lei, Chris J. Vargo, Zixuan Pan, Weicong Ding, and Prakash Ishwar. "Big Social Data Analytics in Journalism and Mass Communication: Comparing Dictionary-Based Text Analysis and Unsupervised Topic Modeling." *Journalism & Mass Communication Quarterly* 93 (2016): 332–59. doi:10.1177/1077699016639231.

Haidt, Jonathan, and Jesse Graham. "When Morality Opposes Justice: Conservatives Have Moral Intuitions that Liberals May Not Recognize." *Social Justice Research* 20, no. 1 (2007): 98–116.

Hainmueller, Jens, Andrew B. Hall, and James M. Snyder, Jr. "Assessing the External Validity of Election RD Estimates: An Investigation of the Incumbency Advantage." *Journal of Politics* 77.3 (2015): 707–720.

Han, Gang. "New Media Use, Sociodemographics, and Voter Turnout in the 2000 Presidential Election." *Mass Communication and Society,* 11 (2008): 62–81.

Han, Lori Cox, and Caroline Heldman. *Rethinking Madam President: Are We Ready for a Woman in the White House?* Boulder, Colorado: Lynne Rienner Publishers, 2007.

Hansen, Glenn J., and William L. Benoit. "The Role of Significant Policy Issues in the 2000 Presidential Primaries." *American Behavioral Scientist* 44, no. 12 (2001): 2082–2100.

Hanson, Gary L., Paul M. Haridakis, Audrey Wagstaff Cunningham, Rekha Sharma, and J.D. Ponder. "The 2008 Presidential Campaign: Political Cynicism in the Age of Facebook, MySpace, and YouTube." *Mass Communication and Society,* 13 (2010): 584–607.

Harris, Mary. "A Media Post-Mortem on the 2016 Presidential Election." MediaQuant, November 14, 2016, http://www.mediaquant.net/2016/11/a-media-post-mortem-on-the-2016-presidential-election.

Hayes, Danny, and Jennifer L. Lawless. "A Non-Gendered Lens? The Absence of Stereotyping in Contemporary Congressional Elections." *Perspectives on Politics* 13 (2015): 95–118.

Hayes, Danny, and Jennifer L. Lawless. *Women on the Run: Gender, Media, and Political Campaigns in a Polarized Era.* New York: Cambridge University Press, 2016.

Hayes, Danny. "Party Reputation, Journalistic Expectations: How Issue Ownership Influences Election News." *Political Communication* 25 (2008): 377–400. doi:10.1080/10584600802426981.

Haynes, Audrey A., Julianne F. Flowers, and Paul-Henri Gurian. "Getting the Message Out Early: Candidate Strategy and the Invisible Primary." *Political Research Quarterly*, 55 (2002): 633–52.

Hazen, Don, Kali Holloway, Jenny Pierson, Jan Friel, Les Leopold, Steve Rosenfeld, Michael Arria, Ilana Novick, and Janet Allon. "Why Donald Trump Won—and How Hillary Clinton Lost: 13 Theories Explain the Stunning Election." *Salon*, December 26, 2016, http://www.salon.com/2016/12/26/13-theories-on-why-trump-won-and-how-clinton-lost_partner/.

Heim, Kyle. "Framing the 2008 Iowa Democratic Caucuses: Political Blogs and Second-Level Intermedia Agenda Setting." *Journalism and Mass Communication Quarterly* 90, no. 3 (2013): 500–519.

Heldman, Caroline, Susan J. Carroll, and Stephanie Olson. "'She Brought Only a Skirt': Print Media Coverage of Elizabeth Dole's Bid for the Republican Nomination." *Political Communication* 22 (2005): 315–335.

Heller, Nathan. "The First Debate of the Twitter Election." *The New Yorker*, September 27, 2016. Accessed March 27, 2017, http://www.newyorker.com/culture/cultural-comment/the-first-debate-of-the-twitter-election.

Hemphill, Libby, Jahna Otterbacher, and Matthew A. Shapiro. "What's Congress Doing on Twitter?" Proceedings of the 2013 Conference on Computer Supported Cooperative Work (2013): 877–886.

Herrman, John. 2016. "Inside Facebook's (Totally Insane, Unintentionally Gigantic, Hyperpartisan) Political-Media Machine," *The New York Times Magazine*, August 25: 1–14, http://www.nytimes.com/2016/08/28/magazine/inside-facebooks-totally-insane-unintentionally-gigantic-hyperpartisan-political-media-machine.html?_r=1.

Herrnson, Paul S. "The Roles of Party Organizations, Party-Connected Committees, and Party Allies in Elections." *The Journal of Politics* 71, no. 4 (2009): 1207–1224.

Herrnson, Paul S., and Jennifer C. Lucas. "The Fairer Sex? Gender and Negative Campaigning in U.S. Elections." *American Politics Research*, 34 (2006): 69–94.

Herrnson, Paul S., Atiya Kai Stokes-Brown, and Matthew Hindman. "Campaign Politics and the Digital Divide: Constituency Characteristics, Strategic Considerations, and Candidate Internet Use in State Legislative Elections." *Political Research Quarterly* 60:1 (2007): 31–42. doi: https://doi.org/10.1177/1065912906298527.

Hess, Amanda. "Memes, Myself and I: The Internet Lets Us All Run the Campaign." *New York Times*, November 6, 2016, https://www.nytimes.com/2016/11/06/arts/memes-myself-and-i-the-internet-lets-us-all-run-the-campaign.html?_r=0.

Higgins, Caroline. 2012. "The 2012 Presidential Campaign and Social Media: A New Age?" *Flip the Media*, August 31, http://flipthemedia.com/2012/08/the-2012-presidential-campaign-and-social-media-a-new-age/.

Hindman, Matthew. 2009. *The Myth of Digital Democracy*. Princeton: Princeton University Press.

Hockley, William E. "The Picture Superiority Effect in Associative Recognition." *Memory & Cognition* 36, no. 7 (2008): 1351–1359.

Hong, Sounman, and Daniel Nadler. "Which Candidates do the Public Discuss Online in an Election Campaign?: The Use of Social Media by 2012 Presidential Candidates and Its Impact on Candidate Salience." *Government Information Quarterly* 29, no. 4 (2012). 455–461.

Hootsuite. "The 2016 Presidential Candidates on Instagram, Ranked." Accessed on March 2, 2017, https://blog.hootsuite.com/the-2016-presidential-candidates-on-instagram-ranked/, 2015.

Huckfeldt, Robert, and Jeanette Morehouse Mendez. "Moths, Flames, and Political Engagement: Managing Disagreement Within Communication Networks." *The Journal of Politics* 70, no. 1 (2008): 83–96.

Huckfeldt, Robert, Paul E. Johnson, and John Sprague. *Political Disagreement: The Survival of Diverse Opinions Within Communication Networks.* Cambridge University Press, 2004.

Huff, Connor, and Dustin Tingley. 2015. "'Who Are These People?' Evaluating the Demographic Characteristics and Political Preferences of MTurk Survey Respondents," *Research and Politics*, July-September: 1–12.

Instagram. "600 Million and Counting." Press release. December 21, 2016. Accessed March 27, 2017, https://instagram-press.com/2016/12/21/600-million-and-counting/.

Instagram. 2016. "Press Page." Instagram. Accessed November 1, 2016, https://www.instagram.com/press/.

Ireland, Emilienne, and Phil Tajitsu Nash. *Winning Campaigns Online: Strategies for Candidates and Causes,* 2nd ed. Bethesda, MD: Science Writers Press, 2001.

Isaac, Mike, and Sydney Ember. "For Election Day, Twitter Ruled Social Media." *New York Times,* November 8, 2016. Accessed March 27, 2017, https://www.nytimes.com/2016/11/09/technology/for-election-day-chatter-twitter-ruled-social-media.html?_r=0.

Itzkoff, Dave. "As Letterman Moves On, Late-Night Success Is Unmoored From TV." *The New York Times.* Last modified May 10, 2015, https://www.nytimes.com/2015/05/11/arts/television/as-letterman-retires-late-night-tv-faces-a-changing-landscape.html.

Iyengar, Shanto, and Donald R. Kinder. *News that Matters: Television and American Opinion.* Chicago: University of Chicago Press, 1987.

Iyengar, Shanto, and Nicholas A. Valentino. "Who Says What? Source Credibility as a Mediator of Campaign Advertising." In *Elements of Reason: Cognition, Choice, and the Bounds of Rationality*, edited by Arthur Lupia, Mathew D. McCubbins, and Samuel L. Popkin, 108–29. New York: Cambridge University Press, 2000.

Jackson, Natalie. "HuffPost Forecasts Hillary Clinton Will Win 323 Electoral Votes." *Huffington Post,* November 7, 2016, http://www.huffingtonpost.com/entry/polls-hillary-clinton-win_us_5821074ce4b0e80b02cc2a94.

Jacobson, Gary C. *The Politics of Congressional Elections,* 8th ed. Boston: Pearson, 2013.

James, Meg. "Political Ad Spending Estimated at $6 billion in 2016," *Los Angeles Times,* November 8, 2015, accessed on March 1, 2017, http://www.latimes.com/entertainment/envelope/cotown/la-et-ct-political-ad-spending-6-billion-dollars-in-2016-20151117-story.html.

Jamieson, Kathleen Hall. *Beyond the Double Bind: Women and Leadership.* New York: Oxford University Press, 1995.

Jamieson, Kathleen Hall. *Packaging the Presidency: A History and Criticism of Presidential Campaign Advertising.* 3rd ed. New York: Oxford University Press, 1996.

Jamieson, Kathleen Hall. *Electing the President, 2012: The Insiders' View.* Philadelphia, PA: University of Pennsylvania Press, 2013.

Jamieson, Kathleen Hall, Allyson Volinsky, Ilana Weitz, and Kate Kenski. 2015. "The Political Uses and Abuses of Civility and Incivility," in Kate Kenski and Kathleen Hall Jamieson, *The Oxford Handbook of Political Communication.* New

York: Oxford University Press, online. http://www.oxfordhandbooks.com/view/10.1093/oxfordhb/9780199793471.001.0001/oxfordhb-9780199793471-e-79#oxfordhb-9780199793471-e-79-bibItem-28.

Jenkins, Henry, Sam Ford, and Joshua Green. 2013. *Spreadable Media*. New York: New York University Press.

Johnson, Dennis W. *Campaigning in the Twenty-First Century: Activism, Big Data, and Dark Money*. Routledge, 2016.

Johnson, Jenna, and Matea Gold. "Trump Calls the Media 'The Enemy of the American People.'" *The Washington Post*, February 17, 2017, https://www.washingtonpost.com/news/post-politics/wp/2017/02/17/trump-calls-the-media-the-enemy-of-the-american-people/.

Johnson, Thomas J., and David D. Perlmutter. "Introduction: The Facebook Election." *Mass Communication and Society* 13, no. 5 (2010): 554–559.

Johnson, Thomas J., and Barbara K. Kaye. "Credibility of Social Network Sites for Political Information Among Politically Interested Internet Users." *Journal of Computer-Mediated Communication* 19, no. 4 (2014): 957–74.

Jones, David A. "Why Americans Don't Trust the Media: A Preliminary Analysis." *The Harvard International Journal of Press/Politics* 9 (2004): 60–75.

Jost, John T., and David M. Amodio. "Political Ideology as Motivated Social Cognition: Behavioral and Neuroscientific Evidence." *Motivation and Emotion* 36, no. 1 (2012): 55–64.

Jost, John T., Jack Glaser, Arie W. Kruglanski, and Frank J. Sulloway. "Political Conservatism as Motivated Social Cognition." *Psychological Bulletin* (2003): 339–375.

Jungherr, Andreas. "The Logic of Political Coverage on Twitter: Temporal Dynamics and Content." *Journal of Communication* 64 (2014): 239–59. doi:10.1111/jcom.12087.

Jungherr, Andreas. "Twitter Use in Election Campaigns: A Systematic Literature Review." *Journal of Information Technology & Politics* 13 (2016): 72–91. doi:10.1080/19331681.2015.1132401.

Kahn, Kim Fridkin. "Gender Differences in Campaign Messages: The Political Advertisements of Men and Women Candidates for U.S. Senate." *Political Research Quarterly*, 46.3 (1993): 481–502.

Kahn, Kim Fridkin. "The Distorted Mirror: Press Coverage of Women Candidates for Statewide Office." *Journal of Politics* 56 (1994): 154–173.

Kahn, Kim Fridkin. *The Political Consequences of Being a Woman*. New York: Columbia University Press, 1996.

Kahn, Kim Fridkin, and Edie N. Goldenberg. "Women Candidates in the News: An Examination of Gender Differences in U.S. Senate Campaign Coverage." *Public Opinion Quarterly* 55.2 (1991): 180–199.

Kahn, Kim Fridkin, and Ann Gordon. "How Women Campaign for the U.S. Senate: Substance and Strategy." In P. Norris (Ed.), *Women, media, and politics* (pp. 59–76). New York, NY: Oxford University Press, 1997.

Kahn, Kim Fridkin, and Patrick J. Kenney. *The Spectacle of U.S. Senate Campaigns*. Princeton, NJ: Princeton University Press, 2000.

Kahn, Kim Fridkin, and Patrick J. Kenney. *No Holds Barred: Negativity in U.S. Senate Campaigns*. Upper Saddle River, NJ: Pearson, Prentice-Hall, 2004.

Kaid, Lynda L. "Newspaper Treatment of a Candidate's News Releases." *Journalism Quarterly* 51, no. 1 (1976): 135–157.

Kaid, Lynda L. "Political Web Wars: The Use of the Internet for Political Advertising." In *The Internet Election: Perspectives on the Web Campaign in 2004*, edited by Andrew P. Williams and John C. Tedesco, 67–82. Lanham, MD: Rowman & Littlefield, 2006.

Kamarack, Elaine. "Increasing Turnout in Congressional Primaries." Brookings Institution (2014). Accessed January 9, 2017. https://www.brookings.edu/research/increasing-turnout-in-congressional-primaries/.

Kang, Michael S. "The Year of the Super PAC." *The George Washington Law Review* 81, no. 6 (2013): 1902–1927.

Kapko, Matt. "Twitter's Impact on 2016 Presidential Election is Unmistakable." CIO. November 3, 2016. Available at: http://www.cio.com/article/3137513/social-networking/twitters-impact-on-2016-presidential-election-is-unmistakable.html.

Kaplan, Noah, David K. Park, and Travis N. Ridout. "Dialogue in American Political Campaigns? An Examination of Issue Convergence in Candidate Television Advertising." *American Journal of Political Science* 50 (2006): 724–36. doi:10.1111/j.1540–5907.2006.00212.x.

Kaufhold, Kelly, Sebastian Valenzuela, and Homero Gil de Zuñiga. "Citizen Journalism and Democracy: How User-Generated News Use Relates to Political Knowledge and Participation." *Journalism and Mass Communication Quarterly* 87 (2010): 515–529.

Kenski, Kate, and Kathleen Hall Jamieson. "Political Communication: Looking Ahead." In *The Oxford Handbook of Political Communication*, edited by Kate Kenski and Kathleen Hall Jamieson, online version. Oxford University Press, 2016. doi:10.1093/oxfordhb/9780199793471.013.86.

Kenski, Kate, Bruce W. Hardy, and Kathleen Hall Jamieson. 2010. *The Obama Victory*. New York: Oxford University Press.

Kernell, Samuel. *Going Public: New Strategies of Presidential Leadership*. Washington, DC: CQ Press, 1986.

Kernell, Samuel. *Going Public: New Strategies of Presidential Leadership*, 3rd edition. Washington, DC: CQ Press, 1997.

Khalid, Asma, and Scott Detrow. "How Trump and Clinton Are Framing Their Closing Arguments." *NPR*, October 26, 2016, http://www.npr.org/2016/10/26/499321154/clinton-and-trump-the-final-sprint.

Khan, Laeeq. "Trump Won Thanks to Social Media." *The Hill*, November 15, 2016, http://thehill.com/blogs/pundits-blog/technology/306175-trump-won-thanks-to-social-media.

Kim, Kihan, and Maxwell McCombs. "News Story Descriptions and the Public's Opinions of Political Candidates." *Journalism and Mass Communication Quarterly* 84, no. 2 (2007): 299–314.

Kim, Sei-Hill, Dietram A. Scheufele, and James Shanahan. "Think about It This Way: Attribute Agenda-Setting Function of the Press and the Public's Evaluation of a Local Issue." *Journalism and Mass Communication Quarterly* 79, (2002): 7–25.

Kim, Yoejin, William Gonzenbach, Chris Vargo, and Youngju Kim. "First and Second Levels of Intermedia Agenda Setting: Political Advertising, Newspaper, and Twitter during the 2012 Presidential Election." *International Journal of Communication* 10, (2016): 4550–4569.

Kim, Yonghwan. "The Contribution of Social Network Sites to Exposure to Political Difference: The Relationships Among SNSs, Online Political Messaging, and Exposure to Cross-Cutting Perspectives." *Computers in Human Behavior* 27, no. 2 (2011): 971–977.

King, Amy, and Andrew Leigh. "Beautiful Politicians." *Kyklos* 62 (2009): 579–593.

King, Pu-tsung. "The Press, Candidate Images, and Voter Perceptions." In *Communication and Democracy: Exploring the Intellectual Frontiers in Agenda-Setting Theory*, edited by Maxwell McCombs, Donald L. Shaw, and David H. Weaver, 29–40. Mahwah, NJ: Erlbaum, 1997.

Kiousis, Spiro. "Compelling Arguments and Attitude Strength: Exploring the Impact of Second-Level Agenda Setting on Public Opinion of Presidential Candidate Images." *Harvard International Journal of Press-Politics* 10 (2005): 3–27.

Kiousis, Spiro, Philemon Bantimaroudis, and Hyun Ban. "Candidate Image Attributes: Experiments on the Substantive Dimension of Second Level Agenda Setting." *Communication Research* 26, no. 4 (1999): 414–428.

Klofstad, Casey A., Anand Edward Sokhey, and Scott D. McClurg. "Disagreeing About Disagreement: How Conflict in Social Networks Affects Political Behavior." *American Journal of Political Science* 57, no. 1 (2013): 120–134.

Knibbs, Kate. "Instagram is Growing Faster than Twitter, Facebook, and Pinterest Combined." Accessed November 11, 2016, http://www.digitaltrends.com/social-media/instagram-is-growing-faster-than-twitter-facebook-and-pinterest-combined-in-2013/, 2014.

Kohut, Andrew, and Lee Rainie. "Internet Election News Audience Seeks Convenience, Familiar Names." Pew Research Center. Last modified December 3, 2000. Accessed February 20, 2017, http://www.pewinternet.org/2000/12/03/internet-election-news-audience-seeks-convenience-familiar-names/.

Kolowich, Steve. "The Life of 'The Party Decides.'" *The Chronicle of Higher Education*, May 16, 2016, http://www.chronicle.com/article/The-Life-of-The-Party/236483.

Kreiss, Daniel. "Seizing the Moment: The Presidential Campaigns' Use of Twitter During the 2012 Electoral Cycle." *New Media & Society*, 2014.

Kreiss, Daniel. *Prototype Politics: Technology-Intensive Campaigning and the Data of Democracy*. Oxford University Press, 2016.

Kreiss, Daniel, and Creighton Welch. "Strategic Communication in a Networked Age." In *Controlling the Message: New Media in American Political Campaigns*, edited by Victoria Farrar-Myers and Justin S. Vaughn, 13–31. New York: New York University Press, 2017.

Krieg, Gregory. "How Did Trump Win? Here Are 24 Theories." *CNN*, November 10, 2016, http://www.cnn.com/2016/11/10/politics/why-donald-trump-won/.

Krueger, Brian S. 2002. "Assessing the Potential of Internet Political Participation in the United States: A Resource Approach." *American Politics Research*, 40 (5): 476–498.

Ku, Gyotae, Lynda L. Kaid, and Michael Pfau. "The Impact of Web Site Campaigning on Traditional News Media and Public Information Processing." *Journalism & Mass Communication* 80, no. 3 (2003): 528–547.

Kuipers, Giselinde. "Media Culture and Internet Disaster Jokes: Bin Laden and the Attack on the World Trade Center." *European Journal of Cultural Studies* 5 (2002): 450–470.

Kuipers, Giselinde. "Where Was King Kong When We Needed Him? Public Discourse, Digital Disaster, Jokes, and the Functions of Laughter After 9/11." *The Journal of American Culture* 28 (2005): 70–84.

Kushin, Matthew James, and Masahiro Yamamoto. "Did Social Media Really Matter? College Students' Use of Online Media and Political Decision Making in the 2008 Election." *Mass Communication and Society* 13, no. 5 (2010): 608–30.

Kuziemko, Ilyana, Michael I. Norton, Emmanuel Saez, and Stefanie Stantcheva. "How Elastic Are Preferences for Redistribution? Evidence from Randomized Survey Experiments." *The American Economic Review* 105, no. 4 (2015): 1478–1508.

Kwak, Haewoon, Changhyun Lee, Hosung Park, and Sue Moon. "What is Twitter, a Social Network or News Media?" Paper presented at the Proceedings of the 19th International Conference on World Wide Web, Raleigh, NC, 2010.

Lai, K. K. Rebecca, Alicia Parlapiano, Jeremy White, and Karen Yourish. "How Trump Won the Election According to Exit Polls." *The New York Times*, November 8, 2016.

LaMarre, Heather L., Kristen D. Landreville, Dannagal Young, and Nathan Gilkerson. "Humor Works in Funny Ways: Examining Satirical Tone as a Key Determinant in Political Humor Message Processing." *Mass Communication and Society* 17 (2014): 400–23.

Landis, J. R., and Koch, G. G. "The Measurement of Observer Agreement for Categorical Data." *Biometrics* 33, no. 1 (1977): 159–174.

Lang, Marissa. 2016. "2016 Election Circus: Is Social Media the Cause?" *San Francisco Chronicle*, April 5.

Lapowsky, Issie. (2015, August 18). Political Ad Spending Online is About to Explode. *Wired*. http://www.wired.com/2015/08/digital-politcal-ads-2016/.

Lassen, David S., and Adam R. Brown. "Twitter: The Electoral Connection?" *The Social Science Computer Review* 29, no. 4 (2011): 419–436.

Lau, Richard, and Gerald M. Pomper. "Effects of Negative Campaigning on Turnout in U.S. Senate Elections, 1988–1996." *Journal of Politics* 63 (2001): 804–819.

Lau, Richard, and Gerald M. Pomper. *Negative Campaigning: An Analysis of U.S. Senate Elections.* Oxford: Rowman and Littlefield, 2004.

Lau, Richard R., and Daniel P. Redlawsk. *How Voters Decide: Information Processing in Election Campaigns.* Cambridge: Cambridge University Press, 2006.

Lawless, Jennifer L. "Female Candidates and Legislators." *Annual Review of Political Science* 18 (2015): 349–366.

Lee, Jayeon, and Young-shin Lim. "Gendered Campaign Tweets: The Cases of Hillary Clinton and Donald Trump." *Public Relations Review* 42 (2016): 849–855.

Lee, Michelle Ye Hee. "Donald Trump's False Comments Connecting Mexican Immigrants and Crime." *The Washington Post*, July 8, 2015, https://www.washingtonpost.com/news/fact-checker/wp/2015/07/08/donald-trumps-false-comments-connecting-mexican-immigrants-and-crime.

Lenz, Gabriel S., and Chappell Lawson. "Looking the Part: Television Leads Less Informed Citizens to Vote Based on Candidates' Appearance." *American Journal of Political Science* 55 (2011): 574–589.

Leslie, Katie, and Jordan Rudner. "Clinton, Trump and Gender Dynamics Pose 'Unprecedented Political Spectacle' at Presidential Debate." *Dallas Morning News*, September 23, 2016, http://www.dallasnews.com/news/politics/2016/09/23/clinton-trump-gender-dynamics-pose-unprecedented-political-spectacle-presidential-debate.

Lever, Rob. "Twitter Shakes Up U.S. Election Campaign." *News* 24. August 26, 2012. Available at: http://www.news24.com/SciTech/News/Twitter-shakes-up-US-election-campaign-20120826.

Lichter, S. Robert, Jody C Baumgartner, and Jonathan Morris. *Politics Is a Joke!: How TV Comedians Are Remaking Political Life.* Boulder, CO: Westview, 2014.

Lipinski, Daniel, William T. Bianco, and Ryan Work. "What Happens When House Members 'Run with Congress'? The Electoral Consequences of Institutional Loyalty." *Legislative Studies Quarterly* 28, no. 3 (2003): 413–429.

Macha, Sarah. "Media Coverage of Female Presidential and Vice Presidential Candidates and Voter Perceptions of Competency." MA Thesis, Sam Houston State University, 2012.

Marcus, George E., W. Russell Neuman, and Michael MacKuen. *Affective Intelligence and Political Judgment.* Chicago: University of Chicago Press, 2000.

Martin, Jonathan, Maggie Haberman, and Alexander Burns. "Lewd Donald Trump Tape Is a Breaking Point for Many in the G.O.P." *The New York Times*, October 8, 2016, https://www.nytimes.com/2016/10/09/us/politics/donald-trump-campaign.html.

Mason, Winter, and Siddharth Suri. "Conducting Behavioral Research on Amazon's Mechanical Turk." *Behavior Research Methods* 44, no. 1 (2013): 1–23.

Matthes, Jorg. "The Need for Orientation towards News Media: Revising and Validating a Classic Concept." *International Journal of Public Opinion Research* 18, no. 4 (2006): 422–444.

Mazza, Ed. "Donald Trump's Taco Bowl Hilariously Backfires." *The Huffington Post*, May 6, 2016, http://www.huffingtonpost.com/entry/donald-trump-taco-bowl_us_572bf20be4b096e9f090e1c5.

McAlone, Nathan. "James Corden Never Looks at His Ratings, Only His YouTube Numbers." *Business Insider.* Last modified October 14, 2016. http://www.businessinsider.com/james-corden-only-cares-about-youtube-2016-10.

McCabe, David. "Welcome to the Social Media Election." *The Hill,* August 17, 2015, http://thehill.com/policy/technology/251185-welcome-to-the-social-media-election.

McCombs, Maxwell E. *Setting the Agenda: The Mass Media and Public Opinion.* Malden, MA: Blackwell Publishing Inc., 2004.

McCombs, Maxwell. "A Look at Agenda-Setting: Past, Present, and Future." *Journalism Studies* 6, no. 4 (2005): 543–557.

McCombs, Maxwell E., and Donald L. Shaw. "The Agenda-Setting Function of Mass Media." *Public Opinion Quarterly* 36 (1972): 176–87. doi:10.1086/2F267990.

McCombs, Maxwell, Esteban Lopez-Escobar, and Juan Pablo Llamas. "Setting the Agenda of Attributes in the 1996 Spanish General Election." *Journal of Communication* 50, no. 2 (2000): 77–92.

McCombs, Maxwell, Donald L. Shaw, and David H. Weaver. *Communication and Democracy: Exploring the Intellectual Frontiers in Agenda-Setting Theory.* New York: Routledge, 2013.

McCombs, Maxwell, Juan Pablo Llamas, Esteban Lopez-Escobar, and Federico Rey. "Candidate Images in Spanish Elections: Second-Level Agenda-Setting Effects." *Journalism and Mass Communication Quarterly* 74, no. 4 (1998): 703–717.

McGinley, Ann C. "Hillary Clinton, Sarah Palin, and Michelle Obama: Performing Gender, Race, and Class on the Campaign Trail." *Denver University Law Review* 86 (2009): 709–725.

MediaMiser. "The Top 15 U.S. Newspapers by Circulation." Last modified on November 11, 2016, from https://www.mediamiser.com/resources/top-media-outlets/top-15-daily-american-newspapers/.

Meeks, Lindsey. "Aligning and Trespassing: Candidates' Party-Based Issue and Trait Ownership on Twitter." *Journalism & Mass Communication Quarterly* 93:4 (2016): 1050–1072. doi: 10.1177/1077699015609284.

Meraz, Sharon. "Is There an Elite Hold? Traditional Media to Social Media Agenda Setting Influence in Blog Networks." *Journal of Computer-Mediated Communication* 14, no. 3 (2009): 682–707.

Meraz, Sharon. "The Fight For 'How To Think': Traditional Media, Social Networks, and Attribute Agenda Setting." *Conference Papers — International Communication Association*, 2009.

Mérola, Vittorio, and Matthew P. Hitt. "Numeracy and the Persuasive Effect of Policy Information and Party Cues." *Public Opinion Quarterly* 80, no. 2 (2016): 554–62.

Messner, Marcus, and Marcia Watson Distaso. "The Source Cycle: How Traditional Media and Weblogs Use Each Other as Sources." *Journalism Studies* 9, no. 3 (2008): 447–463.

Messner, Marcus, and Bruce Garrison. "Study Shows Some Blogs Affect Traditional News Media Agenda." *Newspaper Research Journal* 32, no. 3 (2011): 112–126.

Metzgar, Emily, and Albert Maruggi. "Social Media and the 2008 U.S. Presidential Election." *Journal of New Communications Research* 4 (2009): 141–65.

Metzgar, Emily, and Albert Maruggi. "Social Media and the 2008 U.S. Presidential Election." *Journal of New Communications Research* 4:1 (2009): 141–165.

Mitchell, Amy, and Rachel Weisel. "Political Polarization and Media Habits." Pew Research Center, 2014.

Morrill, Jim, and Bryan Anderson. "In NC, Trump Mocks Accuser: 'She's a Liar.'" *The Charlotte Observer*, October 14, 2016, http://www.charlotteobserver.com/news/politics-government/campaign-tracker-blog/article108260817.html.

Mueller, Melinda, Matthew Cain, Mariah Wallace, and Samantha Sarich. "Gender, U.S. House Campaigns, and the Twitterverse." In *Social Media and Politics: A New Way to Participate in the Political Process*, edited by Glenn W. Richardson, Jr., 89–110. Santa Barbara: Praeger, 2016.

Murray, Rainbow. *Cracking the Highest Glass Ceiling: A Global Comparison on Women's Campaigns for Executive Office*. Santa Barbara, CA: ABC-CLIO, 2010.

Musangi, Jennifer. "'A Zimbabwean Joke Is No Laughing Matter': E-Humour and Versions of Subversion," 161–175, in Sarah Chiumbu and Muchaparara Musemwa, eds., *Crisis! What Crisis? The Multiple Dimensions of the Zimbabwean Crisis*, Human Sciences Research Council (2012): 3–286.

Mutz, Diana C. *Hearing the Other Side: Deliberative Versus Participatory Democracy*. Cambridge University Press, 2006.

Mutz, Diana C., and Byron Reeves. "The New Videomalaise: Effects of Televised Incivility on Political Trust." *American Political Science Review* 99, no. 01 (2005): 1–15.

Neuman, W. Russell, Lauren Guggenheim, S. Mo Jang, and Soo Young Bae. "The Dynamics of Public Attention: Agenda-Setting Theory Meets Big Data." *Journal of Communication* 64, no. 2 (2014): 193–214.

Neustadt, Richard E. *Presidential Power: The Politics of Leadership from FDR to Carter*. New York: John Wiley and Sons, 1980.

New York Times. "The Times Interviews John McCain." Last modified July 13, 2008. Accessed January 10, 2017, http://www.nytimes.com/2008/07/13/us/politics/13text-mccain.html.

New York Times. "Who's Winning the Presidential Campaign?" February 2, 2016, http://www.nytimes.com/interactive/2016/us/elections/presidential-candidates-dashboard.html.

Newman, Bruce I. *The Marketing Revolution in Politics: What Recent US Presidential Campaigns Can Teach Us About Effective Marketing*. University of Toronto Press, 2016.

Nielsen. *2016 Nielsen Social Media Report*. New York: Nielsen Company, 2017.

NORC Center for Public Affairs Research. 2016. *The Frustrated Public: Views of the 2016 Campaign, the Parties, and the Electoral Process*. Issue Brief. http://www.apnorc.org/projects/Pages/HTML%20Reports/the-frustrated-public-americans-views-of-the-election-issue-brief.aspx.

Norpoth, Helmut. "Primary Model Predicts Trump Victory." *PS: Political Science & Politics*, 49 (2016): 655–58.

Nussbaum, Matthew. "Pence Says He Was 'Offended' by Trump's Remarks About Groping Women." *Politico*, October 8, 2016, http://www.politico.com/story/2016/10/pence-says-he-was-offended-by-trumps-remarks-about-groping-women-229355.

O'Keefe, Ed, and Matea Gold. "Jeb Bush and Allied Super PAC Raise an Unprecedented $114 Million War Chest." *The Washington Post*, July 9, 2015, https://www.washingtonpost.com/politics/jeb-bush-and-allied-super-pac-raise-an-unprecedented-114-million-war-chest/2015/07/09/652e1206-2651-11e5-b72c-2b7d516e1e0e_story.html.

Oring, Elliott. *Engaging Humor*. Illinois: University of Illinois Press, 2003.

Owen, Diana. 2009. "The Campaign and the Media," in Janet M. Box-Steffensmeier and Steven E. Schier, eds. *The American Elections of 2008*. New York: Routledge, 9–32.

Owen, Diana. "Media: The Complex Interplay of Old and New Forms." In *New Directions in Campaigns and Elections*, edited by Stephen K. Medvic, 145–162. New York: Routledge, 2011.

Owen, Diana. 2013. "The Campaign and the Media," in *The American Elections of 2012*, Janet M. Box-Steffensmeier and Steven E. Schier, eds. New York: Routledge, 21–47.

Owen, Diana. 2014. "New Media and Political Campaigns," in *The Oxford Handbook of Political Communication Theories*, Kate Kenski and Kathleen Hall Jamieson, eds. New York: Oxford University Press, Chapter 53.

Owen, Diana. 2015. "The Political Culture of American Elections," in Georgiana Banita and Sascha Pohlmann, eds., *Electoral Cultures: American Democracy and Choice*. Heidelberg: Universitatsverlag, Publications of the Bavarian American Academy, 205–224.

Owen, Diana. 2017. "Twitter Rants, Press Bashing, and Fake News: The Shameful Legacy of Media in the 2016 Election," in *Trumped: The 2016 Election that Broke All the Rules*, Larry J. Sabato, Kyle Konkik, and Geoffrey Skelley, eds. Lanham, MD: Rowman and Littlefield, 167–180.

Paivio, Allan. *Imagery and Verbal Processes*. Hillsdale, NJ: Erlbaum, 1979.

Parkin, Michael. *Talk Show Campaigns*. New York: Routledge, 2014.

Parmelee, John H. "Political Journalists and Twitter: Influences on Norms and Practices." *Journal of Media Practice* 14, no. 4 (2013): 291–305.

Parmelee, John H. "The Agenda-Building Function of Political Tweets." *New Media & Society* 16, no. 3 (2014): 434–450.

Parmelee, John H., and Shannon L. Bichard. *Politics and the Twitter Revolution: How Tweets Influence the Relationship between Political Leaders and the Public*. New York: Lexington Books, 2012.

Parmelee, John H., John Davies, and Carolyn A. McMahan. "The Rise of Non-Traditional Site Use for Online Political Information." *Communication Quarterly* 59, no. 5 (2011): 625–40.

Parsons, Bryan M. "Social Networks and the Affective Impact of Political Disagreement." *Political Behavior* 32, no. 2 (2010): 181–204.

Pasek, Josh, Eian More, and Daniel Romer. "Realizing the Social Internet? Online Social Networking Meets Offline Civic Engagement." *Journal of Information Technology and Politics* 6 (2009):197–215.

Patterson, Dan. 2016. "Election Tech: Why 2016 Is the First Made-for-Social Media Campaign." *Tech Republic*, March 26. http://www.techrepublic.com/article/election-tech-why-2016-is-the-first-made-for-social-media-campaign/.

Patterson, Thomas E. *Out of Order: An Incisive and Boldly Original Critique of the New Media's Domination of America's Political Process*. New York: Vintage Books, 1984.

Patterson, Thomas E. "News Coverage of the 2016 National Conventions: Negative News, Lacking Context." *Harvard Kennedy School Shorenstein Center on Media, Politics, and Public Policy*, July 11, 2016, https://shorensteincenter.org/news-coverage-2016-national-conventions/.

Patterson, Thomas. "News Coverage of the 2016 General Election: How the Press Failed the Voters." *Shorenstein Center*, December 7, 2017. https://shorensteincenter.org/news-coverage-2016-general-election/.

Patterson, Thomas, and Robert McClure. *The Unseeing Eye: The Myth of Television Power in National Elections*. New York: Putnam, 1976.

Perrin, Andrew. "Social Media Usage: 2006–2015." Pew Research Center. Last modified October 8, 2015. Accessed December 20, 2016, http://www.pewinternet.org/2015/10/08/social-networking-usage-2005–2015/.

Petrocik, John R. "Issue Ownership in Presidential Elections, With a 1980 Case Study." *American Journal of Political Science* 40 (1996): 825–50.

Petrocik, John R., William L. Benoit, and Glenn L. Hansen. "Issue Ownership and Presidential Campaigning, 1952–2000." *Political Science Quarterly* 118 (2003): 599–626. doi:10.1002/j.1538–165X.2003.tb00407.x.

Petrocik, John R., William L. Benoit, W. L., and Glenn J. Hansen. "Issue Ownership and Presidential Campaigning, 1952–2000." *Political Science Quarterly*, 118 no. 4 (2003): 599–626.

Pew Research Center. "Wide Partisan Differences Over the Issues That Matter in 2014." Pew Research Center, September 12, 2014. http://www.people-press.org/2014/09/12/wide-partisan-differences-over-the-issues-that-matter-in-2014.

Pew Research Center. 2014. *Cell Phones, Social Media and Campaign 2014*. Research Report. November 3. Washington, D.C.

Pew Research Center. *Instagram Demographics*. Washington, D.C.: 2015. Retrieved from http://www.pewinternet.org/2015/08/19/mobile-messaging-and-social-media-2015/2015–08–19_social-media-update_09/.

Pew Research Center. "Social Media Fact Sheet." Accessed February 20, 2017. http://www.pewinternet.org/fact-sheet/social-media/.

Pew Research Center. "Campaign Exposes Fissures Over Issues, Values, and How Life Has Changed in the U.S." (2016). Accessed January 9, 2017. http://www.people-press.org/2016/03/31/1-views-of-the-primaries-press-coverage-of-candidates-attitudes-about-government-and-the-country/.

Pew Research Center. 2016. *2016 Campaign: Strong Interest, Widespread Dissatisfaction*. Research Report. July 7. Washington, D.C.

Pew Research Center. 2016. *Election 2016: Campaigns as a Direct Source of News*. Research Report. July 18. Washington, D.C.

Pew Research Center. 2016. *The Political Environment on Social Media*. Research Report. October 25. Washington, D.C.

Pew Research Center. 2016. *The 2016 Presidential Campaign: A News Event That's Hard to Miss*. Research Report. February 4. Washington, D.C.

Pew Research Center. "How the Presidential Candidates Use the Web and Social Media." August 15, 2012, accessed on March 1, 2017, http://www.journalism.org/2012/08/15/how-presidential-candidates-use-web-and-social-media/

Pew Research Center. "Partisanship and Political Animosity in 2016." Last modified June 22, 2016. http://www.people-press.org/2016/06/22/partisanship-and-political-animosity-in-2016/.

Pew Research Center. "2016 Campaign: Strong Interest, Widespread Dissatisfaction." July 7, 2016. Accessed March 27, 2017. http://www.people-press.org/2016/07/07/2016-campaign-strong-interest-widespread-dissatisfaction/.

Pew Research Center. "Election 2016: Campaign as a Direct Source of News." Accessed on November 11, 2016, from http://assets.pewresearch.org/wp-content/uploads/sites/13/2016/07/PJ_2016.07.18_election-2016_FINAL.pdf.

Pew Research Center. "The Political Environment on Social Media." (2016). Accessed January 9, 2017. http://www.pewinternet.org/2016/10/25/the-political-environment-on-social-media/.

Pew Research Center. "As Election Nears, Voters Divided Over Democracy and 'Respect.'" Last modified October 27, 2016. http://www.people-press.org/2016/10/27/as-election-nears-voters-divided-over-democracy-and-respect/.

Pew Research Center. "The State of the News Media 2013." Pew Research Center, 2013. http://www.stateofthemedia.org/2013/newspapers-stabilizing-but-still-threatened/22-top-25-daily-newspapers/.

Pew Research Center. "Social Media Usage: 2005–2015." October 8, 2015, accessed on March 1, 2017, http://www.pewinternet.org/2015/10/08/social-networking-usage-2005-2015/.

Plouffe, David. 2009. *The Audacity to Win*. New York: Penguin.

Pompeo, Joe. "*Wall Street Journal* Editor to Face Critics." *Politico*, February 8, 2017, http://www.politico.com/media/story/2017/02/gerry-baker-wall-street-journal-trump-newsroom-tensions-004928.

Popkin, Samuel L. *The Reasoning Voter: Communication and Persuasion in Presidential Campaigns*. University of Chicago Press, 1994.

Prior, Markus. "Media and Political Polarization." *Annual Review of Political Science* 16 (2013): 101–127.

Qui, Linda. "Is Bernie Sanders a Democrat?" *Politifact.com*, February 23, 2016. http://www.politifact.com/truth-o-meter/article/2016/feb/23/bernie-sanders-democrat/.

Rainie, Lee, Aaron Smith, Kay Lehman Schlozman, Henry Brady, and Sidney Verba. 2012. *Social Media and Political Engagement*. Research Report. Washington, D.C., October 19, 2012.

RealClearPolitics. "General Election: Trump vs. Clinton." November 7, 2016, http://www.realclearpolitics.com/epolls/2016/president/us/general_election_trump_vs_clinton-5491.html.

Reingold, Beth. *Representing Women: Sex, Gender, and Legislative Behavior in Arizona and California*. Chapel Hill: University of North Carolina Press, 2000.

Reuters. "Prediction Markets: Jeb Bush Likely to Beat Donald Trump for 2016 Republican Nomination." *Newsweek*, August 26, 2015, http://www.newsweek.com/jeb-bush-donald-trump-prediction-markets-polls-366122.

Richardson, Glenn W., Jr., *Pulp Politics: How Political Advertising Tells the Stories of American Politics*. Lanham, MD: Rowman & Littlefield Publishers, 2008.

Ridout, Travis N., and Kathleen Searles. "It's My Campaign I'll Cry if I Want To: How and When Campaigns Use Emotional Appeals." *Political Psychology* 32, no. 3 (2011): 439–458.

Ridout, Travis N., Michael M. Franz, and Erika Franklin Fowler. "Sponsorship, Disclosure, and Donors: Limiting the Impact of Outside Group Ads." *Political Research Quarterly* 68, no. 1 (2015): 154–166.

Roberts, Marilyn, and Maxwell E. McCombs. "Agenda Setting and Political Advertising: Origins of the News Agenda." *Political Communication* 11, no. 3 (1994): 249–262.

Roberts, Marilyn, Wayne Wanta, and Tzong-Horng (Dustin) Dzwo. "Agenda Setting and Issue Salience Online." *Communication Research* 29, no. 4 (2002): 452–465.

Rogers, Everett, James Dearing, and Dorine Bregman. "The Anatomy of Agenda—Setting Research." *Journal of Communication* 43, no. 2 (1993): 68–84.

Rogers, Simon. "What Fuels a Tweet's Engagement?" Twitter. Accessed April 1, 2017, from https://blog.twitter.com/2014/what-fuels-a-tweets-engagement, 2014.

Rogstad, Ingrid. "Is Twitter Just Rehashing? Intermedia Agenda Setting Between Twitter and Mainstream Media." *Journal of Information Technology & Politics* 13 (2016): 142–58. doi:10.1080/19331681.2016.1160263.

Romano, Aja. "The Year Social Media Changed Everything," *Vox*, December 31, 2016. http://www.vox.com/2016/12/31/13869676/social-media-influence-alt-right.

Romer, Daniel. "Time Series Models." In *Capturing Campaign Dynamics 2000 & 2004*, edited by Daniel Romer, Kate Kenski, Kenneth Winneg, Christopher Adasiewicz, and Kathleen Hall Jamieson, 165–243. Philadelphia, PA: University of Pennsylvania Press, 2006.

Rosenberg, Shawn W., Lisa Bohan, Patrick McCafferty, and Kevin Harris. "The Image and the Vote: The Effect of Candidate Presentation on Voter Preference." *American Journal of Political Science* 30 (1986): 108–128.

Ross, Phillip. "Photos Are Still King on Facebook." *SocialBakers*. Accessed April 1, 2017, from http://www.socialbakers.com/blog/2149-photos-are-still-king-on-facebook, 2014.

Ross, Phillip. "Photos Get the Most Engagement on Twitter." *SocialBakers*. Accessed April 1, 2017, from http://www.socialbakers.com/blog/2306-photos-get-the-most-engagement-on-twitter, 2014.

Ross, Phillip. "Three Trends that Dominated Social Video in . . . " *SocialBakers*. Accessed April 1, 2017, from http://www.socialbakers.com/blog/2489-three-trends-that-dominated-social-video-in-2015, 2016.

Royston, Patrick. "Multiple Imputation of Missing Values: Update of Ice." *Stata Journal* 5, no. 4 (2005): 527.

Rucker, Philip. "Trump Belittles McCain's War Service, Sparking Stern Republican Backlash." *Washington Post*, July 19, 2015, https://www.washingtonpost.com/politics/trump-belittles-mccains-war-service-sparking-stern-republican-backlash/2015/07/18/e9f814c6–2d7e-11e5-bd33–395c05608059_story.html.

Saad, Lydia. "Trump Leads Clinton in Historically Bad Image Ratings" *Gallup*, July 1, 2016. http://www.gallup.com/poll/193376/trump-leads-clinton-historically-bad-image-ratings.aspx.

Santana, Arthur, and Lindita Camaj. "Facebook as a Campaign Tool during the 2012 Elections: A New Dimension to Agenda Setting Discourse." *Journal of Social Media in Society* 4, no. 2 (2015): 106–137.

Sapiro, Virginia, Katherine Cramer Walsh, Patricia Strach, and Valerie Hennings. "Gender, Context, and Television Advertising: A Comprehensive Analysis of 2000 and 2002 House Races." *Political Research Quarterly* 64, no. 1 (2011): 107–119.

Savransky, Rebecca. "Trump Compares Twitter to Owning His Own Newspaper." *The Hill*, April 3, 2016. http://thehill.com/blogs/ballot-box/presidential-races/275046-trump-compares-twitter-to-owning-his-own-newspaper.

Sayre, Ben, Leticia Bode, Dhavan Shah, Dave Wilcox, and Chirag Shah. "Agenda Setting in a Digital Age: Tracking Attention to California Proposition 8 in Social Media, Online News, and Conventional News." *Policy and Internet* 2, no. 2 (2010): 7–32.

Scheufele, Dietram A., and Matthew Nisbet. "Being a Citizen Online: New Opportunities and Dead Ends." *The Harvard International Journal of Press/Politics* 7 (2002): 55–75.

Scheufele, Dietram A., Matthew C. Nisbet, Dominique Brossard, and Erik C. Nisbet. "Social Structure and Citizenship: Examining the Impacts of Social Setting, Network Heterogeneity, and Informational Variables on Political Participation." *Political Communication*, 21, no. 3 (2004): 315–338.

Schipper, Burkhard C., and Hee Yuel Woo. 2016. "Political Awareness, Microtargeting of Voters, and Negative Electoral Campaigning." Research Paper. University of California, Davis. http://faculty.econ.ucdavis.edu/faculty/schipper/polaw.pdf.

Schlesinger, Robert. "Done Deal." *U.S. News & World Report*, October 28, 2016, http://www.usnews.com/opinion/thomas-jefferson-street/articles/2016-10-28/7-reasons-why-hillary-clintons-win-over-donald-trump-is-a-done-deal.

Schmierbach, Mike, and Anne Oeldorf-Hirsch. "A Little Bird Told Me, So I Didn't Believe It: Twitter, Credibility, and Issue Perceptions." *Communication Quarterly* 60, no. 3 (2012): 317–37.

Schoenbach, Klaus, and K. Weaver. "Finding the Unexpected: Cognitive Building in a Political Campaign." In *Mass Media and Political Thought: An Information-Processing Approach*, edited by Sidney Kraus and Richard M. Perloff, 157–176: Beverly Hills, CA: Sage, 1985.

Schreckinger, Ben. "Trump Attacks McCain: 'I Like People Who Weren't Captured.'" *Politico*, July 18, 2015, http://www.politico.com/story/2015/07/trump-attacks-mccain-i-like-people-who-werent-captured-120317.

Schultheis, Emily. "Report: Donald Trump Aides Took Away Candidate's Twitter Access," November 6, 2016.

Seitz-Wald, Alex. "Donald Trump's Ugly Electoral Map." *MSNBC*, May 5, 2016, http://www.msnbc.com/msnbc/donald-trumps-ugly-electoral-map.

Semiatin, Richard, ed. 2013. *Campaigns on the Cutting Edge*, 2nd ed. Washington, D.C.: CQ Press.

Shafer, Jack. "How Trump Took Over the Media by Fighting It." *Politico*, November 5, 2016, http://www.politico.com/magazine/story/2016/11/2016-election-trump-media-takeover-coverage-214419.

Shapiro, Matthew, and Libby Hemphill. "Politicians and the Policy Agenda: Does Use of Twitter by the U.S. Congress Direct *New York Times* Content?" *Policy and Internet* 9, no. 1 (2017): 109–132.

Shah, Dhavan V., Jack M. McLeod, and So-Hyang Yoon. "Communication, Context, and Community: An Exploration of Print, Broadcast, and Internet Influence." *Communication Research* 28 (2001): 464–506.

Shah, Dhavan V., Jaeho Cho, William P. Eveland, and Nojin Kwak. "Information and Expression in a Digital Age: Modeling Internet Effects on Civic Participation." *Communication Research* 32 (2005): 1–35.

Shaw, Donald L., and Maxwell McCombs. *The Emergence of American Political Is-sues*. St. Paul, MN: West, 1977.

Shifflet, Shane. "A Divided America: Election Results Reveal the 2016 Presidential Contest to Be One of the Most Polarizing in Recent History. Donald Trump Benefited as More Counties Voted Republican by Wider Margins Than in 2012." *Wall Street Journal*, November 10, 2016, http://www.wsj.com/graphics/elections/2016/divided-america.

Shifman, Limor. "Humor in the Age of Digital Reproduction: Continuity and Change in Internet-Based Comic Texts." *International Journal of Communication* 1, (2007): 187–209.

Shirky, Clay. "The Political Power of Social Media: Technology, the Public Sphere, and Political Change." *Foreign Affairs*, 90 (2011): 26–38.

Shoemaker, Pamela J., and Tim P. Vos. *Gatekeeping Theory*. New York: Routledge, 2009.

Shogan, Colleen J. "Blackberries, Tweets, and YouTube: Technology and the Future of Communicating with Congress." *PS: Political Science and Politics* 43, no. 2 (2010): 231–233.

Sides, John. "The Origins of Campaign Agendas." *British Journal of Political Science* 36 (2006): 407–36. doi:10.1017/S0007123406000226.

Sides, John. "The Consequences of Campaign Agendas." *American Politics Research* 35 (2007): 465–88. doi:10.1177/1532673X07300648.

Sifry, Micah. 2012. "The Rise and Fall of Social Media in American Politics (And How It May Rise Again)," *TechPresident*, November 6, http://techpresident.com/news/23103/rise-and-fall-social-media-american-politics-and-how-it-may-rise-again.

Sigelman, Lee, and Emmett H. Buell. "Avoidance or Engagement? Issue Convergence in US Presidential Campaigns, 1960–2000." *American Journal of Political Science* 48, no. 4 (2004): 650–661.

Sims, David. "What Conan O'Brien Means to Late-Night's Weekly Future." *The Atlantic*. Last modified January 10, 2017, https://www.theatlantic.com/entertainment/archive/2017/01/what-conan-obrien-means-to-late-nights-future/512633/.

Skaperdas, Stergios, and Bernard Grofman. "Modeling Negative Campaigning." *The American Political Science Review* 89, no. 1 (1995): 49–61.

Slaby, Michael. 2013. "From Politics to Public Policy: Part 3: How Campaign Lessons Can Amplify Your Work: Embrace the Change," *Stanford Innovation Review*, April 9.

Smith, Aaron. "The Internet's Role in Campaign 2008." Pew Research Center. April 15, 2009. http://www.pewinternet.org/~/media//Files/Reports/2009/The_Internets_Role_in_Campaign_2008.pdf.

Smith, Aaron, and Maeve Duggan. "Online Political Videos and Campaign 2012." Pew Research Center. November 2, 2012, http://www.pewinternet.org/files/old-media/Files/Reports/2012/PIP_State_of_the_2012_race_online_video_final.pdf.

Smith, Aaron. 2014. "Cell Phones, Social Media, and Campaign 2014." Research Report. Pew Research Center, November 3, Washington, D.C. http://www.pewinternet.org/2014/11/03/cell-phones-social-media-and-campaign-2014/.

Soergel, Andrew. "Divided We Stand: Political Polarization Drives Presidential Race to the Bottom." *US News and World Report*, July 19, 2016, http://www.usnews.com/news/articles/ 2016–07–19/political-polarization-drives-presidential-race-to-the-bottom.

Statista. "Outside group spending in United States political cycles from 1990 to 2016 (in U.S. dollars)." https://www.statista.com/statistics/611303/outside-spending-in-us-political-cycles/.

Statista. "Outside spending for and against major parties in the 2016 U.S. presidential election (in U.S. dollars)." https://www.statista.com/statistics/611844/outside-spending-for-and-against-parties-2016-us-presidential-election/.

Stenberg, George. "Conceptual and Perceptual Factors in the Picture Superiority Effect." *European Journal of Cognitive Psychology*, 18, no. 6 (2006): 813–847.

Stevenson, Peter W. "A Brief History of the 'Lock Her Up!' Chant by Trump Supporters Against Clinton." *Washington Post*, November 22, 2016, https://www.washingtonpost.com/news/the-fix/wp/2016/11/22/a-brief-history-of-the-lock-her-up-chant-as-it-looks-like-trump-might-not-even-try.

Stewart, Emily. "Donald Trump Rode $5 Billion in Free Media to the White House." *The Street*, November 20, 2017. Accessed March 27, 2017, https://www.thestreet.com/story/13896916/1/donald-trump-rode-5-billion-in-free-media-to-the-white-house.html.

Stromback, Jesper, and Spiro Kiousis. "A New Look at Agenda-Setting Effects—Comparing the Predictive Power of Overall Political News Consumption and Specific New Media Consumption across Different Media Channels and Media Types." *Journal of Communication* 60 (2010): 271–292.

Stromer-Galley, Jennifer. "On-line Interaction and Why Candidates Avoid It" *Journal of Communication* 50.4 (2000): 111–132.

Stromer-Galley, Jennifer. 2014. *Presidential Campaigning in the Internet Age.* New York: Oxford University Press.

Stroud, N. J. *Niche News: The Politics of News Choice.* Oxford: Oxford University Press, 2011.

Sweetser, Kaye D. "Partisan personality: The psychological differences between Democrats and Republicans, and Independents somewhere in between." *American Behavioral Scientist* 58, no. 9 (2014): 1183–1194.

Sweetser, Kaye, Guy J. Golan, and Wayne Wanta. "Intermedia Agenda Setting in Television, Advertising, and Blogs during the 2004 Election." *Mass Communication & Society* 11, no. 2 (2008): 197–216.

Swers, Michelle. *The Difference Women Make: The Policy Impact of Women in Congress.* Chicago, IL: University of Chicago Press, 2002.

Swift, Art. "Americans' Trust in Mass Media Sinks to New Low." Gallup, September 14, 2016, http://www.gallup.com/poll/195542/americans-trust-mass-media-sinks-new-low.aspx.

Swigger, Nathaniel. "The Online Citizen: Is Social Media Changing Citizens' Beliefs About Democratic Values?" *Political Behavior* 35, no. 3 (2013): 589–603.

Sydney Morning Herald. "YouTube Hitler Parodies Go Viral." *Stuff.* Last modified September 30, 2008. http://www.stuff.co.nz/technology/651645.

Taber, Charles S., and Milton Lodge. "Motivated Skepticism in the Evaluation of Political Beliefs." *American Journal of Political Science* 50.3 (2006): 755–769.

Tanner, Mike. "A Funny Thing Didn't Happen on the Way to the Web." *Wired*. November, 13, 1997. http://archive.wired.com/culture/lifestyle/news/1997/11/8518.

Tatum, Sophie, "Pictured with Taco Bowl, Trump Proclaims, 'I Love Hispanics!'" *CNN*, May 6, 2016, http://www.cnn.com/2016/05/05/politics/donald-trump-taco-bowl-cinco-de-mayo/.

Tedesco, John C. "Issue and Strategy Agenda-Setting in the 2000 Presidential Primaries." *American Behavioral Scientist* 44, no. 12 (2001).

Tedesco, John C. "Issue and Strategy Agenda Setting in the 2004 Presidential Election: Exploring the Candidate-Journalist Relationship." *Journalism Studies* 62, no. 2 (2005): 187–201.

Tetlock, Philip E. "Cognitive Style and Political Belief Systems in the British House of Commons." *Journal of Personality and Social Psychology* 46, no. 2 (1984): 365–375.

Tetlock, Philip E. "A Value Pluralism Model of Ideological Reasoning." *Journal of Personality and Social Psychology* 50, no. 4 (1986): 819–827.

Tetlock, Philip E., Jane Bernzweig, and Jack L. Gallant. "Supreme Court Decision Making: Cognitive Style as a Predictor of Ideological Consistency of Voting." *Journal of Personality and Social Psychology* 48, no. 5 (1985): 1227–1239.

Thomas, Sue. "The Impact of Women on State Legislative Policies." *Journal of Politics*, 53 (1991): 958–976.

Thomas, Sue. *How Women Legislate*. New York, NY: Oxford University Press, 1994.

Thorson, Kjerstin, and Chris Wells. 2015. "Curated Flows: A Framework for Mapping Media Exposure in the Digital Age." *Communication Theory*, online first.

Timm, Jane C. "Trump on Hot Mike: 'When You're a Star. . . . You Can Do Anything' to Women." NBC News. October 7, 2016.

Towner, Terri L. "Information Hubs or Drains?: The Role of Online Sources in Campaign Learning," in *Handbook of Research on Citizens Engagement and Public Participation in the Era of New Media*, ed., Marco Adria and Yuping Mao. (IGI Global, 2017), 157.

Towner, Terri L., and David A. Dulio. "The Web 2.0 Election: Does the Online Medium Matter?" *Journal of Political Marketing* 10 (2011a): 165–188.

Towner, Terri L. 2013. "All Political Participation is Socially Networked? New Media and the 2012 Election," *Social Science Computer Review*, 31 (5). http://journals.sagepub.com/doi/full/10.1177/0894439313489656.

Towner, Terri L. "The Influence of Twitter Posts on Candidate Perceptions: The 2014 Michigan Midterms." In *Media, Message, and Mobilization: Communication and Midterm Elections*, edited by John A. Hendricks, and Daniel Schill, 145–167. New York: Palgrave, 2016.

Towner, Terri L. "The Infographic Election: The Role of Visual Content on Social Media in the 2016 Presidential Campaign." In *The Presidency and Social Media: Discourse, Disruption, and Digital Democracy in the 2016 Presidential Election*, edited by John Allen Hendricks and Dan Schill. New York, NY: Routledge, forthcoming.

Towner, Terri L., and David A. Dulio. "An Experiment of Campaign Effects during the YouTube Election." *New Media and Society* 13, no. 4 (2011): 626–644.

Towner, Terri L. and David A. Dulio. 2012. "New Media and Political Marketing in the United States: 2012 and Beyond." *The Journal of Political Marketing,* 11(1–2):95–119.

Towner, Terri L., and Caroline Lego Muñoz. "Boomers versus Millennials: Online Media Influence on Political Perceptions and Media Performance." *Social Sciences* 5, no. 4 (2016): 56.

Towner, Terri L., and Caroline Lego Muñoz. "Baby Boom or Bust?: The New Media Effect on Political Participation." *The Journal of Political Marketing,* forthcoming, 2016.

Trent, Judith S., Robert V. Friedenberg, and Robert E. Denton, Jr. *Political Campaign Communication: Principles and Practices,* 7th ed. New York: Rowman & Littlefield, 2011.

Tresch, Anke, Jonas Lefevere, and Stefaan Walgrave. "'Steal Me if You Can!' The Impact of Campaign Messages on Associative Issue Ownership." *Party Politics* 21 (2015): 198–208. doi:10.1177/1354068812472576.

Trippi, Joe. *The Revolution Will Not Be Televised.* NY: HarperCollins, 2004.

Trump, Donald J. "Remarks on the Clinton Campaign of Destruction." Press release, October 13, 2016, https://www.donaldjtrump.com/press-releases/remarks-on-the-clinton-campaign-of-destruction.

Trump, Donald, and Tony Schwartz. *Trump: The Art of the Deal.* New York: Random House, 1987.

Tumulty, Karen, and Philip Rucker. "Trump Roils First Debate Among GOP Contenders." *The Washington Post,* August 6, 2015, https://www.washingtonpost.com/politics/donald-trump-dominates-raucous-republican-debate/2015/08/06/b8a5f0e6-3c79-11e5-8e98-115a3cf7d7ae_story.html.

Twitter 2016. US House: A public list by Twitter government. Accessed November 1, 2016. https://twitter.com/gov/lists/us-house.

Twitter Counter: Check Your Own Twitter Stats. http://twittercounter.com/ (retrieved November 9, 2016).

Uberti, David. "How Political Campaigns Use Twitter to Shape Media Coverage." *Columbia Journalism Review.* Last modified December 9, 2014. Accessed December 20, 2016, http://www.cjr.org/behind_the_news/how_political_campaigns_use_tw.php.

USA Today. "Donald Trump's Unpresidential Campaign: Our View." August 31, 2015, http://www.usatoday.com/story/opinion/2015/08/31/donald-trump-megyn-kelly-jorge-ramos-attacks-editorials-debates/71429356/.

Uscinski, Joseph E., and Lilly J. Goren. "What's in a Name? Coverage of Senator Hillary Clinton During the 2008 Democratic Primary." *Political Research Quarterly* 64 (2010): 884–896.

Vaccari, Cristian, et al. 2015. "Political Expression and Action on Social Media: Exploring the Relationship Between Lower- and Higher-Threshold Political Activities Among Twitter Users in Italy." *Journal of Computer-Mediated Communication,* 20: 221–239.

Van Aelst, Peter, Jesper Strombäck, Tori Aalberg, Frank Esser, Claes de Vreese, Jörg Matthes, David Hopmann, Susana Salgado, Nicholas Hubé, Agnieska Stępińska, Stylianos Papathanassopoulos, Rosa Berganza, Guido Legnante,

Carsten Reinemann, Tamir Shaefer, and James Stanyer, "Political Communication in a High Choice Media Environment: A Challenge for Democracy?"
Annals of the International Communication Association 41 (2017): 3–27. doi:
10.1080/23808985.2017.1288551.

Van Dijck, Jose. *The Culture of Connectivity: A Critical History of Social Media.* New
York: Oxford University Press, 2013.

Vargo, Chris J., Ekaterina Basilaia, and Donald L. Shaw. "Event versus Issue:
Twitter Reflections of Major News—A Case Study." In *Communication and Information Technologies Annual (Studies in Media and Communications, Volume 9),*
edited by Laura Robinson, Sheila R. Cotton, and Jeremy Schulz, 215–39. Bingley, UK: Emerald Publishing Limited, 2015. http://www.emeraldinsight.com/
doi/full/10.1108/S2050-206020150000009009.

Vavrek, Lynn. "2016 Endorsements: How and Why They Matter." *The New York
Times,* July 29, 2015, http://www.nytimes.com/2015/07/30/upshot/2016-
endorsements-how-and-why-they-matter.html.

von Hippel, Paul T. "Regression with Missing Ys: An Improved Strategy for Analyzing Multiply Imputed Data." *Sociological Methodology* 37, no. 1 (2007).

Vraga, Emily K. "Party Differences in Political Content on Social Media." *Online
Information Review* 40, no. 5 (2016): 595–609.

Vraga, Emily K. "Which Candidates Can Be Mavericks? The Effects of Issue Disagreement and Gender on Candidate Evaluations." *Politics & Policy* 45, no. 1
(2017): 4–30.

Vraga, Emily K., D. Jasun Carr, Jeffrey P. Nytes, and Dhavan V. Shah. "Precision
vs. Realism on the Framing Continuum: Understanding the Underpinnings of
Message Effects." *Political Communication* 27, no. 1 (2010): 1–19.

Vraga, Emily K., Kjerstin Thorson, Neta Kligler-Vilenchik, and Emily Gee. "How
Individual Sensitivities to Disagreement Shape Youth Political Expression on
Facebook." *Computers in Human Behavior* 45 (2015): 281–289.

Walgrave, Stefan, and Peter Van Aelst. "The Contingency of the Mass Media's
Political Agenda Setting Power: Toward a Preliminary Theory." *Journal of Communication* 56 (2006): 88–109. doi:10.1111/j.1460-2466.2006.00005.x.

Wallsten, Kevin. "Agenda Setting and the Blogosphere: An Analysis of the Relationship between Mainstream Media and Political Blogs." *Review of Policy
Research* 24, no. 6 (2007): 567–587.

Wang, Sam. "The Comey Effect." *Princeton Election Consortium,* December 10,
2016, http://election.princeton.edu/2016/12/10/the-comey-effect/.

Wanta, Wayne. "The Messenger and the Message: Differences across News
Media." In *Communication and Democracy: Exploring the Intellectual Frontiers of
Agenda-Setting Theory,* edited by Maxwell McCombs, Donald L. Shaw, and Da-
vid Weaver, 137–151. Mahwah, NJ: Erlbaum, 1997.

Wanta, Wayne, and Salma Ghanem. "Effects of Agenda Setting." In *Meta-Analysis
of Media Effects,* edited by Jennings Bryant and Rodney Carveth. Mahwah, NJ:
Erlbaum, 2000.

Wanta, Wayne, Guy Golan, and Cheolhan Lee. "Agenda Setting and International
News: Media Influence on Public Perceptions of Foreign Nations." *Journalism
and Mass Communication Quarterly* 81 (2004): 364–377.

Weaver, Al. "'Not Serious Politics': Krauthammer Dismisses 'Rodeo Clown' Donald Trump." *The Daily Caller*, July 6, 2015, http://dailycaller.com/2015/07/06/not-serious-politics-krauthammer-dismisses-rodeo-clown-donald-trump/.

Weaver, David H. "Audience Need for Orientation and Media Effects." *Communication Research* 7, no. 3 (1980): 361–376.

Weaver, David H., and Jihyang Choi. "The Media Agenda: Who (or What) Sets It?" In *The Oxford Handbook of Political Communication*, edited by Kate Kenski and Kathleen Hall Jamieson. Oxford University Press, 2014. doi:10.1093/oxfordhb/9780199793471.013.37.

Weaver, David H., Maxwell McCombs, and Donald L. Shaw. "Agenda-Setting Research: Issues, Attributes, and Influences." In *Handbook of Political Communication Research*, edited by Lynda L. Kaid, 257–282. Mahwah, NJ: Erlbaum, 2004.

Weaver, David H., Doris Graber, Maxwell E. McCombs, and Chaim H. Eyal. *Media Agenda Setting in a Presidential Election: Issues, Images, and Interest*. New York, NY: Praeger, 1981.

Weber, Christopher, Johanna Dunaway, and Tyler Johnson. "It's All in the Name: Source Cue Ambiguity and the Persuasive Appeal of Campaign Ads." *Political Behavior* 34, no. 3 (2012): 561–584.

Wells, Chris, Dhavan V. Shah, Jon C. Pevehouse, JungHwan Yang, Ayellet Pelled, Frederick Boehm, Josephine Lukito, Shreenita Ghosh, and Jessica L. Schmidt. "How Trump Drove Coverage to the Nomination: Hybrid Media Campaigning." *Political Communication* 33 (2016): 669–76. doi:10.1080/10584609.2016.1224416.

Wesleyan Media Project and The Center for Responsive Politics. "WMP/CRP Special Report: Outside Group Activity, 2000–2016." (August 24, 2016). http://mediaproject.wesleyan.edu/wp-content/uploads/2016/08/DisclosureReport_FINAL-5.pdf.

West, Darrell M. *Air Wars: Television Advertising and Social Media in Election Campaigns, 1952–2012*. Thousand Oaks, CA: SAGE, 2014.

White, David Manning. "The 'Gate-Keeper': A Case Study in the Selection of News." *Journalism Quarterly*, 27 (1950): 383–390.

White, Ian R., Patrick Royston, and Angela M. Wood. "Multiple Imputation Using Chained Equations: Issues and Guidance for Practice." *Statistics in Medicine* 30, no. 4 (2011): 377–99.

Williams, Andrew P., and John C. Tedesco. *The Internet Election: Perspectives on the Web in Campaign 2004*. Lanham, MD: Rowman & Littlefield, 2006.

Williams, Bruce, and Michael X. Delli Carpini. "Monica and Bill All the Time and Everywhere: The Collapse of Gatekeeping in the New Media Environment." *American Behavioral Scientist* 47, no. 9 (2004): 1208–1230.

Williams, Christine B., and Girish J. "Jeff" Gulati. "Social Networks in Political Campaigns: Facebook and the 2006 Midterm Elections." Paper presented at the 2007 annual meeting of the American Political Science Association, Chicago, Illinois, August 30–September 2, 2007.

Williams, Christine, and Jeff Gulati. "Facebook Grows Up: An Empirical Assessment of its Role in the 2008 Congressional Elections." Paper presented at the Annual Meeting of the Midwest Political Science Association, Chicago, IL (2009).

Wilson, Reid, and Joe Disipio. "Clinton Holds Huge Ground Game Advantage Over Team Trump." *The Hill*, October 22, 2016, http://thehill.com/campaign/302231-clinton-holds-huge-ground-game-advantage-over-team-trump.

Wolbrecht, Christina. *The Politics of Women's Rights: Parties, Positions, and Change.* Princeton, NJ: Princeton University Press, 2000.

Wood, Natalie T., and Kenneth C. Herbst. "Political Star Power and Political Parties: Does Celebrity Endorsement Win First-time Votes?" *Journal of Political Marketing* 6, no. 2–3 (2007): 141–158.

Woolley, Julia K., Anthony M. Limperos, and Mary Beth Oliver. "The 2008 Presidential Election, 2.0: A Content Analysis of User-Generated Political Facebook Groups." *Mass Communication and Society* 13, no. 5 (2010): 631–652.

Xenos, Michael, and Patricia Moy. 2007. "Direct and Differential Effects of the Internet on Political and Civic Engagement," *Journal of Communication*, 57 (4): 704–718.

Yamamoto, Masahiro, and Matthew J. Kushin. "More Harm than Good? Online Media Use and Political Disaffection Among College Students in the 2008 Election." *Journal of Computer-Mediated Communication*, 19 (2014): 430–445.

Yan, Holly. "Donald Trump's 'Blood' Comment about Megyn Kelly Draws Outrage." *CNN*, August 8, 2015, http://www.cnn.com/2015/08/08/politics/donald-trump-cnn-megyn-kelly-comment/.

Zucker, Harold. "The Variable Nature of News Media Influence." In *Communication Yearbook*, edited by Brent Ruben. New Brunswick, NJ: Transaction, 1978.

Index

About the Contributors

Monica Ancu studies the role of the Internet, especially online social media, in political campaigns. Within this framework, she investigates how political candidates, mass media, and voters use social networking websites, blogs, online advertising, etc., and how these online channels affect political campaigning and political behavior. Her research spans over a decade of elections, as she looked at every U.S. general and midterm election cycle since 2004. She also is interested in political advertising and media framing of political events. Her research has appeared in *Journalism Studies, American Behavioral Scientist, Journal of Broadcast and Electronic Media*, as well as in several books about online and social media campaigning in the 2008 and 2012 presidential elections. She received her PhD degree in mass communication from the University of Florida in 2006.

Mandi Bates Bailey is an associate professor of political science at Valdosta State University in Valdosta, GA. Her research focuses on public opinion, political behavior, and the impact of stereotypes. In addition to chapters published in *LGBTQ Politics: A Critical Reader* and *Homer Simpson Goes to Washington: American Politics Through the Lens of Popular Culture*, Mandi's research has been published in *The American Review of Politics* and *The Social Science Journal*.

Jody C Baumgartner is a professor of political science at East Carolina University. He received his PhD in political science from Miami University in 1998, specializing in the study of campaigns and elections. He has several books to his credit, including *Modern Presidential Electioneering: An Organizational and Comparative Approach* (2000); *Checking Executive Power* (2003), co-edited with Naoko Kada; *The American Vice Presidency Reconsidered* (2006); *Conventional Wisdom and American Elections: Exploding Myths, Exploring Misconceptions* (2007), written with Peter Francia; and *Laughing Matters: Humor and American Politics in the Media Age* (2007), co-edited with Jonathan Morris. He has also written or collaborated on three dozen articles and book chapters on political humor, the vice presidency, and other subjects.

Kayla J. Brown is an undergraduate student at Sam Houston State University.

Bethany A. Conway-Silva is an assistant professor in the Communication Studies Department at California Polytechnic State University. Her research interests include campaign use of new media, incivility in politics, and the application of social network analysis to news construction.

James N. Druckman is the Payson S. Wild Professor of political science and associate director of the Institute for Policy Research at Northwestern University. He studies preference formation and political communication. He recently co-authored the book *Who Governs: Presidents, Public Opinion and Manipulation* (2015). He also is co-Principal Investigator of Time-Sharing Experiments for the Social Sciences. More information about Professor Druckman can be found at: http://faculty.wcas.northwestern.edu/~jnd260/.

Heather K. Evans is an associate professor in the Department of Political Science at Sam Houston State University. Her primary research interests are political engagement, competitive congressional elections, female representation in the discipline, social media (Twitter), and the effect of entertainment media on political attitudes. Her book, *Competitive Elections and Democracy in America: The Good, the Bad, and the Ugly*, was published in 2014.

Christine R. Filer is a PhD candidate in the Department of Communication at the University of Arizona. Her current research focuses on political campaigns, candidate character, and social media.

Peter L. Francia is professor of political science and co-director of leadership studies at East Carolina University. He is the author of numerous academic publications on the subjects of campaign finance, interest groups, public opinion, and American elections. His major works include *The Financiers of Congressional Elections: Investors, Ideologues, and Intimates* (2003), co-authored with John C. Green, Paul S. Herrnson, Lynda W. Powell, and Clyde Wilcox; *The Future of Organized Labor in American Politics* (2006); *Guide to Interest Groups and Lobbying in the United States* (2012), co-edited with Burdett A. Loomis and Dara Z. Strolovitch; and three editions of *Conventional Wisdom and American Elections: Exploding Myths*,

Exploring Misconceptions (2008, 2010, and 2016), co-authored with Jody C Baumgartner.

Casey Frechette is an assistant professor at the University of South Florida St. Petersburg. He teaches in the department of journalism and media studies, with a focus on digital journalism. Before joining USFSP, Casey was an interactive learning producer with Poynter's News University, a leading online journalism and media training program. He was an adjunct at Poynter for three years and continues to teach in the Institute's programs. At the University of New Mexico's Technology and Education Center, Casey produced multimedia lessons for Navajo students for four years. He has 15 years of web development and eLearning experience.

Girish J. "Jeff" Gulati is an associate professor of political science at Bentley University who earned his PhD from the University of Virginia. Dr. Gulati's areas of expertise are on the U.S. Congress, campaigns and elections, e-government, and telecommunications policy. He is an elected member of the executive board for the Informational Technology & Politics section of the American Political Science Association and serves on the editorial boards of the *Journal of Information Technology & Politics* and *Journal of Political Marketing*. He has previously taught at Wellesley College and the Ralph Bunche Summer Institute. Additionally, he has designed studies assessing higher education programs and policies, election polls, and surveys for non-profits, interest groups, and local governments.

Kate Kenski is an associate professor in the Department of Communication at the University of Arizona. Her current research focuses on campaign use of new media, incivility in online forums, and multimedia teaching strategies to mitigate cognitive biases.

Martin J. Kifer is an associate professor of political science and director of the Survey Research Center (SRC) at High Point University. His research and teaching interests include political campaigns and new media, survey research methods, political opinion, and U.S. foreign policy. He has served on a Capitol Hill legislative staff and as an analyst for political and public policy consulting firms. His academic work has appeared in journals such as the *American Political Science Review* (with James N. Druckman and Michael Parkin). The SRC's HPU Poll conducts periodic election year surveys analyzing national and state campaigns, often focusing on the North Carolina electorate.

Mark D. Ludwig is a professor at California State University, Sacramento, where he teaches courses in political communication, public opinion, and journalism. He holds a PhD in Political Science from Claremont Graduate University, an MA in Communication from California State University, Fullerton, and a BS in Journalism from the University of Illinois at Urbana-Champaign. His research has centered on the intersection of politics and mass communication, with a particular focus on digital media. Before becoming a teacher, he worked as a newspaper editor for about 20 years.

David S. Morris is a visiting assistant professor at Tulane University. His research focuses on political and educational inequality, political behavior and new media, the American educational system, and school security and student behavior.

Caroline Lego Muñoz is an associate professor of marketing at Fairleigh Dickinson University (College at Florham) where she teaches Digital Marketing, Principles of Marketing, Consumer Behavior, and Marketing Research. Her specialization is consumer behavior and social media. Dr. Muñoz has published in numerous journals such as the *Journal of Consumer Behaviour*, *Journal of Business Research*, *Journal of Political Marketing*, *Journal of Marketing Education*, *Marketing Education Review*, and *Journal of Business Education*. Her research has explored the influence of reference groups within virtual communities/discussion boards, regifting, the integration of social media in pedagogy and marketing curriculums, and the role of social media in political campaigns.

Steven Nawara is an assistant professor of political science at Lewis University. He specializes in public opinion, voting behavior, elections, and American politics. His research has been published in *Political Behavior*, *Presidential Studies Quarterly*, and the *Journal of Elections, Public Opinion and Parties*.

Diana Owen is an associate professor of political science at Georgetown University in the Communication, Culture, and Technology graduate program of which she is a cofounder. She served as director of Georgetown's American Studies Program for a decade. She is the author of *Media Messages in American Presidential Elections* (1991), *New Media and American Politics* (with Richard Davis, 1998), and *American Government and Politics in the Information Age* (with David Paletz and Timothy Cook, 2nd ed., 2015). She is the co-editor of *The Internet and Politics: Citizens, Voters, and Activists* (with Sarah Oates and Rachel Gibson, 2006); *Making a Difference: The Internet and Elections in Comparative Perspective* (with Richard Davis, Stephen Ward, and David Taras, 2009); and *Internet Election Campaigns in the United States, Japan, Korea, and Taiwan* (with Shoko Kiyohara and Kazuhiro Maeshima, expected August 2017). She has published widely in the fields of civic education, political engagement, media and politics, political socialization, and elections and voting behavior. Her current research explores the relationship between civic education and the development of citizenship orientations as well as new media's role in politics. She has conducted studies funded by the Pew Charitable Trusts, the Center for Civic Education, and Storyful/News Corp, among others. She is the co-principal investigator on the James Madison Legacy Project of the Center for Civic Education which is funded by a SEED Grant from the U.S. Department of Education.

Michael Parkin is an associate professor of politics at Oberlin College and Director of the Oberlin Initiative in Electoral Politics. His research and teaching interests focus on mass political behavior and campaign strategies. His work includes a book, *Talk Show Campaigns: Presidential Candidates on Daytime and Late Night Television* (2014), and articles in journals such as the *American Political Science Review* (with James N. Druckman and Martin J. Kifer), *Political Research Quarterly*, and the *Journal of Political Marketing*.

Anne-Bennett Smithson is a PhD candidate in the Department of Communication at George Mason University. Her research focuses on how candidates frame political messages in both traditional and new media. She is particularly interested in how candidates present political disagreement and leverage emotional appeals in campaign communications. Her work has been published in *Journal of Computer-Mediated Communication*, *Health Communication*, and *Journal of Information Technology & Politics*.

Terri L. Towner is an associate professor of political science at Oakland University in Michigan. Her research focuses on American politics, public opinion, new media coverage of elections and political institutions, and the politics of race, class, and gender. Her research has been published as book chapters and journal articles, most recently in: *The Journal of Women, Politics & Policy, The Journal of Political Science Education, Presidential Campaigning and Social Media: An Analysis of the 2012 Election, The Journal of Political Marketing, The Social Science Computer Review, Web 2.0 Technologies and Democratic Governance: Political, Policy and Management Implications, New Media & Society, Techno-Politics in Presidential Campaigning: New Voices, New Technologies, and New Voters,* and *The Howard Journal of Communications*.

Eric Tsetsi is a doctoral student in the Department of Communication at the University of Arizona. His primary research interests include communication technologies, political communication, and media effects.

Emily K. Vraga is an assistant professor in the Department of Communication at George Mason University. Her research focuses on how individuals process news and information about contentious political, scientific, and health issues, particularly in response to disagreeable messages they encounter in digital media environments. She is especially interested in testing methods to limit biased processing and misinformation and encouraging attention to more diverse content online, especially through social media websites. Her work has been published in top communication journals such as *Journal of Communication*, *Journal of Computer-Mediated Communication*, and *Political Communication*.

Christine B. Williams is a professor of political science at Bentley University who earned her PhD from Indiana University. Teaching interests include American national elections, parties and interest groups, and the media. Publications and research interests include political socialization, women and politics, media and politics, teaching with the World Wide Web, and curriculum issues (reform, process, content, assessment). Formerly taught at Mount Holyoke College and State University of New York, College at Fredonia. Recipient of the Joseph M. Cronin Award for Excellence in Academic Advising. Recipient of a research grant from the Joan Shorenstein Center on the Press, Politics and Public Policy at Harvard University.

Tiffany Wimberly is an undergraduate student at Sam Houston State University.